Tyler Hendricks

THE
CRAFT AND BUSINESS OF
SONG
WRITING

· T H E ·
CRAFT AND
BUSINESS OF
SONG
WRITING

BY JOHN BRAHENY

Writer's
Digest
Books

Cincinnati, Ohio

The Craft and Business of Songwriting. Copyright © 1988 by John Braheny. Printed and bound in the United States of America. All rights reserved. No part of this book may be reproduced in any form or by any electronic or mechanical means including information storage and retrieval systems without permission in writing from the publisher, except by a reviewer, who may quote brief passages in a review. Published by Writer's Digest Books, an imprint of F&W Publications, Inc., 1507 Dana Avenue, Cincinnati, Ohio 45207. First edition.

93   92   91   90   89   88   5   4   3   2   1

Library of Congress Cataloging-in-Publication Data

Braheny, John, 1938-
   The craft and business of songwriting.

   Bibliography: p.
   Includes index.
   1. Popular music—Writing and publishing. I. Title.
MT67.B65   1987   784'.028   87-31744
ISBN 0-89879-284-3

Design by Clare Finney
Music engraving by Mok Lau, Lau's Music Engraving Company, Cincinnati, Ohio

Pages 308-311 constitute an extension of this copyright page.

Contents

Acknowledgments

There are many people who, both directly and indirectly, helped to write this book. It's impossible to put them in any order of rank, so I'll do it in a roughly chronological order.

My parents, William and Cecilia, who always encouraged me to do my best at whatever I did. My brothers, Dan and Kevin and my sister, Mary, who did the same.

My friend and partner, Len Chandler, with whom I've been growing and learning and dreaming since we started the Los Angeles Songwriters Showcase in 1971. Without his support and his taking on an extra work load while I worked on this book (and his reminders that my sentences are too long) this couldn't have been written. The LASS office staff, and Joy Wildin in particular, who shared that extra load with great patience.

The LASS sponsor, BMI, and in particular Ron Anton, Ed Cramer, Thea Zavin and Frances Preston, whose support allows us to continue to find new ways to help songwriters. *Music Connection* magazine publishers, Michael Dolan and Eric Bettelli, who asked me to write a column for their new magazine in '77 and Mandi Martin-Fox, who convinced me I could do it.

My wife, Jo Ann, whose love and support allowed her to put up with a home in which every available surface was covered with "the book," vacations dreamed of but not (yet) taken, weekend plans cancelled and other inconveniences too numerous to mention. Thank God she has a great sense of humor. Her good ideas and critiques and countless hours of typing also helped shape this book.

My friend and agent for this book, Ronny Schiff, who persistently pursued getting it published and contributed her expertise on the print music business. My editor at Writer's Digest Books, Julie Whaley, who believed in this project. Her relentless encouragement, critiques, and suggestions pushed me to make this a much better book than it would otherwise have been.

Many friends have read various parts of this book and contributed information and critiques. They include hit songwriter Alan O'Day, publisher Dude McLean, A&R exec Neil Portnow, music business consultant Thomas A. White, attorneys Michael Fletcher, Jeffrey Graubart, Kent Klavens, Al Schlesinger, Jack Whitley and Gary Wishik. Literally hundreds of other music industry pros have contributed to my understanding of the craft and business of songwriting and the ability to teach it.

I also want to thank thousands of hopeful and successful songwriters whose songs continue to enrich my life. This is a kind of payback and, I hope, an investment in encouraging you to give us all more great songs.

David "Cat" Cohen, whose "Theoretically Speaking" column I had admired so much when he was a fellow *Music Connection* writer, that I asked him to contribute the "Writing Music" chapter. And Chris Blake, whose "The Imagination of the Listener" provides such valuable information on how lyrics are effectively communicated.

THE GENDER QUESTION
Since both men and women work in all facets of the industry, and since I didn't want to have to write "him/her, he/she" throughout the book, I arbitrarily used either pronoun.

Introduction

Welcome to my book. Before I start showing you around the place, I think it's only right that I tell you why I brought you here. The reason is that I know you're out there slaving over a cold piece of paper and a hot guitar, keyboard, or computer. You have dreams of writing hit songs, becoming a recording artist, a producer, or anything that will bring you recognition and/or money (or at least buy you a tuna fish sandwich) for doing what you love to do. You care enough about doing it well that you're willing to invest some time in research and development to make sure you're not missing any tricks that helped others be successful. And you also want to make sure you don't make some dumb business move that could blow all your progress.

So I thought that, instead of giving you that information one on one for the next few years (which I wouldn't mind, really), it would be much smarter for me to bring you all here at once. It will also help me buy my own tuna fish sandwich.

How did I know you were out there? Easy. You've been calling me with your problems, fears, and dreams for over sixteen years, and I think I've returned most of your calls.

How do you know I'm giving you good information? Trust me! (This is the last time you should accept *that* answer.) But seriously, the question deserves a serious answer, so if you'll come with me for about two minutes I'll give you some background on how this "music information junkie" has fed his habit and can help to feed yours.

The Los Angeles Songwriters Showcase (LASS), which Len Chandler and I founded in 1971, filled a need by providing a focus for songwriting activities and information. Sponsored by Broadcast Music Inc. (BMI), the showcase drew the song-hungry music industry pros to a weekly gathering of the best new songwriting and writer/performer talent around. Stevie Nicks and Lindsey Buckingham, Stephen Bishop, Karla Bonoff, Wendy Waldman, Warren Zevon, R. C. Bannon, Kieren Kane, Chick Rains, Oingo Boingo, Alan O'Day, Jules Shear, Janis Ian, Lone Justice, Robbie Nevil, and Concrete Blonde are among the thousands of writers and writer/artists showcased since then.

We found that many of the writers we auditioned exhibited raw talent but little understanding of songwriting craft that could make their songs more commercially viable. Those writers whose songs we rejected wanted to know why. To offer them some constructive help, we looked for ways to explain those basic principles that seemed to be the common denominators of artistically and commercially successful songs. We also needed information about the music business so we could counsel the writers who were on the brink of making major career decisions. Several circumstances helped us to develop the information we needed.

In 1972, the LA Songwriters Showcase (then called the Alternative Chorus Songwriters Showcase) began a weekly music industry interview session. It has given us the ongoing opportunity to question hundreds of industry pros including hit songwriters and producers, attorneys, publishers, record company executives, recording artists, managers, record promoters, radio personalities and program directors, club owners, and others. Largely because of this experience, publishers Michael Dolan and Eric Bettelli asked me to write a songwriting column for their new biweekly, *Music Connection Magazine*, in 1977. The magazine has subsequently developed into one of the country's best music publications.

During the next six years, I wrote over 150 "Songmine" columns on all aspects of the art, craft, and business of songwriting. It was a golden opportunity to consolidate and focus the information derived from this unique vantage point.

In 1979, we created "Cassette Roulette" at the Showcase, in which a different guest-publisher is invited to critique songs each week. "Pitch-A-Thon," an extension of that idea, brings in a different producer or record company A&R (artist and repertoire) representative each week to screen songs for specific recording projects. These weekly events have given us and our audiences the opportunity to observe the critical processes of hundreds of publishers, producers, artists, and record company representatives. In addition, our friends in the industry, who believe there's no such thing as a dumb question, have always been willing to share their information with us whenever we ask. And we do ask.

So there's my background. As you might imagine, for an information glutton it's been an endless banquet. Because the industry continues to evolve, so does the information. That's why you and I will never stop learning about it. But at least this book will give you a good start.

SONGWRITING PRINCIPLES

There are no absolute rules or formulas for songwriting. For every "rule," you'll find a song that broke that rule and succeeded. The music industry has many "right" ways to do anything, including writing hit songs.

If you want to write successful songs, instead of learning "rules," you need to be aware of principles, the freedoms and restrictions of the medium for which you want to write, and have at your command a wide range of options with which to solve each creative problem.

This book will provide you with these options. In most cases you'll find that you already know them instinctively but haven't ever seen them in writing. In recognizing them you'll commit them more strongly to memory and use them more often and more effectively.

Writing a great song is only part of being a successful songwriter. Unsung thousands possess the talent and craft to write great songs, but without understanding the business and the knowledge of how to protect your creations and get them heard by those who can make them successful, those songs are like orphans.

This book explains in plain language how the music industry works, relative to you, the songwriter or writer/performer. It will demystify and humanize what can often feel to a newcomer like a cold, monolithic, and impersonal industry.

Success in the music/entertainment industry requires a combination of talent, love for the art and craft, hard work, a tremendous amount of persistence, and a good dose of dumb luck. To capitalize on dumb luck, you need to be ready when opportunity drops out of the sky. To be ready for the big break, you have to pull your craft and business together. By reading this book (and others recommended in this book), by listening and analyzing all forms of popular music, especially the music you love, and by meeting as many people in the business as your circumstances will allow, you'll be maximizing your chances for success.

CAN SONGWRITING BE TAUGHT?

Can you learn to write songs from a book? Are songwriting classes a waste of time? Critics of songwriter education say it's a waste, that "You're born with knowing how and, if you're not, there's nothing you can do to get it." Since classes in the craft of songwriting are usually accompanied by some business information, there may be a few among the critics who fear education because they can no longer take advantage of writers' ignorance. But for the most part, music industry pros recognize that they actually benefit from informed writers who understand the business and how to approach it in a professional manner.

In terms of craft, I do believe that, though you may have been born with a predisposition to music and language skills, it's more important to have been raised in an environment where you were encouraged to question, read, and express yourself verbally and musically and were given positive strokes for it. Some people with the natural talent and drive will pick up what they need to know about the craft by trial and error as they go. Many others with as much talent need, by way of classes, books, and workshops, to be provided with a supportive environment and a base of information to help their creativity bloom.

Though trial and error is a great teacher and will never be replaced by classes and books, the time you can waste in the "school of hard knocks" may also be devastating to your ego and your will to persevere. "If I knew then what I know now" has been a sad commentary on too many wasted careers. So getting as much information as early as possible about both craft and business can save you years.

Assuming that you're starting with some talent, imagination, and a love for music and/or language, there are basic principles involved in being a good and commercially successful songwriter that *can* be taught; primarily, you'll be organizing material that you already instinctively know and putting it in a context that helps you remember it when you need it. All types of artists need a knowledge of the media in which they work, their limitations, freedoms, and properties. Painters need to know about the properties of acrylics, oil paints, and watercolors, the types of brushes and canvas, the mechanics of visual perspective. They need to train their eyes.

As songwriters, you need to train your ears. For you, it's important to know, for instance, that Top 40 radio, musical theater, and film all have different requirements for the way songs are written. It's important to have the choice of many different ways to achieve dynamics in a song, and to know why an artistic choice would work in one situation and not in another. Awareness is a tool that can save time and get you what you want much faster. Knowledge serves your inspiration.

Great songs are a combination of substance and form. Substance is what you're saying and form is the way you communicate it.

You *can't* be taught inspiration or imagination. You *can* be taught ways to get in touch with what you have to say and how to effectively communicate it. It's sad to hear songs on the radio with great form and zero substance. It's sadder for me to know that you're out there with something to say that could make me laugh, cry, think about something in a new way, and otherwise enrich my life, but don't know how to do it. This book's for you!

PART ONE

THE
CRAFT

Creativity and Inspiration

CREATIVITY: WHAT IS IT AND DO YOU HAVE IT?

The subject of creativity has always been a fascinating one because we, as songwriters, are so dependent on the muse that it becomes very important that we understand and make some attempt to control it. Stimulating creativity and keeping it flowing past the dreaded spectre of "writer's block" are very real battles, particularly for those whose livelihoods depend on constant creative output. Hence there have been many studies and theories put forth on how creativity works, who's "creative," and who's not.

Psychologists who study creativity have found there are several qualities that are shared by most creative people. It may be useful for you to see how many of these apply to you. Don't be discouraged if you don't possess all of them. This is a broad generalization.

1. **You're a risk-taker.** You don't play it safe. You take intellectual and emotional risks (like submitting your songs for criticism).
2. **You have a talent in a particular area**, and since you're reading this book, we'll assume it's in language or in music.
3. **You tend to think for yourself** and make up your own mind about things. You feel that you, and not fate, luck, or society, are in control of your life.
4. **You're a nonconformist** and you may often find yourself going against the grain.
5. **You're playful.** You like to try new things or new ways of looking at or doing things just for fun.
6. **You have a sense of humor.** You tend to see the humor in novel or incongruous situations that others may not see.
7. **You find it easy to entertain yourself** and seldom get bored.
8. **You're a daydreamer** with a rich fantasy life. You can get totally lost in a fantasy and be oblivious to everything else.
9. **You can function in a state of confusion.** You can tolerate ambiguity. This quality can help you look at more than one side of a problem. You find yourself saying, "It could be this way, but on the other hand. . . ." You can be comfortable in either structured or unstructured situations in which there are no clear directions or guidelines.
10. **You enjoy complexity**—it's intriguing and challenging. You have an

2

ability to see complex relationships between seemingly unrelated situations or ideas.
11. **You're flexible.** You can usually figure out a variety of novel solutions for any problem.
12. **You're self-motivated, persevering, and passionate** about what you do. You work at something until you finish it.

Creative people also have the ability to absorb, digest, and organize external stimuli, reshape them into something novel, and recommunicate them in an art form. To a noncreative person, telephone touch tones are just sounds they hear when they make a call. To a creative person they may become the basis of a melody that can eventually become a full-blown composition. To a creative person a combination of words overheard on an elevator unlocks the memory of an old love affair. The writer's lover stepped into an elevator after a last traumatic goodbye. The conversation not only produced a memory but a song title, "Going Down for the Last Time." The songwriting process gave the writer a therapeutic way to deal with that experience. For an uncreative person it was just another conversation.

Dr. Roland Jefferson, a psychiatrist, novelist, and screenwriter, believes that there are three categories of creativity. Some people have genetic predispositions to visual creativity including painting, photography, sculpture, and architecture. Others have inherited abilities to use words. Lyricists, poets, novelists, and journalists fall into that category. The third is an ability to internalize and manipulate auditory stimuli. This would include musicians, composers, and sound engineers. He says it's not uncommon for creative people to possess combinations of these talents such as the composer/lyricist or the composer with the ability to visualize his music. Obviously novelists and screenwriters, actors, and filmmakers, use a visual/auditory and verbal combination.

Psychologist Dr. Eugene Landy has helped such creative people as Alice Cooper, Richard Harris, and Brian Wilson, and his theory is that everybody is creative in some way. Most people are more creative in fantasy than in reality. The people who actually act out some of these creative fantasies are what we call "professional" creative people and are actually a deviation from the norm. In reality, says Dr. Landy, you have to be a little "not normal" in order to create, because in that process you put forth things that people normally don't express, either because of social restriction or fear of exposing their own personal "secrets." When you turn this into a form of creative expression, you deal with it in a healthy way.

DEVELOPING YOUR CREATIVITY

If you think you're creative, you probably are. Since you're reading this book, you're searching for ways to make the most of the talent and creativity you already have. Psychologists have been working for eons to gather all the information you need. Here are some of the highlights.

Dr. George Gamez is a psychologist and songwriter who specializes in helping people develop their creativity through self-hypnosis and visualization techniques. Self-hypnosis or auto-suggestion emphasizes achieving a "state of receptivity" to suggestions you give yourself. Visualization involves picturing yourself being who you want to be and/or doing what you want to do the way you want to do it. Both techniques have been used successfully to help develop a positive self-concept which is, in turn, related to our self-expectations and consequent behavior. Statements like "I'm not a very good songwriter," "I'll never be that good," or "I just don't think commercial," become self-fulfilling because they both reflect and reinforce a negative and limiting self-image. Developing a positive self-image can help you, not only in writing songs but in being effective in dealing with the industry, something that involves perseverance and overcoming the fear of rejection.

STAGES IN THE CREATIVE PROCESS

Psychologists who specialize in creativity generally agree that the creative process goes through four stages. Relating them to songwriting they are:

1. **Preparation**—the gathering of the physical tools and the establishment of form, theme, and style. In a broader sense, it involves your music education, life experiences, and the development of your unique viewpoint and style.
2. **Incubation**—the unconscious process leading to creation in which, given the theme or problem, the subconscious works on a solution.
3. **Illumination**—the outward stage at which words and music are initially created, written down, or taped. During this stage we should *suspend the inner critic,* be spontaneous, and allow a free flow of ideas. Too often we stop the flow by being too self-critical, by working on a detail of rhyme or meter. Ideas flow from each other, and a tangent idea may be better than the original if we don't stop ourselves before we can get to that tangent.
4. **Verification**—the stage at which we *need* to be critical, looking at the song as a product, in an objective and detached way, rewriting, polishing, looking for the right meter and rhyme. Separation of the illumination and verification stages is crucial.

People in the music business always seem to be telling you to listen to the radio. But how do you listen and what do you listen to? The following Listening Exercises help unite your whole body in the process of songwriting. Every time you do one, you create a sensory memory that goes along with the song you're hearing. Eventually, when you're writing, you can use these memories to help trigger your creative process. You can start a "groove" going by dancing or by "conducting" the band or imagining the chords your "air guitar" is playing. Imagery is a powerful tool to creativity, and the more of our senses we integrate into the process, the more easily we create.

4

LISTENING EXERCISES

The following are some exercises that will help you listen to the radio in ways that will improve your writing.

Pick one instrument and listen to it all the way through a song. Become aware of the sound of the instrument, its tone, timbre, or character. Is it soft, mellow, hard-edged, piercing? Can you vocally reproduce it as a vowel or consonant sound? *Oooo, uuuu, rrrrr, ssss, mmmm,* or percussive *t* or *p* or *k* sounds (called plosives) are all quite different. Noting a sound's likeness to one of these will help you recall it for later reference.

Also think about the function of the instrument in the overall arrangement. Is it a *sustain* function like a string section, providing a chordal or single note "pad" that "grounds" and contrasts with all the other parts? Background vocals, strings, horns, and sustained guitar chords often provide that function.

Does it provide a *rhythm* function? All percussion certainly does. Bass, guitar, and keyboards can provide a combination of *rhythmic, chordal,* or *melodic* functions in the arrangement. Listen to how those functions change within each song.

If you've got some rhythm in your bones and love to dance, pick out an instrument and "assign" it to your right arm, another instrument to your left. "Assign" the bass to one or both feet, and "conduct" the song by dancing it out. Play some "air" guitar, drums, bass, or keyboards.

Pretending you're playing the instrument may seem silly if you're shy and conservative, but as a creator, it's your job to stretch yourself out. Listen to the melody line and try to visualize it as an actual line. Is it jagged and angular, or smooth and flowing? Are there significant differences between the melodies in the verses and those in the choruses and bridges? Sing along whenever you can. Sing or, in some other way, vocalize the instrumental parts as well as the lead vocals.

So what good does all this do? It helps to give you a valuable perspective on the various functions of instrumental parts in an arrangement. Because a songwriter is more effective if he or she can also wear arranger and producer hats, it's valuable to have a sense of what to put in and what to leave out of a demo and to have a ready repertoire of dynamic musical "tricks."

If you're a lyricist who doesn't play an instrument or sing, it's essential to get a "feel" for vocal phrasing against a rhythm track. What helps your growth is to be aware of the way your words can be stretched and bent in performance in ways that you seldom see when they're on paper. You become more aware of the variations of forms available, of which words do and don't "sing," and where and when to use them.

MOTIVATION—OVERCOMING THE BARRIERS

To become more creative, it's important not only to know how to enhance creativity but to be aware of what can kill it. Psychologist Teresa Amabile, writer of *The Social Psychology of Creativity* and *Growing Up Creative*, has conducted many tests to find out the following, which I've adapted to songwriting situations.

Dr. Amabile tested the "intrinsic motivation principle" of creativity, and found that *people will be most creative when they feel motivated primarily by the interest, enjoyment, satisfaction, and challenge of the work itself, not by external pressures.* Among the external pressures are:

1. **Evaluation**—Concern with what someone else will think of your work. We all need love and approval and it's easy to allow that need to become your motivation. You can learn about your craft in a classroom situation, from a music publisher (or from a book) and do exercises to develop skills. These skills may be evaluated by your teachers as part of your learning process. But you need to shut out that concern for outside approval *while you're creating.*
2. **Surveillance**—Like the above, if someone is literally watching you work, it can kill creativity. You tend, again, to want to please them instead of yourself. Even imagining someone is listening or watching can be inhibiting. But surveillance can enhance your performance of previously learned motor skills. When you're performing live, the audience can inspire you. That's obviously different, though, than someone standing over you while you're working something out.
3. **Reward**—When you focus entirely on the goal or reward—the gold record, the recording deal, the hit single, or the money—something dangerous can happen. Once you get it, you could be robbed of your internal motivation. You'll also tend to write in a way that takes the path of least resistance and minimal exploration to get to the next reward. On the other hand, giving yourself a treat for work that you feel good about is positive because the motivation and reward remain internal.
4. **Competition**—People will be more creative when they're less conscious of competing during the process. Again, if you're focused on competition, you'll tend to let someone else's reaction determine whether you should be satisfied with your own work.
5. **Restricted choice**—The more restricted you are in your choice of ways to achieve your goal, the less creative you'll be. You'll tend to internalize the restrictions rather than the freedoms you have in achieving the goal. In songwriting, you'll focus on the parameters rather than on the many options within the parameters. The solution is to recognize the problem and psych yourself out of it.

When you get to a point where you can no longer enjoy the process and you're overwhelmed by the externals (thinking, for example, "This song needs to be a hit," or "If I don't get this recorded, I'm worthless") you're entering "creative burnout." You're no longer writing for yourself and you're doing it for all the wrong reasons. If you're a professional writer you're probably in a situation in which you need to please someone else as well as yourself. Even at that, there will be times when your publisher will say, "That's good, but could you change this verse?" and you'll have to say, "No, this is for me and I don't care if it doesn't get recorded." Sometimes, when you're writing with that kind of freedom, writing from your heart and your emotional core, that's the very thing that will make your song appealing to another artist and an audience.

So the operating principle in all this is that, to operate at peak performance during the creative process you should be motivated internally by the spirit of play and exploration and forget about what anybody else might think. You'll have plenty of time to think about that later.

INSPIRATION: PHILOSOPHIES

I've asked many hit songwriters whether they write from craft or inspiration. Some view writing as a profession, a job, pure craft. They're very disciplined about it and never refer to the cosmos as a source of inspiration. They actively look for song ideas in everything they read, watch, listen to, and experience. They give little credit to inspiration and approach songwriting as they would a 9 to 5 job that they enjoy. The craft of songwriting is described as a game of organizing ideas, a kind of word engineering and problem-solving experience. It's like a big puzzle in which the "pieces" come from rhyming dictionaries, thesauruses, and real life, and in which there are several right ways to construct the "picture." Their knowledge of the most effective construction principles gives them a goal and methods which help them put this picture together clearly.

Most amateur writers and many writer/artists fall into another general category. I'll call them "inspiration" writers which, I should add, doesn't mean that those in the first category never get inspired. Only that, in this one, they rely on inspiration rather than craft. My profile of hard-core inspiration writers is that they won't rewrite, feeling that the magic moment they got from the Creator and put on paper is sacred, and will only write when inspired. It's that attitude that will stand in the way of success for these writers, regardless of how wonderful their inspirations are.

Publishers don't like to work with this type of writer. Many "inspiration" writer/artists have had short careers because their first LP contained the best of their songs to date. They had ten years to write them. When they need to turn out ten more songs for their second album they face the dreaded "sophomore plunge." They discover that they're too tired to be inspired when they're on the road for six months and when it comes time to get back in the studio they no longer have the luxury of waiting for the inspiration. If they don't have discipline and command of their craft at that point, they're in trouble.

People who sit down and write a hit song in ten minutes are usually those who have the craft down so well that they don't think about it. It's automatic. They get the idea, focus on exactly what they want to say, and the rest of it comes easily. "If you think of a great title, the song writes itself" is a typical statement for that phenomenon. On the other hand, pro writers (even ones who *have* written a hit in ten minutes) will more typically write pages to get one great line or will write several mediocre-to-good songs for every song they'd consider great. There are also writers who find it difficult to discuss their creative processes and downplay the craft involved in their work. They deny making conscious craft decisions. The songs, nonetheless, show organized thought processes and good command of the craft.

I believe that many successful writers have unconsciously acquired their craftsmanship by osmosis. They've been emotionally affected by so many great songs for so long that they instinctively know, for instance, when there "needs" to be a chorus or bridge, when a lyric line could be stronger, etc. They go by "feel," but behind it there's been a subconscious analytical process developing. When a writer plays me a nine-line song with twelve verses, a "chorus" that occurs only once, and no rhymes at all, I know I'm not listening to a natural writer who has unconsciously learned the craft. I'm prompted to ask whether the writer has ever listened to the radio.

There are dangers inherent in both extremes. I've heard writers who are trying so hard to write a well crafted, formula "hit" that they forget about imagination and originality and end up with songs that remind me of the "people" in the science fiction film *Westworld* who look great on the outside but have nothing inside but machinery. On the other hand, I've heard writers with great ideas but no discipline or knowledge of how to communicate them. All that good inspiration goes to waste.

In contrasting "craft" and "inspiration" writers, I'm depicting two extremes. Ideally, the inspiration is recognized as only the beginning of the songwriting process. The *craft is at the service of your inspiration* and gives you the confidence and a dependable vehicle to communicate those inspirations in a way that an audience can easily understand and enjoy.

DEVELOPING A "SONGWRITER'S CONSCIOUSNESS"

Regardless of which songwriting philosophy you subscribe to, it's helpful to learn how craft and inspiration work together when we create.

There's a popular theory with which I agree: the human mind is a complex computer that responds only according to the way it's been programmed. The problems occur when we give the computer conflicting messages like "I'd love to write a hit song!" and "I'm not a good enough musician to be a songwriter" or "I don't know how." Your mind just sits there and says "Let me know when you decide." Giving yourself a positive "I am a songwriter" program is very important to what I call "songwriter consciousness." Once you grasp some of the basic principles of what makes songs "work," the world can become an endless supplier of ideas that you then know what to do with. "Songwriter consciousness" filters everything through this network of "idea inspectors" who sit there on duty watching for a big juicy idea to come down the road. They've already been trained to see it coming, so they start getting excited when they see one. Sometimes an idea is low key and subtle and they don't see it right away. Sometimes it's one they're already familiar with and doesn't seem exciting anymore. Some ideas have worn out their welcome and, because he's bored with those, an inspector may miss a part of them that's still worthwhile. But to those juicy ones that are fresh and original, the inspector will say "Wait a minute, Juicy, I'm not letting you by till we can play awhile and check out your potential. You may be just the one we're looking for!"

In short, "songwriter consciousness" is the readiness to recognize what could be a good song idea. If you have it, you'll start to find ideas everywhere.

BEING READY

You're lying in bed, half asleep in that twilight zone where ideas just seem to pop into your head. You've got one! It rolls out like a movie in your mind, a great concept, exciting lines, you see it all. You've had a hard day at work and your body doesn't want to move to get a pen and paper. "It's such a good idea," you say to yourself, "No way I'll forget this one."

The next sound you hear is the alarm clock. You're up, showered, breakfasted, and on the job. About noontime you remember that you had an idea for a song last night but you can't quite recall what it was. Another great idea down the tubes. That could have been the hit that paid the rent for the rest of your life! Do you think now it would have been worth it to keep a pencil and paper by your bed? Or easier yet, but more expensive, a cassette recorder? (The advantage of the recorder is that you can also capture melody and phrasing.) Have one or the other with you always. Have an extra pad and pencil in your car for those freeway daydreams, too. Driving time, and those times between being asleep and awake, seem to be when the brain allows the best communication between the conscious and subconscious. That's fertile, creative territory. Protect it!

Every writer I know has some kind of book or other place to store those little pieces of paper they collect with lines or fragments of ideas. You should have one, too. When you get a chance to write, you've got lots of ideas in front of you. It's a good idea to periodically transfer them from those scraps of paper into a notebook. In the process, you reinforce your memory of them and make it easier to link them with other ideas or phrases with which they'll fit.

There will be times you'll get an idea in a situation where it won't be socially acceptable to whip out your pen and start writing. In those situations, like at formal social gatherings or in mid-conversation, you can use what Len Chandler calls "The Weak Bladder Syndrome" and depart for the restroom to work in private.

You may also want to write about someone you're with at the time. That's when it's beneficial to have a personal brand of shorthand. I know one writer who developed a whole code of geometric symbols that only he could understand. Many writers are very candid about their personal relationships and have difficulty expressing negative feelings a lover is not yet aware of. You can say "This isn't really about us, it's just something I'm creating from the memory of another relationship," or "It's about a friend's romance," or "Don't get paranoid. I'm a songwriter and I make this stuff up! I don't want to have to worry that every time I write something you're going to think it's about us." Of course, depending on the circumstances and what you wrote, any of those approaches could sound utterly ridiculous, so don't quote me.

Since you never know where or when a great idea is going to appear, the only thing you can control for sure is your readiness to catch it when it falls on you. Be prepared!

FINDING YOUR OWN CREATIVE PROCESS

Every writer eventually finds her own process (or more than one) for creating. Though it's a good idea to explore many, your own unique personality will determine an approach that's comfortable and productive for you.

It's important not to put yourself down for having a creative style that's different from someone else's. Don't worry about which style works for someone else unless you want to collaborate with that person, in which case your styles should be compatible. Here are some of the more typical ones.

If you're a *"deadline"* writer, you're part of a very large breed. You've got a lot going on in your life and need an external force to make you put this song on the front burner. Someone says, "I need this by tomorrow morning. The artist will record it at 10 A.M." Your adrenaline starts pumping and every synapse in your brain is working full out. The ability to write and rewrite well under deadline pressure is extremely valuable, since those opportunities happen constantly in the music business. If you get a reputation for being able to deliver, you get the jobs. If you're the type of person who needs deadlines to get things done, but don't happen to have any external deadlines, find a way to trick yourself into one. Making an appointment to show a publisher or producer a new song or booking studio time to record a demo are great ways to create your own deadlines.

If you're a *"total focus"* writer, you like to sit down with a project and proceed to devote your total attention to it until it's finished. No other projects. No diversions or distractions. Straight-ahead concentration from start to finish, no matter how long it takes. You polish each line as you go.

If you're a *"scattered"* writer, you may have several songs going at once, get bored or burnt out with one and work on another, going back to the first later, maybe with fresh ideas generated by working on the others. You're the kind of writer who has difficulty sustaining interest. You'll work for awhile, look for inspiration in the refrigerator, make a sandwich, watch TV, go back to work, stop, make some phone calls, take out the garbage, back to work, stop, read a magazine, back to work again. You may feel guilty for not keeping at it but, in fact, the song is getting written in your subconscious as you do all those other things.

If you're a *"project"* writer, you work best in some kind of framework with an established goal or motivation ("I'll pay you a thousand dollars to write a theme for a play in two weeks.") You have a direction, a framework, and a motive. You may be very creative within that type of situation but otherwise you're not very productive. Recognizing that, you need to search for projects—people with your approach frequently write for TV series, films, and commercials.

Some writers can only write when they're alone. Some can write in a roomful of people with the radio and TV going at the same time. Some need silence. Some, though they might be equally adept at writing words and music, are more productive in a collaboration.

Getting ready to "commit" to writing may involve a common process that Len Chandler calls "sharpening pencils." You seem to be doing everything but writing. You're cleaning the house, preparing the writing space, and actually sharpening pencils. You make sure you have your "sure-fire hit" songwriting pencil and paper and maybe your "great idea" hat. This is a kind of ritual that is very valuable because it's getting you ready and priming your creative pump. While you're doing it you're probably actually working on the song without realizing it.

You may think you *must* be the only writer in the world who goes through this craziness, or that if you were a *real* pro you wouldn't have to. Wrong! Yours may be a unique ritual, but most writers have one.

Your approach may incorporate elements of more than one of those listed here, and it may also change with time and experience, but it's important for you to realize that whatever works for you is right.

BREAKING WRITER'S BLOCK
You're sitting in front of a blank piece of paper, just *knowing* that you've come up with all the ideas you'll ever come up with and that anything you *do* think of has already been written. You try your brand-new pen with the easy glide point but can't convince it to write anything. You go through all your customary rituals but still nothing happens.

At this point, you've landed where every other writer has been at one time or another: The Planet of the Dry. It *is* comforting, in a way, to know you're not the only writer in the world who has ever felt totally stupid.

Though there are those who deny there's anything such as writer's block, to deny it is to acknowledge that it exists. For some people, denial *is* the best way to deal with it. Whatever works! Here are some of the other ways writers have dealt with this problem.

1. Just start writing anything: a grocery list, a letter to the editor, anything to jumpstart your creative engine and get something on the blank page.
2. Psych yourself out of the pressure to produce a hit or great work of art. Focus on having fun. Remind yourself that nobody else will ever see your bad work.

3. Create an atmosphere. Listen to your favorite artist's records. Listen to music that puts you in a mood, and savor it.
4. Find other places to write: the beach, the woods, on a mountain, in a car, in a bus station, a noisy restaurant, a dance club. Try writing at a different time of day.
5. Just forget about writing altogether. Relax, have some fun, go to a movie, go bowling, bicycling, whatever.
6. Try the stream-of-consciousness or problem-solving techniques explained in this chapter.
7. If you're a musician, play scales you don't usually play, put on a record you don't normally listen to, and learn solos from other instruments. If you're a guitarist, for instance, learn a Bach violin solo and maybe try playing it back at half-speed or learn a jazz sax solo.
8. Find a new collaborator.

It's possible that none of the above will work. At that point it may be useful to dig a little deeper.

Writer/psychotherapist Lynne Bernfield says, "Being blocked doesn't mean that you don't want to produce, are self-destructive or lazy, have dried up or been deserted by the muse. It is a coded message from your unconscious telling you that something must be attended to, and, as such, is a blessing in disguise." She believes that one of the things to be attended to is "unfinished business" in other areas of our lives. We won't allow ourselves to start new business till we've "finished" that old business. So try to identify it and deal with it. You *will* get through this!

Two other effective methods merit more of an in-depth explanation. Even if you don't feel you're blocked, they're great ways to get started.

STREAM-OF-CONSCIOUSNESS
One approach is the *stream-of-consciousness* technique. It's used in what Dr. Gamez described earlier as the "illumination phase" of the creative process in which spontaneity is encouraged and the "inner critic" is ignored. It's a great way to generate ideas. This is a technique used by many successful writers.

In an interview by Theresa Ann Nixon for the LASS *Musepaper* in 1984, Paul McCartney discussed a prose piece he'd been working on:

So when my hand didn't know what to put on the paper, my head just said to my hand, "Write! Put it down. It doesn't matter what you say, just put it down. Even if it's all mistakes. Just put it down." I got this method of just forcing my hand to write, no matter what it was. And later I talked with Quincy Jones about this when we were doing "The Girl is Mine" with Michael Jackson. He said he had gotten this book twenty years ago that had changed his life, where the fellow explained that there were two aspects to a creative act. One was just to create it, just do it. The other was judicial, checking everything. He said the biggest mistake everyone makes is to try to do the two at once. And suddenly—ding!—that's exactly what my problem is. In all those years with essays in school, you know, I was trying to get

CREATIVITY EXERCISE

You hear a friend use an interesting phrase and you write it on a notepad, napkin, your hand (or you memorize it). Later on you're noodling with your piano, guitar, or whatever is handy, turn on your cassette recorder and forget it's there. Next, you grab some chords, maybe just play a bass line, get a nice groove going with your feet, get an attitude going—sad, bittersweet, mad, haughty, playful, loving, romantic—picture yourself with that attitude talking to someone, and just say out loud everything you can think of that relates to the situation that you're remembering or creating.

It's strange to hear yourself talking out loud when you're alone, but the more you do it, the less strange it becomes. You want to rhyme this line? If it doesn't just appear, forget it. Keep going. Don't stop the flow; you'll fix it up later, but get all the ideas out there for now. Babble on awhile. None of it has to make much sense or have any continuity at this stage. You can influence the direction of the flow by describing a scene, a setting, or a feeling. If there is another person in this setting, consider your relationship to him. What motivates that person and dictates your attitude toward him? What does he/she say? What do you say? What happened before and what happened after? If you get off on a tangent, that's okay because the tangent may take you to a better place. Don't worry, just keep rapping.

All talked out? Rewind the tape and listen back. Yes, you'll think some of it is total nonsense, but did you really think everything you said would be profound? Some of the stupid stuff may be a bridge to something better. This line could have smoother meter, a better flow, if you changed a couple of words.

Now you're into the "verification phase" of the process. Be critical. Pull out all the good lines and ideas. Write them down, leaving plenty of room to rewrite and add other lines that you think of. Now is the time to pay more attention to form, continuity, rhyme schemes, meter. You may find that most of those were established during that free-form session and now they just need to be rethought and looked at a little more closely. You may discover that what you thought was the chorus works better as a verse or vice versa. Perhaps what you thought was the first verse should be the last. Maybe the first phrase you wrote down that triggered this whole process is no longer nearly as good as other ideas the process produced.

13

that wonderful opening. . . . When you try to do everything at once, there's just no time. Your brain can't cope. You'll kill all your enthusiasm and creative spirit by checking your spelling and going to see "is this the right word, is it clever enough? Will the L.A. Times *critic like it if I say 'hobgoblin'? Yes, there is a better word. Or shall I just say, 'demon'? No. Hobgoblin. No, demon." And you've just spent half a bloody hour.*

What happens during the "stream-of-consciousness" process is that you pull out a lot of ideas and make a lot of creative hookups and links that you might not ordinarily make when you're trying too hard. You also avoid getting hung up trying to make something rhyme or make your meter tight at the expense of flow and focus. Once you've filled a few pages, you'll have a better concept of how to structure the idea and you'll also have come up with some great lines, some rhythms that those lines may suggest, and some good rhymes that will feel natural because you'll be writing closer to the way you think and speak. At that point you can start a new page with the best lines you've come up with. The Creativity Exercise on page 13 is a sample scenario of that process, using a tape recorder.

Keep in mind, while you're in the critical phase, that nothing is sacred. Don't get married to a line that's great by itself but doesn't seem to fit the rest. Put it away in your collection of great lines and use it to trigger another session. As a matter of fact, don't throw anything away. If you're working on paper, don't erase. Draw a single line through the reject. If you work with a word processor, cut or copy sections you don't want to another area. If you're working on tape, always save your tapes. Not only can you return to them for musical ideas, but should you ever be involved in an infringement case, they may be helpful to show the process by which you arrived at your finished song.

PROBLEM SOLVING

Another creative springboard is the *problem-solving* technique in which you make up arbitrary "problems" to solve creatively.

In a way, writing a good title before you write the song is an exercise in problem solving. The problem is to find a great way to set up the title and pay it off. Maybe the title suggests a mood and the "problem" is to maintain and heighten the mood. Maybe the title suggests a story to develop.

The fact is that a substantial amount of the creative process involves problem solving anyway. Like putting together a crossword puzzle, it's word and music architecture and design.

The following Exercise in Problem Solving will give you some ideas to build on. If you ever run into trouble getting started, just pick one of your premises at random and link it with a lyric idea from your collection. Remember that trying to make the puzzle work is a great exercise of your creativity and will force you into "solutions" you may not have otherwise come up with. At the same time remember that creativity is a fluid process and if the exercise only serves to get you started it has done its job. If you ever run into trouble getting started, just pick one of your premises at random and link it with a lyric idea from your collection. Remember

EXERCISE IN PROBLEM SOLVING

In the absence of a "real world" creative problem, simulate one or come up with an arbitrary premise or set of parameters. Here are some samples:

An eight-bar verse with a nine-bar chorus.
A 120 tempo.
The bass with a maximum of four notes every two bars.
Rapid fire sixteenth-note lyric in the verse, half-note lyric in the chorus.

A ten-bar verse (two five-bar sections), eight-bar chorus.
A maximum of five chords.

A 28½-second jingle for a teddy bear, conveying warmth, playfulness. (You'll have to name the bear.)
A ten-second "donut" (a hole in the lyric for dialogue) fifteen seconds from the start.
Write the jingle for a female vocalist.

Create several of these "puzzles" to solve. Mix and match information on:

Form (number and length of sections, bars per section)
Tempo
Time signature(s)
Key
Melodic mode
Number of chords per section or song
Number of instrumental tracks
Density of instrumental parts
Mood
Rhyme scheme
Lyric density

that trying to make the puzzle work is a great exercise of your creativity and will force you into "solutions" you may not have otherwise come up with. At the same time remember that creativity is a fluid process and if the exercise only serves to get you started it has done its job.

Remember too, that many musical and lyrical innovations have resulted from *creative accidents* in which the artist had the presence of mind to recognize a good idea that he accidentally stumbled across on his way to something else. Taking advantage of those situations requires that you maintain an open mind and that you stay flexible.

DEVELOPING GOOD WORK HABITS

Not everyone can form consistent writing habits. Many of the most successful writers have schedules that allow for very little consistency. Developing a regular pattern or schedule for your writing, however, can have valuable advantages. Say you make a commitment to yourself or, even better, to a collaborator, that you're going to meet every Saturday from 9 A.M. till noon to write. First, you'll feel better that you're no longer procrastinating. Second, getting something accomplished every week will do a lot for your self-confidence, and third, it activates a psychological phenomenon that's very productive.

When your subconscious knows that next Saturday at 9 A.M. it has to have some new ideas or to solve a creative problem from last week, it works on it while you do other things. The same phenomenon is at work when you can't remember someone's name. You finally give up until an hour later when the name seems to pop into your mind from nowhere. It actually just moved from storage in the "back" of your mind to the front because you had assigned the task of finding it to your subconscious.

Hit songwriter Tom Snow ("He's So Shy," "You Should Hear How She Talks about You") likes to get an idea started at the end of a writing session but saves developing the idea till the next session. He says it keeps him excited about working on the idea and by the time he gets into it, his brain is already cooking. The technique is one of Snow's personal methods of manipulating his creative juices. You should learn to develop techniques that suit your own personality.

Subject Matter

FINDING IDEAS

Your subject, of course, is the raw material of songwriting. Coming up with that fresh sounding "hook" phrase, or an idea that hasn't been stated in quite the same way before, is important if you want to be viewed as a creative writer. You'll need to develop your ability to recognize and generate lyric ideas from a variety of everyday sources. This chapter will explore some specific places to look for ideas and a few general subject areas with hints on how to approach them effectively.

Sources for song ideas are everywhere. Here are a few that are endlessly productive:

News and human interest programs on radio and TV. Talk shows on radio and TV are extremely popular and elicit an incredible array of emotional problems and conflicts from their callers and in-studio audiences. Each day's topic usually deals with current news events or ethical problems. These shows involve the general public in often passionate interchanges that reflect human conflicts. Check to see if there are any shows in your area that are hosted by psychologists discussing personal problems. These are particularly juicy, especially on radio where the callers are anonymous. They're a tremendous education in human behavior as well. As you listen, remember that it's not just the subjects you're listening for, but the language with which people express themselves.

The networks present special, in-depth programs on a variety of informative and controversial topics. You'll find yourself agreeing or disagreeing and, in the process, solidifying your own point of view. So again, it's not just the topic of the program you're looking at, but a distillation of your personal viewpoint which will work its way into your songs.

TV soap operas and prime-time dramas. The writers of these shows are also listening to the talk shows for ideas.

Listening to music on the radio is really stimulating, especially on the freeway where the creative half of your brain is daydreaming. I've half-heard lines of songs on the radio and said to myself, "What a great line!" only to discover to my pleasure that, when hearing it again, it wasn't really the line I thought I'd heard after all. By some strange approximation of vowel sounds it had triggered a new line that I could use.

It can be a productive exercise to ignore the song you're hearing and use the rhythm section or "feel" to build your own song on. It'll help you to come up with an interesting phrasing of lines that you may not have thought of otherwise. It's also important to listen to the radio to maintain a sense of what's happening in the marketplace and to get familiar with the new artists.

Poetry and books with great colloquial dialogue are inspirations and "triggers" for new ideas. Also check these reference books which contain a wealth of ideas: *A Dictionary of Contemporary and Colloquial Usage, Dictionary of American Underworld Lingo, Dictionary of American Slang, Dictionary of American Idioms,* and *The Wordwatchers Handbook* (see Bibliography).

Conversations with friends or discussions you overhear will provide some great titles, especially if the language is particularly distinctive or colorful. Most of the great lyricists I've interviewed tell me they're conversation "voyeurs." Give yourself the challenge of finding one good line, idea, or title in a five-minute slice of conversation from any source. It's a great way to demonstrate to yourself what a wealth of material is available almost everywhere.

Examine your own life experiences. Think about your feelings toward your lover or romantic situations, positive or negative, past or present, and turn those feelings into actual dialogue or a story. Some writers only write from personal experience. Don't forget that, like a novelist, you're a creator and if you hear someone else's story and it moves you, chances are it'll move others, too. You can also change or embellish or totally fabricate a story that will move or entertain people just as much. It's called "poetic license," not dishonesty.

Once you "program" your subconscious to look for ideas, it'll automatically do it. But you have to help, by getting ideas down on paper or computer or tape recorder as soon as possible or your subconscious won't believe you're serious. The "idea inspectors" will say, "We pick up on these great ideas but the turkey never does anything with them. Why should we bother?"

THE COMMERCIALITY OF SUBJECT MATTER—MASS APPEAL

At some point before, during, or after a song is written, it behooves a writer to decide whether the song idea itself is "commercial." Now don't get defensive! I'm not saying that every song you write must appeal to the lowest common denominator. At the risk of repeating this message too many times, I'll say again that you should write everything and anything your creative impulses trigger. At some point though, if you want to make a living at songwriting, you've got to develop some perspective on your songs. The one you wrote about your second-cousin's appendicitis may be important to you personally but everybody else will say, "So what?" You need to decide which of your songs are going to be meaningful in some way to a mass audience before shopping them to publishers or producers. Lots of different kinds of songs can work. Larry Groce's "Junk Food Junkie" was an "off the wall" song but everybody identified with it and made it a hit.

RELATABLE THEMES

Occasionally a monster will emerge with far more than the basic ingredients. One of the classics was "I Will Survive," the #1 hit that Freddie Perren and Dino Fekaris wrote for Gloria Gaynor in 1979. Along with the great groove and production, the song had a lyric idea that made its popularity continue long after that groove and production would have burnt out by repetition. The lyric was an anthem for women, something positive from someone who sounded like she knew what she was talking about, with a story that sounded familiar. The message was positive: that no matter how her lover had treated her before, she didn't have to take it anymore because she had found a new self-respect.

One of the most important functions of a song is to give people a vehicle to express hopes, dreams, and inner conflicts that they might otherwise keep inside.

Songs have a way of uniting us by defining those common strings that bind us together. Dan Hill's "Sometimes When We Touch" expressed the apparent contradictions, the love/hate aspects of an intense relationship. Those of us who've been there may have felt like we were a little crazy for having those kinds of feelings and were relieved to hear someone else express them. We were even more relieved that hundreds of thousands of other people loved the song.

"Torn Between Two Lovers" was both a country and pop hit because it expressed an old situation in a new and more sensitive way. Few people may approve of "cheatin'," but they may still know how it feels to love more than one person at the same time. The Madonna hit, "Papa Don't Preach," explores one of the sad choices of a pregnant teenager.

Often the more "commercial" songs are the ones that not only express more personal situations and feelings, but do it in a way that everyone else can easily understand and identify with.

BEING BELIEVABLE

Hopefully, the values and experiences reflected in your songs are either ones you feel comfortable with or that reflect your own situation. If you're a writer/artist, a major part of your appeal will be that people will identify with your point of view. Don't take a different point of view on every record—people will never really learn who you are. Also, as an artist, be leery of recording a song that you're not completely comfortable with. You may be doomed to playing it for years. If you're a nonperforming writer, you're not so restricted; you can write "for the market" or from the point of view of the artist.

CLEVERNESS

Beyond the considerations we've just discussed, there are some stylistic considerations that affect the commerciality of a song. One of those is *cleverness*. Country music is the obvious home of the clever word play, the new twist on an old cliché, and the lyrical "turnaround." Some examples are "Lying Time Again," "Yippi Cry Yi," "Nothin' Sure Looked Good On You," and "Wishful Drinkin." The old pop tune, "I Had Too Much to Dream Last Night," is another example of the kind of cleverness designed to stick in the listener's mind. The lyrical "turnaround" with the surprise ending has wide appeal. A good example is Rupert Holmes's "Escape (The Piña Colada Song)," in which a husband and wife, growing bored with each other, both respond to a "personal" ad describing someone they'd love to meet, only to discover each other again. "Tie a Yellow Ribbon 'Round the Ole Oak Tree," by Irwin Levine and L. Russell Brown, was another in that genre that was a huge crossover hit.

To pure "heart" writers, that kind of song may seem trite and contrived. "Punch line" songs run the risk of wearing out their welcome quickly, like a joke you've heard too many times. The only thing that makes a song like these worth hearing again is a great storyteller and an interesting story leading up to the punch line. The appeal is probably even broader if the song illustrates some common problem or philosophy like Harry Chapin's "Taxi" or Rupert Holmes's "Escape."

The more conversational and natural the lyric feels and the more vivid the visual imagery, the less contrived they seem. In other words, the trip should be as rewarding as the destination. "The Gambler," by Don Schlitz, was a very cleverly contrived story and even though the use of a deck of cards as an analogy for life wasn't a new idea, the song's natural, rhymed, colloquial language and movie-like imagery made it a wonderful piece of work.

CROSSOVER RECORDS

If you're concerned about selling records, you must appeal to a large section of the record-buying population. Consistently at the top of the "best seller" and "most played" lists are "crossovers," which you'll hear a lot about in the recording industry.

A crossover record is one that can be played on more than one radio format. Crossover artists include Michael Jackson, Stevie Wonder, Lionel Richie, Madonna, Whitney Houston, Steve Winwood, and Prince, whose records regularly get played on R&B (rhythm and blues), pop, adult contemporary (AC, an "easy listening" or "mellow rock" format), and urban contemporary (R&B and pop/rock combination) radio stations.

The music of Kenny Rogers, Paul Davis, Anne Murray, Crystal Gayle, and Dolly Parton gets played on country, pop and adult contemporary stations. Many rock artists get air time both on pop and AOR (album-oriented rock) stations, and occasionally on adult contemporaries. Crossover potential, in fact, is based more on the record than the artist. Record companies frequently promote different songs on an album in different radio formats. The principle of crossover is that the more radio stations that air the record, the more people will hear it and be motivated to buy it. Video and film exposure are still other avenues that can further contribute to the power of a crossover song, record, and artist.

20

THEMES OF LOVE

Of all possible song themes, love is the most popular. No other subject is as universal, no other human need so emotionally rich, provocative, and potentially traumatic. A quick survey of the top singles in any category of the trade charts will show that over 75 percent of their subject matter pertains to love or lust. We spend most of our lives looking for it, exulting in it, or losing it.

To illustrate, I've broken the subject down into several categories based on the span of a relationship, with a variety of samples for each: **Feeling the need:** The longing to love and be loved has inspired some classics: "Lookin' for Love," "When Will I Be Loved?," "Dream Lover," "Looking for Another Pure Love," and "You Can't Hurry Love."

I think I've just found her (or him): This is the part where you've just seen someone, you think you might be in love already, and you're scoping out the situation: "Da Doo Ron Ron," "I'm Into Something Good," "I Saw Her Standing There," "Like to Get to Know You," "I've Just Seen a Face," "Pretty Woman," "Sharing the Night Together," "Must Be Somebody's Baby," and "Love, Or Something Like It."

The big come-on: A formidable category, since so many love and lust games are played out to a background of popular music. It encompasses both the bold and tender: "Let's Spend the Night Together," "Kiss You All Over," "I'm in the Mood for Love," "Feel Like Makin' Love," "Lay Lady Lay," "Sexual Healing," "Make Yourself Comfortable," "I'm Ready," "Tonight's the Night," and, of course, hundreds more.

This is it, I'm in love: For better or worse you've passed the point of no return: "Fooled Around and Fell in Love," "For Once in My Life," "Can't Help Falling in Love," "It's So Easy," "Truly," "Baby I Love You," "How Sweet It Is," "Your Song," "My Girl," "My Own True Love," "True Blue," "Nothing's Gonna Stop Us Now." This may possibly be the biggest category of love songs.

The honeymoon is over: Or "The Thrill is Gone," "Don't Be Cruel," "Cold as Ice," "Suspicious Minds," "We Can Work It Out," "This Masquerade," "Sometimes When We Touch," "You've Lost That Lovin' Feeling," "You Don't Bring Me Flowers," "Love on the Rocks," "You Keep Me Hanging On."

Cheating: Songs of infidelity, guilt, suspicion, and jealousy are popular, despite their negativity, because they're great drama and everyone can identify with those feelings and experiences: "Lying Eyes," "If Loving You is Wrong," "Me and Mrs. Jones," "Your Cheatin' Heart," "Ruby, Don't Take Your Love to Town," "You Belong to Me," "I'm Losing You," "Who's Cheatin' Who," "Him," and "What She Don't Know Won't Hurt Her."

Leaving: Along with cheating, the trauma of goodbye is an emotional minefield, with heavy pathos: "I'd Rather Leave While I'm In Love," "For the Good Times," "By the Time I Get To Phoenix," "Bye Bye Love," "Don't Think Twice, It's All Right," "Breaking Up is Hard to Do," "If You Leave Me Now," "I've Been Loving You Too Long," "It's Too Late," "I Will Survive," and "Fifty Ways to Leave Your Lover."

Remembering how it used to be: After the breakup and the passage of time, the more positive among us tend to fondly remember the good times and forget the bad. If we've been on the losing end, there's a profound sense of loss and longing that has created some classics: "I Can't Stop Loving You," "Love Has No Pride," "Time in a Bottle," "As Tears Go By," "Tears on My Pillow," "Hello Walls," "Funny How Time Slips Away," "San Francisco Bay Blues," "I'm Sorry," "She's Gone," "Same Auld Lang Syne," "Yesterday," "I'll Be Over You."

Philosophy: It's also human nature to aid the recovery process by trying to provide a rationale and perspective for it all. "All in Love is Fair," "Only Love Can Break Your Heart," "The Things We Do for Love," "It's All in the Game," and "The Rose."

Sex sells just about everything. It is an international preoccupation, particularly for those in the prime record-buying age groups. A look at any week's *Billboard* Hot 100 singles chart shows that outright sex themes are still prime song lyric topics.

Radio wasn't always as tolerant as it is now. If writers wanted to get that powerful, money-making air play they had to avoid the subject, or be very clever about it. In the early '50s, even songs like "Teach Me Tonight," as tame as it sounds today, were considered risqué. See how jaded we've become?

Throughout history there's been a wealth of bawdy balladry. During the '60s folk revival, Oscar Brand ("Bawdy Songs and Backroom Ballads"), Ed McCurdy ("When Dalliance was in Flower") and others resurrected volumes of it to record. A lot of hard-core album cuts exist today that you won't hear on the radio. A heavy division has always existed between what can be sold on record and what's considered fit fare for the air, but in the past few years that division seems to have all but disappeared and if a song isn't getting air play it's more likely because it doesn't sound like a hit than because it's offensive. There are rock stations that fifteen years ago would have been shut down for playing songs that seem commonplace today. Public attitudes are always in a state of change though, and a songwriter must always be aware of those changes. In light of the AIDS epidemic, songs that seem to encourage casual sex are now being viewed by many as irresponsible and dangerous.

If you're going to write about sex, the next big question is, "How?" I've said before that the songwriter must reflect his own personal attitudes about the subject, no matter how self-indulgent, sexist, debauched, or immature they may be.

The important thing is that those of you who have more positive attitudes about sex should get your songs to the marketplace as well. Along with all the TV shows and films that seem to encourage teenage sex (and drug use), we also have a strong media campaign that says, "Just say no." Unless songwriters want to invite censorship, we must make sure there are alternative philosophies and values offered to impressionable minds. Songs like Jermaine Stewart's hit, "We Don't Have to Take Our Clothes Off

(To Have a Good Time)," offer a positive alternative to songs that are more sexually exploitative.

The treatment of sex in a song may be subtle or explicit. Explicitness gets old fast and ultimately is not as stimulating as a song that is more clever, subtle, sensuous, perhaps using *double entendre.* It's been said that the mind is the most sensitive erogenous zone. Use your imagination and creativity to stimulate it. It takes little imagination or craftsmanship to say, "Let's Do It," which also risks being a turnoff. David Gates's standard, "Make It With You" let the listener use the phrase not only in a sexual sense, but in the sense of building a successful relationship. Songs like that, with titillating titles but with broader, multilevel meanings and good craftsmanship, not only sell well but are more satisfying for a longer time as a listening experience.

THE CENSORSHIP ISSUE

Sex-oriented lyrics of varying degrees of explicitness can be found in all styles of music. Those in rock music, for some reason, are increasingly under fire by self-appointed guardians of our national morality. These elements have raised the spectre of music censorship which, if it materializes, would constitute a major barrier to self-expression.

Perhaps the focus has also made us aware of the power lyricists wield. Songwriters, who spend a substantial part of their careers attempting to gain some acceptance by the industry, are unaccustomed to imagining a ten-year-old kid singing their lyrics. That reality (after the song is a hit) has caused many writers to reassess their responsibility to the listener. Whether or not you allow this pressure to influence your creative choices, the responsibility should not be taken lightly.

There will always be critics who will only listen to part of what you say and misinterpret based on that incomplete knowledge. Some have been known to condemn a song about drugs without realizing it's an *anti*-drug song. In a situation like that, you should at least have the satisfaction of knowing that you *did* write the song you *intended* to write.

Sex is not only a major human drive but a major topic on TV, in novels and in our own conversations. It can't be ignored and won't ever go away. To censor sex as a song topic would be like asking songwriters not to write about love.

MESSAGE SONGS

Most songwriters, particularly in the early stages of their development, seem motivated primarily by the need to express some kind of emotional turmoil. Most often it's "my baby left me," or "I'm so lonely," or "he/she's cheatin' on me"—all negative scenarios. We may think our experience is unique, that we're the only one able to feel such pain. But intellectually, we know how common this situation really is. In times of heavy stress, our ability to think rationally is temporarily on vacation.

Consequently, when the professional songwriter in us looks back on those songs after we've cooled out, we're amazed at how trite and unimaginative those "agony" songs are. Not that agony or other strong emotion doesn't occasionally spawn something profound; but most often, it just spawns self-indulgence. There's nothing wrong with writing songs during these periods as therapy. Just don't get the idea that because you wrote something in a heavy emotional state, it's automatically going to produce a fantastic song.

Another song genre that grows out of a strong emotional state, though often a more positive one, is the message song. Even though it's positive, it may have similar results as the "agony" song unless you're careful. Here's an example:

You've just had a religious experience, and must tell the world about your revelation. The spirits have laid a great truth on you and as a musician and songwriter, you're uniquely qualified to spread the word.

So you dash off a song. After all, this is a very important message, and you don't want to bother with all those crass commercial techniques like rhyme and meter. They seem so unimportant next to the innate power of the message. You just know that when you sing it, everyone within earshot will automatically share your feelings.

Wrong! Suddenly, as you play the song for a publisher, or even for someone on the street, reality becomes a new revelation. You realize this person a) doesn't care, b) has heard it all before and it doesn't make any more sense now than it ever did, or c) he already shares your belief and is bored by the way you stated it. You've told it the way you felt it, but failed to *communicate* it to someone who needs the message, or failed to move someone who already knows it by not presenting it in a fresh, new way.

Very few "message" songs actually communicate their message. If the lyric is weak, the music has to be doubly strong to make up for it. The Beatles' "All You Need is Love" is one of the most trite lyrics on paper, but it works, thanks to the Beatles' fame, an interesting melody, a 7/4 time signature, and strong production. Without a powerful musical vehicle, the words have to stand on their own.

Len Chandler and I have a phrase, "man on the mountain," for a particularly preachy kind of stance. It translates to "I, at my tender age, have gone to the mountaintop and learned the secret of the universe. And now, from this lofty perch, I'm going to tell all you unfortunate, unenlightened people how to live your lives."

As a listener, I have one demand: Don't preach to me! If I want to be preached at, I'll go to church. If I need guidance, I'll look for someone with credentials.

I'm not anti-message songs. On the contrary, I don't think there are enough effective ones around. I'd just like writers to take their messages

24

seriously enough to devote some time and craft to ensuring I receive them.

Now that I've told you what doesn't work, what does?

Some people might respond to the sledge-hammer, preachy "You've got to . . . ," "You'd better . . . ," "Don't ever . . ." school of thought, but more of us would probably rather be led gently than driven to enlightenment with a whip.

The most effective songs are the ones that involve me in a scene I'm a part of, or one I feel is cut so realistically from the fabric of life that I could be part of. Jesus, Buddha, and all the great religious leaders used parables to get their messages to masses of people, to relate those messages to people's everyday lives. The Good Samaritan was one of Jesus's greatest hits. Wouldn't you feel great if you wrote a song that 2,000 years later still taught the same message as strongly as it did when it was written?

One of the best contemporary examples of this type of song comes from the late Harry Chapin and his wife, Sandy. The message, that we should all try to spend more time with our parents and children, is important in a time when all of us have so many activities that keep us away from each other. The Chapins could have written a song that said, "You'd better spend time with your families or the family unit will be destroyed." Sledge-hammer! No poetry, too general, impersonal, and pompous. Instead, they wrote "Cat's in the Cradle."

CAT'S IN THE CRADLE
Words and music by Harry Chapin and Sandy Chapin

> My child arrived just the other day
> He came to the world in the usual way
> But there were planes to catch and bills to pay
> He learned to walk while I was away
> And he was talkin' 'fore I knew it,
> and as he grew he'd say
> "I'm gonna be like you, Dad
> You know I'm gonna be like you."
>
> And the cat's in the cradle and the silver spoon,
> little boy blue and the man in the moon.
> "When you comin' home Dad?" "I don't know when,
> But we'll get together then; you know we'll have a good time then."
>
> My son turned ten just the other day
> He said, "Thanks for the ball, Dad, come on let's play.
> Can you teach me to throw?" I said, "Not today,
> I got a lot to do." He said, "That's okay."
> And he walked away but his smile never dimmed,
> it said, "I'm gonna be like him, yeah,
> you know I'm gonna be like him."

And the cat's in the cradle and the silver spoon,
Little boy blue and the man in the moon.
"When you comin' home Dad?" "I don't know when,
But we'll get together then; you know we'll have a good time then."

Well he came from college just the other day
so much like a man I just had to say,
"Son I'm proud of you, can you sit for a while?"
He shook his head and he said with a smile,
"What I'd really like, Dad, is to borrow the car keys
see you later, can I have them please?"

And the cat's in the cradle and the silver spoon,
Little boy blue and the man in the moon.
"When you comin' home Son?" "I don't know when,
But we'll get together then; you know we'll have a good time then."

I've long since retired, my son's moved away
I called him up just the other day.
I said "I'd like to see you if you don't mind."
He said, "I'd love to, Dad, if I can find the time.
You see, my new job's a hassle and the kids have the flu,
but it's sure nice talkin' to you, Dad, it's sure nice talkin' to you."

And as I hung up the phone, it occurred to me,
he'd grown up just like me. My boy was just like me.

And the cat's in the cradle and the silver spoon,
Little boy blue and the man in the moon.
"When you comin' home Son?" "I don't know when,
But we'll get together then; you know we'll have a good time then.

The Chapins didn't give us any "shoulds" here. They didn't have to. They held a mirror up to life that made listeners think about their relationships with their parents, and did it with real-life dialogue and situations we've all been in. They also did it from a first-person point-of-view.

The point-of-view is very important in message songs. It's effective to describe a situation in terms of your own personal involvement. If you're offering a message, you're really being a kind of salesman. Testimonials are always very effective sales devices. A good approach is to let people in on your own discovery—what got *you* so excited that you wanted to tell us about it. Your enthusiasm will motivate us without your having to preach to us. The first-person (I, we) approach, assuming you put the song together in a way that makes people want to sing along with you, lets your audience internalize the message by saying "I" or "we" along with you.

Another effective point-of-view is that of the seemingly uninvolved storyteller. This type of song doesn't moralize because, if the story is told

26

well, there's no need for it. One of the most powerful examples is Bob Dylan's "Ballad of Hollis Brown," about a man who kills his family and himself rather than see them starve to death because he can't find a job. Dylan wrote many other powerful songs in this way. Stevie Wonder's "Living for the City" and "The Way It Is" by Bruce Hornsby are other good examples.

I don't mean to imply that there are only a few approaches to writing effective message songs. What I'm focusing on here are ways to write for mass audiences who don't necessarily share your point of view. You can use a "sledge-hammer" approach as a rallying song for people who are already on your side. You can use humor, satire, anything that *works*. And don't forget that the music is also important in helping people to hear the message *and* remember it.

Message writers generally choose *not* to collaborate, perhaps for fear their message will somehow become compromised. In fact, they may be compromising their ability to get that song to a wide audience. If you can write a powerful lyric but are a little shaky in the music department, look for someone who composes well in a contemporary style. The music is such a powerful vehicle for delivering the message that it shouldn't be taken lightly. Social and political message songs occasionally become hits. A controversial message may help a song gain notoriety but it's still the power of the performance, the music, and the record that makes a radio station play it. Your message deserves the best of all ingredients.

NOVELTY SONGS

Every writer seems to have at least one crazy, off-the-wall novelty song written just for fun. The spirit can be as infectious and as much fun for an audience to hear as it was for the writer to write.

Novelty songs, however, are extremely difficult to place with an artist. Aside from a very few artists such as Ray Stevens ("The Streak," "People's Court"), Jim Stafford ("Spiders and Snakes"), Ross Bagdassarian (The Chipmunks), Weird Al Yankovic ("Eat It"), and Pinkard and Bowden, who have built careers on novelty records, most artists and their producers and record companies view novelty records, particularly for new artists, as career killers. If an artist gets a hit on a novelty record, it's next to impossible to get radio to accept any kind of serious music from the artist after that. If you feel you've got a terrific novelty song, forget pitching it to publishers. Instead, pitch it directly to the few artists who do them, their managers or producers. It's a long shot, but one which might work.

The Dr. Demento show is a nationally syndicated radio program featuring novelty material from unknown writers. "Weird Al" got his start there. Contact the show at: Dr. Demento, %The Demento Society, P.O. Box 884, Culver City, CA 90230.

Another approach is to pitch your song to a non-novelty artist who might use it in a live performance. Most artists like to lighten up their stage act by inserting a funny song. They'll often hire writers to create such "special material" for the act based on the personality of the artist and the function the material needs to fulfill in the act. Contact the artist's manager. If they like it, chances are (even if they use it in the act) they won't record it, so charge them a fee for using it.

Be careful, though, if you write parodies of well-known songs. Though it may be considered a fair use area, you could still be subject to a lawsuit. The safest approach is to get permission from the publisher first. (See "Copyright Infringement/Plagiarism," page 135.)

CHRISTMAS SONGS

Every year I get a few Christmas songs in the mail. They're almost invariably on lead sheets (lyrics with musical notation) with no tape. I've never understood why, since I rarely get lead sheets anymore. Neither does most of the rest of the industry unless the song is going to be recorded. It tells me that these are probably people who haven't had much contact with the industry. Maybe they figure that if they could just write one good Christmas song, like "White Christmas," they'd be set for life. Unfortunately, I've never received a Christmas song in the mail to get very excited about. Not because they didn't feel right in the summertime, but because they didn't exhibit the craftsmanship that all songs need in order to be competitive.

But let's assume that they did. What does the Christmas market look like? I spoke with publishers and other industry folks and the consensus was that it's an even bigger long shot than trying to get a hit record. Obviously, the first barrier is that the song is seasonal, not the kind people will buy year 'round. The real barrier, though, is that a record needs air play to become a hit, and few stations allot that much time for Christmas music.

Veteran publisher Jay Lowy explains that a few years ago, right after Thanksgiving, the radio rotation of Christmas songs would begin and escalate until most stations had a couple days' worth of solid Christmas fare at Christmas eve and day. The air play of those songs was encouraged by the stations' ad salesmen to stimulate Christmas shopping activity for their accounts.

Now, with few exceptions, stations keep playing their regular hits with only an occasional holiday song thrown in. They figure their audience isn't tuning in to hear Christmas music. Unless a major artist like Kenny Rogers records a Christmas LP, Lowy adds, it's seldom worth it for a record company to ship records for a short period of time, then pay to have the leftovers shipped back. The retailers would rather use their stockroom space for records that sell year 'round.

If the song fits a contemporary rock or other mass-appeal radio format, it's more likely to get played on those stations than something like "White Christmas," but it would still help if you had a contemporary superstar to help it along.

Print: Ronny Schiff, an independent agent for print music projects, says that she knows of several Christmas songs which have become successful in the educational market by virtue of having great choral arrangements. These were popularized mainly by word of mouth among choral directors and presented in annual school and church pageants. One of the best examples is Albert Burt's "Do You Hear What I Hear?" Another is the Ukrainian folk song "The Carol Of The Bells," which was popular as a choral piece for generations before someone recorded a pop Christmas arrangement.

The "back door" method, says Schiff, is the best for this type of song. When she was working for publishers in New York a few years ago, she saw many people plugging Christmas songs to recording artists but not one she knew of was successful. "We Need A Little Christmas" still gets performed frequently on TV shows but since it was from *Auntie Mame,* not only a popular play but a movie, it got widespread exposure automatically. Schiff adds that Christmas songs sell best in books and not in individual sheet music. This, I suspect, reflects the fact that people will go for a book of standards first and it takes continued popularity of an individual song before it starts being included in the books.

TV: Every year major artists do Christmas TV specials. Your song may have a shot at one with some ingenuity, good timing and contacts, or a good publisher. Otherwise that new song that's needed by the special is written "for hire" by musical directors who work for the show.

Contemporary Christian and Gospel: This part of the industry is in a growth period and may be more receptive than pop radio to Christmas songs with a religious message.

If you're a long-shot player and an excellent writer, if you're willing to start pitching your songs in July and to work for years to develop a standard, you may be one of the few who gets a big royalty check for Christmas.

The Media and the Listeners

THE MEDIA

Let's assume you're a songwriter who ultimately wants your songs to reach the public. As much as you'd like to just wave that magic wand and have everyone automatically hear them, the reality is that, before that happens, your song must pass judgment by a whole series of people. Publishers, producers, record company A&R representatives, record promoters, radio program directors and club owners all, in their own ways, decide in which medium your music belongs or whether your music is appropriate for their particular medium.

When we attend a classical music concert we expect to hear long compositions with several different movements. In a film, we expect to hear music that creates mood, that enhances and heightens the action and drama.

When we turn on a pop, country, R&B, rock, or other contemporary music station, we know we'll hear songs that will hold our attention with excellent production and arrangements, that have frequent and regularly recurring changes in lyrical, musical, and rhythmic texture and fairly predictable form. On an album-oriented rock (AOR) station, we know (at least we hope) we'll hear cuts that run longer than those on Top 40 stations, that are of higher intensity and maybe more adventurous subject matter.

In musical theater, the songs reveal characters' personalities and help tell the story. When a character sings a song, the lyric and music must feel natural to that character. However, they don't *need* to be structured like radio songs unless they're also intended for air play. Since theater is a visual medium, it already holds our attention and isn't as dependent on the type of "reach out and grab you" dynamics that radio needs.

The point is that every medium has both restrictions and freedoms that are created by the function of that medium, the needs of the industry, and the expectations of the audience. The more we understand the medium in which we want to work, its principles and forms, the better we can manipulate it.

A POEM IS NOT A LYRIC

In the print medium, we have an exceptional legacy of poetry in all languages. Much of that poetry also lends itself to recitation and may, in fact, be written specifically to be recited. It is one of a poet's creative options, and if he chooses it, he knows that there are certain words or syllables that won't flow comfortably in speech but will work fine on paper. Other words that can conjure pictures when spoken passionately don't have nearly as much impact on paper. Dylan Thomas's poetry, though it does work on paper, was clearly written to be recited, and recordings of him or Brendan Behan reciting it can bring tears to the eyes. The point is that poetry lives in the media of print and speech. Lyrics, on the other hand, live elsewhere.

A common misconception is that songs are poetry put to music. An immense number of treasured lyrics do work as well on the printed page as in a musical context. Writer/artists such as Jackson Browne, Joni Mitchell, Bob Dylan, Paul Simon, Carly Simon and others possess vocal and writing styles so integrated that an unusually poetic phrase feels right at home in their styles, but would not work comfortably in another artist's style. How many Joni Mitchell songs can you imagine other artists performing without imitating her style?

Performers such as these are considered "album artists." In other words, we buy their albums, not because they have a hit single, but because we like their style and like who we perceive them to be. We're likely to read their lyrics on the album liners and allow them a little more "poetic license," a little more abstraction and a few more obscure references that we're challenged to figure out. We don't mind because we're already fans.

The point is, though some lyrics work as poetry, a good poem does not necessarily make a good lyric. The obvious difference is that a lyric must function with music; it must be sung. A poem written for the printed page alone can use graphic style and unusual placement of words on a page to emphasize subtleties in meaning. It's not expected to rhyme. It can use sight rhyme (*board, bored*). It can indulge in abstractions, because if the words aren't readily understood, our eyes and minds can stop for as long as we need to let them sink in and bounce around in the brain.

Much of what is referred to as "poetry" is really verse. The difference is that between substance and form, imagination and craft. Verse is really anything that conforms to accepted metrical rules and structure. Anyone can write good verse that rhymes and has accurate meter, but if it's devoid of substance and imagination, it's still not poetry.

Good lyrics need to have all those attributes and more—and less. In an interview with Oscar-winning lyricist Dean Pitchford ("Footloose"), I asked what he felt was the difference between poetry and lyric since he had been a poet prior to becoming a lyricist:

I think poetry, in its final form, is on the page. Maybe when it's read, it achieves something else, but poetry is on the page. Lyric is only 50 percent of the work of a song, and it's spare. It can't be very full or fleshed out. Otherwise you don't leave much room for the music to do anything, or for the interpretation of the singer, which is why I learned very early on that you don't read lyrics to people who aren't in the music industry. It doesn't read, it doesn't speak, and a musician could maybe hear it like the song it could become, but a lyric is not a finished thing. You also have to resist the temptation to fill all the corners, to expand to fill your space. People hand me these typewritten sheets saying, "What do you think?" and it looks like the Gettysburg Address—long extended lines and they're very erudite and smart and there's lots of thought and inner rhymes and alliteration, but there's no space for the music.

The lyric, like a poem, seeks to imaginatively express an idea or emotion in a condensed, yet powerful way. Music helps it do that. Eddy Lawrence Manson is a top film scorer and teacher. In his classes he asks a student to walk across the room the same way several times. Each time, he plays different music expressing different moods behind the walk. Each time the music expresses a different idea about what that person is feeling, where he or she is going. You can do that to a lyrical phrase with different music, too. The right (or wrong) music can give that spare and lean phrase exactly the right or wrong meaning. New lyricists have a tendency to minimize the importance of the music as an aid to delivering their message.

Unlike poetry, the words in a lyric must be able to be sung well. Words like "orange" are not only impossible to rhyme, but difficult to sing. A lyricist must be able to imagine someone singing the words.

In writing lyrics for radio songs, we need to remember that in a quick three minutes the listener doesn't have time, as in poetry, to wonder what the words really mean.

A SONG IS NOT A RECORD

Making a record is a craft in its own right. Today, the craft of making a record or tape involves the combined skills of singers, musicians, arrangers, producers, and recording engineers. Their creativity and command of the technology involved can transform a mediocre song into a wonderful sonic experience. But they'll never make it a great song. A great song has a life of its own. It will move you even if it's sung *a cappella.* It can be sung by different artists in different eras with the same results.

Many writers voice the complaint, "My song is better than a lot of stuff I hear on the radio, so why doesn't anyone want it?" They're usually right, but what they've failed to recognize is the difference between a "hit record" and a "hit song."

The appeal of the *record* may be based primarily on any of the combination of ingredients aside from words and melody: a powerful vocal performance, an artist or group with a unique identity or sound, a great arrangement, or business considerations such as timing or promotion. There are a lot of hit *records* that we can't remember the melody to, or the lyrics; perhaps we just remember the hook line. We may even find ourselves humming the bass line. Those aren't songs—they're records.

You can't write a *record* unless you're in control of that recording situation as a producer or artist (though you *can* put together a demo that suggests the ingredients that give the producer a blueprint to work from.)

I've bought records solely on my love of the finished product, even though I couldn't hum the melody or had no understanding of the lyric. Peter Gabriel's "Shock the Monkey" was one of them. I played the record over and over and even after I *saw* the lyrics, I had no idea what he was talking about. It communicated nothing to me as a song, but I enjoyed it as a listening experience. Had he written a great song to go with that experience, it would have been a classic.

Those of you who record your own material will, I hope, remember that the more you approach your art and craft with a desire to communicate and a commitment to excellence, the more powerfully an audience will experience it.

Some producers and artists strive for the best product possible by seeking out the best songs available, whether they write them themselves or go for "outside" (other writers') songs. Others, more concerned about collecting royalties than turning out a quality product, would rather record a mediocre song of their own than go for a great song by someone else. It's up to the record buyers whether they'll continue to subsidize mediocrity.

WRITING FOR RADIO

In the many interviews Len Chandler and I have done with radio program directors, we've frequently been reminded that radio personnel don't consider themselves to be in the record business. They're in the ADVERTISING business. They'll play or do whatever will make the largest possible audience listen. The bigger the audience, the more money advertisers will pay to sell everything from acne medicine to insurance. The approaches vary widely, from high energy Top 40 (or 20) stations, with hard sell styles, to instrumental Muzak-type stations, where the commercials register almost subliminally. Some stations seek to reach a wide variety of listeners and age groups, with music that's interesting and not too high-energy. This used to be called MOR (Middle of the Road) or "Easy Listening," but is now classified as AC (adult contemporary). Others attempt to pinpoint a specific "market" with classical music, country, soul, or Top 40 pop.

The competition is very heavy between radio stations, particularly between those with similar formats. They're obsessed with preventing "dial outs." Once they have you tuned in, they don't want you to go away. Consequently, one of the most important requirements for music on the radio is that it holds the listener's attention. While it's true that holding someone's attention on the radio is accomplished by a combination of song, artist, and production, you need to start with a song that lends itself well to radio. The following chapters will help you create that type of song.

SONG LENGTH

The greatest percentage of hit radio songs used to be approximately three minutes long. Today they may be as long as four minutes and sometimes longer. You rarely hear them much longer than that because radio wants to play more songs yet keep more space for commercials. Knowing this, few publishers, producers, and record companies want to buck those kinds of odds by signing/producing/recording a longer song. They also know that exceptionally long songs won't get maximum "rotation," that is, the number of times per hour or day a song gets played. They'd rather a short song got played once an hour than a long one every three hours. With a higher frequency of air play you, as a writer, will make more money from BMI or ASCAP, the performing rights organizations. (See Chapter 9, "Where Your Money Comes From.") It's interesting to note that, when radio was much tougher about keeping songs down to three minutes, record companies were known to put 2:59 on the label of a single that really maybe ran 3:04, just for that extra edge!

A great story is told about country superstar Buck Owens, who had a radio background before his career as a recording artist. Knowing that DJs frequently had less than three minutes to go before a newsbreak or commercial, too short to play a three-minute record and maybe too long to fill with idle chatter, he fashioned his first hits to two minutes or under and let the DJs know it. Consequently, he got lots of air play in those awkward time slots.

Radio personnel *will* play a longer song if there is such an incredible public demand for it that they might lose listeners to another station. However, that song had better be able to hold an audience's attention from beginning to end and make them want to hear it again.

Michael Jackson and other major artists get away with long songs on hit radio because everyone wants to hear these artists. A common practice is to edit a record for different functions: a short version for the radio single and longer versions for AOR (Album-Oriented Radio) or for the dance club market.

Something else to be considered in the length of the song is the *introduction.* "Intro" lengths vary, but it's generally considered that for a slow song approximately ten seconds of introduction is optimum. For an upbeat dance tune, twenty seconds or more can work because, if it grabs your body, you'll keep listening.

Even though these general time guidelines are important, it's *more* important that the intro be easily identifiable and *musically interesting.* It should involve changing textures, adding instruments, or other arrangement devices to keep it developing. Nothing induces boredom faster than an intro that "goes nowhere."

A unique, identifiable introduction will make a radio station's program director pay attention. If he pays attention, he feels his audience will too. Just a warning, though: DJs love to talk over intros. Many people find it irritating (myself included) but it gets back to radio trying to save more time for commercials. Some DJs just get excited about having sound tracks behind their raps. It's a common practice to include the time of the intro on the DJs' promotional copies, so they'll know how long to talk.

SINGLES, ALBUMS, AND LIVE PERFORMANCES

The ability to distinguish between the requirements of these three different media and art forms can eliminate a lot of confusion for a writer or writer/performer.

Let's start with live performance. It's not unusual to have a writer/performer play me a mediocre-to-fair song and be shocked when my response is less than enthusiastic. He'll say, *"The people* love these songs when I play them in the clubs and, after all, aren't *they* my audience?" Yes, they *are* your audience and they'll almost always respond to a high-energy, enthusiastic performance, a heartfelt delivery, and to a performer with conviction and personal charisma. The positive response a writer/artist gets from a club performance can be very misleading when he doesn't separate the performance from the song.

The writer/artist often takes his performance ability for granted. He may be relatively new to songwriting and writing songs in which he's invested a lot of himself. The songs, in his mind, take the focus and he consequently assumes that people are applauding the songs rather than the performance.

When we go to a club and plunk down ten dollars in cover charges and possibly twenty dollars or more on drinks for a date, we're willing to go more than halfway to be entertained. We *want* a performer to be good and we're easily pleased. Give us a performer with the qualities mentioned above and we can be ecstatic. Take the same songs on audio tape to a hard-nosed publisher or a record company A&R rep who's separating the performance from the song and looking for a hit and it's a whole new situation. These businesspeople can't *see* the performance, be moved by the charisma, and communicated to via facial expressions and body language; the song has to stand on its own. This is particularly true for publishers, who have to convince another artist to record the song.

A lot of music works in clubs that wouldn't work as a hit single. A ten-minute vamp will work for a dancing crowd and a ten-minute guitar or drum solo can bring a club or concert crowd to a frenzy, but put it on a "hit format" radio station, and the same person who loved it in concert may turn the dial.

You'll be learning more about the qualities of hit singles in the following chapters. Let it suffice here to say that the dynamics needed for a hit single can certainly work in a club though the reverse is not necessarily true, particularly as it relates to the length of the record.

Albums are another medium altogether. Generally speaking, albums allow more creative latitude, particularly for self-contained bands and writer/artists. "The Doors" were a good example. The group's hit singles were a completely different listening experience from their concerts or albums, both of the latter being much more spontaneous and unpredictable. They could stretch the forms and create tremendous tension with long repetitive vamps that would never work in the group's hit singles. Longer, more dramatic songs were possible, coming closer, in fact, to musical theater. Most great performing artists and bands present an audience with quite a different experience in concert than on record.

Albums have always been a more viable medium for jazz artists and for rock and soul fusion instrumentalists because the longer format gives them an opportunity to showcase their performance skill and that of other band members. Also, when we buy an album rather than a single, it's usually because we like the artist already and are willing to invest our attention and time in sharing this adventure with them. We'll read the liner notes, follow the lyrics, and generally pay attention in a way not far removed from the attention we pay at a concert. It doesn't have to *demand* our attention like a hit single. It already has it.

Given that, then, the album has an obligation not to betray the buyer's trust. We're all tired of having been seduced by a hit single and profoundly disappointed by a mediocre album with mundane and unmemorable songs and performances. Personally, I'll forgive an artist for being adventurous on an album, even if it falls short of my expectations, but not for copping out by giving me empty "filler" just to have an album to sell.

THE LISTENER: KNOW YOUR AUDIENCE

Most writers give little conscious thought to who they're writing for. They may write primarily for themselves and automatically reach an audience of their peers who share their emotional problems, social scene, political concerns, colloquial language, and musical styles. They're a reflection of what is happening around them, and they're popular because of it. They aren't deliberately writing for a target demographic group. They *are* that group. Self-contained writer/artists and groups like the Rolling Stones may not only keep an audience who grew up with them, but also continue to appeal to an audience maybe twenty years younger who can still identify with their attitudes. On the other hand, the Stones still write about the same things they wrote about twenty years ago.

If you want the creative challenge of writing songs for artists in different styles of music than the one(s) you've been most at home with, you need to do some stretching. The challenge is to analyze the appeal of an artist and the characteristics of his or her audience. Then write a song in that artist's style. Immerse yourself in the artist's work. Listen to the radio stations that play his records. Buy some of them yourself, especially recent successful ones.

Be careful not to make quick, stereotyped judgments or harbor any negative attitudes about the style. I counselled a writer, for instance, who expressed interest in writing country songs. I asked who his favorite country artists were and he said, "I don't know. I never listen to country. In fact, I don't even like it! It just seems like it would be easier to write than pop and more artists record songs they don't write." I told him to forget it. The motivation was all wrong.

It's difficult enough to come up with something worthwhile even when you know and love a style. Having the wrong attitudes about a kind of music you haven't really lived with or made a thorough study of can easily get you way off track. You have to know, for instance, that complex melodies and chord changes, while jazz fans may love them, don't work in most country songs. Abstract lyrics that might spark a pop or rock piece would turn off a country audience.

One of the most common problems in targeting listeners comes from inappropriate combinations of music and subject matter. For instance, heavy metal appeals to primarily young, white males age twelve to eighteen. A romantic lyric like "Looks Like We Made It" doesn't make it in heavy metal; rebellious lyrics do. Attitude is very important in rock and roll. A hard, frantic edge in the music needs attitudes that aren't soft, mushy, or tender. Groups like Journey and Genesis appeal to both young men and women because there's room in their image and repertoire to do romantic ballads as well as rockers. The point is that you need to understand who an artist's audience is to write effective material.

Visualize the audience you're writing the song for. A writer once played me a song involving a man propositioning his wife's best friend. He reminds her he's still in love with his wife, so she shouldn't think about getting too involved. Musically, it was a mellow pop ballad, a style that appeals primarily to women, and the song was obviously directed to a woman. But the song had a few obvious flaws. The audience is being asked to identify with the best friend. Even if we assume she liked the guy and was flattered by the come-on, she would not feel great about hearing him say he was still in love with his wife! The other category of potential record buyers—wives—are not going to enjoy a song in which the husband propositions her best friend. So the song effectively negated the very audience that would be most drawn to the musical style. If he had thought, to start with, how his audience would feel hearing the song, he would not have made those mistakes.

Whether you're writing a song for yourself or for someone else, if you want it to sell to an audience, it's important to have an idea who they are and how they will respond.

Chris Blake was an interview guest and song critiquer for a weekly LASS event, and I had an opportunity to discuss with him what makes songs "work" for an audience. I found him to be even more obsessed with the subject than I was, to the degree that he had spent a lot of time in research. I was even more pleased to see how well he articulated that research and decided that the material was important enough to be included in this book. Chris has a book of his own in mind, but graciously consented to my use of the following part of his material.

THE IMAGINATION OF THE LISTENER
by Chris Blake

Imagination plays a large part in our perception of a song. The imagination converts words into experiences, turning songs into old friends that we want to hear again and again. The hit song lyric is one which, one way or another, gives the imagination what it needs to do that job, simply, easily, and completely.

The theater of the imagination performs twenty-four hours a day. It literally cannot *not* function but as a mechanism it has certain characteristics—certain ways of acting and reacting—which we, as writers, need to know about.

Much remains to be learned about the human imagination and how it works, but a review of some of what has been found so far could make a difference to your work as a lyricist. I'm going to spare you the specific references and "technical" talk that is in much of the scientific literature. (For those who enjoy that sort of thing, see the Bibliography.) But I do want to point out some specific characteristics of the imagination which have been confirmed by scientific research and are totally relevant to the job of the song lyricist.

The imagination is a stimulus-response mechanism. That is, it will not act unless acted upon, at which point it will act (or more properly, react) totally automatically.

What stimulates the imagination is just about any "cue" which it perceives. To keep it simple, we can talk about "cues" as *internal* and *external.*

Internal cues are those which originate from within—from thoughts, associations, and memories. Fantasies and daydreams are good examples of the imagination responding to internal cues. While it's important to notice that the imagination itself cannot originate a stimulus, it can and does respond to its own images all the time. All of us who have ever been guilty of daydreaming (while that half-finished lyric sits unattended in front of us) have been caught up in what the people in the lab jackets call an "associative response chain"—really an instance of the imagination taking off on its own material and going on and on.

This ability of the imagination to entertain itself is one of your major concerns as a lyricist. For now, just know that it is a relatively "weak" phenomenon. It is easily interrupted by external stimuli which, because they exist in present time, appear to hold a much stronger demand for the attention of the imagination. That ringing phone with all its potential for who might be calling, will stop a daydream every time. Sometimes, that's a shame.

External cues are just what they sound like—the sights, sounds, smells, and touch sensations—the whole world we perceive outside us. We take them in and interpret them in our own experience, giving them meaning and order in our own "reality." We then attempt to communicate our realities to one another using a set of mutually agreed-upon sounds we call "words." These words, when spoken and heard, become powerful external cues to the imagination—the cues we, as lyricists, are primarily concerned with right now.

Nowhere is the stimulus-response characteristic of the imagination clearer than in the domain of words. The imagination can't resist them. Indeed, it's a good thing! Were it not for the ability of our imaginations to convert words into images, we simply could not communicate with each other. (Nor could we communicate with ourselves, for it is in our imaginations that we put the world together.) But, let's keep it simple.

It's 6:30 A.M., and Larry, fanatic that he is, is going out jogging. This morning he's trying a new running route and, as he heads out the door, his roommate, Max (who has run the new route before) yells after him to "watch out for the dog."

As Larry goes down the steps he wonders, as he always does, why he's doing this crazy thing. But not as hard as he's wondering what Max was talking about. Dog? What dog? Watch out? Why? Larry has been hooked. And his imagination is off and running (faster than Larry, probably).

Before we find out what happened, let's take a look at what went on inside Larry's head after the dog warning. It may seem a dry exercise but as a lyricist this had best become a well-practiced way of thinking for you.

Larry's mind now launches into an enormous amount of activity, but let's just touch on the highlights. *"Watch out for the dog."* What does that mean? It's not just automatic—he's got to remember—what, exactly, does "watch out" mean, and what is a "dog"?

Well, Larry's no dummy. He is now somewhere in the "watch out for the dog" ballpark in his mind, with a vague kind of picture of what those words mean to him. And there he would remain if he didn't have an imagination. But he does have one, and because it's an automatic response mechanism, it reacts automatically to the words.

Now, the imagination is not a selective machine. That is, it doesn't make choices for us. It is programmed to retrieve from the files and project on our "screens" exactly what it's told to—no less. And what is in our files—our memory—on any given subject? Only *every experience, thought, fantasy, emotion, and impulse we've ever had which we associate, however loosely, with that subject.*

Poor Larry! All he ever did was decide to take a new running route. Let's listen in while his imagination does what it is built to do:

Dog. Yessir, coming right up. Hmm, let's see, 'dog'. . . ah, here it is— Lassie, Rin-Tin-Tin (excitement),—German Police dogs, big, teeth (fear),—memory of being bitten by Mrs. Smith's Doberman (fear, pain, anger),—old Fido and me playing on the front lawn (happy),—Fido grew old and had to be put to sleep (sad),—your parents bought you a new puppy, but he had to be housebroken (disgust),—and so on . . .

As much as all this information is, it's just a fraction of what Larry has filed away with the word "dog."

But, his roommate wasn't just talking about any "dog." He was talking about a "watch out" kind of dog:

Hmm, let's see, "Watch Out"—Oh, yeah, it's right here—pain, anger,—what Mom said just before I burned my hand on the stove (fear, pain),—it's what you're supposed to do because Santa Claus is coming to town (confused),—what that kid shouted at me just before the baseball hit me in the head (pain),—what a roommate would say if I were about to go running past a man-eating dog—(fear, anger) . . .

So now, Larry's imagination has "watch out" and "dog" files on tap. It puts them together and begins to feed Larry the following kinds of images:

Rabid wolves chasing starving children through the Russian woods

(terror),—Mrs. Smith's Doberman resurrected from the past and wait-
ing for me just around the corner (fear),—Cujo crouched behind the
next bush waiting,—The Big Bad Wolf,—packs of wild dogs, led by an
evil-minded little mutt who looks suspiciously like Fido . . .

All this sounds a little silly but, to Larry, these kinds of images don't
seem silly at the time. The point is to notice the enormity and the complex variety of the information which becomes available to Larry's
imagination from just a few words.

And he can't help himself. Notice that nothing about Larry's wild
imagining was voluntary. Unless he particularly enjoys being afraid, we
have to think that Larry probably wished he could think of something
else while running. What I hoped to demonstrate is that the imagination (given appropriate cues) will do its thing, no matter what. It is a
stimulus-response mechanism.

But please notice that the imagination is literally "wild" and has no
discipline to it. *You,* the writer, must realize that you set off this same
crazy process in the listener's head with every word you write; and it is
you who must bring discipline to the listener's imagination. You need
to impose controls on it in order to keep it somewhere in the domain in
which you intend it to be.

Your tool for this job of channeling imagery is the *specificity* in your
words. It's why God invented nouns and verbs and modifiers—adjectives and adverbs—tools to specify *exactly* who, what, where, when,
how, and why.

As we saw with Larry, the imagination will come up with the whole
crazy "file" unless it gets further directions. The quality of the image
will be generalized and nonsensical.

The tendency of the imagination is to quit the job under these conditions—for reasons we shall see—or to re-create only one particular
image for arbitrary reasons, and *it may or may not be the image you
want the listener to experience.*

Experiment for yourself. How intensely can you become involved
with the following words?

Car
Book
Musical instrument

Not very, huh? You may have chosen to focus on one image that had
personal meaning in your experience. The problem is that *I meant you
to see:*

My great 1982 Porsche 928 with the broken right tail light
My paperback book with a blue cover and the words "Gifts
of God" printed in gold on the front
My old white Telecaster guitar with the broken B-string
and the missing volume knob

While the examples may seem arbitrary, the implications for your work are direct. You want the listener's imagination to re-create what *you* want it to; and for that, you need to be specific, or the imagination will abandon you, your words, and your song and wander off down god-knows-what corridors of its own. It may pay more attention to other more specific and immediate information—the car ahead, the fight he had with his wife last night, or whatever.

It's called "getting bored," and it is astonishing how often we simply *bore* listeners away from our songs by refusing to give them specific items to imagine.

The imagination is a restless and highly distractable child, full of all good intentions and no self-control. If you want its attention, you'd better keep it busy with specific tasks.

But what tasks? Read on.

The imagination is an "analog information" mechanism, that is, it can only create pictures out of the information already stored in the mind's experience. Larry's "dog" emerged as a composite of many past real and imagined events, feelings, and pictures. Nothing really new was a part of that image, save possibly some new combinations of old information.

The phrase "floating in space" can only be imagined by memories of experiences we've already had—none of which, of course, include really floating in space. The feeling of semiweightlessness we've had floating in water—various remembered scenes from sci-fi movies—perhaps the sensation of room and freedom around us (because we've heard space is empty, vast, and infinite). All sorts of images, feelings, and sensations occur, but all of them are taken from experiences real and imagined that we've already had. Nothing new. The imagination literally cannot deliver to us the experience of floating in space but it tries hard (as it's designed to do) to re-create the experience out of old bits and pieces of information available to it. Our experience of the words can only be "imaginary" because we cannot come up with the real thing.

This is the primary reason why songs must be built on universal themes. As a songwriter, you simply cannot write about things which are outside of most people's experience and expect them to be able to relate to—to become involved in—the song through their imaginations. If they cannot relate *at the level of their imaginations,* the song becomes meaningless simply because they don't have the machinery to deal with it. Their reaction, of course, is one of instant frustration and turnoff. And your song doesn't get listened to.

It's amazing how often songwriters seem to believe they can get around this one. I wish I had a dime for every song I've heard from people who want to crash into the commercial market and yet who write about such obscure items as working on the floor of the stock market, the intricacies of shifting through ten different truck gears, and the tactics employed in 19th-century sea battles.

It's one matter to use specific detail to contribute to a universal emotion (plot). It's another to write your song exclusively about something with which you're familiar but about which a large block of listeners would have no experience or little knowledge.

Just remember to be very careful about the ideas, metaphors, and images you use in your song and keep a ruthless eye out for the possibility that you are excluding large blocks of people from participating in your song. One of the chief villains here are songs that are totally about marriage or totally about divorce. You have to remember that lots of people have neither been married nor divorced.

Mental images are complete neurophysiological events, meaning that they occur in the brain and throughout the body simultaneously.

"Unreal" as imagined experiences are, they actually can produce the experience of reality. It's a testimony to how powerful the imagination truly is that we don't just "imagine" the sensation of weightlessness; we feel it. Indeed we react emotionally and physically to images in our mind. Our bodies produce what scientists call "secondary sympathetic responses" to mental imagery. The word *red* causes "red" activity in the parts of our eyes that react to color; the word *ouch* causes muscle contraction. And nerve endings truly react to the phrase, "the touch of your hand."

Notice for yourself the number of song titles and lyrics which use images which suggest or involve physical action:

"Stop, in the Name of Love"
"Please Help Me, I'm Falling"
"If I Said You Had A Beautiful Body (Would You Hold It Against Me?)"
"Beat It"

The list would be nearly endless. The usefulness of such physical action imagery is obvious when you consider the fact that we react to mental images with actual physical sensation and action. In short, lyrics which involve such demands in their imagery hook the listener not just from the standpoint of their beauty or cleverness but from a physical standpoint as well. Remember that the imagination responds automatically to words. You literally tell it what to do and it is helpless not to respond. If you give clear, simple, precise directions to it, you can produce powerful *emotional* and *physical* events in the listener.

Are you beginning to understand just how totally listeners are "hooked" by a good lyric? We don't *have* images; we *do* them. We imagine with our whole selves.

We can produce audio "images," feeling and sensation "images," and so forth. We can, in fact, "image" just about any experience we've ever had, think we've had, or imagine we've had, and you as the songwriter, can direct us to do that if only you are clear in your directions and keep in mind the response characteristics of the imagination.

But you must realize some of the imagination's limits. Chief among these is its inability to re-create conceptual abstractions. An abstraction, for our purposes, is a subjective, usually very general, piece of information.

An abstraction just floats there. It's not grounded in specificity (who, what, where, when, or why). It is nonspecific and the imagination, because it works the way it does, doesn't know what to do with it and isn't interested. Try to imagine such external cues as "decency," "belief," "transcendent," "wonderful," "beautiful," and so forth. Abstractions lack focus.

On the face of it this creates an alarming problem for songwriters. For the worst abstractions of them all are the body of words that refer to the emotions, one of which is "love."

So how do you write a song about an emotional state such as love? Your goal is to involve the listener as deeply as possible by writing words which are usable by his imagination so that he can re-create the words of the song. The very words you would think the listener wants to hear—all about "love," "sad," "sorrow," "you hurt me," "I need you"—are abstractions the imagination cannot process.

The key to resolving this dilemma is simple enough. First, remember that listeners want "the real thing," information accessible to their imagination as they listen. Second, notice that abstractions *are* convenient for organizing and labeling our life experiences but they are most definitely not life itself.

For the fun of it, let's look at the abstract phrase, "falling in love." At the risk of offending the romantic poet in all of us, those words don't really refer to anything at all. They are only a kind of organizing label system, a file into which we put what for each of us have been unique and very real experiences. When I remember "falling in love" (the last time it happened to me), what I remember was:

being able to think of nothing else except Betsy
feeling lightheaded and slightly dizzy when I was around her
losing my appetite
daydreaming about us together
making plans for our future
wishing time would go faster so that I could be with her
having my phone bill quadruple
loving the smell of her perfume on my sweater

And on and on. Even that list is not too specific, but I *know* it brought you into a more real contact with my experience of "falling in love" than the phrase itself ever could. Are you beginning to get the drift?

Life is not an abstraction. It is moment to moment—real, specific, and concrete. And so it is that when the imagination re-creates life it can only do so with specific and concrete images. Thus, when you write lyrics, you must give the mind the kind of cues and information it needs to do its job or it won't bother with the information.

Abstractions simply do not work in the imagination. They, in fact, serve to turn it away.

And yet it is true that songs are about abstractions. I refer you to Jack Smalley's excellent book, *Lyrics, Lyrics, Lyrics,* published by Simon and Schuster, in which the author asserts that there are just seven possible "plots" to a commercial song: Love, hate, loneliness, happiness, sadness, jealousy, and revenge. Every one of those words is an abstraction—every one of them is basically unusable by the imagination—and every one of them refers to what is at the heart of universal commerciality.

Nonetheless, it does present an apparent contradiction. How does the writer write about abstract emotions in a way which engages and involves the listener so he can participate in the song? How do you give the imagination the concrete specifics it needs to kick into gear? The answer lies in those questions. *The successful lyricist writes about abstractions through the use of detailed, concrete, specific (nonabstract) information.*

Two classic and fine examples of what I'm talking about are in the songs, "Miss Emily's Picture" and "The Gambler."

"Miss Emily's Picture," recorded by John Conlee, is about a man who's lonely, blue, and missing "Miss Emily" terribly. But notice how dry that description is. The vehicle—the medium—through which the writer Hollis R. De Laughter communicates those feelings are simple, repeated descriptions of the act of looking at Miss Emily's picture. Notice that that is *a physical act* which you can imagine and participate in. Remember the number of times you've looked at pictures of someone very special to you. The idea is easy to re-create in your imagination. Absolutely nowhere in the song does the singer talk about missing Emily, or how he loved her, or anything else like that; and yet the impact of those emotions is profound and lasting. It is a very emotional song in which not one emotion is ever *mentioned by word.*

"The Gambler" outlines a whole philosophy of living. And if Don Schlitz, the writer, had gone at it directly it could have been one of that year's ten worst songs. If, instead of telling us about when to "hold 'em" and when to "fold 'em," he'd said something like:

It's important to know when to persist in trying to achieve your goals, and when to give up.

You have to know when to decide to give up what you're doing gradually, and to know when to give up quickly.

You should never make a judgment about how your life is going while it's going on.

There'll be plenty of time to look back to see how it all went, after your life is over.

Those statements are an attempt at a straight, conceptual description of "The Gambler's" philosophy. It's what we all know he meant. But, obviously, the words are simply *poison* in terms of retaining our interest and involving us in the song. As ludicrous as the examples seem, many songwriters actually write their lyrics at this level of abstraction. The lyrics are accurate. They say what the songwriter wants to say. They have meter and rhyme. But they are extraordinarily uninvolving and boring.

Examine your songs rigorously to be sure you're not falling into the trap of settling for abstractions when you _could express your abstractions in a way which would be alive and imaginable—preferably in the form of some kind of action_—for the listener. Notice that "The Gambler" got its job done by delivering the abstraction but doing so using the action metaphor of a poker game.

The imagination is addicted to action. Notice in your imagination the difference between: "the red brick" and "the brick flew toward the store window."

It's not that the imagination cannot handle the idea of "the red brick." It's okay as images go. It has a color. It has a form we're all familiar with. It's concrete (so to speak). You can feel it. You can see it. You might turn it around in your imagination and examine it, and (with some encouragement) spend enough time to really get into its "brickness." But the chances are you'd get bored fast and lose interest.

That is because mental images have a rapid decay rate. Research shows that images last less than a second, and visually speaking, are not too clear in the first place. The picture in your "mind's eye" is somewhat granular (something like a snowy television picture) with best definition and clarity in the center of the picture and degeneration of that image away from the center. So we "see" our images for only a very short time and they are not too clear to start with. This is true for _one image_, for that _one instant_ in time.

So to stay with that brick long enough to produce any involvement, one must re-create the image a number of times in succession. Re-creating the same image is not something the imagination does too eagerly. Try it and you'll see. The imagination quickly gets bored with the same item over and over again. And when the imagination gets bored, it wanders (away from your song).

What keeps the imagination on target and involved is action. The reason is that action demands change in an image—usually movement—and that allows the imagination to re-create a new image each time. This keeps the quality of imagery fresh and our involvement more complete. The image of the brick headed toward that store window is a cue for a whole series of images which the imagination cannot resist.

Here's another experiment. Try to remember the last blue-eyed person you saw. Notice whether or not your imagination is re-creating that person in one image or in action. Are you not remembering your blue-eyed person _doing something?_ Try the image in "freeze-frame" (no action) and notice how fast it fades away.

The only way the imagination can sustain an image is if that image involves some sort of action. Among other things, this is the problem the imagination has with abstractions: there's no action. They may suggest action, cause a desire for action, or even describe a whole se-

45

ries of actions, but an abstract word does not refer to action itself nor does it describe a specific action.

"Sorrow," for example, is a fairly specific abstraction but it is not truly useful for producing an image. If the image of sorrow—the imagined *experience* of sorrow—is what you want to deliver, try "falling teardrops," "aching feeling," "breaking heart," and so forth. Such action words will produce the *experience* of "sorrow," and make your lyrics come alive—seem lifelike, in the listener's imagination. In a sense, because of the mental and physical effects of images, the good writer will allow the listener to *do* sorrow.

Hit writers understand this double need for action and abstraction and strive to combine the two:

"Love's Been a Little Bit Hard on Me"
"Crazy in the Night (Barking at Airplanes)"
"The Sound of Goodbye"
"Total Eclipse of the Heart"
"Please Help Me, I'm Falling"
"You Really Go for the Heart"
"You Left Your Love All Over Me"

Each title mentions the abstraction itself but gives it action metaphorically. Imagine if Juice Newton's hit written by Gary Burr were titled "Love's Been a Difficult Experience," rather than "Love's Been a Little Bit Hard on Me." It's the action which hooks us.

The imagination functions at its best with simple images. This is implicit in the examples we've already seen. An image lasts in the mind for only a short time. The "field of image"—the vision of the "mind's eye"—resembles our true field of vision, with objects being clear toward the center and increasingly indistinct toward the edges. For these two reasons—its short "memory" and limited field of clear vision—the imagination engages best with *simple images.* It does its job best when requested to produce one, single object or action which it can place right in the center of its field of vision. Notice the ease with which you can produce the image: "Lipstick on Your Collar" vs. "The Marks of Cheating are All Over You."

While some would-be hit writer might try his hand at that second line, as an image it is overly complex. The tendency of the imagination is to abandon the task if the image is too complex and varied. One "broken white feather" stays in your imagination far longer than "a flock of many colored seabirds." Specific, simple images get more mileage out of the imagination than groups of things do. It's why songs which deal with "I" or "you" (meaning a specific person), work better than "people" songs—"everybody" songs. Such message songs run the risk of providing too much for the imagination to handle. ("The Gambler" got away with it mostly because of the specific setting of a conversation between the old man and the singer and because of the specific imagery of a poker game.)

When imagery becomes too complex and varied, the imaging process is no longer free and experiential but rather becomes more like mental work. And mental work is not what the listener has in mind when he turns on the radio.

Look through your songs to find those places where you could narrow down your images to one single item—one specific instance—one emotion—one moment in time. I know you're trying to sum up all of life and capture it in a three-minute pearl of wisdom. But, believe me, your goal will elude you if you try to do it in one song. A song which tells the truth about one simple moment in time can deliver the experience of living more vividly than all the writings of philosophers over the ages.

With all due deference to you poets out there, *life—moment to moment*—is outrageously simple. The imagination knows it. The listener knows it. Everybody knows it. So keep it simple. Cut narrow and cut deep.

The risk to the writer (and one of the reasons many writers avoid simplicity) is that simplicity and specificity render one vulnerable. Your simple song could be—and may be—simply awful (especially when you're trying out an unusual story, theme, plot, etc.). It's far safer to stick with tried and true banalities and abstractions, that "sound like" other great songs you've heard.

The problem is that, while there is much to be learned from other songs, there is really no "safe harbor" for a songwriter. If he/she hides, so will the song.

So, say what you've got to say directly and take your lumps. You'll be surprised at how few "lumps" there are when you write "straight." It's part of growing professionally.

But don't write in code. Write "user friendly" songs and remember the users listen with their imaginations. Let them.

Enjoy.

Chris Blake is a songwriting teacher and has done several Cassette Roulette sessions at LASS, revealing himself to be an excellent critiquer. He has served as manager of Nashcal Music, the West Coast subsidiary of the Nashville-based Fischer Music Group, and his songs have been recorded by Moe Bandy, Joe Stampley, John Conlee, Johnny Carver, Billy "Crash" Craddock, Dotsie, and others.

Writing Lyrics

When we think in terms of the population of the world there are very few people who have the opportunity and talent to communicate their feelings and opinions to anyone beyond their immediate family, friends, or co-workers. Politicians use the electronic media. Actors do, too, but they're usually speaking someone else's thoughts. Novelists and journalists, when they're allowed to speak freely, may reach a large audience but its numbers are still fairly limited.

Radio, TV, and films have become the vehicle by which most people receive information from the rest of the world. These media share a form of communication that reaches and influences people all over the planet: music. As a skilled songwriter, you wield a tremendous power to communicate to millions of people. That realization (along with your desire to prove to your relatives that you can make a living at this) should make you want to do your best.

In this chapter I'll discuss various techniques and principles that will help you express your lyrics as effectively as possible so that when you get that opportunity to talk to the world, they'll love listening.

SIMPLICITY

I asked hit producer John Ryan what he felt was one of the most important common denominators of successful songs. It was a question I had asked many others, and the reply is almost always the same:

Simplicity—in saying something that everyone experiences in his or her life, but doesn't know quite how to say. You're taking a song out of your head and giving it to an artist or performing it yourself. Then you have to try to get someone else to receive your communication. You're not doing it just for yourself. You want someone else to feel what you feel about life, maybe challenge them.

When hit songwriter/producer/publisher Jack Keller was critiquing songs one night, he remarked to songwriters several times, "You've got too many ideas here. Focus on one idea, and build your song around it."

We've all read how-to manuals that say things like "insert the strand in the elliptical aperture," when they could say "put the thread through the hole in the needle" or "thread the needle." Applying that example to lyric writing, two common problems are saying more than you need and not saying clearly what you mean. Have you ever had a friend with whom you communicated so well that you could convey a whole idea in two words that would mean absolutely nothing to anyone else who heard them? Made you feel clever, didn't it? Sorry, but you can't bring that friend with you into the songwriting game. Instead of setting up a very private communication that excludes everyone else, the big game is to make yourself understood by as many listeners as possible.

A songwriter once played me five songs, none of which made any sense. She wanted to know why the songs didn't work for me. I read her back a few lines and asked what they meant. Some of her explanations were worth whole songs in themselves, but nowhere in what she had written could I make the connection until she told me the background. She had a song called "Geraldine" that made no sense until she told me that Geraldine was the name of a truck. I told her I thought it was a lesbian love song. The writer was intelligent and talented, but she was playing an intellectual game with her lyrics. She seemed to be saying, "How obtuse and clever and abstract can I make this so it's challenging to listen to?" The songs were so challenging, they weren't worth bothering to figure out.

Ironically, the most accessible lyric of the five was her first song, which she said was "too simple" for her and she didn't like much anymore. Those abstract lyrics in her other songs might work as poetry, since we could look at the words for as long as we needed to decipher the message. But when we also have music to focus on and the song is presented on a dance floor, a jukebox, or a car radio, tricky lyrics only make us feel as though we're missing something. She asked, "What about art? Do you think I should write commercial crap?" I said, "No thanks, we seem to have an overstock in that department. Think about the art of songwriting as the ability to communicate an idea or a feeling in a unique, interesting, enjoyable way."

If your lyric doesn't attempt to communicate, you're operating in a vacuum, which is fine if you just want to write for yourself. You can derive some benefits from keeping a personal diary, but if you want to make a living writing, your songs have to communicate their messages easily to others.

FOCUS

Another critical aspect of effective lyric writing is focus. *You should be able, in one word, to describe the emotion or mental state that a song expresses.* Happiness, sadness, love, hate, jealousy, and resentment are just some of the emotions we've all felt. Any of these could be, in a broad sense, the subject of your song, provided you focus down to specifics.

Beginning songwriters tend to want to settle on the first thing that comes out of their heads whether it's focused or not. While it doesn't hurt to write all your thoughts down, you need to zero in on a single idea. You may want to express that idea as a story or just explore different aspects of it. Many successful songs don't follow a linear "story line" or plot. But if you do write about a feeling, make it just one.

You should also be able, in a short phrase, to describe what the song is

49

about. On pages 21-22, I listed several subject areas as they related to love relationships. "I think I've just found her (him)," "Remembering how it used to be," and "Cheating" all describe what a song is about.

EXERCISE IN FOCUS

Several basic questions will help you brainstorm an idea or to help you bring the idea into focus after that initial inspiration:

Who is singing the song? Male? Female? You? Someone else?

What is the point-of-view? Someone who's been left? Someone who's leaving? Someone who's sad? Angry? Lonely? Happy?

Who is the song being sung to? A lover? Someone you'd like to meet? The general public? A friend? God?

What does the singer want to accomplish? To express love or other emotion? Give people a philosophy? Teach something? Criticize? Arouse?

As a purely commercial consideration, you should also ask: is this a subject or attitude an artist, other than myself, would be interested in expressing? For example, if you write a song with the message, "I'm a thoroughly despicable person," you have to ask yourself how many recording artists you'll find who want to record a song like that even if they believe it about themselves. Generally speaking, artists will stay away from songs that are depressing, express negative attitudes, or make them appear unlikable.

As an exercise, listen to a few songs on the radio and write down one line for each that expresses what the song is about. Then do it with your own songs. If you have trouble condensing them, they're not focused.

Attitude, which in a songwriting context means an aggressively stated point-of-view, is another factor that requires consistency and focus. Though we most commonly find rock songs that express an attitude, it's very important in first-person songs (I, me, my) of any style. Billy Joel and Bruce Springsteen's songs have attitude. Listen to the attitude of Cyndi Lauper's "Girls Just Wanna Have Fun," the Pointer Sisters's "I'm So Excited," Dolly Parton's "9 to 5," Michael Jackson's "Billie Jean," or Timbuk 3's sarcastic, "The Future's So Bright, I Gotta Wear Shades." If attitude is an important ingredient of your song, it needs to be consistently maintained by the lyrics and supported by the music.

TITLES

A strong title can go a long way toward ensuring that industry people and the general public will remember your song.

Of course, you don't *have* to have a great title to have a hit song. Look at any list of Top 10 songs and you'll see titles that are dull and ordinary, as well as titles that are imaginative and intriguing. Lionel Richie's "Lady," with an ordinary, straightforward one-on-one love lyric and a wonderful melody and performance, didn't suffer commercially from a simple title. Some very intriguing titles have failed to live up to their promise in the body of the song musically or lyrically.

For the most part, if you're searching (as you should be) for a way to say something in a fresh and unusual way, you're likely to arrive at an imaginative title in the process. Concept and title are so wedded that, particularly in country music, some writers don't even begin to write a song until they have a great title/concept. It's a very common and practical way to start. Sometimes, if you have the right title, the song practically writes itself.

Pretend you're a publisher with two tapes in front of you, one called "I Love You" and another called "Silent Partners." Which one do you think you'd be most interested in hearing? You've already heard "I Love You" twenty times this month. You've never heard "Silent Partners," but it's an interesting concept that makes you start guessing right away what the song's about. If it's interesting to you, it might just interest a producer, artist, or program director.

If you can come up with a short title phrase that embodies a concept, it's easier to focus your lyric from the beginning. Here are some hit titles that are intriguing in themselves: "You're So Vain," "Mama Told Me Not to Come," "What a Fool Believes," "Old Bridges Burn Slow." Some titles stick in the mind because of unusual word combinations: "Undercover Angel," "Mandolin Rain," and "Karma Chameleon."

Not only is the *concept* of the title important, but you'll increase its memorability if it *sounds* "catchy." A "catchy" title has a combination of a pleasing meter and some poetic device like alliteration (a repetition of consonants): "*Doo Wah Diddy Diddy*," "*Baby's in Black*," "*We Can Work It Out*," or assonance (repetition of vowel sounds): "*Owner of a Lonely Heart*," "Bl*i*nded by the L*i*ght," or rhyme: "*Okie from Muskogee.*"

Common phrases from everyday language also become more memorable in songs: "You Ain't Seen Nothing Yet," "Knock on Wood," "I Heard It Through the Grapevine," "I Can't Go for That." Twists of common phrases also work: "Stop! In the Name of Love," "(Love Is) Thicker than Water."

Aside from the benefits derived from a phrase that's catchy, clever, and conceptual, in most successful songs the real magic of the title comes from the way it fits with the music and is supported by the rest of the lyric. That combination can make an otherwise mundane title seem profound. City and state name titles are a good case in point. Jim Webb's love stories and majestic melodies made "Galveston," "By the Time I Get to Phoenix" and "MacArthur Park" special places in our minds. The whole sound and

51

feeling of the Mamas and Papas' "California Dreamin' " could make someone feel nostalgic about California whether they'd been there or not. Hoagy Carmichael and Stewart Gorrell's classic "Georgia on My Mind" does the same.

Sometimes a musical figure or the emotional intensity of the music itself suggests a title. This is a spontaneous process that resembles a sort of musical Rorschach test: "What does this chord, riff, or melody make you think of?" It's a process in which the musician shuts down that very practiced intellectual approach and gets very close to his emotional core. A good groove can be hypnotic, put you in a mood, and trigger ideas and phrases that you might never come up with while you're staring at a piece of paper.

Place that good title in the strategic first or last line of your chorus (or verse, depending on the form), ensuring that it will be repeated several times during the song. You can then practically guarantee it will be remembered. If it's easy to remember, a potential record buyer knows what to ask for at the record store or on the radio request line. This is an important commercial consideration. Many potential hits may have been lost for lack of an obvious title in the right place.

Another commercial reason to craft a unique title is that, occasionally, a common one like "I Love You" gets mixed up with another song called "I Love You" and someone else gets your royalties through computer or human error. That's a fate neither you nor the other writer deserve.

FIRST LINES

The first words from a singer's mouth are critical, particularly if they're the first words you've ever heard from that artist. It all goes into that evaluation you make as a listener about whether or not you like the record. So with your writer's hat on, you need to think about how strongly you can interest the listener with that first line or lines. When a publisher or producer hears that first line, he's deciding whether to keep listening or turn it off, too. If it doesn't sell him, he's not optimistic about selling it to an artist.

Don't fall prey to the temptation to start with "I'm just sittin' here (a) writing this song (b) thinking about you, or (c) looking at the . . ." or "Woke up this mornin' . . ." (didn't we all?) or other equally uninteresting clichés. Though these might be penciled in to get your motor running, when you get down to a rewrite they should be the first things that get penciled out.

Your first line should set the tone for the whole song and make us want to hear what comes next. "You're a rich girl, and you've gone too far 'cause you know it doesn't matter anyway," starts Darryl Hall's "Rich Girl." The line gives us the title, an attitude of disapproval, and arouses our curiosity about how she's gone "too far" and what it is that "doesn't matter." "Some men find her sexy, some men disagree, but if she's not, it's because she doesn't want to be" tells you something important right away about Dolly Parton's "Working Girl." "You ask me if I love you and I choke on my reply," opens Dan Hill's and Barry Mann's "Sometimes When We Touch" with a powerful taste of the heavy drama to come. Rupert Holmes begins his infidelity song "Him" with a minimovie scene: "Over by the window there's a pack of cigarettes. Not my brand, you understand. Sometimes she forgets." Notice all these openers immediately give you the pronoun that begins to establish the cast of characters (*You're, her, you/me, my, she's*).

You can set your first scene by asking several questions. Their answers will contribute to what you want your lyric to accomplish.

1. Where is it taking place? Is it important to the song? What kind of a place is it? Are there evocative features? If you allude to a particular country or city, the mountains, beach, etc., be careful of passive "picture postcard" openers that don't carry with them action, flavor, attitude, or emotional charge. "Ten miles west of Houston," "In a dirty downtown doorway," "At home in your love," "Halfway into Heaven" are all about places, either geographical or emotional.

2. Can the hour, day, season, or year offer a flavor that enhances the emotional impact of your song? Think of the number of songs that use "morning" or "night" to evoke a mood.

3. If the song is addressed *to* someone, is there something arresting you can say, as Daryl Hall does in "Rich Girl"?

4. If the song is *about* someone, can you say something that immediately gives a picture or a quick personality sketch, as in "Working Girl"?

5. Is there an *active image* you can use? Stephen Geyer and Bill La-Bounty's "Hot Rod Hearts" opens with "Ten miles east of the highway, hot sparks burnin' the night away. Two lips touchin' together, cheek to cheek, sweatshirt to sweater." Very graphic. Another minimovie.

6. If you're expressing an emotion, can you do it in a *poetic* or *dramatic* way? "I feel so out of place," for instance, just kind of lays there. Contrast that with George Gobel's line, "The world's a tuxedo and I'm just a pair of brown shoes." Of course, that type of cleverness isn't always the answer—it depends on the tone you want to establish. Michael McDonald and Patrick Henderson could have said, "Even though I'm with you, I still feel lonely," but instead used a poetic "Darlin', I know I'm just another head on your pillow" ("Real Love").

A listener should have the answers to the "who, what, when, and where" by the end of the first verse, as well as know the song's attitude and mood. But most importantly, the listener should be persuaded to keep listening, no matter how you accomplish it, with your lyric, your music, or better, by both.

RHYME

I'd guess that over 99 percent of all commercially successful songs use rhyme. Why is it so important? What rhymes do or don't work?

There's a reason why people still remember the nursery rhymes of childhood. The rhymes are strong and predictable, the meter is solid and consistent. Together, rhyme and meter act as an effective trigger to the memory. How many lyrics do you think you'd remember if nothing rhymed? Rhyme has other values as well. It can create a sense of symmetry and completion, and it offers an opportunity to enhance the power of a line by giving it an established "stage" to deliver a payoff.

Rhyme is a tool you can't afford to ignore. To deliberately drop it just to be different isn't a sensible attitude for someone trying to be a successful songwriter. Not that there aren't exceptions to the rule, but when you want the odds in your favor, you use every tool you have.

TYPES OF RHYME

Perfect—Stressed sound that ends the line is *identical,* preceding consonant is different: god/quad, action/fraction, variety/society

Imperfect, near, false, slant, oblique, or half-rhyme—Common and quite acceptable in pop music. It *approximates* rhyme and some would argue strongly that it shouldn't be called rhyme at all, but assonance. Anyway, let the nitpickers argue. Sometimes you just can't find a perfect rhyme to fit your meaning and you *do* find the imperfect "near" rhyme as in port/fourth, loss/wash, around/down, shaky/aching.

Masculine or "one rhyme"—single-syllable rhyme, as in pack/rack or a multisyllable word in which the *last* syllable rhymes, as in compro-*mise*/ido*lize.*

Feminine or "two rhyme"—Two-syllable rhymes, with the stress on the first. The vowels and inner consonants must match, as in maker/shaker, masquerading/degrading.

Three rhyme—The last three syllables rhyme and the consonants that precede them differ, as in *m*edium/*t*edium, *fa*cilitate/reha*b*ilitate.

Open rhyme—Rhymes that don't end in hard consonants. Use them wherever possible on notes that are to be held, as in glow/snow, fly/try.

Closed or stopped rhyme—Rhymes that end in a consonant (*b, p, d, t, q,* and *k*) that makes us close our mouths and that can't be sustained when sung. *M, n, l,* and *r* can be sustained. *V, f, z,* and *s* can be sustained but don't sound very pleasant. *S*'s drive recording engineers crazy. Pay close attention to these "singability" factors as you write your lyrics.

Internal, inner, or inside rhyme—End rhyme, of course, occurs at the end of the line. Internal rhyme occurs within the line, as in "The fate of the great state."

RHYME SCHEMES

To make rhyme work as a memory tool, you must be consistent. Once you establish a rhyme scheme for your verses, it's best to use the same pattern in *all* the verses. That same verse pattern in the choruses and bridge, however, could get monotonous, so it's better to establish one rhyme scheme for the verse, one for the chorus, and yet another for the bridge. You can introduce a subtle element of surprise this way without affecting the predictability of the song. Another way to surprise the listener is to either precipitate or delay the rhyme. It can be used with any rhyme scheme and the rhyme can occur at any of the underlined positions in the last line:

Ta TUM Ta TUM Ta TUM Ta
Ta TUM Ta TUM <u>Ta TUM</u>
Ta TUM Ta TUM <u>Ta TUM</u> Ta
<u>Ta TUM</u> <u>Ta TUM</u> Ta TUM <u>Ta TUM</u> <u>Ta TUM</u>

Here are the most common rhyme schemes:

1.	a	*more*	(Rhyming all four lines.) Usually too predictable. This gets old fast.
	a	*score*	
	a	*floor*	
	a	*door*	
2.	a	*trust*	(Rhyming second and fourth line) Has flexibility and the element of predictability (b) without the boredom.
	b	*guess*	
	c	*hurt*	
	b	*mess*	
3.	a	*luck*	(Rhyming first and second lines, third and fourth lines)
	a	*stuck*	
	b	*brave*	
	b	*save*	
4.	a	*able*	(Rhyming first, third, and fourth lines)
	b	*still*	
	a	*cable*	
	a	*stable*	
5.	a	*making*	(Rhyming first and third, second and fourth lines)
	b	*good*	
	a	*taking*	
	b	*could*	
6.	a	*friend of mine*	(Rhyming first and second lines)
	a	*send a sign*	
	b	*try*	
7.	a	*when*	(Rhyming first, second, and third lines)
	a	*then*	
	a	*men*	
	c	<u>*know*</u>	or
	b	*stand*	(First, second, and third PLUS last lines of adjoining verses)
	b	*band*	
	b	*land*	
	c	<u>*show*</u>	

55

There are other variations. These forms are often doubled, for instance. Given that one of their functions is to help us remember, rhymes in any consistent position in the line may work. In the English language, though, there is an *expectation* that the *primary* rhymes come at the ends of the lines. Because they're in a powerful position it becomes extra important that they enhance—or at least don't distract the listener—from the mood and meaning of the song.

In musical theater the rhymes are expected to be perfect (unless the character wouldn't rhyme perfectly). It's not so much a question of whether the rhymes work, but of how they're judged by critics who hold the power of life and death over a production. Musical theater boasts a long history of exceptional craftsmanship and they aim to keep it that way. Whenever you start to think it's too hard or impossible to come up with perfect rhymes in a context that makes them feel perfectly natural, study the masters. For instance, listen to the songs in the Barbra Streisand film, "Yentl," for the work of lyricists Alan and Marilyn Bergman. We need such standards to remind us that it's still possible to put in the extra effort and come up with perfect rhymes without sacrificing naturalness.

SOME COMMON PROBLEMS WITH RHYME

A common failing among songwriters is to say what you want to say in the first two lines and, instead of finding an equally strong statement to finish the verse, settling for a weaker line for the sake of the rhyme. Sure, you save some work, but you've also effectively weakened your song. Better to have written several versions of the first two lines to come up with an end word that offered more rhyming possibilities. Don't reach for the easy rhyme if it dilutes your efforts. And beware of these possible rhyming pitfalls:

Inversions involve twisting the order of words so as to use a rhyme which wouldn't naturally occur at that point. It almost always feels awkward. Here's an example:

I never knew how much I'd missed
Until your candy lips I kissed.

In this situation, I'd go for "lips" as the end rhyme, even though it lacks the perfection of "missed/kissed." "Till I kissed your candy lips" just feels more natural.

Identities are not rhymes. Identities are: the same words, words with the same consonant preceding the same final sound (buy/goodbye), words that sound identical even though spelled differently (homonyms) like "bear" and "bare," "no" and "know." You won't get arrested for doing this; it's just lazy writing. Common exceptions include building of parallel constructions like, "Gonna talk about it/Gonna shout about it/Gonna sing about it/There's no doubt about it," which uses the "shout/doubt" rhyme before the last word. Also acceptable is the repetition of a variation of a line for emphasis: "Goin' downtown, goin' way downtown."

Slang is a great source of new rhymes and many hits have been based on slang words and expressions. The only drawback is if you're trying to write a song people will record twenty years from now. By then, the slang we use today may sound really dumb. Would anybody record a song today with "the cat's meow" or "23 skidoo" in it? Even "groovy" sounds dated, and not so long ago it felt absolutely appropriate in Simon and Garfunkel's "59th Street Bridge Song."

Colloquial Pronunciation has a problem similar to slang. Here the drawback is not change in fashion, but the reduced ability of other artists to record the song. It's good to be able to tailor a song to a particular musical style, like country or R&B, and use the pronunciations common in that style (e.g., to rhyme *thang* (thing) with *hang*, or *pain* and *again*). But bear in mind, you're limiting the coverage of those songs to artists who are comfortable with those styles and pronunciations.

THE EXCEPTIONS

We hear more songs these days that don't rhyme. In most cases, they're from self-contained bands. They write their own material and aren't that interested in having other artists record the songs. Because they aren't exposed to the same industry scrutiny, they have a more wide-ranging creative palette from which to paint their songs. More power to them. If you can get your message across to your audience without the use of rhyme, there's no rule that says you have to use it. Be aware though, that laziness is not a good enough reason to ignore a powerful tool.

Even in pop music there are examples of songs that don't use rhyme. The standard "Moonlight in Vermont" is a good example; more recently, Lionel Richie's "Lady," a major hit for both him and Kenny Rogers, doesn't rhyme. So, why do they work? There are several possibilities: 1) They're both exceptional melodies, 2) One of rhyme's functions is to help us remember the lyric, and both of those lyrics, especially "Moonlight in Vermont," are simple enough to remember without it; 3) In the case of "Lady," the melody's construction is such that it doesn't, through rhythm and meter, set up a *rhyme expectation*, so we don't ever miss it.

The constant creative challenge is to find the best rhymes possible and still retain the flow of natural speech patterns, while at the same time not compromising content and mood. If you read the lines aloud they should feel as natural as conversation. Every line presents a new challenge and it may be that, after exploring the possibilities, you'll need to choose a less-than-perfect rhyme. It's more important that you opt for naturalness, mood, or clarity of content over convenience or cleverness for its own sake.

RHYMING DICTIONARIES AND THESAURUSES

Some writers look at rhyming dictionaries as a crutch, as though it was cheating to use one. If you've been writing for any time at all, you probably know the most natural possibilities for rhyme. But when you're really stuck, it's always good to know that there's somewhere you can go *quickly* to make sure you have the best rhyme possible for the line. I've also run across rhymes in such sources that instigated a whole new thought pattern. The human mind has such wonderful facility for "connecting the dots" between seemingly unrelated images and words that anything you feed it can become an ingredient for something new.

A friend of mine once put a few hundred descriptive adjectives in his computer and just ran them through to fill in the blank in a line. The results were often comical, occasionally profound, and usually words that he would have had difficulty coming up with "off the top of his head." This is one of the things a good rhyming dictionary can do for you. And the more you use it, the more you develop a storehouse of rhyme possibilities in your mind.

All rhyming dictionaries contain thousands of words that you'd never use in a song. You'll also be able to come up with colloquialisms that aren't in the dictionaries and make up your own words, so don't let yourself get too attached. *The Modern Rhyming Dictionary* by pro lyricist Gene Lees and Clement Wood's *The Complete Rhyming Dictionary* are both good ones.

When you're looking for a particular word and can only come up with a word that's somewhere in the neighborhood, you need a thesaurus. It will give you words or phrases that mean the same or almost the same thing (synonyms) or the opposite (antonyms) as well as words and phrases that are only remotely related. It incorporates slang and lists words by part of speech. Using a thesaurus is like a treasure hunt in which each new discovery can send you on yet another exciting journey. It's an indispensable tool. *Roget's International* is my favorite.

POETIC DEVICES

The great poets have used many devices throughout history that are regularly put to work by songwriters in the service of a great lyric. At their best, these devices go consciously unnoticed, like the subtle spices in a gourmet dish. Though you might not identify them right away, you know that without them the dish wouldn't taste nearly as good. Only when the chef tells you what the spices are, do you start to separate and recognize them in the overall taste. That's ideally what poetic devices should do. Our attention shouldn't be drawn from the overall meaning and flow of the lyric to these devices. If they're overused, or too obvious, our attention goes to them. They say, "Look here, see how I did this! Clever, eh?"

Some songs, however, substitute cleverness for content and don't pretend to be serious at all. Cole Porter was noted for his cleverness, but that style of writing, though admirable for its skill, is no longer in vogue. The skill of contemporary writers is in achieving the naturalness of common speech and using the devices in a subtle way. Here are some of the most common ones:

Alliteration is the repetition of accented consonants. This is a device that can get ridiculous if carried to extremes but if used with taste, can be subtly effective. Dan Fogelberg in "Same Old Lang Syne" writes "She would have *l*iked to say she *l*oved the man, but she didn't *l*ike to *l*ie."

Assonance is when the stressed vowels in a word agree, but the preceding consonants do not, as in "You won't be going home"

Similes are comparisons using the word "as" or "like." "Straight as an arrow," "hard as a rock" and "sleeping like a log." Don't settle for these common-place clichés though. If something comes to your mind that you've heard before try for a new one. In Paul Simon's "Crazy Love, Vol. II" from the "Graceland" album, he gives us "Sad as a lonely little wrinkled balloon."

Metaphors are also comparisons that don't depend on "like" or "as." Simon and Garfunkel's "I Am A Rock" is an example. It would have been a simile if it had been written "I'm Like A Rock" but not nearly as effective. Another good example is Steve Geyer and Bill La Bounty's "Hot Rod Hearts." A line from it goes "Hot rod hearts, out on the boulevard tonight/ Here come those hungry sharks, up from the bottom for another bite." He's not talking about real sharks, but about a kind of people and their activities that resemble a bunch of sharks gathering for the kill. It wouldn't have been nearly as powerful to say, "They look like a bunch of sharks. . . ."

In their hit "Out of Touch," Hall and Oates use, "Smoking guns, hot to the touch/would cool down if we didn't use them so much," as a metaphor for arguments breeding more arguments in a relationship.

Allegory is a device that allows the writer to treat an abstract idea with concrete imagery. In other words, you can tell a story on both material and symbolic levels. Paul McCartney's "Ebony and Ivory" uses the image of black and white piano keys working together as an allegory for racial harmony.

Personification is attributing human characteristics to inanimate objects: "When the ground started rolling, I heard the buildings scream." In George Michael's "Careless Whispers" he sings, "Guilty feet have got no rhythm."

Hyperbole is an obvious exaggeration to drive home a point. The Beatles' "Eight Days a Week" is an example. "You're a hurricane" is both hyperbole and a metaphor.

Irony is saying the opposite of what you mean, or pointing up the incongruities of a situation. Rick Christian's "I Don't Need You," sung by Kenny Rogers, is an example. Randy Goodrum and Steve Kipner's "If She Would Have Been Faithful," points up the irony of having to painfully lose a lover to be able to win a new one.

Antithesis sets two opposing ideas against each other for contrast. Michael Hazelwood and Albert Hammond's "It Never Rains in Southern California," ("it pours") worked effectively this way.

Characterization is the creation and representation of convincing characters. Always look for a line of dialogue or an image that says a lot more about the character or situation. In Lennon and McCartney's "Eleanor Rigby," when she "picks up the rice in the church where a wedding has been" we get a profound sense of her loneliness. Jerry Jeff Walker's "Mr. Bojangles" is a beautiful example of characterization. Janis Ian's "At Seventeen" was a masterful character study. Even though it contained very personal details, the way Ian wrote it allowed us all to experience once again the often agonizing process of growing up.

PROBLEMS WITH PRONOUNS

One of the most common problem areas in lyric writing is the use of pronouns. Pronouns take the place of both proper nouns (Paul Simon, Los Angeles, Laurel Canyon) and common nouns (songwriter, city, canyon). The words pronouns replace are referred to as "principals." Here are five rules for the use of pronouns, all established in the interest of clarity:

1. Make it clear what the pronoun you're using is a substitute for.
2. The principal must be close by so the listener doesn't get confused about what the pronoun stands for.
3. Avoid putting *two* principals close by or the listener won't know which one the pronoun represents. "When John talked to Joe, he realized that he was getting old but not wise." Was it John or Joe who was getting old?
4. Avoid having one pronoun represent two principals at once. "He was rich but he was poor." Was principal #1 rich and principal #2 poor, or is there only one principal involved?
5. If possible, avoid placing the pronoun before its principal. "She heard the message he delivered but didn't believe the messenger." It takes the listener a few seconds to make the connection that "he" is the messenger.

Be very careful about the number of pronouns you use in a song. Without realizing it, you can create a maze in which only you know who's saying what to whom. "She said she thought he loved her more than she loved him, and she wouldn't recommend that he move in." There are at least three different ways that line could be interpreted. If you can read the line at your leisure, you can probably figure them out, but when the line goes by in seven seconds in a song, you're in trouble.

On the other hand, pronouns serve a valuable function when they're used properly. They can help you guide the listener away from vagueness by letting them know exactly who is saying or doing what.

Pronouns are important in establishing point-of-view. Certain creative decisions need to be made by the songwriter. The options are:

Relating the song in the first person (I, me, we). *"I was on my way to nowhere"*

Having the singer address the song to the second person (you). *"You Are So Beautiful."*

Relating a song about something or someone else (he, him, she, her, it, they, them). *"He's a real nowhere man . . ."*

The choices you make are based on clarity and impact. For instance, it's usually very effective to deliver a heavy philosophical message in the first person ("Here's what happened to me") or in the third person, in which you tell a story about someone else and we understand the message in our own way. Second-person messages ("You should . . .") can alienate the singer from the listener by implying that "I don't need this message but you do," but second-person positive sentiments ("You're wonderful." "You deserve the best.") are very powerful.

Some writers use "you" as a substitute for "I" in a rhetorical sort of way. "What do you do when you fall in love with someone you can't have?" We read this as "What do *I* do . . . ?" The approach puts distance between the singer and a hurtful problem by using "you" instead of "I." There's no wrong or right here. The impact of the pronoun you choose can vary with each song. It's always a good idea to check out all the possibilities to create the most powerful emotional statement. "I can't pretend that I don't hurt" may be better than "You can't pretend that you don't hurt" because, when the listener sings along, he is singing about himself rather than an anonymous "you."

The most common-sense rule to follow in all of this is to try to put yourself in the place of the listener, no matter how emotionally involved you may be in expressing your personal feelings. It's a difficult thing to do in the heat of passionate inspiration, so it's a good idea to put a song away for a few days to allow yourself to look at it more objectively.

For an in-depth look at the psychological principles behind the effectiveness of visual imagery and figurative language, see Chapter 3, "The Imagination of the Listener."

PROSODY AND METER

Prosody is the agreement of lyric and music. If the lyric has an "up," positive message, it would generally be unwise to use a melody in a minor key. Minor chords are used better in songs of pain, longing, despair, loss, and sadness.

Ideally, you want the emotional tone of the music to enhance the message of the lyric. It's possible, however, that your message might be enhanced by doing just the opposite of what feels natural, for effect. Examples are Bertolt Brecht and Kurt Weill's "Mack the Knife" and Country Joe McDonald's "Fixin' to Die Rag." But that should be a conscious choice, not an accident.

If Jim Webb had written the melody to the line, "Up, Up and Away" or Curtis Mayfield to the line "Move on Up" as a series of *descending* notes, the result would have sounded ludicrous. That's the extreme, but it's a graphic example of the importance of prosody.

Other factors also contribute to good prosody. Watch for combinations of words that could be *heard* as other words. "What do I know?" "What a Wino?" "Let the winds take hold," "Let the wind stay cold," " 'Scuse me while I kiss the sky" " 'Scuse me while I kiss this guy." ('Scuse me Mr. Hendrix, I know what you said, but somebody could get confused.) A similar problem exists with adjoining words that end and begin with the same sound. The phrases "teach children" and "strange journey" will give a good singer an anxiety attack unless there's plenty of space in between to allow the tongue to recover. Anyway, I'm sure you get my point. Make certain that what a listener hears is what *you want* them to hear and that the singer can easily sing what you write.

The best way to make sure your lyrics will sing well is to sing them as you write them. Sing your lyrics at the tempo they'll be performed. Words may look fine on paper or sing easily at a slow tempo but will tie a singer's tongue in knots when you increase the tempo even a little.

If the words feel at all awkward in your mouth, or don't sing smoothly, change them.

Some words like *long* and *cool* carry their own emotional meanings that feel wrong when connected to short choppy notes. Action words like *jump, run, crash,* and *flash* may feel out of place in a slow ballad but right at home in a high-intensity rocker.

One of the most important tools in the service of prosody is lyric meter. Its skilled use allows you to *emphasize natural speech patterns and tie them effectively to the musical pulse and melody.* It helps make the words fit comfortably with the music without putting the accents on the wrong syllables or squeezing too many words into too little musical space.

If you were paying attention in English class instead of day-dreaming about being a rock star, you would probably already know about what follows. You just didn't think you'd ever need to use it, right?

Why do you need to know about meter? You may not need to remember the names of the patterns, but you should know that they are options to be considered and that they can be used for emotional effect and for variety. Few things are more deadly than an entire lyric in perfect iambic pentameter, and the melodies to those lyrics don't usually save them. So lets go back to English class again.

The groupings of stressed and unstressed syllables and words are called "metric feet." We usually hear them in groups of two or three. Those most commonly used in poetry and lyric use are:

NAME OF FOOT	SCANSION	EXAMPLES	ACCENT
iamb	˘ ´	ĭn-sáne, gŏod-bý, tŏ-níght fŏr gŏod	ta TUM
trochee	´ ˘	héal-tȟy, lóv-ĕr, mo-nĕy	TUM ta
anapest	˘ ˘ ´	gŏ-iňg óut, ma-kiňg sénse, ŭn-dĕr-stánd	ta ta TUM
dactyl	´ ˘ ˘	po-ĕ-tȟy, úl-tĭ-măte, Í'm ŏ-kăy, ýou're ŏ-kăy	TUM ta ta
spondee	´ ´	dówn-tówn, stár-shíp, héad-loňg	TUM TUM
amphibrach	˘ ´ ˘	bĕ-líev-iňg, cŏn-cérn-iňg, Ĭ lóve ĭt	ta TUM ta

The emotional impact of a song can be greatly influenced by your choice of meter. Spondees (TUM TUM) have a very deliberate feeling. Iambic pentameter (Ta TUM/ta TUM/ta TUM/ta TUM/ta TUM) is the most commonly used meter and has a long history in English poetry, probably because it's closest to human speech. It's good for seriousness. So are dactyls (TUM ta ta).

Three-foot meters, particularly anapests, have a lightness about them that doesn't suit them for particularly heavy subject matter (Ta ta TUM/ta ta TUM/ta ta TUM).

Though overuse of the same meter can be monotonous, just enough repetition can create tension to set a listener up for a dynamic change of meter.

In songwriting, you need to repeat the metric feet in a way that not only makes them fit comfortably with the musical pulse, but *emphasizes the intended meaning of the lyric.*

As an illustration, let's take a line that could have several meanings and "work it" to find its best setting:

I **need**/you **in**/my **life**/
(Iambic)

A duple meter (two syllables per foot) emphasizing "need," "in," and "life." "In" doesn't take the emphasis particularly well because it's a weaker word.

or

I need/**you** in/**my** life/
(Trochee)

Another duple meter emphasizing "I," "you," "my." Feels more natural.

I need **you**/in my **life**/
(Anapest)

A triple meter (three syllables per foot) emphasizing "you" and "life."

or

I **need** you/in **my** life/
(Amphibrach)

emphasizing "need" and "my."

Depending on the length of notes and rests, these versions could be done in either 4/4 or 3/4 time.

Try your own melodies with these variations. Sing them out loud. You'll find your melodies changing with each variation to *accommodate the meaning of the line and the musical meter.* This is a process that should happen regardless of whether you're writing a melody to lyric, lyric to melody, or lyric alone. Once you get used to it, the process goes very fast.

Let's try a straight 4/4 with equal emphasis on each note.

```
        1   2   3   4    1   2   3   4
4/4    /   /   /   /    /   /   /   /
       I  need you  in      my  life
```

It feels a little stiff this way and "life" held this long is a little strained. Better to make "life" a beat shorter and end in a rest.

How about emphasizing 1 and 3?

```
        1   2   3   4    1   2   3   4
4/4    /   -   /   -    /   -   /   -
       I  need you  in     my  life
```

Not bad, but it would again be awkward to hold "life." You can also add to the emphasis of "you" by raising the melody on that word.

Still emphasizing 1 and 3, you can use a "pickup," starting the lyric before the downbeat.

```
        1   2   3   4    1   2   3   4
4/4    /   -   /   -    /   -   /   -
       I need you  in   my   life
```

This gives you the chance to use the accents *and* maintain your choice of emphasis.

```
        1  and  2  and   3  and  4  and
2/4    /   -    -   -    /   -    -   -
       I need you  in   my   life
```

By using eighth notes, you can emphasize "need" and "life." It also gives the line more urgency.

Let's try leaning on the backbeat, 2 and 4:

```
        1   2   3   4    1   2   3   4
4/4    -   /   -   /    -   /   -   /
       I  need you  in     my  life
```

We're still accenting the "in" here, but can deemphasize it by raising the melody on both "need" and "life."

Still accenting the backbeat you can delay the line and try an eighth note feel again:

```
        1  and  2  and   3  and  4  and
4/4    -   -    /   -    -   -    /   -
       I  need you     in  my  life
```

This one feels good, too.

Now let's switch to 3/4 waltz time:

```
        1   2   3     1   2   3
3/4    -   -   /     -   -   /
       I  need you    in  my  life
```

A little stiff—too predictable.

```
     1   2   3   1   2   3   1   2   3
3/4  -   /   -   -   /   -   -   /   -
     I need      you in      my life
```
A little smoother with more room for a singer to play with the words.

```
     1   2   3   1   2   3   1   2   3
3/4  /   /   -   /   /   -   /   -   -
     I  need you in  my      life
```
More interesting, less predictable.

or with a pickup . . .

```
       1   2   3   1   2   3   1   2   3
3/4    /   -   -   /   /   -   /   -   -
     I need      you in  my      life
```
Again, more interesting with room for a singer to move.

In this chapter, I've explored the major areas that will concern you as a lyric writer. There's a lot more to learn. If you're serious about being a songwriter you'll read everything you can on the subject (see the Bibliography for some suggestions), but there's no better and faster way to improve than to write constantly. When you do, you'll create your own examples and encounter problems that will give a practical context to what you read.

Constructing a Song
Words and Music Together

No matter how creative and powerful lyrics or melodies may be by themselves, they take on a whole new life and a whole new power and magic when they're together. The song is greater than the sum of its parts. Whether you're a specialist at one or the other or a genius at both, an essential aspect of your craft is the understanding of how to make the parts fit together to create that magic. In this chapter I'll cover the elements of songwriting that relate most to words and music as a whole.

FORM

The form, also called the format, of your song, is its basic shape or organization. In this section I'll discuss how the components—verses, choruses, bridges and pre-hooks—work together to ensure listener interest; how to best use the basic forms and variations, and how to analyze form so you can continue to stay abreast of contemporary trends.

Much has been said about "the formula" of a hit song or, in an often derogatory sense, about "formula music." There was a time in the '50s and early '60s when most rock songs had hardly more than three different chord progressions. If a song didn't conform to one of them, the odds were heavy against its becoming a hit. So the chord progression formulas perpetuated themselves. The 1-6m-4-5 (C-Am-F-G) progression spawned hundreds of hits like "26 Miles," "Silhouettes," and "Earth Angel." They may seem dated and boring to the terminally jaded but the record-buying teenagers at the time weren't at all bored. The success of the remakes of those old hits proves they're appealing again to a fresh audience.

Those old progressions had enough familiarity to make us feel at home with new records and new artists. We kept buying those clichéd changes. They were predictable. We already knew our parts and could sing along. Non-rock songs were based more on melody than on chord progressions and, in that way, avoided those melodic clichés. But no matter whether a song is based on chord changes, or melody, or rhythm, some basic structural forms and variations will continue as they have for many, many years for a simple reason: *they work.*

Again, I must add that there are exceptions, where the time-tested forms have been expertly manipulated and stretched, by sheer force of production and arrangement, as well as by firmly established writer/artists who can still experiment with little fear of failure. Hopefully, they—

and you—will continue to experiment and stretch those boundaries. Once you have an understanding of the elements of form, what they do and why, you'll be able to challenge yourself to go beyond the familiar as you write your own songs.

People have an unconscious desire and need for symmetry; and the repetition of rhyme, melody, and form satisfies that need. The repetition of form also sets up a degree of predictability that's reassuring and comfortable to a listener, a solid base on which we can create surprises without taking our audiences too far into uncharted territory. The manipulation of form is an important game to know. The classical composers all learned form as a basic part of their training and for you, as a popular songwriter, to be able to make conscious choices about form, is to be in control of your art.

THE COMPONENTS OF FORM: VERSE

The verse is the major vehicle for conveying the song's information. It also serves, lyrically and musically, to "set up" or lead inevitably to either the chorus, the bridge, another verse, or a title/hook line. If it doesn't do one of those things well, it's not working. Verses have certain basic characteristics:

1. The lyric, from verse to verse, is different or contains substantial new information each time. It may contain elements of previous verses (such as the title line if there's no chorus)—called the refrain.

2. The melody is essentially the same each time we hear it though there's room for variation and some flexibility to accommodate the lyric. The reason for keeping the melody the same is that once listeners are familiar with it, it becomes easier for them to focus on the changing lyric.

CHORUS

The chorus is sometimes incorrectly referred to as a "refrain." In the sense that we refer to it in contemporary songwriting, the chorus crystallizes, focuses, and distills the intent, emotion, meaning, and essence of the song into a succinct, simple, and easily remembered statement. (Musicians sometimes use the term "chorus" to refer to the playing of the entire melody of a song, particularly in the 32-bar AABA form.) While verses usually concentrate on detail, the chorus can make a broader statement that bears more repetition. If the verse is the meat or the fiber, the chorus is the juice. It's the segment most people in the industry refer to as "the hook." The basic characteristics of the chorus are:

1. The melody is the same each time we hear it.
2. The title preferably appears in at least the first and/or last line and possibly more.
3. The lyric is usually the same each time although you may want to use some new lyric information in subsequent choruses to develop the story. A good example would be a "turnaround," commonly used in country music, in which the "twist" is not revealed until the last chorus.

Even though there may be reason for you to change the lyric, there's a very practical reason for you to keep at least a substantial part of it the same. *You want listeners to learn your song quickly and easily.* If they hear the same chorus three times during the song, they can go away singing it. If you change all or even some of the lyric and music of the chorus every time, you make it harder for the listener. If you have information in the verses that you want people to think about, and it's at all complex, the chorus should let a listener relax with its simplicity to allow the verse information to sink in. Be aware that, in a song, the listener's attention is divided between the lyric *and* the music, making it extra important to retain simplicity. So even when you feel you need to change the chorus lyric, a substantial amount of it, particularly the title line, should remain the same and be repeated every time.

BRIDGE

Also called a "release" or "break," the bridge can provide a variety of important functions in a song. Musically, the bridge helps to relieve the "boredom factor" and is therefore placed about two-thirds of the way into the song, where people may begin to tire of melodic repetition. It zaps the listeners back to attention and helps them refocus if you don't already have them totally under your spell. The bridge can add drama to your song in many ways. *Musically,* you can use any of the devices used to achieve contrast described in the "Song Dynamics" segment later in this chapter.

The bridge can also be purely instrumental. The melody should sound as different as possible without sounding like it belongs in another song. *Lyrically,* it offers you the opportunity to change gears. You can reiterate the philosophy of the song in a whole new way by changing the "person" (going from "they" or "you" to "I," for example) going from concrete, specific imagery to the abstract and philosophical or vice versa, using it as an "aside" or serving the function of a third party storyteller as the Greek chorus did in ancient drama. Basic characteristics of the bridge are:

1. Its melody is different from either the verse or the chorus though occasionally a portion of the verse or chorus melody may be recapped in the position of a bridge.
2. It's entirely optional.
3. It most commonly occurs once but occasionally is repeated in an extended verse/chorus form. What keeps it from acting like a chorus in that situation is that it doesn't contain the hook/title, and if put together right, its melody inevitably carries it back to the verse or chorus, therefore making it difficult to end with.
4. It's rarely over eight bars long. After all, it's supposed to be a diversion, not a whole piece in itself. It may be two bars or two lyric lines or *whatever is needed* to fulfill the function.
5. Generally speaking, it doesn't contain the title/hook, but that's certainly not law. That decision may depend on how much repetition of

the title/hook you already have in the song. If you don't have much, it might be smart to use it again.

PRE-HOOK

"Pre-hooks" are melodic segments that are different from the verses, chorus, or bridge. They're used extensively in contemporary music, primarily in pop and R&B. Pre-hooks are known by many other names (*climb, lift, "B" section, pre-chorus, setup*), probably because there was no universal term for them and people just made up their own. Producers seem to favor pre-hooks to help create an additional level of dynamics and interest to keep a song exciting, particularly in up-tempo dance songs where extra length and faster tempo make a straight verse/chorus form feel too repetitive. When you first hear a pre-hook, it almost sounds as if it's going to be the chorus till you hear the chorus that follows.

Musically, a pre-hook should increase the tension to a point where there's a great sense of relief going into the chorus. Hall and Oates's "I Can't Go for That" is a great example. The Bee Gees used the pre-hook to great advantage as well in "Shadow Dancing," "Staying Alive," and "Night Fever," and Diane Warren and Albert Hammond used it in their Starship hit, "Nothing's Gonna Stop Us Now." In many cases, pre-hooks rule out the need for a bridge though if the song needs it, go ahead. "Nothing's Gonna Stop Us Now" uses one, and so does the Aretha Franklin/George Michael duet, "I Knew You Were Waiting (For Me)" by Climie and Morgan. The basic characteristics of pre-hooks are:

1. They directly precede the chorus.
2. They usually precede the chorus *each time* but may be dropped after the first couple of times if you can find a way, musically, to get back to the chorus without it.
3. Lyrics can be the same each time or different. Melodies are the same.
4. Length varies, like the bridge, from one line to four. Usually they're no more than eight bars.

Here's a classic example of a song that uses a pre-hook, a second pre-hook, and a bridge:

YOU'VE LOST THAT LOVIN' FEELIN'
Words and music by Barry Mann, Cynthia Weil and Phil Spector

A—verse   *You never close your eyes anymore when I kiss your lips*
             And there's no tenderness like before in your fingertips

B—pre-hook   *It makes me just feel like crying, baby*
             'Cause baby, something beautiful's dying

C—chorus   *You've lost that lovin' feelin'*
             Wo-o that lovin' feelin'
             You've lost that lovin' feelin' now it's gone, gone, gone wo wo

| A—verse | *And there's no welcome look in your eyes when I reach for you* |
| | *And girl, you're startin' to criticize little things I do* |

| B—pre-hook | *It makes me just feel like crying, baby* |
| | *'Cause baby, something beautiful's dying* |

C—chorus	*You've lost that lovin' feelin'*
	Wo-o that lovin' feelin'
	You've lost that lovin' feelin' now it's gone, gone, gone wo wo

D—bridge	*Baby, baby, I'd get down on my knees for you*
	If you could only love me, like you used to do
	We had a love, a love, a love you don't find every day
	So don't, don't, don't let it slip away

E—pre-hook 2	*I said baby, baby, baby, I'm beggin' you please*
	I'm beggin' you please
	I need your love (I need your love) I need your love,
	So bring it on back (bring it on back) now bring it on back
	Now bring it on back, you've got to—

C—chorus	*Bring back that lovin' feelin'*
	Wo-o that lovin' feelin'
	Bring back that lovin' feelin' 'cause it's gone, gone, gone
	and I can't go on wo wo woh

Note: The addition of the second pre-hook was a surprise that took the emotional pitch and tension of the song even higher with the repetition of short phrases, then surprised us with "Bring back . . ." instead of "You've lost. . . ." Though some of the lyric changed in the last chorus, the hook had already been well established earlier and the last chorus preserved the repetition of "lovin' feelin'."

ANALYZING FORM
Before getting into the forms themselves, I'll explain how you can analyze the song forms you hear.

To start, consider the first melodic segment you hear—whether it's a verse or chorus—as "A." The next complete melodic section (that's a different melody than "A") you designate "B," the third "C." Repeats of any melodic segment are assigned the same letter they got the first time. Count bars or measures starting at the downbeat as follows: for 4/4 time, 1-2-3-4, 2-2-3-4, 3-2-3-4, 4-2-3-4, etc. For 3/4 waltz time, 1-2-3, 2-2-3, 3-2-3, 4-2-3, etc. When the next melodic segment starts, begin counting at bar one again. Enter the total number of bars in each segment. Be sure to include any instrumental breaks, using "ins" or a dash, or some other shorthand to designate them, along with the number of bars they run. You'll end up with a diagram that looks like this: A-8, A-8, B-8, A-8; or A A B A or A B C ins A B C.
8 8 8 8   8 8 8 2 8 8 8

Here's a more graphic way to lay it out quickly so you can easily add extra bars and make notes. Each of the slash marks represents a beat (in 4/4 time).

```
INTRO     1 / / / 2 / / / 3 / / / 4 / / /
A         1 / / / 2 / / / 3 / / / 4 / / / 5 / / / 6 / / / 7 / / / 8 / / /
B         1 / / / 2 / / / 3 / / / 4 / / /
INS       1 / / / 2 / / /
A         1 / / / 2 / / / 3 / / / 4 / / / 5 / / / 6 / / / 7 / / / 8 / / /
B         1 / / / 2 / / / 3 / / / 4 / / /
```

Do this exercise periodically while you listen to the radio. It will give you a repertoire of basic forms and, more importantly, show you a wide range of variations that work, such as extra bars of music between sections and unexpected chord changes. Even though you'll find the forms falling into predictable patterns, it's often the variations that create the sense of surprise that takes a song enough out of the commonplace to make it special and exciting.

Note how form contributes to the memorability of a song by achieving a balance between predictability and surprise, interest and boredom, how it ensures repetition of melody and/or lyrics, and how all that is carried out in a commercially acceptable time limit.

THE BASIC FORMS

AAA

A Verse with title/hook in first or last line
A
A

This is an old form used a lot in folk music but occasionally with good results in contemporary songs as well. There is no chorus or bridge. The title line usually appears in the first or last line. Occasionally, there are two repeated lyric phrases, one in the first *and* one in the last line. The form can have any number of verses. You'd use it if you had a lot of important lyric content such as in a story song but wanted to eliminate the time spent on repetition of choruses. You get your needed repetition from the repeated lyric lines and repeated melody. In the absence of the chorus that "sums up" the song, you'll want the verses to end with a dramatic kind of "payoff" line.

Examples: "I'll Walk the Line" (Johnny Cash), "Turn, Turn, Turn" and "Where Have All The Flowers Gone?" (Pete Seeger) "The Rose" (Amanda McBroom), "By the Time I Get to Phoenix" (Jim Webb), "Ode to Billie Joe" (Bobbie Gentry), "The Times They Are a Changin' " and "With God on Our Side" (Bob Dylan), "Wreck of the Edmund Fitzgerald" (Gordon Lightfoot), "Do That to Me One More Time" (Toni Tennille), "Gentle on My Mind" (John Hartford), "Fiddlin' Man" (Chick Rains, Jim Ed Norman, Michael Martin Murphey).
Variations: There are variations of this form, like Don Henley's "Dirty Laundry" which uses a short refrain between every couple of verses. It's

not a standard AAA because the refrain isn't a part of the basic melodic structure of the verse, but the refrain misses being a chorus by being very short and not containing the hook line, which *is* contained in the verse.

Bruce Springsteen's "Born in the U.S.A." is musically an AAA. Though it has a chorus, its melody is the same as the verses. That's very unusual, and if you had written this song instead of "The Boss," your publisher would have demanded a rewrite. Without a powerful performance the song would be musically boring.

Another variation of the AAA form is an extension created by repeating part or all of the last line. The special focus on that line, however, makes it important that it be the title line. A short instrumental section or melodic instrumental hook can be used to break the potential monotony.

Caution: The AAA form is usually used in ballads because at a slower tempo, we don't get bored with the melodic repetition. You need to be careful to make the melody as interesting as possible without getting too complex to be easily remembered. This is generally accomplished with a melodic variation in the last two lines of each verse. Hum any of the examples mentioned above to see what I mean.

A A B A (Four eight-bar sections)

A   Title/hook in first or last line
A
B   New melody and lyric
A

Variations

A   Title/hook in first or last line
A
B   New melody and lyric
A
B   Repeat B section with or without new lyric
A   Repeat first A, or part of first A and part of second A, or part of first A and new lyric
A   Repeat second A

AABA is a classic song form with a long and popular history. At one time, it was considered *the* song form. It's short, concise, melodically seamless, and easy to remember. It's still used in all styles of music, though least in hard rock. It's also used most frequently in slow or mid-tempo ballads, since its 32 bars (four eight-bar sections) make for a very short song at fast tempos. There are variations which can accommodate faster tempos and the need for more room to tell the story. You'll find your own as the need arises.

Hook/title placement is usually in either the first or last line of the verse, but it can occur in both ("Yesterday," "Don't Give Up On Us Baby"). In rare cases, the title will also be recapped in the "B" section though the object is to go to a new place in that section, both musically and lyrically.

Examples: "Just the Way You Are" and "She's Always a Woman to Me" (Billy Joel), "When Sunny Gets Blue" (Segal/Fischer), "My Way" (Anka/Francois/Revaux/Thibaut), "One Hundred Ways" (Wakefield/Wright/Coleman), "As Time Goes By" (Herman Hupfeld), "Raindrops Keep Fallin' on My Head" (Hal David/Burt Bacharach), "No Getting Over Me" (Aldridge/Brasfield), "Always On My Mind" (Zambon/Thompson/Christopher), "Don't It Make My Brown Eyes Blue" (Richard Leigh), "Saving All My Love for You" and "Tonight I Celebrate My Love" (Michael Masser/Gerry Goffin), and "Fire" (Bruce Springsteen).

VERSE/CHORUS

The varieties of this most popular form provide a maximum of chorus repetition and two or more verses to tell your story.

#1
A Verse
B Chorus
A Verse
B Chorus
A Verse
B Chorus

Version #1 gives you a maximum verse and chorus repetition. A potential problem is that, if you have a lot of melodic repetition *within* each verse or chorus, such as an eight-bar section made up of three two-bar melodies with a slight variation in the fourth two-bar melody line, you may have monotony from too much repetition. In that case, #2 with the substitutions of a bridge for the third verse helps to break it up.

#2
A Verse
B Chorus
A Verse
B Chorus
C Bridge
B Chorus

#3
A Chorus
B Verse
A Chorus
B Verse
A Chorus

Version #3, with the chorus first, can give you more repetition of the chorus in a shorter time. The choice of whether to start with a chorus depends on the lyric development of the song. If it's important to generate a dynamic opener to the song, try the chorus first unless you want the vers-

73

es to build interest and suspense and "set up" the chorus as a payoff. Many Motown hits used variations of this form.

#4		#5	
A	Verse	A	Verse
A	Verse	B	Pre-hook
B	Chorus	C	Chorus
A	Verse	A	Verse
B	Chorus	B	Pre-hook
B	Chorus	C	Chorus

Version #4, with two verses in front, is also a much used form. Its workability depends on a very strong lyric continuity between the first and second verses to offset the delay in getting to the chorus. This is a much greater problem in a slow ballad than an uptempo song because of the additional time it takes to get to the chorus. Every word has to propel the story forward. Repeating of information is deadly. If each of the two verses cover the same information in a different way and don't depend on each other, this may not be the best form to use since you should have a very important reason to delay the hook. If you do need to use two verses, you may want to look for some arrangement devices or write a variation of the first verse melody to help sustain musical interest in the second verse.

You could also consider using your title in the first line of the chorus to avoid even further delay in reaching the hook line. Variations of this form opening with three verses (AAABAB or AAABAAB) are rare, and the two examples that come to mind—Don Henley and Glenn Frey's "Lyin' Eyes" and Don Schlitz's "The Gambler"—both have such exceptional lyric continuity that a chorus any earlier would be an unwelcome intrusion. You'll also occasionally hear an AABAABB variation, particularly on up-tempo songs. Again, those choices will be different for each song but the guiding principle is that you *don't delay the hook unless you have another good way to sustain the listener's interest.*

Version #5 offers the excitement of three different melodic segments. The pre-hook is the segment that makes the difference here. This form works best in up-tempo dance songs where the three segments go by quickly. Many variations are possible with this form, including repeated instrumental versions of any of the segments and instrumental breaks between segments. Here are some examples of how the segments may be arranged:

AABC ABC BC BC or
ABC AC ABC AC or
ABC ABCD BC or
ABC ABCD ABCD, the "D" being a bridge with a new melody, with or without lyrics.

With the increase in the number of dance songs in the four-minute range

74

on the pop and R&B charts, we see much more experimentation with these extended forms. Dance records are developed for pop, rock, and R&B radio and 12″ singles with extended bass response for the dance club market. The records are usually formatted in a way that allows them to be re-edited. This means that an original long version is recorded with segments that can be removed to make a short version for radio or left in for the dance club market or for radio stations that play the long version.

Records earmarked specifically for the dance club market, and not for radio, can break more rules. Since there's a captive audience and you don't need to get their attention and since records well over four minutes are the norm, you can use long, slow-building intros, additional sections, and long instrumental breaks that would be too monotonous on radio. The records' major appeal is based on a relentlessly exciting dance groove. Beyond that, there are no rules and, aside from a few conventional arrangement tricks like dropping out and bringing in instruments, there is a lot of room for creativity in vocal and instrumental textures, particularly for songwriters with arranging and producing skills.

EXERCISES IN FORM

1. Write a song adhering strictly to each of the standard forms mentioned.
2. Analyze the forms of ten current hits. Do this exercise about once a month with ten new songs. It's a great way to stay current and to explore new form variations. Examine the forms and variations and why you think they work. Weekly radio and TV "countdowns" like Casey Kasem's "American Top 40," based on current *Billboard* charts, are good to use for this. There are also countdowns on radio for country and black music.
3. Write songs using new variations of standard forms.

CHOOSING A FORM

Even when your songs come spontaneously, there is a point at which you need to decide which form to use. Usually writers will come up with a single verse or chorus idea first. After that first flash of inspiration and an exploration of what you want the song to say, you'll need to have an idea of the type of form you'll want to use to help you say it more effectively. You may do that unconsciously, as a natural result of having listened to the radio all your life. You just feel where there ought to be a change without really making a conscious evaluation of the reasons. That approach often works just fine. However it has some inherent problems, like the beginning guitar player who writes monotonous two-chord songs because he only knows two chords. You have to remind yourself that what you already know or feel about form could be limiting.

Another problem to choosing form by "feel" is the songwriter's equivalent to "painting yourself into a corner." You might lock into a form that, by the time you've said what you wanted to say, has resulted in a five-minute song that you really wanted to be three minutes. You're now faced with a rewrite that might include a restructuring of the whole song. It's much harder to get out of a corner like that than it is to set it up better in the beginning. Even if you do have to restructure the song because the form you chose didn't quite work—or you had another idea halfway through the song—the important thing is that you make those decisions on the basis of knowing your options.

So what do you consider in your choice of form? If you're starting with the music, tempo is a major factor. If it's an up-tempo song, you may need a form with many sections, like an ABCABCDC or AABABCB, to help sustain musical interest. If it's a slow or mid-tempo ballad, you can use either the longer or shorter forms.

If you're starting from a lyric, the mood and subject matter will dictate the tempo of the music. In other words, "Boogie Fever" wouldn't work very well as a slow ballad and the lyric to "Up Where We Belong" wouldn't be as effective in a fast dance song. Tempo is also determined by the ease with which the lyrics can be sung. If there are lots of words, and the tempo's too fast, you may tie knots in your tongue trying to get them all in. If you want a rapid-fire, one syllable per eighth- or sixteenth-note lyric, you have to be extra careful that the words are easy to pronounce and sing together. It's a good idea to experiment with a metronome by singing the lyric against various tempo settings. Fewer words generally pose fewer problems, but the challenge is to phrase them in an interesting way against the rhythm.

Other tempo variations are possible, of course. But once you've set the tempo and determined how many lyric lines in each segment, you've begun to lock yourself into the form. If it takes one minute to get through a verse and chorus and you're looking for a three-minute song, your options have already shrunk.

You must also consider the amount of lyric needed to tell the story. Though it's always a good idea to condense, the AAA form gives a writer the most room to stretch lyrically. Any up-tempo three or four-section form provides plenty of lyric space with strong musical interest, particularly if you use pre-hooks for new lyric information each time. One-section (AAA) and two-section (ABABAB) forms at fast tempos, though they allow for a maximum of lyric information, can also be melodically boring because the melodies repeat so often.

With a spare, condensed lyric you have lots of options. You can lay it over either an up-tempo track or a slow ballad and, in either case, have plenty of room to accommodate the individual phrasing styles of different artists. You can use any form and ensure a maximum amount of both repetition and musical interest. At slower tempos with a spare lyric though, the lyric carries more of an obligation to be interesting. You're making the listener wait for that lyric to unfold, and it had better be worth the wait. The same is true of the music.

Eventually, like anything else, once you've worked with these forms they'll become second nature to you. You'll also find that you *will* get yourself into problematic situations for which you *will* find creative solutions. A substantial amount of innovation in music is initiated by a need to find a graceful way out of a jam. If you already have a repertoire of solutions, you're ahead of the game.

HOOKS

"Hook" is the term you'll hear most often in the business and craft of commercial songwriting. Well, maybe not as often as "sorry we can't use it," but it's possible that the more you hear about hooks now, the less you'll hear "we can't use it" later.

The hook has been described as "the part(s) you remember after the song is over," "the part that reaches out and grabs you," "the part you can't stop singing (even when you hate it)" and "the catchy repeated chorus." Among the best hook crafters are commercial jingle writers. How many times have you had a jingle stick in your mind and the harder you tried to get rid of it, the harder it stuck? That's a good hook! Here are several categories:

THE STRUCTURAL HOOK
In this category, part of the structure of the song functions as the hook. The most common is the "hook chorus." It repeats several times during the song, and should contain the title or "hook line," usually the first or last line (see "Chorus Construction," page 78). We may also consider memorable "B" sections, particularly in an AABA form, to be hooks, though it's the chorus that's almost universally referred to as the hook.

INSTRUMENTAL HOOKS
Certain melodic phrases in songs may not be part of the vocal melody, yet stick in our minds as if they were. In the last line of the chorus of George Harrison's "Something," following the words "Don't want to leave her now, you know I believe and how . . . ," is a melodic guitar figure that we think of whenever we think of the melody. Though there's no lyric over it, if we heard that figure by itself, we'd be able to "name that tune." The repeated riffs that introduce and run beneath Stevie Wonder's "Superstition" and Michael Jackson's "Beat It" are as memorable as any other parts of the songs. The same is true of the keyboard figure created by studio musician Bill Cuomo under Kim Carnes's version of "Bette Davis Eyes" (written by Jackie DeShannon and Donna Weiss).

Too often, songwriters tend to believe that creating those instrumental hooks is the job of the arranger, producer, or studio musicians. Keep in mind, though, that if those are the hooks that sell the song to the public, they'll sell the song to the producer and artist if you create them first.

STORY LINE HOOK

Have you ever heard a song and afterward couldn't quite remember the melody or the exact words but you could remember the story? Sometimes the story itself is so powerful and evocative that it's the thing that stays in your mind longer than the exact words or melody. Bobbie Gentry's "Ode to Billie Joe" is a classic, as is Kenny Rogers's hit, "Coward of the County," written by Roger Bowling and Billy Wheeler, and Helen Reddy's "Angie Baby," written by Alan O'Day.

PRODUCTION HOOKS

These aren't always within the realm of the songwriter, but today more writers than ever before have access to sophisticated instrumental and recording technology. The sound of demos and master recordings has become very important. Experiment with the way various instruments sound in combination, with electronic keyboard synth "presets" combined with acoustic instruments or natural sounds. You can digitally sample all those sound sources or buy them on disks, tapes, or ROM cartridges and modify them yourself. MIDI (Musical Instrument Digital Interface) technology has made possible an almost infinite variety of sonic combinations. (See "Demos: What You Can Do At Home," page 202.)

Early recording techniques such as "phasing" and "flanging" were later incorporated into electronic boxes that you could use at the tap of a button, and today virtually any sound modification device used in the studio has been converted to some portable form to use at home or on stage.

Certain sounds will evoke certain emotional responses, so you can use them as artistic tools along with lyric and melody to create mood and emotion. One of the most effective hooks is a sound no one has ever heard before. Remember, however, that the technology of creating sounds can be so much fun that you can easily forget that the song is still the most important thing. No matter how exciting those sounds are, they won't make up for a weak song.

Hooks are essential in commercial music. They are points of reference that keep us interested and focused, devices that help us remember, and an entertainment in themselves. Part of your job as a commercial writer is to be able to use as many different types of hooks as possible.

CHORUS CONSTRUCTION

The part of a song people usually remember best, after the first couple of listens, is the chorus. Effective choruses are a magic mix of lyric, melody, and phrasing.

The majority of choruses adhere to certain guidelines. I say "majority" because some songs ignore the guidelines and still win by the strength of their performance, arrangement, and/or production.

For the others, here are some guidelines:

1. The title should appear in the chorus in a way that, by virtue of its placement and/or degree of repetition, we *know* it's the title. If

words or phrases other than the title repeat in the chorus or are placed in strong positions, the listener won't know which is the title. That's strictly a commercial consideration.

2. Keep the information the chorus imparts simple enough for people to remember easily. If you're a literary genius, you may tend to think most choruses are *too* simple. Don't worry about it. They need to be simple.
3. They also need to distill and focus the song.
4. They need to stand repetition.
5. Besides the information, the words of the chorus themselves need to be easily remembered. It also helps if the melody is fun and easy to sing.
6. The action in the verses should not pass the action in the chorus chronologically. Choruses can run from two to eight lines, depending on your definition of a line.

Here are some common lyric constructions:

Repeat the same line two or more times. This one can get monotonous unless that line is fun to sing, it's sung with a style that makes it interesting, and/or it's musically exciting. Examples: Bruce Springsteen's "Born in the U.S.A.," Huey Lewis's "Hip to Be Square" (Lewis/Hopper/Gibson), Lionel Richie's "Dancing on the Ceiling" (Richie/Rios/Frenchic).

First and third line the same, second and fourth lines different. This offers the possibility of a strong "payoff" line to end the chorus. The last line in the chorus is a power position and listeners therefore expect it to be strong and satisfying. Examples: Kenny Loggins's "Meet Me Half Way," (Giorgio Moroder and Tom Whitlock), Bruce Hornsby's "The Way It Is."

First three lines the same, fourth line different. This has some of the potential monotony of #1 and the payoff advantage of #2. The repetition of the first three lines makes for a powerful setup, so the payoff needs to be strong. Examples: Pat Benatar's smash "Hit Me with Your Best Shot (Eddie Schwartz), Will Jennings's and Steve Winwood's "Higher Love."

All four lines different. This doesn't risk monotony and doesn't set up as much of an expectation for a powerful last line as #2 and #3. But give them one anyway. Examples: Larry Henley and Jeff Silbar's "The Wind Beneath My Wings," Smokey Robinson's "Being with You."

The first or last part of each line repeated (almost always the title). This is one of the oldest and most common structures, going back to "call and response" songs in tribal music and Gregorian chant. Examples: Hall and Oates's "She's Gone," Irene Cara's "Fame" (Dean Pitchford and Michael Gore).

The first and last line the same, the second and third each different. This gives you a chance to repeat the hook line at both the beginning and the end. Examples: Anne Murray's "Could I Have This Dance" (Wayland Holyfield and Bob House), Huey Lewis's "The Heart of Rock and Roll."

Now that we have the generalizations out of the way, you should know that chorus structures are far less standardized than song forms. Pick up a copy of *Song Hits* magazine on the newsstand or listen to a Top 40 count-down and try to get a consensus of chorus structures. What you'll find is an incredible degree of diversity, particularly in pop music (more than in country). In fact, a good share of pop hits are there *because* their choruses are unusual.

Let's look at the Pointer Sisters's hit "Automatic" by Brock Walsh and Mark Goldenberg. This is a good example of a chorus that's not really one of the standard constructions, but if there's such a thing as a textbook ex-ample of a creative chorus that works, this is it. It's easy to remember, fun to sing, and gives us both predictability and surprise.

No way to control it
It's totally automatic
Whenever you're around.
I'm walking blindfolded
Completely automatic
All of my systems are down.
Down, down, down
Automatic, automatic

Though the line in which the title appears is different each time, the title is in the same position the first two times we hear it. That, and the closing of the *around*/*down* rhyme, set up enough predictable comfort to make "Down, down, down" a pleasant surprise. The last repetitions of the title line are also a surprise. They're delivered to give each syllable of *au-to-ma-tic* two beats in contrast to the one beat per word of the "downs."

They also gave us both assonance and alliteration with *control/totally,* the emotional imagery and near-rhyme of "No way to con*trol it*," "I'm walking blind*folded*," and "All of my systems are down," the latter line be-ing a perfect compliment to the automatic, techno feel of the music and performance.

Musical construction of a chorus roughly follows the lyric structure, but a tremendous variety of rhythmic and phrasing options is available. Pop music allows for great flexibility in the ways that lyrics can be stretched and spaced and positioned relative to the music, and looking at a lyric on paper only gives us a part of the story.

REPETITION
One of the most important ingredients of successful songs is repetition. Repetition is also one of the keys to teaching almost anything. If you want to teach someone your song quickly, you can't afford not to use it.

Several studies have shown that most listeners have some resistance to hearing something unfamiliar. They'd rather hear a song they already know. I confess to a little disappointment in that revelation, but it shouldn't have been surprising. As writers and musicians, we are always looking for something fresh and new and tend to forget that there's a pub-lic out there who, generally speaking, doesn't share that need for change.

They feel comfortable with the familiar, and uncomfortable with the unfamiliar.

This poses obvious problems for radio stations who'd like to add a new record by a new artist, but whose audience polls say they should keep playing "Stairway to Heaven" instead. The more they repeat those old songs, the more comfortable people feel with them, and the more personal nostalgia they generate. Since radio stations are relying more heavily on listener polls and feedback to program their music, and since listeners can't request what they haven't heard, new writer/artists are between a rock and a hard place.

If you can write songs for established artists, with already familiar and easily identifiable voices and styles, you have an edge, because a new song by Madonna or Whitney Houston or the Oak Ridge Boys is going to get played before an unfamiliar song performed by an unknown artist.

Since your problem with a new song is to break through that resistance, repetition of melodic themes, choruses, or instrumental figures (riffs) will build instant familiarity into a song. Write a chorus that is totally and instantly understandable, simple, easily remembered, and that touches their hearts and/or their feet. By the time the song is finished and the listeners have heard it three or four times, they'll know it and want to hear and sing it again.

As a general guideline, try to get enough repetition without inducing boredom. It's sometimes difficult to determine how much is too much. Lyricists, in general, seem to get bored very quickly and even a very little repetition can make them feel guilty about not doing their job properly. On the other hand, a musician who's just found a great groove will tend to play it till the neighbors have him arrested. This supports the theory that you can get away with more repetition of a short lyric phrase if it's catchy and fun to sing—in other words, if it's "musical" by virtue of its meter, phrasing, rhythm, rhyme, assonance, and alliteration. "Chattanooga Choo Choo," "Your Kiss is on My List," "Little Latin Lupe Lu," and "Owner of a Lonely Heart" all have those "catchy" qualities about them.

Obviously, the amount of repetition you use depends on the purpose of the song, what audience you're trying to reach, and other considerations. We've all gotten bored with some five- to ten-minute dance tunes we've heard on the radio in which three-quarters of the song seems to be repeats of a short riff or lyric phrase.

If we heard the song in a dance club or at a live performance we may not be bored at all. These songs are written primarily to appeal to us on a visceral level, or their mental appeal is one of putting us in a kind of hypnotic trance to "bliss us out." At the other extreme are songs like Billy Joel's "Just the Way You Are," which repeats that one line only at the end of each verse, or story songs like Bobbie Gentry's "Ode to Billy Joe," in which the continuity was so strong that, if it had a chorus, it would have driven us crazy waiting for the next verse. Both of these songs, of course, have memorable repeated melodies. Try to imagine what it would feel like if both songs changed the melody with each verse. We'd have a much harder time paying attention to the lyrics. So the repetition of melody allows listeners to focus more on the lyrics. One of the reasons, I think, why country music melodies have such simple familiarity is that the songs are about 90 percent (my estimate) lyric-oriented, and the familiarity helps the listener concentrate on the words.

Lyric repetition also serves to let the listener's mind rest. If, as a writer, you're giving listeners complex information in the verses, a repeated chorus coming up says, "O.K. You'll only have to concentrate a little longer. When the chorus comes back you can rest your mind and just groove. When it's over you'll know just when to get ready to concentrate again." That "mental set" or "preparation to pay attention" is another psychology-of-learning principle. It's really why you need, in both writing and production, to have "pick-ups" before choruses and verses, intros to songs, drum fills, any little figure or chord change or something that "telegraphs" ahead that there's going to be a change. We like those when we dance, too. They help us to choreograph ourselves.

Repetition of words or short phrases or the first part of a known melody or lyric line is a great tension creator in a song. In order to work, though, it has to substantially "pay off." Otis Redding was great at these. "You got to, got to, got to, got to" and when he finally hits "try a little tenderness," it's a release and a relief and it makes you feel good.

Being too repetitious, though, can wear out your radio welcome fast. We all know songs like that. Pay attention to the ones that do it to you and figure out why. A chorus made up of the same short repeated phrase throughout can be death. Ideally, a song should be a good balance of predictability and surprise without too much of either.

SONG DYNAMICS

Among the most powerful tools to make your songs more commercial and to impress industry pros with your command of the craft are the contrasts and variations I call "song dynamics." Surprisingly, they're the tools most commonly overlooked and underused by amateur songwriters. In this section we'll look at several devices you should have in your bag of tricks and why they work. (Also see Chapter 6, "Writing Music.")

Each record or a song has crucial points at which the audience's attention must be dramatically and positively captured in order to make it effective on radio. I had a very valuable experience that helped to verify my information on this fact.

Len Chandler and I were asked to produce demos of some strong commercial songs by a company that regularly tests records on behalf of producers and record companies. Every Saturday, four hundred young potential record buyers representing several demographic groups sat in a theater and turned a dial on the arm of their seats to indicate responses to a given song ranging from "don't like it" to neutral to "love it." As the song was heard in the theater, lyrics were shown on the screen and, simultaneously, a computer totaling the combined responses of each demographic group drew a graph of that group's reaction so that we could see how they responded at any given moment of the song. From watching those reactions and from the director's interpretations of what we saw, we learned:

1. Intros for ballads should be shorter to get the listener into the body of the song faster. Intros for up-tempo songs can be longer because people get involved physically almost immediately and don't need to wait to get excited and delighted.
2. People will try to identify the voice when it's first heard. If it's familiar, it usually generates a positive reaction. People always feel more comfortable with a voice they know than one they don't because they have to decide whether they even like an unfamiliar singer.

 This phenomenon also contributes to the difficulty of an unknown artist getting exposure on radio. An example of this was an unknown male artist with a beautiful but very high voice who got a negative reaction from the audience. We finally concluded that the audience was turned off because they didn't know whether to identify a male or female—the lyrics didn't immediately establish a gender. Remember that this wasn't Michael Jackson with a readily identifiable voice. It wasn't the high voice in itself that didn't work, it was the lack of gender identity.
3. The reaction at the first sound of a voice is critical to the audience's continued reaction to the record. The longer it takes to respond positively, the harder it is to build interest through the rest of the song. In the absence of a familiar voice, the lyric content of the first line(s) is very important to the audience's response. This is the audience's first exposure to the song and artist and there's an automatic tendency to pay attention when someone starts to sing, just as there is when someone starts to talk. If people don't understand or hear or like what's being said, the reaction will be negative.
4. The "hook" chorus is another critical point in a song. If audience interest doesn't increase perceptibly at the beginning of the chorus and increase throughout, continued positive interest in the remainder of the record is unlikely.
5. As mentioned in #1, in up-tempo records, the interest usually develops quickly since people usually get their bodies pleasantly involved in an infectious rhythm track right away. Ballads take longer to develop interest since musically they're not usually creating high energy excitement. People reflect on ballad lyrics in a more passive way which increases the need for a blockbuster chorus.

In television, the pros say that there should be a new camera angle or other change at least every fifteen seconds to keep the viewer's interest. This principle has an analogy to radio. Since it's true that we remember only a fraction of what we hear compared to what we see, we begin to understand why we're so easily distracted when we listen to the radio. That means that the battle for people's attention on the radio is a heavy one and writers need all the ammunition they can get.

Now that we understand what has to be done, how can we create the necessary excitement to solve the problem?

One of the main components of the "Superlearning" techniques developed by Soviet educators and now used in the West is that teachers vary the tone, intensity, and pitch of their voice frequently as they deliver the material. The effect is that the changes continue to stimulate the student's attention. Since this is the same effect you want to achieve in your listeners, you can use this principle by varying your "voice"—increasing and releasing tension and achieving contrast between different segments of the song. Try out some of these.

> CHANGE THE GROOVE

You can go from a straight "on the beat" feel in the verse to a more syncopated feel in the chorus or vice versa. In other words from emphasizing 1 2 3 4 to 1 *and* 2 *and* 3 *and* 4 *and* like a reggae beat.

> CHANGE CHORDS

Initiate a whole new chord progression for the chorus and another for the bridge. Modulating up or down, playing the same progression only in a higher or lower key, is an arrangement device but one you can build into your demos.

CHANGE TIME

Don't change tempo or pulse if you're going for a radio or dance market record. It's been done by major artists (Paul McCartney on "Live and Let Die," Queen on "We Are the Champions") but it's a very risky business (even to start slow and break into an uptempo dance groove as Donna Summer did on "Last Dance." That record had a difficult time gaining acceptance in the dance market initially because of its slow intro).

Once you've engaged a listener or dancer in the pulse of a song, it's a solid base on which to build other dynamics. On that solid base you can go from 4/4 time to a couple of bars of 3/4 time to increase tension, as the Beatles did on "We Can Work It Out." It can make for an interesting transition between verse and chorus.

CHANGE MELODY

A melodic change in the chorus is probably the most effective song dynamic you can use to make a song memorable and commercially viable. Generally you'll want it to "lift" out of (up from) the verse melody by starting *above* the last note of the verse. That's not a rule, however, and there have been songs that have achieved a contrast by dropping down from the verse—they're just more rare. A change in chord progressions will automatically induce you to change the melody in the chorus. It can also be effective to try to change the chorus melody before you work out new chords. Try playing and singing your verse melody right up to the place where your chorus is supposed to come in. Then stop playing and continue *a cappella.* It also helps to put it on tape so you can avoid the temptation to start playing chords on your instrument.

CHANGE LYRIC DENSITY

The term "lyric density" refers to how close together the words are over a given tempo. A song might have rapid-fire lyrics with one syllable per sixteenth note during the verse, then change in the chorus to one syllable per quarter note in the chorus. Or just the opposite. Many hit songs use that kind of device. "You Light Up My Life" is a good example. The verses, in general, have a syllable per quarter note but when the song gets to the chorus, a new pattern begins. "You" lasts three beats (a whole bar), "light up my" is one syllable per quarter note, and "life" is again a whole bar. The rest of the chorus continues in the same pattern, giving our minds another subconscious cue to remember the lyric and melody.

CHANGE THE METER

Changing lyric meters from line to line or section to section also creates interest. Keeping the same meter through a verse can subtly build tension that can be released when you change it in the chorus. You can also alternate between two different meters every other line. You'll find lots of options here. (See "Prosody and Meter," page 61.)

CHANGE THE RHYME SCHEME

You can have a different rhyme scheme in your verses than in your chorus and/or your bridge. Try not to use the same end rhymes in more than one verse.

If you're a lyricist whose words will be set to music, you should employ changes in lyric density, meter, and rhyme scheme so that eventually, your composer has a head start in creating musical contrasts. Writing lyrics against a metronome pulse or drum machine will help you to "hear" those patterns in a useful context.

These devices have infinite variations and it's in their imaginative use that you exercise your creative muscles. They won't all work on all songs, but they're options you can try on each song. Arrangement devices such as dropping out and bringing in instruments, silence, and changes in intensity, volume, and texture can be used to further give your songs drama. These are devices to explore when you record your demo.

REWRITING

Before demoing any song you'll want to be sure it's the best it can be. Usually the first draft of any song can use improvement. So before your ecstasy about finishing compels you to immediately spend your hard-earned cash on a demo, it's well worth putting your song away for a few days. Being able to look at it more objectively may spare you the frustration of hearing a publisher say, "This is really good, but the second verse needs a rewrite," and knowing you'll have to spend even more to at least rerecord the vocal. Not that a rewrite is a guarantee that it won't happen anyway, but at least you'll know you gave it your best shot.

It's often said that creating successful songs is 10 percent writing and 90 percent rewriting. Writer Parker McGee revealed he had about twenty-two pages of rewrites for his England Dan/John Ford Coley hit, "I'd Really Love to See You Tonight." The song sounded so simple and straight ahead that it seemed it must have just poured right out all at once. But the truth is that it's often very difficult to write something that sounds simple and natural.

To be sure, a few special writers can get close to the finished song the first time around. Their processes are so well honed and they've been at it so long that their creative flow and critical faculties practically work in unison. Even relatively inexperienced writers will find they can occasionally write a song in fifteen minutes practically in its finished form. But even for pro writers, those times are rare. One of the differences between a pro and an amateur writer is that the pro usually recognizes from the beginning that there is a probability that he or she will be able to come up with rewrites to improve the song. The amateur tends to think that everything that comes out of the original, inspired state is wonderful and shouldn't be tampered with.

The latter attitude is the enemy of professionalism. Most writers go through this stage of development with great difficulty. The first time a publisher or producer rejects a song and suggests a rewrite, the writer rebels, thinking, "Who are you to criticize my work? Nobody knows better than I when it's finished or not!" I've watched many writers go through this stage, take the suggestions, rewrite, and be forced to admit to themselves that they really liked the changes they made and felt their songs had become much stronger. Once they have gone through that experience, the perspective makes them much more open to change, particularly if the end result is getting a song recorded or published. This doesn't mean that every criticism you receive is valid just because it comes from a so-called authority, but it is necessary to keep an open mind even if you eventually decide to leave the song unchanged.

Though it may be important to your livelihood that you rewrite for commercial considerations, it's most important to satisfy *yourself* that this is the best work you can do. Hopefully, you want to create something that will continue to be enjoyed for a long time. Five or twenty years from now, you don't want to be embarrassed to hear that song and know that if you'd just been a little harder on yourself, you'd be proud of it.

Sometimes it's valuable to imagine your toughest critic reading your lyric or hearing your song and picking it apart. It may point up flaws that you hadn't noticed before.

Here are some areas to look at for possible rewrites:

1. Make sure your lyrics and music work well together and you haven't placed accents on the wrong syllables or tried to fit too many words together in a short musical space. Words need to be easily sung and comprehended, so make sure that if they are to be sustained, they sound pleasant.
2. Can you substitute an image or action or dialogue line that will con-

dense and heighten the impact of the song? The less wordy a lyric, the more room an artist has to phrase it in his or her style.
3. Is every line important and every word necessary? Hit writer David Gates says that if he can omit a line without affecting the meaning and flow of the lyric, he knows he has to replace that line with a stronger one. Every line should contribute to the overall meaning.
4. Does your song contain the dynamics necessary to hold a listener's attention? Does your chorus stand out melodically from your verses? Can you rearrange rhyme schemes or meter to enhance the difference between sections of your song? Try some alternate melody lines while imagining an appropriate singer performing them. You may find something better than your first idea.

Jack Segal, hit lyricist, super craftsman, and teacher, lays out some rewriting tools in his lyric class that are well worth knowing: Reduction, Inversion, Insertion, and Rhyme Relocation.

REDUCTION
Reduction is the process of shortening of sentences or lines; specifically, making fewer syllables and fewer metric feet. Let's take a line that's seven metric feet,

Aňd thére   Ĭ ẃas   jušt haṅg   iňg ón   tŏ áll   thŏse ẃorn   oŭt liṅes

take out the useless words and cut it down to five feet with a one-syllable pickup:

Ĭ   wăs háng   iňg ón   tŏ áll   thŏse ẃorn   oŭt liṅes

Always look for ways to streamline your lyrics. If the above line was locked into a musical pattern that accommodated the first version, the reduced version would lend itself to a variety of new phrasing possibilities that the first version didn't offer.

INVERSION
Inversion is a tricky form of rhyme relocation, reversing part of the line so a new rhyme word switches from the interior to the end position. As I discussed in the "Rhyme" chapter, it's important to preserve the natural flow of the line and if the inversion appears to have been done only to achieve a rhyme, it feels awkward: "I loved you then, I love you still/Break us up, they never will."

That's an example of a mediocre line gone bad. "I love you still" is an acceptable inversion of "I still love you," but the last line is one you'd never deliver in a conversation and one that should get your poetic license revoked. You could say *they try to* break us up, they never will," and would then have two complete thoughts. If that possibility messes up your meter, you'd have to go back to the first line and look for another end word to give you a new choice of rhymes. In doing so, you might use another form of inversion by inverting the order in the first line to "I love you still, I loved you then" giving you "then" to work with. In this case, you're also reversing the natural time order of "then"/"still" which weakens the line. You could also say, "I love you now" instead of "still" though it does have a slightly different meaning which is an important element for consideration in this jigsaw juggle.

INSERTION

This is filling in the blanks when the desired meter, number of syllables, and the before and after thoughts are all known. You've got your verse or chorus written, your meter established, and you know what you want to say. You realize that there's a weak line in the middle that could be replaced. Now you have a *real* jigsaw puzzle.

Here's an example in something I wrote about a man trying to cope with his wife's addiction. The first draft:

> *She drifted past the mirror but she didn't even look.*
> *A week ago she would have fixed her hair.*
> *I could see that the spark had vanished from her eyes,*
> *And she was too far in the ozone now to care.*

I felt I needed something to replace the third line that said something about the emotional impact, the desperation the man was feeling, since I had already established, both before and after, what was happening to her.

> *She drifted past the mirror but she didn't even look.*
> *A week ago she would have fixed her hair.*
> *I was fading from her life and trying to hold on*
> *But she was too far in the ozone now to care.*

Even that line went through the same process, from "She was shut out of my life and I needed to break through" to "I was fading from her life and I needed to break through," which felt more vulnerable, to the final choice which felt vulnerable but also more helpless.

RHYME RELOCATION

Rhyme relocation is the flip-flopping of rhymes to strengthen the power of the lyric and rhyme. The stronger rhyme-word of the two should come second whenever possible. Inversion is actually a form of rhyme relocation. You get more power out of placing the strongest word as the end rhyme. Some words are more powerful than others, as you can see in these examples: *said/dead, had/bad, dream/scream, well/hell.* Obviously the second word in each pair would evoke the deepest emotional response in the hearer. If you find you have the strongest word first, try to reverse them. It won't always work and ultimately, it's a juggle between the power of the line, power of the word, meaning, and flow. The principle, overall, is always to escalate toward the most powerful word, line, or idea.

If you're writing a story song, save the payoff till the last verse. The last line of every section is a power position because it's where the tension is released. If you blow it with a weak line, chances are that the listener will feel let down enough to have forgotten that brilliant line in the middle of the verse. In the case of lines, an interesting example is in George Michael's hit, "Careless Whispers," "To the heart and mind/Ignorance is kind." If you turned the lines around, you'd get a slightly more natural, conversational feel but you'd lose considerable impact since "Ignorance is kind" is the real payoff line.

If you're writing the lyric first, you have the luxury of performing these changes without restriction. But if the change gives you a different meter, you'll want to follow through with the same meter in the rest of the verses, or the rest of the choruses (if that's what you're changing). If you don't, you'll give your melody writer a nervous breakdown. At times, it's actually easier to make reductions when the melody and lyrics are already married. When you're able to sing a line, you'll notice the awkward little spots where you could drop a word or two and give the singer more time to hang onto a word. It's also easier to feel when an insertion might help to enhance the rhythm of the lyric. Adding a word or two in the right place could help make the song "catchier."

Obviously no hard and fast rules exist about this, but the general principle is that *every word should perform a valuable function for the song. If it does nothing to enhance the rhythm, meaning, or sound of the lyric, it shouldn't be there.*

WRITING ON ASSIGNMENT

Staff writers at publishing companies are often called upon to write on assignment, but even if you're not in that position you'll hear about specific recording projects you'll want to write for on assignment. If you're a "project" writer who works best with specific guidelines, this is a great exercise whether you've been actually given a project or not.

Tailoring songs for a specific artist is a calculated and methodical approach. You may have written down or taped some great ideas during the heat of inspiration but now, in the light of wht you'll learn about your target artist or project you'll look at the ideas with a whole new perspective.

Let's say you have a "prescription" to write. You know that the producer is looking for positive, uptempo love songs for an artist. If you can, get information from the producer about the artist's vocal range, point of view, attitude, and philosophy. If it's not convenient to do that but the artist has previous albums, get them. Make a synopsis of the lyric of each song you hear on these: "He left me but I know I'll get over him," "I've had my problems with other women but I know she'll be different," "My friends think I'm crazy to love you but I don't care," "They all want you but I know what you want," etc. See if the songs the artist records—particularly the successful ones—fall into a consistent pattern. Some artists would never record a "weak" or "victim" song that says, basically, "You can walk all over me and I don't care. I'll still love you no matter what you do." Other artists have practically built their careers on songs with that attitude. Pay attention to the established image of an artist.

You can often get additional information from reading interviews with the artists in trade magazines. When you hear their records check out the kind of melodic passages the artist sings well. Does he/she have a great voice that loves to hold onto long notes and style them? Does the artist not have a great voice, coming off better doing story songs with lots of lyrics and short choppy lines? Does the artist phrase well or have a stylistic trademark that you'd do well to accommodate?

Notice if the artist seems to prefer a particular form. Does he like a form that allows him a minute to "jam" on the hook during a fade? Does she prefer short, four-line choruses with lots of repetition, or four different lines with a strong "payoff" line? Is the song for a group with more involved vocal parts, needing parallel lyric lines to intermesh? Once you've listened to enough of the artist, you can imagine him/her singing your lyrics, and it gets much easier to write for the style. A valuable exercise is to try to write a follow-up song to an artist's last hit, taking into consideration all the artistic factors that you feel contributed to its success.

Some writers hate this approach to writing because they feel it's calculated, uninspired hack-work. Other writers love it because they welcome the artistic challenge of saying something that comes from them but is tailor-made for someone else. They look at the parameters as an architect would look at building a house for a family's specific needs. Matching form with function is the challenge. If the music that comes from this approach seems uninspired, the writer has no one to blame but himself. All those great inspired ideas you wrote on all those little scraps of paper or sang or played into a tape recorder should inspire you again.

Norman Gimbel had the phrase "killing me softly" in his notebook long before Lori Lieberman (who he and co-writer Charles Fox were producing) told him about her emotional reaction to experiencing Don McLean in concert. They used (1) the need to write a song to fit her style, (2) the inspired phrase, and (3) Lori's own experience to put together a fresh and original classic. Many writers I've interviewed have felt that some of their best work was done under deadline or for a specific project.

For a writer/performer writing primarily for yourself, it can be an artistically liberating experience to write for someone else and not be identified with your words, to be able to say something in a way that you wouldn't state it for yourself. It allows you to expand the parameters of your craft and that can't hurt. For nonperforming writers who depend on others to record their songs, tailoring is a valuable discipline to develop.

A possible criticism of this approach is that you may write a song that's too tailored to only one artist. If that artist doesn't cut it, you may end up with a great song that no other artist wants. I don't agree. I believe that if it really is a great song you'll find another artist to cut it, even if you have to rewrite or redemo it.

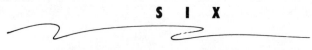

Writing Music

by Cat Cohen

MELODY

Writing melodies for commercial songs is an art unto itself. Though there may be some similarity to classical composition, the priorities of pop melody writing are very different. The basis of most classical writing is building melodic ideas over an extended period of time. In pop writing, short melodic ideas are usually repeated and contrasted without much development, and lead to the main chorus or *hook section* in a relatively short amount of time. The essence of pop composition is repeating these ideas with enough contrast and variation to keep the listener involved.

The starting point of any melody is its INITIAL IDEA or phrase. In 4/4 time, this can be anywhere from a half-measure (two beats) to two measures (eight beats) long. Occasionally, one may find a melodic idea that is four measures long in a slow romantic ballad, but usually this is a feature reserved for art song and classical writing. Short melodic ideas are easier for most people to remember.

Try tapping out one of the short melodic ideas running around in your head. Most songwriters seem to be blessed (or cursed) with these little bursts of inspiration. This is a great place to start, since what often has hooked your unconscious mind will have a tendency to hook others. The challenge of pop melody writing is expanding these ideas into *song sections* and then into *complete songs.* You can learn how to do this by using the techniques of *repetition, variation, contrast,* and *development.*

Take a look at a couple of melodic ideas and see how they can be expanded into songs. Here are two examples.

The first example is long, unfocused, and unworkable, while the second one is short and memorable, easy to develop into the kind of catchy, hooky phrases that sell a song. The basic reason that the first melody is unmemorable is a complete lack of repetition in the phrase, either note-wise or rhythmically. See how the second melody takes the first three notes of the first measure and repeats them.

Now, take the second idea and see how it can be stretched out into eight effective measures.

Start with a one-bar phrase and simply *duplicate* it.

If it's duplicated four times, though, it might get a little too simple-minded.

Some people confuse being "commercial" with being mindlessly repetitive. Yes, you need enough repetition to get immediate recognition and familiarity, but Top 40 stations play the same songs over and over, and a song must have enough variety to withstand repeated listenings. A better way to expand melodic fragments is to *alternate* between two melodic ideas.

Actually, the technique of alternating between melodic ideas is nothing new. It was derived from religious services where the priest, preacher, or cantor alternated singing with the choir or congregation. Contemporary gospel music is a great example of this "call and response." The same structure is also found in blues. Up-tempo music, from folk and square dancing to the "Hokey Pokey" to contemporary dance records, has always been based on this foundation, alternating between right and left, front and back steps.

Two ways of using this alternating technique are—*variation* (with repetition) and *contrast* (with repetition). In *variation,* the second or "re-

sponse" phrase is only slightly different from the "call" or original melodic idea. But this difference, no matter how slight, keeps the melody from becoming too predictable.

In *contrast,* a completely different melody is paired with the original, and the close alternation of the two ideas serves to link them quickly in the listener's mind.

A lot of pop recordings, especially dance records, are structured almost exclusively in this way. Listen and try to analyze "We Are Family" by Sister Sledge, one of the classic dance records of the late '70s, and see how it is composed of variation with repetition. Here it is spread out over an eight-measure section.

WE ARE FAMILY
by Nile Rogers and Bernard Edwards

Some pop styles use more complex phrasing than simple alternation. From Burt Bacharach to Michael McDonald to Barry Gibb to Luther Vandross there is a whole range of more sophisticated approaches to commercial writing. Most of these writers have had some classical background, the kind of instruction that encourages the writer to develop and insert new material. It takes a lot more craft to develop more melodic ideas, somewhat like juggling with three or four balls instead of just two. It is easy to fall into the trap of taking a melody too far away without enough repetition to keep the listener involved. Inexperienced songwriters have a tendency to lose their audience by trying to say too much—through melody or through lyric—in one song.

Here is an excellent example of a more complex melodic composition written by the Gibb brothers (Bee Gees) for Dionne Warwick.

HEARTBREAKER
by Barry, Robin and Maurice Gibb

Once you get a handle on duplicating, alternating, contrasting, and developing melodic ideas, you can combine them to craft more distinctive song sections that still will be within the commercial ballpark. A song that combines these techniques is "What's Love Got to Do with It?" which won the Grammy for Best Song of the Year in 1984 (see next page).

COMPLETING SONGS
Once you are able to write an effective eight-bar song section, the biggest challenge is then expanding it into a completed song. This is where most songwriters seem to get stuck.

One of the best ways of writing an interesting, complete song is by using *contrasting sections*. Why do you need more than one song section in

WHAT'S LOVE GOT TO DO WITH IT?
by Terry Britten and Graham Lyle

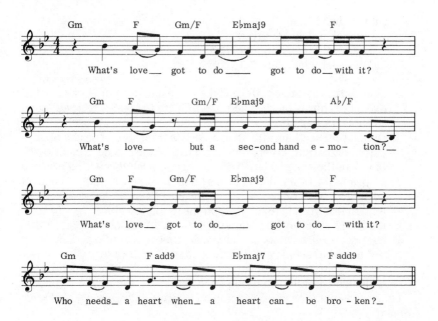

the first place? With few exceptions (remember "I'm Henry the Eighth I Am" by Herman's Hermits?), the record-buying public does not respond to simple one-section songs. To keep a listener involved for a full three minutes or more, you must depart from the main melodic material. *Coming up with the amount of contrast appropriate to the song is perhaps the most difficult and crucial aspect of effective melody writing.*

A good analogy to help understand how contrast functions is to compare a second song section to a vacation. If you stay at home all the time, life can get a little dull. A trip to another place or environment brings relief from monotony and the pleasure of returning home. A trip without much contrast (such as a dash to the supermarket and back) gives neither the enjoyment of leaving or returning. Similarly, a song with melodic departure and return keeps us involved and interested. A lack of change, and we tune out.

Here are some ideas to help you get more contrast in your song sections.

1. **Change the level of your melodic line.** Make the more important section (the hook section) higher in pitch, or use different time values (for instance, change to mostly sixteenth notes instead of eighths and quarters, use long half-notes instead of eighths, etc.).
2. **Change the phrase length.** If your verse is made up of long phrases (two bars or longer), then write shorter ones. Or vice versa. Nothing

95

is more boring than a cookie-cutter four-line verse and a similar four-line chorus, all with the same pat phrase along the lines of

I think that I shall never see
A thing as lovely as a tree
La, dee, dah, dee, dah, dee, dah
La, dee, dah, dee, dah, dee, dah . . .

3. **Change the rhythmic pattern.** If the verse has straight-ahead rhythm, make the chorus more syncopated. Or try the opposite. (See "Song Dynamics," page 82.)
4. **Define your sections with an appropriate transition.** The use of musical "punctuation" is very important to give the listener a clear sense of where the song is "at." You can accomplish this with a break, a stop, a build, or a musical turnaround. If you try to jump unexpectedly into a hook or second verse, the effect may be "arty," but you'll tend to lose your listener. Exceptions to this are album cuts from established artists whose fans look to them for new musical challenges. Top 40 formats don't have the time to let radio audiences figure out what seems puzzling in a song at first. Unless you are purposely going for an unusual song style, it's better to lead your audience carefully from one song section to the next.

Other considerations important in melody writing are *range* and *scale context.*

RANGE

Every singer has a vocal range within which he or she can sing consistently and with professional control. Here is a guideline for ranges of different song styles and for different vocal abilities:

Modest. Less than an octave. This is for the less-skilled singer, talk singer, or sing-along style performer. Country music and simple rock styles often feature performers whose personality far exceeds their ability to sing. Material written for them should never push them beyond their limited range.

Average. Octave and a third or fourth. Two or three notes above an octave is the typical range for most pop singers and styles. There is room for a few dramatic leaps or high notes, but nothing too demanding for the average performer.

Wide. An octave and a fifth and beyond. This is for virtuoso singers, the Barbra Streisands, the Chaka Khans, the Larry Gatlins, and the Lou Gramms of the pop world.

SCALE CONTEXT

Another important consideration is *scale context*. Without getting into an involved theoretical discussion, note that besides the key a song is written in (C major, G minor), the actual scale tones that are used in the melody have a great deal to do with the song's style. Here are a few examples of scale contexts.

Major 7-Tone

INNOCENT MAN
written and recorded by Billy Joel

LOVE THEME FROM 'A STAR IS BORN' (EVERGREEN)
by Barbra Streisand and Paul Williams (Barbra Streisand)

Major 6-Tone

UP WHERE WE BELONG
by Jack Nitzsche, Will Jennings and Buffy Sainte-Marie (Joe Cocker/Jennifer Warnes)

Major 5-Tone (pentatonic)

MY GIRL
by William "Smokey" Robinson and Ronald White (Temptations)

HUNGRY HEART
by Bruce Springsteen (Bruce Springsteen)

Minor 7-Tone (natural)

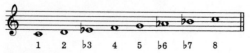

1   2   ♭3   4   5   ♭6   ♭7   8

HEARTS
by Jesse Barish (Marty Balin)

Minor 6-Tone

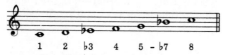

1   2   ♭3   4   5 - ♭7   8

BILLIE JEAN
written and recorded by Michael Jackson

Minor 5-Tone (pentatonic)

1 - ♭3   4   5 - ♭7   8

HEARTBREAKER
by Geoff Gill and Cliff Wade (Pat Benatar)

Ragtime

1   2   ♭3   3 - 5   6 - 8

SIGNED, SEALED, DELIVERED, I'M YOURS
written by Stevie Wonder, L. Garrett, S. Wright, and Lil Hardaway
(Stevie Wonder)

Blues

| 1 | - | b3 | 4 | b5 | 5 | - | b7 | 8 |

THE SUNSHINE OF YOUR LOVE
by Peter Brown, John Bruce and Eric Clapton (Cream)

Mixolydian Mode

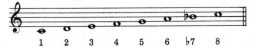

| 1 | 2 | 3 | 4 | 5 | 6 | b7 | 8 |

IS THERE SOMETHING I SHOULD KNOW
written and recorded by Duran Duran

Dorian Mode

| 1 | 2 | b3 | 4 | 5 | 6 | b7 | 8 |

ELEANOR RIGBY
by John Lennon and Paul McCartney (Beatles)

    To summarize, pop melody writing is a specialized craft of balancing repetition and contrast. We can do this by *duplicating, alternating,* and *developing* melodic ideas. We then craft our ideas into *contrasting* sections. Writing within a suitable range and scale context helps pinpoint a song to its potential audience. A knowledge of these aspects enables you to write for specific styles and artists, which is what professional songwriting is all about.

HARMONY

A knowledge of harmony is very important to a professional songwriter. A completed song includes not only lyric and melody, but a chordal accompaniment as well. Harmony is based on the concept of uniting pleasing musical sounds. The chordal sounds used to accompany and arrange our songs bring out their colors, their emotions. Think of a plain melody and lyric as a black-and-white sketch, a song with harmonization as a full-color drawing or painting. Very often, the imaginativeness of its harmonic setting is what gives a song its distinctive appeal.

INTERVALS

In order to understand how chords are constructed, they should be broken down into INTERVALS. The basic unit of measuring intervals in Western music is the half-step. You can find a half-step easily on the piano by simply going up or down the keyboard to the next note whether a black key or white key (C-C♯-D-D♯-E-F-F♯ etc.). All intervals are measured multiples of half-steps thus indicating the specific distances between musical pitches.

Here are the intervals inside the major scale, called *diatonic intervals.*

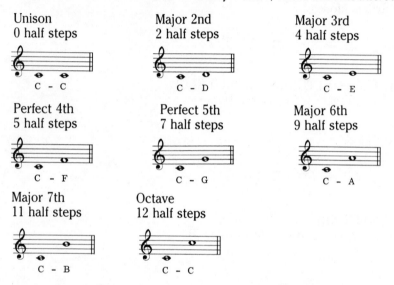

Unison
0 half steps
C - C

Major 2nd
2 half steps
C - D

Major 3rd
4 half steps
C - E

Perfect 4th
5 half steps
C - F

Perfect 5th
7 half steps
C - G

Major 6th
9 half steps
C - A

Major 7th
11 half steps
C - B

Octave
12 half steps
C - C

If you examine this chart, you will see that certain intervals have been skipped over. There are gaps in the major scale, tones that are considered to be outside the major scale. These are the minor intervals, colors which are used to form minor and exotic scales and chords.

Here are the intervals outside the major scale—*chromatic intervals:*

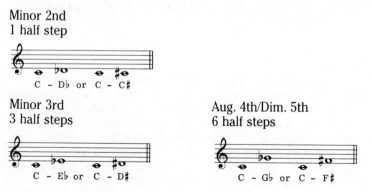

Minor 2nd
1 half step
C - D♭ or C - C♯

Minor 3rd
3 half steps
C - E♭ or C - D♯

Aug. 4th/Dim. 5th
6 half steps
C - G♭ or C - F♯

Minor 6th
8 half steps

C – A♭ or C – G♯

Minor 7th
10 half steps

C – B♭ or C – A♯

The intervals on the unison, 4th, 5th, and octave are called *perfect* intervals because they rarely change, even when the scales change to minor or modal. The 2nd, 3rd, 6th, and 7th intervals are more coloristic, changing in order to form more interesting scale tone colors.

C Major:

Major third   Perfect fifth

C Minor:

Minor third   Perfect fifth

THREE LEVELS OF CHORD CONSTRUCTION

When you play three or more pitches simultaneously, you have played a "chord," and harmony (or disharmony) is created. You can create a whole variety of chordal colors simply by building chords out of various combinations of intervals. The harmonies you may choose depend on the level of chordal sophistication your song requires. Rock, country, and folk styles use mainly simple *triads* (three-note chords), while jazz-influenced styles are written with more complex chords. Most pop and crossover styles tend to be made up of chords midway between these two extremes. **First level of harmony—triads.** The most common triad in pop music is the *major triad,* which has a specific formula of half-steps.

MAJOR TRIAD 4 half-steps + 3 half-steps
(major 3rd)   (minor 3rd)

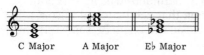

C Major   A Major   E♭ Major

5th scale tone
3rd scale tone
1st scale tone

Another regularly used triad in pop music is the *minor triad,* which lowers the middle tone, the 3rd, a half-step.

MINOR TRIAD 3 half-steps + 4 half-steps
(minor 3rd)   (major 3rd)

C Minor   A Minor   E♭ Minor

5th scale tone
♭3rd scale tone
1st scale tone

A third type of triad is especially common in rock music, the *suspended triad*, which "suspends" the use of the 3rd and replaces it with a 4th.

SUSPENDED TRIAD 5 half-steps + 2 half-steps
                       (4th)   (major 2nd)

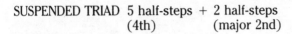

5th scale tone
4th scale tone
1st scale tone

C sus   A sus   E♭ sus

Many songs use chord progressions made up of triadic harmony, like Bruce Springsteen's "Hungry Heart."

| C | Am | F | G | |

Second level of harmony—7ths. For simple styles, triads are all that may be necessary for effective harmonization, but in more middle-of-the-spectrum styles such as country-pop, R&B, and MOR, you'll need more sophisticated chords. For most of these styles, adding a 7th tone above the triads may give a fuller, more polished sound and lead the ear to a more interesting resolution.

Here are some formulas for building 7th chords.

Dominant 7th   Minor 7th   Major 7th

A dominant seventh chord is a *major triad* plus a minor seventh, a minor seventh chord is a *minor triad* with a minor seventh added, and a major seventh chord is a *major triad* plus a major seventh.

It is common for song passages to be harmonized using 7th chords, as illustrated here in a chord progression that can be found in songs like "Even the Nights Are Better," by JL Wallace, Kenneth Bell and Terry Skinner (Air Supply).

| Fm7 | B♭7 | E♭maj7 | Cm7 | Fm7 | B♭7 | C | C | |

Third level of harmony—9ths, 11ths, and complex chords. When you want to write in jazz-influenced harmonies such as R&B-pop, jazz-rock-fusion, Broadway, and pre-1950 pop standards, then even more sophisticated harmonies are called for. These include chords built on 9ths and above, as well as chromatically altered chords (with raised or lowered 5ths, 9ths, 11ths, etc.). This is much too demanding a subject to cover here, but don't be overly concerned. These chords are never used in 90 percent of the music on the charts. They are a specialized sound for a specialized urban audience. For those interested in studying jazz harmony, there are many excellent books on the subject, such as the John Mehegan Jazz Pianist series.

This song passage features complex harmonies, and is used in songs like "Through The Fire," by David Foster, Cynthia Weil and Tom Keene (Chaka Khan).

	–13					
	–9					
Ab add2	C7	Fm7 Ebm7 Ab7	Dbmaj7 Cm7 Fm7	Bbm7	Eb11	

CREATING CHORD PROGRESSIONS

The true art of harmonization is more than knowing which chords to choose; it is often the order in which they progress through the song and how they relate to its melodic shape and emotion that determines their effectiveness. To get a better idea of how chords work together, you need to relate them to a scale context. Chords can be built *diatonically* (using only tones inside a scale) or *chromatically* (using tones inside and outside the scale).

Diatonic chords. Most songs can be harmonized entirely with diatonic chords. Here is how diatonic harmonies are formed inside a C major scale.[1]

I	ii	iii	IV	V	vi	vii°	I		I	IV	V	I		ii	iii	vi
5	6	7	1	2	3	4	5									
3	4	5	6	7	1	2	3									
1	2	3	4	5	6	7	1									

These diatonic chords fall into two groups, *primary chords* and *secondary chords*. The *primary chords* are the ones most people refer to when describing three-chord rock songs such as "Twist and Shout," country-western classics such as "I Walk the Line," and traditional twelve-bar blues. *Secondary chords* are minor triads formed within a ma-

[1] Roman numerals are used in analyzing chords to show at a glance which scale tone the chord is built on; whether the chord is major, minor, or altered in some way; whether a seventh or ninth has been added, etc. The numeral corresponds to the scale degree that is the root of the chord. For instance, in the key of C, a iii chord would be an E-minor triad made up of E-G-B. "Capital" numerals are used for major triads and "lower case" numerals for minor triads. For the iii triad in C to be a major chord, the G would have to be raised to a G♯. But the IV chord—F-A-C—is a major triad automatically. A iii7 would consist of E-G-B-D. If a chord were built on E♭ (an exotic harmony), it would be notated as ♭iii or ♭III depending on whether the chord were major or minor. A degree sign is used after the Roman numeral to show a diminished chord—one in which there is less than a perfect fifth between the root and the "fifth" of the chord. An example in C Major would be the vii°. This triad is made up of B-D-F (while a perfect fifth would be B-F♯). The whole system of using Roman numerals can get rather complicated, but this basic knowledge of conventional symbols will suffice for the examples cited here.

jor scale, and they provide generally darker, more serious shadings of emotion and color. *They allow you to give harmonic contrast in a song without having to change keys.* Diatonic secondary chords can help achieve a sense of departure for our second song section without having to travel too far away harmonically. Diatonic secondary chords are used effectively in song passages like this progression illustrates, in songs such as "Lyin' Eyes," by Henley/Frey (The Eagles).

G	C	G	C	Em	Bm	Am	D	
I	IV	I	IV	vi	iii	ii	V	

Minor diatonic chords. You can do the same thing to the chords in the minor scale.

	i	ii°	(♭)III	iv	v	(♭)VI	(♭)VII	i		i	iv	v		(♭)III	(♭)VI	(♭)VII
	5	6	7	1	2	3	4	5
	3	4	5	6	7	1	2	3
	1	2	3	4	5	6	7	1

Many songs make use of minor diatonic harmony as analyzed in the following chord progression found in songs like "Hearts," by Jesse Barish (Marty Balin).

A♭maj7	Gsus7	G7	Cm	Fm	G7	Cm	
♭VImaj7	Vsus7	V7	i	iv	V7	i	

Chromatic chords. To get even more contrast and more unusual sounds, you may want to experiment with chords that use tones outside your scale context. Here is a list of chords that are "slightly outside," that use only one nonscale tone and do not take you too far out. The Beatles were masters of using one slightly outside chord for temporary "shock value" in an otherwise straightforward harmonization in their songs.

MAJOR

II, III, VI, ♭VII, iv

MINOR

II, ♭II, IV, ii

Song passages using slightly outside harmonies can be found in tunes like "You Won't See Me," by John Lennon and Paul McCartney (Beatles).

C	D	F	C	C	D	F	C	C7	F	Fm	C	C	D	F	C
I	II	IV	I	I	II	IV	I	I7	IV	iv	I	I	II	IV	I

EXOTIC HARMONY

For harmonic effects that are even "farther out," try using one of these chords. They contain more than one nonscale tone and take a song into strange, unexpected places. However, they have to be used carefully and sparingly or your listener may get confused and lose interest.

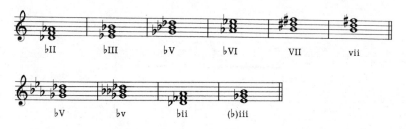

Chord progressions using these unusual harmonies are not uncommon in songs like "Do You Really Want To Hurt Me?," by Hay/Moss/Craig/O'Dowd (Culture Club).

G Bm	Em	G Bm	Em	C G	Am	Bm	B♭	B♭	A♭	A♭	Gm
I iii	vi	I iii	vi	IV I	ii	iii	♭III	♭III	♭II	♭II	i

VERTICAL OR HORIZONTAL CONSTRUCTION

Now that you've seen how a variety of chords can be used to accompany pop melodies, don't overlook the fact that many pop recordings, especially dance records, do not rely on harmony as an important element. In fact, some contemporary records hardly use chords at all. Instead of the traditional vertical construction of a melody with underlying chords, you will find the horizontal construction of a melody accompanied only with a strong rhythmic background, countermelodic riffs and bass lines. That's right, no chords, just riffs!

Here is an example of a song that uses horizontal instead of vertical construction:

BILLY JEAN
written and recorded by Michael Jackson

She was more like a beau - ty queen from a mov - ie scene.

I said don't mind, but what do ____ you mean I ____ am the one ____

As you can see in this section, there are many ways to use harmony to make your songs more effective. Think of chords as coloring agents and learn to choose the appropriate simplicity or sophistication of harmonies to match the style of music you're seeking to write. A good way to get a handle on this is to listen to radio stations in your area and see which ones play songs mostly using triads, which ones play seventh chord songs, and which ones play songs using complex ninths and above. In business, identifying a style of music and targeting the market audience it appeals to is called demographics. Why don't we coin a phrase and call this "harmonigraphics"? Whatever we call it, you can see that the more you know about chords and how they work together, the more versatility you can achieve in your songwriting.

GROOVE
Musicians have long referred to "groove" when describing the basic feel of a song, especially when it feels right. When Duke Ellington wrote "It Don't Mean a Thing If It Ain't Got that Swing," or when that infamous dancer on *American Bandstand* said that she thought a particular song was a hit because "It's got a good beat and you can dance to it," they were talking about groove. It is absolutely essential for a songwriter to learn what gives a song the kind of groove or feel that has "hit" written all over it.

RHYTHMIC ELEMENTS

In more technical terms, you can better understand groove by examining its rhythmic elements: pulse, tempo, meter, rhythmic subdivision, syncopation, and texture.

Pulse. A pulse is simply a regular, recurring beat. For instance, a march (*hup,* 2, 3, 4) is based on pulse. In pop music, an obvious example is the bass drum beat (1,2,3,4) of the disco style.

Tempo. The tempo is the speed of the pulse, the number of pulses per minute. You can understand this by comparing any music pulse to your heartbeat. At rest, our hearts beat at 72-80 times a minute. But get us excited (through uptempo dancing, aerobics, or whatever) and watch our pulse race to 150 times a minute and beyond. Here is a chart showing the relationship of various tempos to pop music function and activity: (Heartbeat = 72 beats per minute: BPM)

60 BPM	90 BPM	120 BPM	150 BPM
Slow Ballad	Moderate	Uptempo Dance	Hyper Drive
"Yesterday," by John Lennon and Paul McCartney (Beatles)	"Crazy for You," by John Bettis and Jon Lind (Madonna)	"Brown Sugar," by Keith Richards and Mick Jagger (Rolling Stones)	"Maniac," by Michael Sembello and Dennis Matkosky (Michael Sembello)

Meter. Meter is the way in which pulses are grouped into measures or bars. Almost all pop music is grouped into 4/4 meter—four pulses (quarter notes) in each measure (or bar). Occasionally, one finds a 3/4 waltz meter with three pulses (quarter notes) in each measure.

Other meters like 2/4, 6/8, 2/2, or more complicated ones like 11/16 or 7/8 exist in classical music and jazz, but are seldom used in pop.

Rhythmic subdivision. The 4/4 pulse of a pop song is the basis for 95 percent of what we hear on the radio today. What's important is to differentiate the rhythms played on rock stations, country stations, soul stations, and easy listening stations. You may need more technical know-how to learn how rhythmic subdivisions help to define a song's style.

A 4/4 measure can be subdivided into any of the following.

March, disco

8th note groove
(rock, MOR, new wave)

1 and 2 and 3 and 4 and

Triplet groove
('50s, blues)

1 and a 2 and a 3 and a 4 and a

Shuffle groove
('40s, be-bop, country, blues, gospel)

1 a 2 a 3 a 4 a

16th groove
(funk, R&B, reggae, half-time rock)

1 e and a 2 e and a 3 e and a 4 e and a

Syncopation. Once you determine the rhythmic subdivision of a groove, the next most important feature that defines style is its syncopation. Syncopation occurs when there are rhythmic accents on the weak inner beats of a groove, *the beats between the pulses*. Dance music is full of syncopated patterns that use one or more of these accents to create rhythmic drive. Syncopated patterns can be found in the rhythm tracks and in the actual melodies of most of today's recorded music.

Examples within each of the four rhythmic subdivisions are listed below.

8th note groove:

WRAPPED AROUND YOUR FINGER
by Gordon Sumner

You con - si - der me____ the young_ ap - pren - tice____

Triplet groove:

JUST LIKE STARTING OVER
by John Lennon

It's been too long since we took the time.___ No

one's to blame. I know time flies___ so quick - ly!

Shuffle groove:

WITH A LITTLE HELP FROM MY FRIENDS
by John Lennon and Paul McCartney

What would you do___ if I sang___ out of tune___

___ would you stand___ up and walk ___ out on me ___

16th note groove:

TOTAL ECLIPSE OF THE HEART
by Jim Steinman

Turn a round_ Eve - ry now and then I get a

lit - tle bit lone - ly and you're ne - ver com-ing round___

Texture. Once you understand how syncopation creates a danceable groove, you'll want to study the finer points of what makes one dance beat distinctive from another, even if they are made up of the same rhythmic subdivision.

Each groove has its own unique "texture," from sparse to moderate to full. Some rhythm tracks move the beat along with just a few notes while others use many more. Here are examples of sparse and full grooves in eighth-note and sixteenth-note subdivisions:

Sparse 8th bass line:

SHE BLINDED ME WITH SCIENCE
by Thomas Dolby and Joe Kerr

Full 8th bass line:

LIKE A VIRGIN
by Billy Steinberg and Tom Kelly

Sparse 16th bass line:

DON'T YOU GET SO MAD
by Jeffrey Osborne, Donald Freeman and Michael Sembello

Full 16th bass line (techno):

found in songs like
HEART OF GLASS
by Deborah Harry and Chris Stein

People in the record industry are looking for songs with the groove already built in. Knowing how to place your song in its best rhythmic setting will give your writing the competitive edge that says "Play me on the radio!"

David "Cat" Cohen enjoys a multi-faceted career as a songwriter, independent producer, keyboard teacher and author. A songwriter with major credits (Cheryl Lynn, Syreeta, Freddie Hubbard), he is a member of ASCAP and NARAS. Cat teaches classes at his studio in Los Angeles as well as lecturing at the LASS Songwriter Expo and other writer-oriented events.

Collaboration

WHY TWO (OR MORE) HEADS ARE BETTER THAN ONE

A substantial percentage of the world's most popular songs are collaborations. Consider the wealth of material that's come from teams like Lerner and Loewe; Rodgers and Hammerstein; Kander and Ebb; Bacharach and David; Rodgers and Hart; the Gershwins; Mann and Weil; Holland, Dozier, and Holland; Lennon and McCartney; Goffin and King; Sedaka and Greenfield; Barry and Greenwich; Leiber and Stoller; the Bergmans; Foster and Rice; Hall and Oates; Fleming and Morgan; and on and on.

Look at the *Billboard* charts any week and you'll find that more than 70 percent of the titles on the country and black music charts (more than 50 percent on the Hot 100 Chart) are cowritten. Today's song market is so competitive that professional writers can't afford to settle for less than the best, so they often elect to team up with other specialists.

Though this chapter is devoted to collaboration, it should be noted here that it isn't necessarily the best or the only way to write. Hit writer Randy Goodrum ("You Needed Me," "Bluer Than Blue") has written successfully with and without a collaborator, and in this 1984 interview in the LASS *Musepaper* he expressed some opinions about each:

First of all I'm not a collaborative writer as a rule. I started off writing for years and years on my own. Most everything that I have ever had that was big was written totally by me except for this year [Goodrum collaborated with Steve Perry on "Oh Sherrie," "Foolish Heart" and six others on an album]. But there are dangers with collaboration. At least from my experience, it can water down and lose a sense of uniqueness. I was in a seminar one time and somebody said, "Gee when I heard 'Bluer Than Blue,' I thought, how is he going to rhyme 'closet'?" I said, "feel like it." I rhymed it, not closet. Well, if I had been cowriting, chances are we would have said, "Let's don't use 'closet'." We would have thrown it out, yet it's a little bit more unique of a line than other songs that I've cowritten. . . . Sometimes the art has to have a little bit of a rough edge in there, in a charismatic sort of sense. There has to be some abandon to it. You just rewrite and rewrite and rewrite and sometimes it's not logical what makes greatness. You know, it's just this little muse that comes along. He doesn't have a business suit on or anything, and it tickles. . . .

So I think with collaboration, it's good to get something that makes you just jump up and down, and if it can be better than what you can do on your own, that's incredible. Or if you can arrive at a place that neither of

111

you can get by yourselves. . . . I wrote two songs with Michael McDonald for his solo album, and I am proud to say that neither of us has ever written anything like the two songs we came up with. They were totally in another place. So that's a nice way to look at cowriting also.

Here are several other good reasons why writers collaborate:

1. **A writer may have more talent as a lyricist than a composer or vice versa.** It's important that you objectively assess your strengths and weaknesses. Obviously, if you're a good lyricist with marginal musical skills, you should look for a composer. Your ego may need to see only your name on the "words & music by" line at the top of the page, or maybe you just want all the royalties yourself. The bottom line though, is that the song must be as good as it can possibly be, regardless of who did what.

   Many talented musicians/arrangers can put together the music but don't feel the lyric is important enough to warrant a collaborator. They risk seriously limiting the artistic and commercial potential of the songs. Even Earth, Wind & Fire's Maurice White, to his credit, decided to collaborate with hit lyricist Allee Willis ("Boogie Wonderland" and "September") to increase the already fantastic appeal of their records.

2. **Writers often tend to get trapped in their own musical and lyrical clichés, and a collaborator can supply fresh ideas.** When you pick up your guitar your fingers automatically go through a familiar and comfortable set of chord changes, picking styles, or rhythm patterns. Out of these established patterns come melodies much like those you've written before. It's easy to get into a creative rut. At that point you need to get a chord book and work out some new chords and progressions, listen to the radio and discover some new grooves, or find a collaborator whose style you like.

   Even professional writers aren't always productive and may need the input of other writers. They may write great ballads, but need to team up with someone when it comes to uptempo songs or another style.

3. **Writing with someone else disciplines your writing habits.** Many people seem to function better on deadlines and always wait until the last minute, while thinking up all kinds of other projects to avoid the task ("I can't possibly create with a dirty house/broken guitar string/out-of-tune piano.") This avoidance syndrome is a way of signaling and priming the subconscious to start working on the project at hand. At the eleventh hour, when you have to produce, the brain sends a signal to the subconscious that says, "It's time to give me all those ideas" and, like magic, they're there.

   Many writers will avoid writing altogether if there are no deadlines. Those who function best on that kind of "crisis" basis *set up* deadlines for themselves. One good way is to find a collaborator and plan on a regular day to get together and write. You know you'll have to come up with some ideas to work on before that deadline, and that subconscious preparation process will operate on an ongoing basis if it knows that every week (or every day) that deadline will arrive.

4. **A partner will furnish a constant feedback and critique.** You're stuck for a rhyme and eager to finish the song. You put together the first thing to come into your head and say, "It's okay, I've heard stuff on the radio that rhymes 'rain' with 'again.' Maybe some British guy'll cut it." A conscientious collaborator is there to say, "WRONG! Let's see if we can find something else." Maybe you're a lyricist and your collaborator is a singer and can say, "I'll want to hold this note in the melody, so could we use another word instead of 'garbage'? Obviously it can keep you at your best and help you both grow commercially and artistically.

5. **The more collaborators on a song, the more people there are networking to get the song recorded.** If each writer has several industry contacts for whom he can play the song, you'll have that many more opportunities to get the song published or recorded.

MEETING YOUR MATCH

Finding the perfect partner can be a difficult process. At best, no matter how you go about it, you'll have the same odds on finding the perfect collaborator right away as you'd have walking into a singles' bar and finding a marriage partner. The two situations have a lot in common. You're dealing with a whole range of personalities, personal habits, expectations, previous experiences, egos, and lifestyles. With collaborators you can add musical and literary influences, business know-how, and aggressiveness.

But there are a few ways to get started and narrow the odds. Like a singles' bar, you go to where other people are looking, too. You put an ad in a music-oriented periodical like the LASS *Musepaper, Music Connection, The Overture* (Musicians Union), or the newsletter of your local songwriters organization. Placing an ad in your local newspaper is probably a waste of time because readers don't generally look for cowriters there. A better bet is to make little signs that you can put up on bulletin boards in music and record stores, the Musicians Union, or clubs that feature your kind of music. If you're a lyricist, it's also a good idea to put your signs on college music department bulletin boards so composition students can find you.

The ad or sign should include the styles with which you're most comfortable, the instrument(s) you play, your favorite lyricists/composers and your credits, if any. If you're looking for a lyricist and are in a working band, have a production deal, do your own publishing, or have an exclusive publishing deal, mention that too. This tells the serious lyricists that you have serious prospects for their work.

Another approach is through professional organizations. National Academy of Songwriters (NAS) has a collaboration service for members. Musicians Contact Service (MCS) has composer/lyricist listings containing relevant style and bio information. For a fee of $20 per year you can list your own information and be sent a list of potential collaborators. The Songwriters Guild of America also has lyricist/composer listings for different regions of the country. This service is for members only. (See appendices for lists of "Organizations.")

If you're in Los Angeles, attend the L.A. Songwriters Showcase (LASS) and you can "audition" anywhere from 70 to over 100 potential collaborators at their weekly Cassette Roulette and Pitch-A-Thon publisher and producer screening sessions. Since you can hear the tapes anonymously you can evaluate other writers' work and approach the ones you like. In Nashville, attend the weekly critique sessions by the Nashville Songwriters Association International or any of the many "writers nights" at local clubs. These are among the best opportunities to screen a writer's work before meeting in person. All workshops, clubs, and showcases offer that opportunity. Joining local or national songwriter organizations or music associations is also a great way to make contacts.

In any of these situations you may hear a singer/songwriter whose music is excellent but whose lyrics are weak, or vice versa. You might, diplomatically, ask that person if he or she would consider collaboration. There's a definite advantage in writing with someone who's out there exposing those songs to the public and the industry. It's also advantageous to your growth to write with those you feel are as good or, preferably better, writers than you.

Try to meet as many people as possible in all areas of the industry. Publishers, though they seldom sign staff lyricists, often like to know of good lyricists that they can hook up with good composers, or with other writers on their staffs. Producers may be working with groups who could use the services of a strong lyricist. Recording engineers are also good contacts. Lyrics or music sent out cold in the mail to publishers or producers is almost never read or listened to.

CAN THIS MARRIAGE WORK?

After finding a collaborator who's stylistically compatible, you have the sometimes difficult task of developing a good rapport and business relationship with that person.

One successful songwriter says, "My ego is my biggest problem when I collaborate. I have to keep reminding myself that I'm collaborating with this lyricist because I really respect her work and when she offers a suggestion or asks me to change part of my melody to accommodate a lyric, I should give it a shot." The ego problem in this example was caused, in part, by the fact that the writer had written the words and music himself for years and found it difficult to readjust his habits.

A negative and quarrelsome attitude can destroy any type of partnership, especially with people who are sensitive and involved with such emotional issues as exposing their vulnerable psyches. It's not always easy to deal with someone who tells you your "baby" is ugly. We all want to believe that because the baby comes from us, it's already perfect. Remember that you're both trying to make your song pretty. Even when you're writing alone, the ability to step back and look at your song objectively is a quality of professionalism. When you're working with someone else, that professional attitude becomes doubly important because criticism is a necessary part of the process—a good partner won't let you ignore a flaw. It is, in fact, one of the primary benefits of collaborating.

If you really do feel strongly about a line a cowriter has rejected, a few calm reasons why you think it works may convince your partner to leave it in. If you find yourself fighting too hard for it, it may be more productive to spend the time and energy looking for a new line. Alan and Marilyn Bergman's rule is: If one collaborator doesn't like the line, it goes. With nearly endless alternatives, they're confident they'll eventually find a line they both like.

The one thing to keep foremost in your mind is that you're both trying to create the best song possible. All criticism and response should be directed toward that goal rather than to protecting your ego. Don't defend something just because you wrote it or because you'll get a bigger percentage if you contribute more (a good argument for a straight 50/50 split of writers' royalties from the beginning—see "Business Considerations," page 118).

You'll need to learn not only to accept criticism graciously but also to give it constructively. Critiquing is an art in itself. When you're beginning a relationship, it's crucial that any criticism be given as gently and positively as possible. As your routine develops and you get more comfortable and trusting with each other you'll probably work out some shorthand to speed up the process. As you communicate better, you'll also get to know which buttons *not* to push. There's a big difference between saying, "What a dumb line!" and "Let's make that line stronger." The former is an unqualified putdown. The latter acknowledges a line could be better, offers a challenge, and implies faith in you and your partner. It's important that you continuously acknowledge your partner's talent and compliment good ideas. Criticism becomes much easier in an atmosphere of respect. If you find few causes for compliments, you should be writing with someone else.

Approaches to collaboration are as varied as the combinations of individuals involved. It's important to find out right away how your prospective partner likes to work. Here are some of the variables:

Writing lyric or music alone, and getting together later. Some people become uptight when their partner is in the same room. It disturbs their creative flow. They may be open to criticism and change later, but they need to get something to work from first. Some lyricists would rather write to a finished melody and vice versa. This method is well-suited to correspondence. Some who write this way will send a melody or lyric to several writers in succession and say, "Take this lyric (or tune) for a week and see what you can come up with. It gives a writer a chance to hear several versions of his material. And it saves the hassle of waiting endlessly for a collaborator to finish a song—a very common problem.

To make that situation work, however, you should have an agreement in writing ahead of time that it won't be a complete song unless you both agree on the finished product. Otherwise, legally, it *is* a complete work. I should also mention that it's unethical to give a lyric or music to more than one potential collaborator at the same time *without their knowledge.* They should have the option to agree to that type of speculative situation or not. They may choose to spend their time more productively elsewhere and it's disrespectful of you to not allow them the choice.

For yourself, it's always a good idea to ask if anyone else is working on the same assignment you've been given. Publishers have been known to not volunteer that information and writers rightfully resent it.

Writing together in the same room. Writers who work this way love the give-and-take of instant feedback. They enjoy the excitement and high energy level that can happen when two collaborators really start to "cook." It's particularly good for artists who write both lyric *and* music, so ideas can be stimulated and shared in both areas. With this type of collaboration, your compatability becomes more important. What is your most creative time of day? Can you work every day or once a week? Do you like each other and not feel intimidated?

Regardless of the approach, you'll need stylistic compatibility and also need to decide whether you or your partner also want to collaborate with others. As in all other partnership efforts (including marriage) a spirit of compromise and understanding are the keys.

NAS board members and songwriters Pat and Pete Luboff have this to say about collaboration:

The paperwork is easy to deal with. The relationship with a creative partner is the hard part. The give-and-take process can be a stimulation which may be pleasant or devastating. To avoid the latter, it's important to collaborate from strength, not weakness. One of our cowriters says, "You have to feel you're very good to be able to collaborate, or you won't have the security to let things go. If you're not secure in your writing, you get that ego thing of trying to prove yourself with every line you write. You should collaborate to make it better, not because you can't do all of it by yourself."

Pete Luboff continues:

The most important thing to keep in mind while writing alone or collaborating is that you're writing because you love it and the purpose is to have a good time. I go crazy every time I see Muppet character Don Music, songwriter on Sesame Street, banging his head into his piano keys and screaming, "I'll never do it, I'll never get that line." I've been there so many times myself. Fortunately, Don has Kermit the Frog to help him over the rough spots. All we have is our sense of humor and lots of patience.

It's a useful technique to play records of a specific artist while warming up to a song. This way, you create your own assignments. Check the label to make sure the artist does sing songs written by other writers. Playing the current hit single and trying to write the next one is a good job to take on.

Harold Payne, NAS board member and songwriter for Bobby Womack, Mary and Leon Russell, Candi Staton, and others, had these words of advice to offer:

You can collaborate on an assignment or an organic basis. You should decide at the beginning if you want to be commercial. If you do, what artist could record it? If you are writing a song that's more production-oriented, do you have the facilities among you to make the kind of demo that song needs? If we have a particular assignment to write for an artist, we do research, listen to something like it, and buy the artist's latest album.

EXERCISE IN COLLABORATION
You can practice collaborating with the world's best writers before you approach your friend next door. How? Take any song that has been a hit or that you simply admire. If you want some lyric writing practice, write new lyrics to the melody. If you want to try out your melody writing, put a new melody to those lyrics. Now, you can take what *you've* created to another writer without telling them how you did it, and they'll write the new missing part. The advantage of this trick is that while you're writing, you learn about how successful songs are structured, where rhymes go, where the title is placed, how long the song is, how many bars to each section, where the melody rises and falls, and some of the other things we've discussed. And you know your finished product is based on a successful structure.

If there's no particular assignment, we might work from a title. Both parties must be enthusiastic before looking at each other's ideas. It's chemistry that makes us go on a particular one. You should have a few different ideas, in case your first choice doesn't work, so someone doesn't feel forced to work on something they're not interested in.

Or you can just get together and have a conversation casually. I call that the organic approach. It's for the pleasure of it. It's an opportunity to stretch out a bit and establish a rapport. Take whatever comes as a result of the interaction, no pressure. If something gets done, that's almost extra. It's also okay if you decide not to write together or not to write that particular idea. You have to be comfortable about saying, "That doesn't turn me on." It has to flow. Meet once a week, don't be afraid if there's no progress. Some obstacles are dislodged just by getting together.

A good way to start the collaboration going is to have a title session. We do this by talking about the world in general, what's happening in the news, what is happening to the way people relate to each other. Then we might decide whether we want to write an up song or a down one. Most of the time, we decide on the "up" side, because we want to be commercial, and positive songs tend to be more commercially acceptable. Then we might decide on a general area, like two people who have gotten back together after being split up. Then, we have to find a unique way of expressing that idea. We might throw around some titles of songs that have already been written on the subject, just to give a clearer idea of where we're heading. Or, we might just throw around titles on various subjects from lists that we've made on our own. Or, we might talk about something that happened in the life of a friend that we feel would make a good story. These conversations over dinner make writing a pleasant social thing, rather than just another task to sit down to after a hard day of earning a living.

BUSINESS CONSIDERATIONS

Let's assume that you've found a lyricist and/or composer whose words or music feel like the magic ingredient you need to write great songs. You find that you can work well together and the first thing you know you've got a fantastic song. You say, "Great, let's find a publisher!" Your partner says, "Oh, I guess I forgot to tell you—I've got my own publishing company so I'd like to publish the song." At that point the song may be in trouble. You may rightfully ask whether your partner's company is capable of properly promoting the song. Does the company have the connections to get the song recorded? You're better off not having a publisher at all than to have the song tied up with an inadequate one. At least you'd be free to place the song with a good publisher.

If you find yourself in this situation, you might request that if your partner's company doesn't get the song recorded in six months or a year, that he give up his publishing interest and the two of you look for a publisher together. You might also set up your own company and split the publishing, but jointly agree to the above reversion clause. Or you may agree to bring in a third publisher at which point you both will give an equal share of the publishing (or all of it) to the new party. (See Chapter 9, "Publishing," for more on this subject.)

Another possible scenario is that you have a super song and an interested publisher, but you wrote the song with someone last year and since you had no agreement, you can't assign his share of the ownership of the copyright to the publisher. You haven't seen your collaborator since you wrote the song and can't find him. The publisher, fearful of future legal problems, decides not to publish it. If you had, on paper, granted the power of attorney to each other, either of you could have put that publisher at ease.

You also need to agree on a division of the writers share of the royalties. Your collaborator may have supplied a title for a song but you wrote the rest of it. You might feel you did most of the work and should get 90 percent of the money. Your partner may feel that without the title, which supplied the premise, there wouldn't *be* a song. You may both be right but that kind of bickering could destroy a very promising collaborative effort. It's generally agreed that if you get together with the intention of writing a song or to establish an ongoing writing relationship, you split the writers royalties 50/50. If one of you is a lyricist and the other writes music, it's a pretty straightforward arrangement. It tends to get a little touchy if each of you write music and lyrics or if the contributions are more difficult to quantify. There's more room for argument about who contributed the most. That's why it's best to agree on equal shares ahead of time.

Hit writer/producer Jay Graydon, who received a Grammy for "After The Love Has Gone" with David Foster and Bill Champlin, says that he often functions as David Foster's editor. "When I've written with David, 70 percent of the time I'm saying, 'I don't know, David. Now try this. Yeah, I like that.' And another sixteen bars down the road I'm saying 'Yes, yes, no, yes.' He would write all the time by himself if he didn't need that extra input." About royalty splits Graydon says, "Years ago the split was 50/50, music writer and lyric writer. These days, if there are three people on a tune, it's split in thirds no matter who does what."

On some of the Lennon/McCartney tunes, one undoubtedly contributed more than the other on individual songs but they just didn't want to fight over it every time so they divided the royalties equally.

Here are some other possible situations you may have to deal with:

1. You've written the song and you take it to someone else to "tighten it up" and that person contributes a new hook or changes the song's direction. How much writer credit will he get? At the time you bring your song to the writer you should try to work it out based on what you want him to contribute.
2. You take your song to an artist who wants to "personalize" it and changes something. For this he wants writer's credit. This is a very common and potentially volatile situation, with several factors to weigh:
   a. Is this an important cut? With an established artist there's no question about it. But even with a new artist the song could be a major hit or end up on a hit album. Any recording credit may therefore be important to you.
   b. How extensive are the changes? "Personalizing" the song by changing a "she" to a "he" does not warrant a writer's credit. If the artist wants more extensive changes and you want to accommodate him, offer to make them yourself. Get as much information as you can about what the artist is looking for and present several rewrites. If the artist seems unreasonably resistant to your changes, you have to face the reality that you may lose the cut unless you allow him to rewrite or just give him the credit. You can swallow your pride and walk to the bank, walk away with your pride (and your empty pockets), or tell the artist you can't change this song but suggest that you write something together from scratch. If it's just a matter of financial incentive for the artist to record the song, you also have the publisher's share of the royalties to offer if you publish the song yourself. (See "When in Doubt, Negotiate" in Chapter 10.)
   c. How badly does the artist want the song? If he thinks it's good enough he's torn between wanting the writing credit and money and possibly blowing a potential hit. You're in the same position, too, except that you may also be motivated by anger that someone would have the gall to demand credit for your work.

While many artists wouldn't think of asking for undeserved credit (and royalties), others do it in a New York minute. You ultimately have to decide whether it's worth it to your career to give up a portion of those royalties and credits.

3. A publisher suggests changes and wants a writer's credit. Generally speaking, this is the publisher's job, and she shouldn't ask. It would depend, of course, on how substantial the contribution is—and it can get a little touchy, but it should be *your* decision.

Aside from the considerations of who gets what, you may encounter other difficult situations. Maybe you decide later that for some reason you want a new lyric to a song you've already written with someone. Is it okay to change? Not without your cowriter's permission. What if your melody writer wants a new foreign language lyric? Do *you* still get paid?

All these potential problems point to the need for collaborators *to get all the business straight before they get into the music.* There are few things more frustrating than knowing you've written a winner but can't do anything with it.

PRELIMINARY BUSINESS MEETING

K.A. Parker is a professional lyricist, five time American Song Festival winner, and former staff writer for Motown's Stone Diamond Music who has taught lyric writing at U.C.L.A. and for the Los Angeles Songwriters Showcase. Her suggestions for conducting a business meeting and list of considerations for collaborators (she uses it in her classes) is the best I've seen and, with her permission, I offer them to you minus the more extensive discussions of the ones I've already covered.

CONDUCTING THE BUSINESS MEETING

Setting up a business meeting is like buying fire insurance: you may not think you need it until it's too late. The things that you'll be discussing will only be necessary if and when the songs you write with your collaborator turn out to be good enough to be published, recorded, and released. Of course, there's no way to know this until you actually start working together. But, assuming you believe in your own potential, and in that of your collaborator (and there's no reason to work with another person unless you do), I am going to assume that you agree that a meeting of the minds on business matters is necessary before you begin work on music matters.

Don't fall into the trap of thinking that just because your potential collaborator is "nice," that ironing out the business will be a snap later on. Most of us are "nice" when we are trying to impress others. But greed does amazing things to people and business is about money, after all. Ego, dreams, and money make a powerful brew. Many successful songwriters have ended up giving their royalty income to the lawyers who were left to sort out the disagreements between two "nice," talented people.

The business meeting has three basic rules:

Never conduct a business meeting at the same time as a creative meeting. You'll need to be organized, closed, and tough to do business. You'll need to be flexible, open, and childlike to be creative. Don't try to be both at the same time—it won't work. Conduct your business in a neutral place, like a coffee shop, on a day when you're not planning to work together at all. Having a meal together is a nice idea. It softens the whole affair, limits the time frame (usually not more than an hour), and makes it easy to exit if you see that it's not going well. Of course, if things do go well, it helps to bond the relationship, too.

Come prepared. You may very well end up educating your new partner if he is less informed about the business than you are. Make copies of information you want him to read. Back up your opinion with resources. Take notes or tape the meeting for future reference. Make a checklist or agenda of the items you want to discuss. Be prepared to draw a letter of agreement for signature at a later date, based on the discussion. A business meeting is not a good time to be under the influence of alcohol or drugs of any kind. Have your drink when the meeting is over.

Go with a positive attitude. Don't enter the meeting with tales about how you got screwed before and you're doing this to protect yourself. Assume good will and go from there. You're building a team and every team needs goals, guidelines, regulations, and direction. Don't be defensive. More than anything, the session should be an information-gathering interview. If you conduct it well, it should save you from any hostile confrontations in the future.

Now that you know the rules, what specifics do you discuss? Here's a list. You may want to eliminate some of these points or include some of your own, but all the basics are here:

1. Is your information current—name, address, phone number, Social Security number, birthdate and affiliation (ASCAP, BMI, SESAC)—on your partner? This will go in your files and be used when you fill out the copyright forms on your songs. The minute you create a copyright (i.e., a song) together, you must keep up to date on this information. I remember vividly how I felt when a publisher wanted a song of mine badly, but finally passed when my collaborator could not be found. Most publishers will not be interested in publishing half a song. Keep in touch!

2. How does your partner feel about publishing? Does he have his own publishing company? Is it active? Does he want *your* publishing as well? How does he feel about working with the major publishers? Should a contract be offered to them on the tune? Is he interested in working with a small, untried publishing company?

3. Does your partner have aspirations to be a recording artist? Do you? Will either of you want to keep all the best songs for yourself? This is a source of major conflict with many collaborators and should be thoroughly discussed before the work begins. There is nothing more frustrating than holding back a great song on the chance that your partner might get signed—or seeing all your best

songs go to another person, if you're the one with artistic aspirations. Be frank about this issue.

4. When is a song completed? Ideally, it's when BOTH of you say so. That's okay if one of you isn't a perfectionist or a procrastinator. Clashes of temperament will be a sore spot here unless you come up with a set of rules about this. What if you disagree? How many times do you rewrite after a critique session? After the demo is complete, will you be willing to go back in and make major changes?

5. How prolific are you? Your partner? If one of you writes every day and one of you only writes when you're inspired, that can be very frustrating for the more prolific of the two. Do you or your partner need deadlines? Pressure? How long will you give a lyric or melody to your partner before you expect to see some activity on his part? What do you do when one of you wants the song finished and the other one doesn't want to finish it, or can't?

6. When do you bring in a third party to work on the song? Ideally, it's when you BOTH agree you've reached a dead end. Who will you bring in? Again, in an ideal situation, it should be a mutually agreed-upon third party. But you need to discuss this thoroughly. *Never bring in a third party to work on a song without telling your partner.* You'd be surprised how often this is done and it usually means the end of the partnership.

7. What about splits? This is a major bone of contention in many relationships where one party writes both words and music and the other party only writes one or the other. *Professional writers split everything right down the middle, no matter who does what. When a third party is called in, everything is divided into thirds.*

8. What about demos? Where do you do them? Who decides which songs to do? Who pays for them and how? Who produces, who engineers, plays, sings? Generally, the fees are split exactly like the song, 50/50. But what if one partner owns a studio and can play all the instruments, etc.? Does he charge the other partner for the demo costs? This is an individual matter and both parties should feel comfortable with whatever arrangement is made, regardless of how they work it out.

9. What connections do each of you have? Would either of you feel comfortable in using them? Is one of you more aggressive? Do either of you go to L.A., New York, or Nashville on a regular basis? How will you get your songs heard by publishers, producers, or artists? Do either of you belong to professional organizations such as the Los Angeles Songwriters Showcase, National Academy of Songwriters, the Nashville Songwriters Association, or The Songwriters Guild? Would either of you be willing to join to get professional feedback, pitch songs to producers and publishers and so forth? Most partnerships die quickly when they are without goals. Once you spend the time and money required to write and demo your songs—then what? Are either of you prepared to move to L.A.,

Nashville, or New York to better promote your work?
10. How do each of you feel about songwriting competitions? Who pays the entry fee and how will the winnings be split?

Creating music successfully with your partner will depend on the flexibility and willingness to work things out that each of you brings to the relationship. If the songs you produce are great, the incentive to work out the snags will be greater. It might help if you adopt the belief that people are more important than songs. If you don't believe that, then maybe you should write alone.

STANDARD CONTRACT

The following is a standard cowriters contract with comments to help you tailor it to your own situation.

COLLABORATORS' AGREEMENT
This Agreement is entered into on _____,
19___ with respect to the following musical composition(s):

_____

_____

The undersigned songwriters have collaborated in the creation of the aforementioned song(s) with the following understanding:

1. No songwriter shall be responsible to any other songwriter for expenses incurred in the preparation or presentation of the song(s) unless agreed upon.

2. All sums received from exploitation of the song(s), as well as all approved expenses incurred, will be divided as follows:

Writer's name   Percent share

_____   _____

_____   _____

3. _____ wrote all of the lyrics to the song(s).
   _____ composed all the music to the song(s).

continued

123

[NOTE: IF THE WRITERS HAVE MADE VARYING CON-
TRIBUTIONS TO THE MUSIC AND LYRIC, AND THERE IS
NO PRECISE SPLIT IN RESPONSIBILITY FOR EACH, AN
ATTEMPT TO IDENTIFY INDIVIDUAL CONTRIBUTION IS
OF VIRTUALLY NO USE.]

4. If the song(s) are not [*signed to a publishing agreement/
   commercially recorded/commercially released*] by
   _____, 19___, we may each withdraw
   our respective creative contributions to any song(s) not
   meeting such requirement, and the other(s) shall have no
   remaining claim to income from any use then made by the
   creator thereof. [NOTE: AGAIN, THERE IS LITTLE PUR-
   POSE TO THIS CLAUSE UNLESS THE DIVISION BETWEEN
   LYRICAL AND MUSICAL CONTRIBUTIONS IS CLEAR-
   CUT.]

5. [*One or more of the writers*] shall have the only right to issue licenses for any use whatsoever of the song(s). [*or*] All
   of us shall have equal rights to issue licenses for any use of
   the song(s), but must pay appropriate shares of any money
   received as specified in Paragraph 2 above. [*or*] Any of us
   may grant licenses for any use of the song(s), but only after
   obtaining written approval of all of the others.

6. [*One of the writers/All of us/Any of us with approval, etc.*]
   may authorize changes to the lyric or melody of the song(s)
   and may reduce the shares of all of us in equal proportion
   to compensate any new songwriter(s) adding such creative
   changes. [NOTE: IF THERE IS A DEFINITE DIVISION BE-
   TWEEN LYRICAL AND MUSICAL CONTRIBUTIONS
   AMONG THE ORIGINAL WRITERS, REDUCTIONS FOR
   CHANGES MAY BE APPROPRIATELY CATEGORIZED BY
   THE TYPE OF CHANGE AND ASSESSED AGAINST THAT
   WRITER.]

7. [*One of the writers*] is hereby granted full power of attorney [*or*] [*All of the writers*] are each granted full power of
   attorney to assign any rights or grant any licenses respect-
   ing the song(s) in the event that the others are unavailable
   to give their approval for any period in excess of
   _____ days. [NOTE: IN SOME CIRCUMSTANCES,
   WHERE ONE WRITER MAY BE FAR MORE KNOWLEDGE-
   ABLE IN MUSIC INDUSTRY MATTERS, OR WHERE ONE
   WRITER INSISTS ON RESERVING A SONG FOR HIS OR

HER PERFORMING GROUP'S USE ONLY, IT MAY BE AP-
PROPRIATE TO GRANT THAT WRITER THE EXCLUSIVE
RIGHT TO GRANT LICENSES AND ASSIGN RIGHTS
WITHOUT APPROVAL OF THE OTHERS.]

8. In the event of any dispute between us regarding the
song(s) or this Agreement, we will submit the matter to
binding arbitration in (the largest nearby city) under the
rules of the American Arbitration Association or any local
arbitration association upon which we otherwise agree.

Signature   Soc. Sec. Number   Address and Phone

Note: Although it's not critical, you may wish to have this document notarized. In many states, notarization is required for any power of attorney.
Check your state laws as to how a power of attorney is legally granted.

Agreements regarding copyrighted musical compositions may be registered in the Copyright Office in Washington, D.C., if you know the original
copyright registration number. This provides "constructive notice" of the
agreement to the public, so that anyone dealing with a writer acting in violation of the agreement is deemed to have notice of such a wrongful act.
As to companies and individuals who conduct an actual search of copyright office records, a record of the agreement will discourage any transfers or licenses in violation of its terms.

WORKING AS A GROUP

Occasionally you'll pick up a record by a group and see five or six writers
(group members) listed after a title. You think, "Do they expect me to believe that *all* those writers contributed equally to the writing of that
song?" There are, in fact, groups in which all members create lyrics and/
or music together, but in most group situations one writer (or two) usually contributes more than the rest. Maybe the lead singer is responsible for
the melody or someone else has the lyric concept or writes most of the
words. Many bands are formed around a writer/artist or team. There are
bands in which several members contribute their own songs or write with
another group member.

So why, then, should a group decide to share writing credit with all its members if those members don't contribute to lyrics or melodies? For two main reasons, the first financial, the second artistic. On the financial side, there are five major areas in which a group member can make money: 1. Record royalties, 2. Live performances, 3. Songwriting royalties, 4. Publishing royalties, 5. Merchandising. In record royalties, the cold reality is that since recording costs, advances, and other expenses are recouped by the company from your artist royalties, most group members never receive *any* royalties beyond the original advance until they're *very* successful.

Regarding live performances, even subsequently successful groups usually take at least two years from the start of a recording contract to begin making any kind of decent money. "Opening act" status and at least two hit singles (or, for heavy metal bands, substantial touring) are needed to bring in enough revenue to do more than pay touring bills. Merchandising of T-shirts, etc., at concerts can be lucrative but this business also takes time to build.

So, the only sources of income left are from writer royalties or income generated by self-publishing. The songwriting royalties will be earned whether the songs are published by a company outside the group or by a company the group sets up to publish its own (and others') songs. In the latter case, what frequently happens is that an individual or company is hired to administer the group's publishing company for a fee (see chapter 11, "Self Publishing," and "Administration Deals," page 195), and the remaining royalties are divided among the group.

On the artistic side, the philosophy is that everyone in the group contributes his own individuality towards creating the final product and therefore deserves a share of the credit. The final and unique sound of the group is not dictated by the writer/artist/lead singer, etc., but by the interaction of all the members. In other words, if one member left the group, this philosophy says, the sound would be audibly altered.

But, you might ask, "What if the bass player doesn't write lyrics or melodies? How does he justify receiving royalties?" To answer that we have to ignore our traditional concept of the songwriter and instead reiterate that the group is not writing a song as we know it, but creating a *sound,* an element frequently as important to the commercial success of a record as lyrics and melodies. So it's not only important what the bass player plays, but *how* he plays it, what sound modification devices he chooses to use and when. If he's a singer it's important how his voice sounds, how he uses it, and what parts he creates for the vocal arrangement. He may create an instrumental hook in the form of a bass riff that gives the tune a unique identity or serves as the basis (so to speak) for the whole song. So although he hasn't written a word, or a note, his contribution can be extremely important to the success of the record, and ultimately, the group.

It may occur to you that, depending on the situation, all the above contributions can be and often are made by others. The studio musician, arranger, or producer are all paid in other ways and are free to solicit work with anyone else. A group member whose first commitment is to the group doesn't always have these options.

Dividing writer royalties doesn't work with everyone and may give rise to jealousy from those who feel their contribution was more important, especially after the big money starts rolling in. So if you're writing with a group, it is worth considering sharing the credit, especially if you want to attract creative people to your band, and if everyone can perceive each other's contribution as being equally important.

As you can see, collaboration is an option to be seriously considered. It offers many positive advantages, both artistically and commercially. The difficulty in finding a compatible partner and keeping your business straight can be more than compensated for in increased productivity and quality.

PART TWO

THE
BUSINESS

■

Protecting Your Songs

THE IMPORTANCE OF TAKING CARE OF BUSINESS

Now that you've put so much soul and perspiration into writing those great songs, I hope you're not looking at the rest of this book and saying, "Oh, that's just the business stuff. I don't have a business kind of mind, I think I'll skip that part." Or "I'll just get a manager who can take care of all that." Those words have a sad echo for a lot of people I've met over the years whose creativity has been drained and their careers put on hold while they tried to undo by legal means the damage caused by their own ignorance.

There was a time not long ago when there were no books from which someone (who wasn't an attorney) could learn about the business. Now you have no excuse. The following chapters are an introduction to some basics of the music business. It doesn't pretend to teach you everything but it *will* give you plenty of streetwise information about the business that you don't have to be a Ph.D. to understand. At the bottom of it all, as you might have suspected, are common sense and human nature. Don't forget that the music *business* is also very creative. You can exercise your creativity every bit as much by figuring out fresh approaches to getting your songs recorded as you can by writing a song, and succeeding at it can feel just as good.

Your songs and talent are your babies. You want to know when they go out in the world, that they have every advantage. You want them to be protected, to be with people who care about them, to have a chance to do something good in the world and if they're special, to pay your rent in your old age. Reading the rest of this book is a major payment on an insurance policy you owe to those babies.

I'll show you a lot of options in this section, just in case you thought there were only one or two. There are many different ways to deal with your business, and your personal situation may use a combination of them.

Many wonderful, honest, hard-working people exist in this business who want to see you succeed and who are motivated every bit as much by seeing their creativity pay off for you as they are by the financial rewards they'll receive by helping you do it. They take great pride in their work and go through as much frustration and aggravation in their jobs as you do in yours. Reading the rest of this book will help you find those people and get some idea of what happens on *their* end of *your* business. That knowledge will help you make the best kind of business deals, the ones in which everyone is rewarded for his efforts and knows how to work as a team. And it will help you avoid the dishonest people and poor business deals.

YOUR SONG IS YOUR PROPERTY

One of the most important business considerations is protecting your songs. While you may be emotionally attached to your "baby," you have to think of it as a product, or commodity—an "intellectual property."

Our government (and others around the world) have agreed that an artist deserves to retain ownership of his own creations. To encourage creative expression, legislation was enacted so that an artist could expect to be compensated by whoever sought the "right to copy" his work. A creator can assign different rights to different people for different purposes. A sculptor gives a gallery "the right to display." A songwriter can license (or assign) the rights to her song to a music publisher to obtain recordings of her song, reproduce those recordings, and distribute them to the public.

Now we come to the need for a "right to copy," or copyright: How can someone acquire something from you until they are sure it is yours to begin with? Anyone can show me "his" car, even take me for a ride in it, but if there were ever any legal questions regarding that car, we would need to see some proof of ownership.

Countless stories have been told about songwriters who have written some of America's most famous and successful songs and either did not know how to register their own works, or depended totally on someone else to give them proper payment as the creators. Years later, as these songwriters became more educated regarding copyright protection procedures, they realized they had blindly signed over all of their rights to earn any income from their songs.

Fortunately, today there are books (like this one), songwriters organizations, classes, seminars, and other learning opportunities available to help people learn about their rights as creative artists. When a songwriter puts so much work, worry, and love into his art, it seems irresponsible not to know how to protect it.

Before I knew better, I had a fantasy about the Copyright Office in which, when they received my new song, a piano player played it for all the employees just to make sure it was really original. He'd say, "Hey, have you guys ever heard this one before?" In the fantasy, I'd break out in a cold sweat as I prayed that I hadn't accidentally written part of something I'd heard on the radio or in a club somewhere. One by one, the copyright "experts" (who I knew had heard everything) would shake their heads and somebody would say, "Wait a minute! Play the last four bars of that bridge again. No, I thought it might have been 'Earth Angel' but it's okay. Let it pass," and I was home free.

If you have that fantasy, you can now wipe it out in favor of cold reality. The Copyright Office processes somewhere in the neighborhood of a half million copyright registrations every year. Needless to say, they *don't* listen to those songs, but they *do* check over the forms to make sure you've filled them out correctly. If you haven't, they'll send back your application. They also don't check to see if the song is original, since the copyright registration is only a proof of the *date* of registration.

According to the Copyright Revision Act of 1976, which went into effect on Jan. 1, 1978, *original* (original with the creator of the work) songs are entitled to copyright protection from the time they're "fixed" in a tangible medium of expression. This means on paper or "phonorecord," which includes vinyl, tape, compact disc, or software. At the time it's written or recorded, it's considered to be *created.* If you sing your song "live" for an audience, it is not automatically protected. Technically, it's only considered protected when it's recorded or written. Consequently, it's a good idea to tape the song and put the copyright notice on the tape with the date, and even better to obtain a copyright registration before performing it in public. Ideas, concepts, titles, chord or rhythm patterns are not protected—only the specific form of their expression.

LENGTH OF COPYRIGHT PROTECTION
The length of copyright protection is described by the Copyright Office as follows:

Works originally copyrighted on or after January 1, 1978. A work that is created (fixed in tangible form for the first time) on or after January 1, 1978, is automatically protected from the moment of its creation, and is ordinarily given a term enduring for the author's life, plus an additional 50 years after the author's death. In the case of "a joint work prepared by two or more authors who did not work for hire," the term lasts for 50 years after the last surviving author's death. For works made for hire, and for anonymous and pseudonymous works (unless the author's identity is revealed in Copyright Office records), the duration of copyright will be 75 years from publication or 100 years from creation, whichever is shorter.

Works that were created *before* the present law came into effect, but had neither been published nor registered for copyright before January 1, 1978, have been automatically brought under the statute and are now given Federal copyright protection. The duration of copyright in these works will generally be computed in the same way as for works created on or after January 1, 1978: the life-plus-50 or 75/100-year terms will apply to them as well. However, all works in this category are guaranteed at least 25 years of statutory protection.

Works copyrighted before January 1, 1978. Under the law in effect before 1978, copyright was secured either on the date a work was published, or on the date of registration if the work was registered in unpublished form. In either case, the copyright endured for a first term of 28 years from the date it was secured. During the last (28th) year of the first term, the copyright was eligible for renewal. The new copyright law has extended the renewal term from 28 to 47 years for copyrights that were subsisting on January 1, 1978, making these works eligible for a total term of protection of 75 years. However, the copyright *must* be timely renewed to receive the 47-year period of added protection. For more detailed information on the copyright term, write to the Copyright Office and request Circulars 15a and 15t. For information on how to search the Copyright Office records concerning the copyright status of a work, ask for Circular 22.

THE COPYRIGHT NOTICE
Any time you write out the lyric, leadsheet or send a demo tape, put the copyright notice in this form on the first page (or on the tape):

© 1986 John Doe. All rights reserved.

Though technically, a copyright notice is not needed unless the work is published (distributed for sale), it's a good idea to get into the habit of including it.

COPYRIGHT REGISTRATION
Though using the copyright notice automatically secures your copyright, informing other people that you own the song, actually registering it with the Copyright Office (Library of Congress) offers the important proof of authorship and the date of creation you'll need if you ever want to sue someone for stealing your song (copyright infringement). Here's how to register your song.

1. Send in a filled out PA (*Performing Arts*) form which you can obtain free by writing the United States Copyright Office, Library of Congress, Washington, D.C. 20559 or calling them on their 24-hour hot line (202)287-9100. In fact, while you're at it, copyright attorney Jack Whitley suggests you organize a "Copyright Registration Kit" by calling that number and leaving the following message on their answering machine: "My name is _____, my address is _____ (spell unusual names and addresses); I want Circular Numbers R-1, R-1c, R-8, R-9, R-15a, R-31, R-34, R-45, R-50, R-56, R-56a, R-73, Sample Forms PA 1 through 6, and five PA forms with instructions and continuation sheets" (to list additional songs). You'll get all the forms you need for the price of one phone call.
2. Enclose a $10 check or money order made out to "Register of Copyrights."
3. Enclose one copy of the leadsheet (two if the song has been distributed to the public [published] in some visually perceivable form), or a cassette (or record) of the song (two if it's been distributed to the public as a cassette or record). Limited distribution of demo tapes to music industry people doesn't count as distribution to the public.

Complete instructions appear on the copyright registration form. (See Appendix.)

If you rewrite a song on which you've already received a copyright registration you can send in the new version on a Form PA as you did the first, making sure to mention the original registration number.

If you're copyrighting a sound recording (as separate from the individual songs) you need a Form SR (*Sound Recording*). If you want to publicly distribute (publish) a tape or record of your own songs, you can protect both the record and the songs on it with a Form SR. Send two copies of the recording with the registration form. If it's a record, be sure to send the jacket with it.

You can send your registration by First Class mail, though some like to send it registered mail just to have proof that it arrived. It's not uncommon to wait three or four months for the certificate to be returned to you with your copyright registration number. Your work is registered from the time it reaches the copyright office. If you've sent it by registered mail you'll know when it arrived there by the receipt that the post office returns to you.

ALTERNATIVES

If you have many songs and are sending them to publishers and showing them to other writers but can't afford to spend $10 on each one, there are some other ways to protect yourself.

You can register *a large number of songs as an unpublished collection of songs under a single name* (e.g., "The John Doe Songbook #1"). Though you get the same protection as with single songs, there are practical problems.

If someone heard your song, didn't know who wrote it, wanted to record it, and tried to search for it through the Copyright Office, he wouldn't find it because it would be registered under the collective name.

A more practical problem is that, if someone wants to record or publish a song on the collection and you grant them a license using the copyright number of the collection, you risk granting them the license for (*or* ownership of—in the case of a publisher) the whole collection. You have to remember that a new copyright registration number must be obtained on that particular song if the ownership is transferred. In other words, if a music publisher wants to publish your song, you're transferring the ownership of the song to that publisher. As the new owner, he needs to have a new registration number that proves that he now owns it. On your contract with the publisher you'll need to write the registration number of the collection, but make sure you clearly note that you're transferring ownership of only that particular song.

Here are the conditions you must meet to register an unpublished collection:

1. The selections must be assembled in an orderly form (as many songs as you can get on one cassette).
2. The combined selections must have a single title identifying the collection as a whole.
3. The copyright claimant in all the selections and in the collection as a whole must be the same.
4. All the selections must be by the same writer, or, if they're by differ-

ent writers, at least one of the writers must have contributed to each one.

When you make up your tape to send to the Copyright Office, recite the title name of each song on the tape before you record it. If you send leadsheets, make a cover sheet listing all the songs in the collections. Use the PA form for this method. Be sure to keep a duplicate copy of the tape or leadsheet you registered in a safe place along with the registration certificate that will be returned to you.

The "poor man's copyright" is the process of sending yourself your song by registered mail. It's the least reliable "protection" since it could be argued that, with it in your possession, you could have opened it and altered its contents. Also, if your house burned down, you'd have no proof at all that those songs were yours.

REGISTRATION SERVICES

Song registration services provide a quick and inexpensive alternative to federal copyright registration. Registering a song with such a service legally establishes authorship and date of creation should you ever need proof. The most prominent registration service is the National Academy of Songwriters' (NAS) Song Bank at 6381 Hollywood Blvd., Suite 780, Los Angeles, CA 90028 (213)463-7178. The service was set up in 1973 and modeled after a similar service offered by The Writers Guild of America, Inc. It provides a ten-year protection at a very low cost. The fact that it's an established procedure and provides a "disinterested third party" makes it preferable to the "poor man's copyright."

The only disadvantage is that, in the case of infringement, you wouldn't automatically have access to statutory damages (money) the Copyright Law provides if you should win your case with a Copyright Office registration. (See "Copyright Infringement/Plagiarism," below.) You'd have to pursue damages in a civil court.

In evaluating registration services, check to make sure the storage of their files is adequate and safe, and their record keeping is competent.

COPYRIGHT INFRINGEMENT/PLAGIARISM

One of the most common fears of songwriters is that they'll have a song stolen. And while it's been known to happen, plagiarism is less common than the paranoia would indicate. Publishers would rather publish a song than plagiarize it. They'd rather be in line for your next hit than be in court defending themselves in a copyright infringement case.

The more concrete fear is that another writer will steal an idea. Since neither an idea nor a title can be copyrighted, the possibility is greater that another writer might borrow an idea or title and use it as a basis for a new song. There's no real protection for lyric ideas. Throughout the history of literature and music, writers and musicians have borrowed from each other quite blatantly with no apologies for doing so. The originators of musical and literary forms are well documented and the forms are still in use. The storyteller is said to have a choice of 36 basic plots. Beyond that, he's dealing with variations. The idea itself is not as important as how he develops it. The language, characterization, and imagery are what make a story, or a song, special.

If you do come up with a new idea or an unusual variation, but don't craft it well, it is unlikely that it will spark interest. There is, however, the chance that another writer will realize you had a good idea but you didn't do it justice. That person may have the craftsmanship and perseverance to make it work and he would have every right to develop the idea in his own way. If the writer took your idea in a totally different direction and used none of your actual language, it would probably not constitute copyright infringement.

COPYRIGHT INFRINGEMENT

Copyright infringement is a federal crime that occurs when any of the copyright owner's exclusive rights are violated. Those rights cover reproduction, adaptation, publication, performance, and display.

In order to prove copyright infringement, two things must be established: (1) who has ownership of the copyright and (2) whether the alleged infringer actually copied the song. A copyright registration number for that song from the Library of Congress can be admitted as evidence that the song belongs to the person filing the suit.

Whether the copyright is registered before or after the infringement will influence the type of damage compensation for which the plaintiff (the one suing) is eligible. The plaintiff also must prove that the song was infringed upon. If a witness cannot testify that he or she saw the defendant actually listening to and copying the song, the plaintiff has to prove (1) access and (2) substantial similarity.

Access. Access is really "the opportunity to have heard" a song or a "reasonable possibility that it was heard" by the defendant. If you prove that a song was widely known, the courts will assume the defendant heard it. "Widely known" is obvious with recorded songs, particularly hits. Where it gets really sticky is in a case where a writer/performer is traveling around the country singing his/her songs. Though no publishing or recording deals are involved, it's possible that the song could be taped or taught to another writer/performer and a chain of listeners created over which the original writer has no control. If you played a concert in the defendant's town, he could have both "opportunity" and "possibility," but it would be tricky to find any kind of proof.

Substantial similarity. The crucial question is, of course, how similar was the defendant's song to that of the plaintiff? This is where we get into the question of whether it's okay to copy "a few bars" of another work. A popular myth says that more than four bars need to be copied before it constitutes infringement. Not true! On the one hand, there are probably a lot of songs with four-bar passages that are technically the same, but they sound so much different that one would not remind you of the other. But there are other songs that are instantly recognizable in just four notes, such as the first four notes of the old "Dragnet" theme, which establish the identity of the song so strongly that using them would constitute a "substantial taking."

The court uses two tests to determine the degree of similarity. Expert witnesses such as musicologists are brought in to testify about whether the actual melodic construction is the same and whether the general idea of the two works is similar. The other test is for a jury to decide whether, after listening to both songs, they sound alike, or close enough that one could be mistaken for the other, or that the impression to "the reasonable person" is similar. If you listen to George Harrison's "My Sweet Lord" you will understand why he lost the infringement suit by the owners of "He's So Fine." Though it was decided that Harrison didn't deliberately plagiarize the song, he was still found guilty. "I didn't mean to do it" is not a defense.

PUBLIC DOMAIN
Often, a defense in an infringement case is that the defendant did not copy the plaintiff's song, but copied part of a "public domain" song that existed long before the plaintiff's song. A song is in the public domain if, like classical works and traditional folk songs, it was composed before there were copyright laws or no one knows who wrote them. They're also in the public domain when their copyright term has expired.

FAIR USE
Some uses can be made of the works of other writers which don't constitute infringement. These are covered by the doctrine of "fair use." These include criticism (for example, reproducing part of a lyric in a record review), comment, news reporting (using a small portion of another's work as a basis for an editorial comment or a news story that relates to it), scholarship or research (using portions of other works for a thesis or term paper, for instance), and teaching. The latter is the fair use area that most concerns songwriters and composers. Several major music publishing and music educators associations have worked out guidelines for the photocopying of sheet music for classroom use. (See Appendix.)

Four guidelines help define what constitutes fair use: 1) the purpose and character of the use, including whether it's for commercial or for nonprofit educational purposes; 2) the nature of the copyrighted work itself; 3) the amount and substantiality of the portion used in relation to the work as a whole; 4) the effect of the use on the potential market for, or value of, the copyrighted work.

Parody is another category that can be considered fair use. I say "can be" because it also is subject to the above qualifications and if, for instance, you use too much of the original work you may be on shaky legal ground. "Weird Al" Yankovic has made a career of parodying hits but always obtains permission of the copyright owners for the use of their melodies. It's clearly the safest course of action. In some cases, it amounts to more of a professional courtesy than anything else, but at least you're covered. Fair use legal problems are decided by the courts on a case by case basis. Decisions of the courts can then be cited as precedents in future cases.

AWARDING DAMAGES

What can the plaintiff expect to receive if he wins an infringement case? If it can be established how much profit was made by the infringer, or how much monetary damage has been done, it can all be recovered. The plaintiff will probably fare better if it can be proven that the person willfully infringed than if it was unintentional.

It's very difficult to prove damages though, so the plaintiff can elect to seek "statutory damages," an amount set by law to encourage copyright registration. (They figured that if they offered a cash reward they could keep you from being your own worst enemy.) The amount can range from between $250 and $10,000. In order to be eligible to collect statutory damages and recover the attorney fees spent on the trial, the copyright registration must have been obtained before the infringement occurs.

Some publishers will delay copyrighting the song until they get a record released on it. In the case of a published song there is a three month grace period after publication which allows for the situation in which a record is released publicly (a form of publication) and the song is ripped off before the song is actually registered. Meanwhile, the song is protected if it contains a proper copyright notice. If the song is unpublished there is no grace period so it's important to copyright it as soon as possible after you write it.

If you're worried about whether you're infringing on someone else's song, a fear that all writers experience at times, don't let it become an obsession or it will stop the creative juices. If you haven't deliberately lifted something, you shouldn't worry about it. If you have any doubts, just ask someone to listen to the song. You probably know someone who you think has heard everything recorded in the past thirty years. And if the song gets to a publisher there is a good chance that someone will recognize a potential problem. They'll have an interest in avoiding a lawsuit.

What I've discussed here is a simplification of the subject. If you would like to pursue this further or answer other questions about copyright matters, call your local Bar Association and locate a copyright attorney. I also highly recommend *Musicians Guide to Copyright* by J. Gunnar Erickson, Edward R. Hearn, and Mark E. Halloran, published by Bay Area Lawyers for the Arts, Fort Mason Building 310, San Francisco, CA 94123.

AVOIDING THE SONGSHARKS

"Songsharks" are companies and individuals who charge a fee to publish your song or collaborate with you, most commonly to write music to your lyric which they like to refer to as a "songpoem." Others, under the guise of publishing companies, ask you to submit material, then inform you that it just so happens that they've found an album project that your song is perfect for. In fact, what happens is that the "publishing" company sends your song to another branch of their own company that is the "record" company. The latter writes to say that the song is perfect—they just need some money from you first to make sure they can do a good job. You're "double teamed" to make sure the sharks get your money.

Many "songshark" letters have been forwarded to me from songwriters who were concerned about getting ripped off. The most common story is that, out of nowhere, they received a letter asking them to submit material for "review." "Where did they find out about me?" is the common question from writers who've received letters out of the blue from a notorious "record company" who wants to record their material. They're always flattered that someone knows about them. Sorry to burst the bubble, but they get your name and address from the Library of Congress where you copyrighted your song (and that copyright information is then available to the public).

The next most common story is that the writer responded to an ad in a magazine. In either case they received a letter much like the one that follows, a composite of several I've seen from "record" or "production" companies. Their offers usually contain the same catch phrases. Only the names have been changed. I've highlighted the most common statements and sales pitches:

As a songwriter, **you've probably considered having a song recorded** *at one time or another.* **If you've been disappointed** *and you're about to make that decision to just let that song sit unrecorded, Songshark Music Productions would like you to consider submitting it to us.*

Recording companies need new songs. Without them they would cease to exist. Just think how many new songs you hear on the radio, television, and records. **Some day one of them may be yours! Just compare your efforts with songs on the market today.**

Many writers, perhaps like yourself, produce some really good songs. **Your song may be excellent and worthy of recording.** *We are interested in ALL types of material; Popular, Country Western, Gospel, Rock, Ballads, etc.*

We employ professional arrangers, musicians and vocalists to help you accomplish that commercial production that was, before, out of reach. Best of all, after Songshark Music Productions records your song on a commercial record, we will **ship records to disc jockeys and record stores and pay you a ROYALTY for each record sold.**

Songshark Music Productions will record songs of any style, with or without melody (leadsheet). **If you have lyric only, it will be completed with a commercial tune by our professional arrangers.** *If you have a completed song, rest assured our arrangers will adhere to your lyric and melody as much as possible. If you send a tape, make sure it is accompanied by the lyrics or leadsheet along with a self-addressed stamped envelope for its return.*

Have no fear in sending us your un-copyrighted songs or poems. *Songshark Music Productions is a recording company and is not in the business of stealing songs or poems. However, if you wish to stay on the "safe side," have your material notarized and/or send it* **Registered Mail through the United States Post Office.**

You may have real ability and **you must act now, today!** *Let us look over your work, so that we may give you* **our honest opinion.** *Don't just let your poem or song sit around.* **Let us help you get it recorded.**

What a great offer! Songshark Music Productions came along just in the nick of time to save your creative life. But take a closer look at this letter and you'll find clues to tip you off to their questionable business practices.

First they use "If you've been disappointed" as an attention-grabber. Who hasn't been disappointed? Sounds like they're going to get your song recorded for you!

Next the pitch gets heavy. The "just compare" line is typical—and effective. There isn't a writer alive who hasn't heard a song on the radio and said "If that can get on the radio, my song is a cinch!"

Notice that the letter makes no mention of R&B. "Country Western" is a phrase seldom heard anymore. That alone tells you this company is behind the times.

Next they actually promise that *after* they record your song on a *commercial* record (they're already assuming it will be good enough), they'll ship records to DJs and record stores. They'll probably actually do this. They could fulfill this promise by sending it to *two* DJs and *two* record stores. The reality is that they're hoping that *you* will buy the albums, along with all the other writers whose songs are included on it. Songsharks have no real illusions about their ability to get air play on an unknown artist on a compilation record (containing several different singers.) They know that even if a radio station did play one of the cuts from this album and it got good listener response, it would go nowhere because the listeners couldn't buy an *album* of *that* artist. So why should they play it instead of the superstar product from major record labels they're being pushed to play? They wouldn't. If they will play unknown artists, they'd rather play new artists from legitimate small independent record companies.

Notice how Songsharks capitalize "ROYALTY" in the letter as though it's an added bonus, as if they want very badly to prove to you that they're really honest and wouldn't think of ripping you off. Receiving royalties for each record sold is a matter of course, and specific percentages are always negotiated upfront.

Many writers are confused by people who tell them that if they can't write musical notation they haven't "written" the melody. Songsharks want you to believe that "melody" means "leadsheet" or the melody written down. In truth, if someone has created a melody in his head and can sing it into a tape recorder he's "written" it. When someone else essentially puts chords to the melody, writes a chord and/or melody chart, and wants writer credit and half the writers royalties for it, the first writer must decide if that contribution warrants cowriter credit.

But Songshark isn't looking to share the royalties with you as would a legitimate collaborator who believes her contribution is valuable enough to deserve a royalty split. A legitimate collaborator works on your song because she honestly believes you can make a potential hit together, not because a company pays her to write a melody for "any" lyric she's not otherwise motivated to work with, and for "any" lyricist she's never even taken the trouble to talk to.

The Songshark letter assures you the company is "not in the business of stealing songs or poems." Songsharks often refer to lyrics as "songpoems" knowing that the world is full of frustrated poets who think their poems could be used as song lyrics. They might be quite sincere about not wanting to steal your song, but they're being tremendously irresponsible about it. The worst possible protection is the so-called "poor man's copyright," sending your work to yourself registered mail. It's been proven to be legally weak. You notice they didn't suggest you actually obtain a legitimate copyright registration through the Library of Congress. They could just as easily have given you the phone number of the Copyright Office. But they don't care about you. It's in *their* best interest that you don't take time to think about it or check with anyone about this letter.

The last paragraph urges you to hurry and let them help you. This is a prime setup that makes you think this is really an exclusive deal. This actually makes it sound as though you have to be good enough to be able to make use of their services. You're nervous when you send it in, hoping against hope that you have something they'll think worthy to record.

Typically, the next step is that they send you a second letter that says: **Congratulations!** *Out of all the hundreds of songs we receive, (title) has been chosen to appear on our new (title) album which will be* **distributed to radio stations around the country. Just send $400** *to cover production costs so that our experienced and creative team of singers, musicians, and producers can record your song with the* **best possible quality for commercial release.**

There's the zinger. You actually think something might happen and you send your $400. Another letter arrives to tell you there's yet another album you could get your song on if you send *more* money. Once you send your first money they know you're gullible. They know you're not aware that *NO legitimate record company would ever charge you to have your song released on their record.* No legitimate publisher, record company, or demo service writes melodies for a fee.

Demo services, by the way, are legitimate businesses (and demo production seems to be a part of the activities of this songshark company). Some sharks will make a demo of your song under the guise of releasing your song on a record. Demos can usually be done much cheaper elsewhere with your participation, though demo services may legitimately charge for arrangements, leadsheets or chord charts. However, before dealing with any demo production service, you should hear samples of their work. (See "Demo Production Companies.")

Songsharks are very inventive in coming up with new ways to separate you from your money. They'll "publish," "promote," "record," and charge you large "screening" fees, explaining that screening is a standard practice in the industry. Screening *is* a standard practice, but charging for it is considered unethical. In the legitimate music industry, publishers and record companies gamble *their* money on your talent. If you lose, they lose. In the songshark "industry," only you lose. They don't gamble.

Songsharks usually do operate within the letter of the law. Strictly speaking, they *usually* do what they promise. But everyone in the legitimate music industry considers them *unethical* because what they promise and deliver is not what you think it is. Their carefully worded letters create an illusion that bears little resemblance to how the real world of music publishing works. They prey on ignorant people who don't know how to get good information or who would rather harbor their illusions than deal with hard reality.

The songsharks argue that those people don't *want* to deal with the music industry. Songsharks say they're satisfying a need for people to hear their songs in a "finished" product. If that's the case, then sharks are essentially the equivalent of a "vanity press" for poets and authors, another legitimate business, but one that doesn't pretend to be anything else. If songsharks operated like vanity presses, they'd say it costs X amount to produce a master of your song, X amount to press X number of records, and then *you* do what you want with them. If you want them to actually promote your record, they'd tell you it will cost X amount *if* they thought the record is promotable.

Legitimate promotion is expensive. Major labels can spend over $100,000 on a single. Just sending records to radio stations is *not* promoting a record. Promoting records that you don't believe in is the quickest way to get radio program directors NOT to take your calls and to totally lose your credibility.

When songsharks promise to get your songs played on the radio, they deliver that, too. They buy time on small stations in small markets that typically play your song at 3 A.M. You'll receive no performance royalty because the station can't log the airplay. BMI and ASCAP don't recognize songsharks as legitimate publishers, so songsharks can't put BMI or ASCAP next to the title of your song on their record. You thought that, when they said they'd "get it on the radio," they meant everywhere. *No one can promise that,* even promoters for major artists. If they were honest, they'd tell you exactly what they do and how they do it, but songsharks are not in the honesty business.

Where Your Money Comes From

One of the most confusing things to new writers is the source of income from their songs. Though it's not important until one of your songs gets recorded, most of us want to know how much money we can make and how we can get it. "How much money" is impossible to predict because there are so many variables. A song may earn nothing or it may earn millions throughout the life of the copyright. How we get paid is quite simple. There are four major income sources from songs—*mechanical, performance, synchronization* and *print.* The flow chart on page 155 illustrates how these sources relate to the songwriter, and the others who may also get a slice of the pie.

METHODS OF PAYMENT

Mechanical, synchronization, and *print* royalties are collected by the publisher who takes his share and sends you your share, usually quarterly or semiannually. The *performance royalties* are collected by the performing rights organizations—BMI, ASCAP, and SESAC (SESAC also collects mechanical royalties). They will send a quarterly check and statement directly to you and one to your publisher, the amounts divided according to the terms of your publishing contract.

For example, *if you have a standard 50/50 writer/publisher split* the publisher's half will go directly to him, and your half will go directly to you. If you have a 50/50 cowriter split, half of the *writers' share* (25 percent of the total) will go to you directly, the other half to your cowriter. Maybe you're splitting the publishing as well. *If you have a 50/50 copublishing split* and you're the only writer, the other publisher would get a check for 50 percent of the publishing (25 percent of the total). Your own publishing company would get a check for the other half of the publishing (25 percent of the total). As the writer you'd get a check for all of the writer's share (50 percent of the total). In the end you end up with two checks comprising 75 percent of the total.

The following diagrams illustrate the way income is divided between publishers and writers, based on contract clauses that may limit what the writers actually earn. Keep in mind that the 50/50 division is "traditional" and is not an absolute, though the writer should not accept less than 100% of the writer's share. I use 200% as a basis because the publisher's share is nearly always referred to in terms of 100%, i.e., "100% of publishing," "50% of publishing," etc. The "writer's" share may be divided between any number of writers and the "publisher's" share may be divided between any number of publishers.

100% WRITER'S	100% PUBLISHER'S

A

4½% Collection	
97¾% WRITER'S NET	97¾% PUBLISHER'S NET

B

Figure A represents a 50/50 split of gross income. Figure B is the royalty split you get when the contract calls for a 50/50 split of gross income "less costs of collection." The 4½% shown here as an example, is the current fee charged by the Harry Fox Agency for collection of mechanical income only. Other mechanical rights organizations charge different fees. Ideally, for the writer, this cost should be paid by the publisher (Figure C).

100% WRITERS	Collection and administration expenses absorbed by PUBLISHER

C

10%-15% Administration and out-of-pocket costs	
92½% to 95% WRITER'S NET	92½% to 95% PUBLISHER'S NET

D

Figure D represents a 50/50 split of gross income "less administration" and out-of-pocket costs (copyright registration, photocopies, postage, etc.) directly connected to the exploitation of that specific composition. In this example, those costs are shared by the writer and publisher by being taken "off the top" before royalties are divided. Again, the writer should attempt to have the publisher absorb those costs as in Figure C.

SPLIT PUBLISHING

Figure E shows the division of income for a writer who gets "half the publishing." In this most common situation, the "other publisher" usually absorbs costs of collection and administration. In other cases, such as when two writers with their own publishing companies split the income, an independent administration company may be hired. In such a case, the writers' companies may both share those expenses.

| 100% WRITER'S | OTHER PUBLISHER 50% |
| | WRITER'S PUBLISHING COMPANY 50% |

E

MECHANICAL ROYALTIES

Mechanical royalties come from the sale of things mechanical—audio records, tapes, compact discs and, more recently, video tapes and discs—to the general public. The current mechanical rate, called the "statutory rate" set by the Copyright Royalty Tribunal, is 5.25 cents per song per unit sold, so if you have ten songs on an LP, the record company owes the publisher 52.5 cents.

At times, you may be able to negotiate a contract for part of the "publishing" (the traditional 50 percent publisher's share in addition to your 50 percent writer's share). This can occur most often if you're a recording artist or a hot writer with a proven success record. A publisher will make that kind of split if he's excited enough about your songs, is in competition with other publishers for your songs, or if you can convince him/her that you'll personally be very aggressive about pitching the tune to producers and artists.

Collecting the money is a very important part of the publisher's job and often a difficult one. Most publishers contract with agencies such as Harry Fox who issue licenses and collect both domestic and certain foreign mechanical royalties for a fee. (See "Starting Your Own Publishing Company," page 183.) Currently Harry Fox charges 4½ percent of what they collect. Because the agencies collect on behalf of many publishers, they have some power, and they audit the record companies regularly to make sure the publishers get all the royalties they've earned. There is a lot of "creative bookkeeping" in record companies *and* publishing companies. Their objective is to hold on to the money for as long as they can. When interest rates are high they can make a substantial amount of money from the interest on *your* royalties.

The major mechanical rights organizations that publishers will most often work with are listed here:

The Harry Fox Agency
205 East 42nd Street, 18th Floor
New York, N.Y. 10017
(212) 370-5330

The Canadian Musical Reproduction Rights Agency Ltd.
(CMRRA)
56 Wellesley Street West, Suite 320
Toronto, Ontario
Canada M5S 2S4

Copyright Management Inc.
1102 17th Ave. So., Ste. 401
Nashville, TN 37212
Phone: (615) 327-1517

Also, the Songwriters Guild of America collects mechanical royalties on behalf of its members. (See list of "Associations" in Appendix.)

The National Music Publishers Association (NMPA), representing publishers, and The Songwriters Guild of America and the Nashville Songwriters Association International (NSAI), on behalf of songwriters, have waged a continuous battle against the Recording Industry of America Assn. (RIAA) to raise the mechanical royalty rate.

The rate remained at two cents per song, per unit sold, from 1909 to 1978 when it was raised to 2.75 cents. It was raised four times after that, to a rate, effective January 1, 1988, of 5.25 cents per song or one cent per minute, whichever is greater.

As of July 15, 1987, a system for pegging the mechanical royalty rate for the next decade to the Consumer Price Index (CPI) became official. The Copyright Royalty Tribunal will figure the percentage change in the CPI every two years and adjust the mechanical royalty rate accordingly. The system specifies that the adjusted rate shall be no greater than 25 percent of the then-current fee and no lower than the existing fee. The adjusted rate will be rounded to the nearest 1/20th of a cent. The first change was based on the percentage difference between the CPI for December, 1985, and that for September, 1987. After that, the Tribunal is required to use the Index published for September, 1987, and biennially to 1995 to determine revisions in the rates beginning November 1, 1989, and every two years thereafter.

As you might guess, record companies lobbied hard against writers and publishers who sought these increases. There was an unsuccessful attempt to tie the rates to a percentage of the suggested retail selling price of the records and tapes so that when record prices went up, writer/publisher royalties would also be raised. This is the system currently used in Europe.

So how do the numbers work out? A little arithmetic shows that one song on a million-seller LP or single will bring a total of $52,500. When you have a song as a single, you can figure it will be on the LP, too. (And the B-side of a single earns as much mechanical royalty as the A-side since they're both on a "unit sold.") If you have a hit single, then down the road you may also be involved in "Greatest Hits" LPs, the record clubs, and TV packages like "The Top Hits of '85," etc. Promoters of these will usually want you to give them a lower "rate," like maybe three cents. Their philosophy is that it's an extra market for you—a bonus—and they may sell hundreds of thousands of records after the peak sales period of your original release.

THE COMPULSORY LICENSE

The *first time* a composition is recorded, the copyright owner has total control over who records the song and what they're charged. Theoretically, copyright owners could charge even more than the current statutory rate for that first recording but they never do. That first-time control is the reason a producer and artist can be granted a "hold" by a publisher and promised that no one will be allowed to record the song before they do.

After a record of a song has been manufactured and distributed the first time, the 1976 Copyright Act allows anyone else to record the song as long as it avoids changing the basic melody or fundamental character of the work. In other words, no one can do an arrangement of your song and get their own copyright on it. Those who record the song after the first recording must obtain a "compulsory license" and agree to pay the statutory maximum mechanical rate unless they can negotiate a lower rate with the copyright owner. Failure to obtain a compulsory license constitutes piracy.

In addition, they must file a "notice of intention" with the copyright owner and the Copyright Office before they can distribute the records. The licensee is required to make payments and accountings (signed by a Certified Public Accountant) by the 20th of each month for records made and distributed during the previous month and to designate the name of the copyright owner or agent on the record or tape label or container. If this is not done and not remedied within 30 days, the license is defaulted.

The licensee doesn't have to pay if there is no record of copyright registration filed at the Library of Congress.

Compulsory licenses are only granted for records, tapes, and compact discs primarily intended to be distributed to the public for private use.

CONTROLLED COMPOSITION CLAUSES

If you're a self-contained writer/artist, group, or writer/producer looking for a record deal, you should be aware of the increasing practice of record companies to demand a reduced mechanical royalty rate on "controlled compositions" (songs and other musical material in which the copyrights are owned by the act or producer). The current practice is to ask for 75 percent of the statutory rate or less. Your ability to resist their "take it or leave it" approach is entirely dependent on your or your manager's or attorney's assessment of your bargaining power in that particular situation. New acts are particularly vulnerable and frequently give in with the philosophy that any deal is better than no deal.

Record companies have gone so far as to tell an act or producer that even if they choose "outside material" (songs controlled by a publisher or writer other than themselves), the record company will *still* pay only 75

147

percent of the statutory rate, forcing the producer to negotiate for a lower rate from the other publisher or make up the difference from his own pocket. The obvious effect is to reduce the willingness of the producer to record "outside material," possibly reducing the quality of music on the album because the producer or the recording artist must write their own material rather than use well-written songs by other writers.

From the record company's point of view, it's expensive to produce, market, and promote a record, particularly if they have to front the money for a video. They want to cut expenses any way they can.

From your point of view, the record company makes their money from selling records. You make yours from that royalty and without that song, there wouldn't be a record! So though writers and publishers unanimously condemn the practice, it's a reality that you may have to deal with.

PERFORMANCE ROYALTIES: BMI, ASCAP, AND SESAC

Performance royalties are a major source of income for a writer. They're not to be confused with the money a performer makes in public appearances. Performance royalties are monies the copyright owner(s) and songwriter(s) receive when their song is performed publicly. According to the copyright law, nobody can publicly perform a copyrighted song without permission of the copyright owner.

The most common uses of music in public performance are familiar to us all: radio, network and local TV, jukeboxes, Muzak, and live performances. When your songs are played in any of these venues, you, as the writer, and the publisher (whoever owns the copyright) are entitled to get paid for its use. The obvious problem is how to go about collecting the money. Do you call the radio and TV stations all over the country to pay you each time they play your song? Do you send a bill to a club owner because you heard someone play your song there? How do you find out how many times they played it? How do you get them to pay? How do you give them permission to play it there in the first place? The mind boggles at the enormity of the task.

The performing rights organizations, BMI, ASCAP (American Society of Composers, Authors and Publishers) and SESAC (no longer using their original title, Society of European Stage Authors and Composers) are the entities that take care of these problems for you. Through membership in ASCAP or affiliation with BMI or SESAC, you grant them permission to license nondramatic public performances ("small rights") of your compositions. (Dramatic performances, or "grand rights," are those contained in musical theatre, ballet, operas, operettas, etc., in which the story line of the song is dramatized with sets, costumes, props, and so forth. The licenses are granted directly by the copyright owner. A writer or publisher may collect from only one of these organizations for the same song. You may only belong to *one organization at a time.*

How do these organizations collect the money? Generally speaking, radio and TV stations and networks pay annual "blanket license" fees negotiated by the performing rights organizations on behalf of their writer and publisher members. Blanket fees give radio and local and network TV permission for unlimited use of the compositions. Fees are based on a percentage of the advertising revenue received by the stations or networks. The philosophy is that if a station has a 50,000-watt clear channel signal, it's reaching millions of people, enabling them to charge top dollar for advertising.

The independent TV stations have long been waging a campaign to abolish blanket licensing. They don't want to pay you through BMI, ASCAP, and SESAC for using your music. Although they represent only about one percent of their annual budget, the stations claim that blanket licenses are too expensive. They have introduced "source licensing bills" in the Congress and Senate which would require producers (the "source" of the shows) to be exclusively responsible for paying songwriters for the music before it's even performed (broadcast). This would deny continued payment for continued use.

Once the writer had been paid whatever could be negotiated with the producer, the show could be rerun for years without the writer ever seeing another cent. The courts have decided more than once that blanket licensing is the fairest and most efficient way to pay you for the use of your music. If the bills are passed, they will deprive songwriters of financial incentive to pursue writing as a career and ultimately deprive the world of some great music.

Revenues collected from dance clubs are charged according to their maximum legal room occupancy. Other clubs are charged a fee based on their annual entertainment expenses. Concert halls' charges are based on seating capacity and ticket prices. The American Hotel and Motel Association, The American Symphony Orchestra League, The Amusement Machine Operators of America, and The National Ballroom Operators Association all negotiate for their respective types of licenses. There is an annual fee for every jukebox. That money goes into a fund and is divided between the organizations. The organizations also license cable TV, colleges and universities, airlines, retail stores, and many other music users.

How do they know how many times a song is played? Each organization has its own method of determining the number of performances. BMI scientifically chooses a representative cross section of stations to sample each quarter. The stations supply a written record (log) of all music performed. The logs are put through an elaborate computer system which multiplies each performance listed by a factor that reflects the ratio of stations logged to the number of stations licensed. They then make a statistical projection that gives them a figure to approximate the number of "plays" on all stations. Different types or classes of stations are weighed in different ways.

ASCAP uses a method involving taping the stations for a given period of time, sending the tapes to a central place where expert listeners pick out the ASCAP songs, tally them, and make the statistical projections. Both methods have been developed by statistical experts, with the goal of finding cost-effective ways to get the information. The organizations strive to spend less money so that more may be distributed to their writer and publisher members. Both organizations operate on a nonprofit basis, distributing to their members all money not used for overhead. Both monitor all network TV performances by direct census from producers' cue sheets. For local TV they use a combination of sampling, cue sheets, and program listings. BMI accesses data similar to that used by over 110 regional editions of *TV Guide*, giving them a virtual census of all syndicated programs and motion pictures shown on local television. ASCAP uses the printed editions of *TV Guide*. Both BMI and ASCAP distribute foreign performance royalties through reciprocal agreements with foreign performing right societies.

SESAC, by far the smallest of the three, is a for-profit company and pays according to actual dollar value scaled to trade chart positions and pays flat fees for releases of songs on singles and albums. SESAC also analyzes national network and pay TV logs, though it does not have the resources of BMI and ASCAP to do in-depth surveys.

How much do you make each time it's played? It varies in both BMI and ASCAP according to the amount of income generated from all sources during the year or the quarter. Each has an equation that gives them an overall per-play figure based on the type of station, number of plays, and amount collected. BMI offers a bonus system which increases the value of a performance after the song attains certain performance levels. Performance royalties for a song that gets considerable air play (which can continue for many, many years) will generally amount to a great deal more than the money earned from mechanical royalties.

Do performing rights organizations give advances to writers and publishers? BMI and ASCAP are not currently giving advances. They had, prior to the "Buffalo Broadcasting" case, in which independent TV stations sued the organizations to challenge their ability to negotiate blanket licenses. BMI and ASCAP won the case, but did not resume giving advances.

The advances, based on anticipated air play, were a risky business for the organizations. They walked a fine line between giving you your money in advance of earning it and literally shortchanging other writers (collectively) by advancing you money that may not be recouped. They had to know if your song was a single, or album cut, with a major or new artist, if there was a major promotional effort and other factors to determine how much performance income you'd earn in the future.

How else do the organizations help songwriters? The more songs licensed by an organization that are receiving air play, the more money that organization can command in negotiations from the various users. The more money they receive, the more they can distribute to their members. So consequently the three are in competition with each other for actively productive members. So it's in their interest to try to help you before you need to decide which organization to join. If your material merits being published or produced whether you're an individual writer, writer/artist or a self-contained group writing your own material, they'll help you connect with publishers, producers, or record companies. Their representatives are always looking for great new songwriter, writer/artist, and film composer talent.

BMI sponsors the Los Angeles Songwriters Showcase established in 1971 to help educate and connect writers with the industry. ASCAP sponsors regular workshops, and both BMI and ASCAP offer grants to outstanding college student composers. Call the organizations and talk to them about what each offers.

Which is the best? That's the toughest question to answer because there are so many variables—one of the most important being your own needs. The big question is usually "Who pays more?"—a complicated question that depends somewhat on your unique situation. Talk to them all. Believe me, they'll leave no questions unanswered. But remember: How much they each pay may be the biggest question, but it's not the only one. How do they treat you? Is there someone there you can relate to? Do you feel comfortable calling with a question? Those are the considerations that precede your making money at all. The organization you join is your decision alone. Some publishers will automatically put you in one or the other for the mere reason that they prefer filling out one form over another. It's an important decision, however, so don't let anyone else make it for you.

Is there a charge to join? There is a $10 annual fee for a writer to be an ASCAP member. There is no fee to affiliate with BMI or SESAC.

What else do I need to know? Be sure to report any new songs that you have published or recorded to the clearance departments of your performing rights organization. The publisher should also do this, but make sure it's done, and done with the correct cowriting or copublishing percentages, if applicable.

BMI and ASCAP members may cowrite with one another. If the song is licensed by both organizations, each will pay its own writers and publishers. If there is no publisher involved in a song, a BMI writer can collect the full writer *and* publisher share of performance royalties.

Be sure to notify your organization immediately of any change of address so that you'll be sure to get your royalty checks!

BMI
320 W. 57th Street
New York, NY 10019
(212)586-2000

BMI
10 Music Square East
Nashville, TN 37203
(615)259-3625

BMI
8730 Sunset Blvd.
3rd Floor West
Los Angeles, CA
90069
(213)659-9109

ASCAP
1 Lincoln Plaza
New York, NY 10023
(212)595-3035

ASCAP
2 Music Square West
Nashville, TN 37203
(615)244-3936

ASCAP
6430 Sunset Blvd.
Hollywood, CA 90028
(213)466-7681

SESAC
156 W. 56th Street
New York, NY 10019
(212)586-1708

SESAC
55 Music Square East
Nashville, TN 37203
(615)320-0055

SYNCHRONIZATION ROYALTIES

Another important area of income for writers and publishers is the licensing of the right to record the music or song in synchronization (timed to the pictures in a film or TV movie) and the right to perform publicly (that is show in theatres, etc.) the music that's recorded under that "synch" right.

The film or TV producer is responsible for negotiating the synchronization and performance license with the copyright owner (usually the publisher). Several companies including the Harry Fox Agency, Inc. in New York; Copyright Management in Nashville; and the Clearing House in Los Angeles, negotiate synchronization rights between film producers and publishers.

The big question is always, how much money can be made from synch royalties? It's totally negotiable and depends largely on the previous popularity of the song and the way it's to be used. At the bottom rung are instrumental pieces used as background music. Next is "source music," the songs that come from a recognized source in the film such as a car radio or music in an elevator. Then there are featured performances in which we watch a rock band in the film perform a song, or listen to a theme that's prominently featured over the intro or end-credits. If the song has already been a hit and it's a perfect selection for that particular film, it's worth a lot. If it's an unknown song and there's a soundtrack album as well, it may be perceived in the negotiation that a lower "synch fee" might be worked out because the film's exposure of the song may benefit record sales, print, or other promotional areas. Fees are also based on the length of the song and whether it's used in a network or syndicated program.

The negotiations involve a producer's desire to obtain rights to as *many* possible uses for the *longest* possible time in the *most* territories. The copyright owner negotiates to limit them or obtain higher fees for additional time and uses. If you need an in-depth discussion of synchronization licenses including the information on foreign usage, consult the 1985 edition of *This Business of Music* (listed in the Bibliography).

The most common situation is that a film or TV producer asks you to compose a score or songs as a "work for hire" in which the production company becomes the "author" and publisher and which also automatically gives them the "synch rights." This doesn't mean, though, that you won't receive screen credit. That and the fee you receive are a part of your contract negotiations. It's possible, but very difficult, for an unknown writer to retain publishing rights for music in a film. Film companies will fight hard to get them and may not use the song at all if it looks as if they can't get them. From their point of view, having the rights saves them future negotiations for future uses and gives them lots of extra money if their movie helps to make your song a hit. Most of the cases I know in which the writer retained at least some publishing rights were those in which a well-known writer was approached to do the song or score and his/her "clout" helped, or the film company neglected to negotiate rights before mixing the music into the film, leaving the writer in a great negotiating position.

MUSIC IN PRINT

Most writers know little about print music. If you write mass-appeal songs, particularly adult contemporary, MOR, pop, or country, you'll be able to take advantage of a potentially lucrative print market. With the possible exception of the education market, though, the songs will have to become very popular records to make all those piano bar singers, Top 40 bands, and other print buyers want them. Ronny Schiff, an independent agent for print projects, has worked for some of the biggest print companies including Hansen, Warner Bros. Music, and Almo Publications (the latter is no longer in the print business). Here's her rundown on the types of print music publishing:

1. **Sheet Music:** piano/vocal arrangements, often with chord designations for other instruments.
2. **Personality Folio:** collections based on a name artist or writer, e.g., "The Songs of . . . ," "The . . . Songbook." These involve an additional contract called a "name and likeness" contract, which allows the print publisher to use the writer's or artist's name and/or picture. For example, Barry Manilow could negotiate a "name and likeness" contract if someone wanted to do a personality folio that included not only songs he wrote but songs by other writers that he'd popularized. The philosophy is that his picture on the cover will sell that sheet music or folio, whereas the writer's name won't always attract that attention.
3. **Matched Folio:** music from a particular album or musical theater show. These also involve a "name and likeness" contract.
4. **Mixed Folio:** collections based on concepts like "Easy Piano Tunes," "Hits of '87," etc., involving songs from several writers. "Peaceful Easy Feeling," Schiff says, was one of the most popular mixed folios.
5. **Educational:** included in this category are arrangements for choruses, marching bands, concert bands, jazz bands, and orchestras. These are obviously sold to schools, drill teams, drum and bugle corps, and the like. This market gives music great exposure beyond actual sales. How many times in school have you heard the same songs being practiced by the chorus or band? Multiply that by the number of listeners in schools and/or attending sports events, and you get an idea how much exposure is available there. Writers also receive royalties if their songs are used in a televised event or parade.

   The educational print market can be very lucrative, especially for jazz and pop writers. Five thousand copies for a marching band is a big sell. It doesn't sound so big until you realize that arrangements go for $12 to $25 and a publisher will get 10 to 12½ percent of the retail selling price. Choral arrangements of songs can be a good source of revenue, too. Some composers can sell 50,000 copies per year of a song that hasn't even been recorded! It's not unusual for popular choral writers to net $9,000-$10,000 a year for a single tune.

There are also freelance opportunities to compose and arrange for concert, jazz, and marching bands. Schools regularly buy arrangements of original songs as well as hits, but for this you need an understanding of the proficiency levels of different student groups so the parts aren't too difficult for them.

Another area of the educational market is "how to" books (*How to Play Bass Kazoo, Easy Gong Method,* etc.). This is a market for the songwriter who also has teaching skills to use. There's some demand for jazz "how tos," drum methods, and country and rock guitar techniques.

What does the publisher get in print royalties? Retail prices for print music, like everything else, continue to rise. Currently, sheet music publishers will pay your publisher up to 20 percent of the retail selling price. Folio publishers will pay about 12½ to 15 percent of the retail selling price. In cases where the folio contains songs by various writers, this income is pro-rated according to the total number of songs.

What does the writer get? My personal feeling is they get the short end of the stick.

The long-time practice in "standard" publishing contracts has been to offer the writer a "penny" value on sheet music sales, currently about six to ten cents per copy. This means that if your publisher can renegotiate his deal with the print company after a new version of your hit becomes popular, you may still be getting pennies a sheet from your old deal while his share goes up.

Try to negotiate 50 percent *of all royalties received by your publisher from all your print sales.* That way you remain equal partners in all royalties received. The 50 percent is based on a standard writer/publisher split, but should you be able to negotiate one more favorable to you (say, 60/40), the print deal should reflect the same split. Publishers have no justification for giving you less than a 50/50 split on your print deal. In some situations, a publisher may have to lay out some legal fees to negotiate a difficult deal with a print publisher, but that's part of the expense of running a publishing company, just like producing demos and mailing tapes.

RESEARCHING PRINT MUSIC DEALS

If you're a self-published writer or a music publisher, you'll need to have some idea of how to go about looking for and sizing up a prospective print publisher. In the early days, the primary avenue of exposure for songs was selling sheet music and arrangements to the "big bands" and to artists who sang live on radio. With the growing popularity of records, sheet music became dependent on the popularity and style of the recording. As music publishers became more involved in the recording industry, they became less interested in print music and began to contract with those equipped to specialize in print marketing and distribution. Print publishers are further specialized in two major areas: pop, which includes sheet music and folios; and educational, which deals with arrangements for chorus, marching bands, orchestras, school jazz groups, and the like.

Ronny Schiff believes the best method in looking for an effective pop print publisher is to drop in on a few sheet music stores and ask some questions:

How frequently are they serviced with new hit songs? You want a print publisher who calls the stores weekly and provides them with a list of the latest acquisitions. (There's heavy competition between print publishers for the rights to new hits.)

Does the print company keep sheet music in print or do they let it lapse after the song has peaked on the charts?

Is their artwork well done? Are the copies slick and professional?

Do they supply retailers with promotional aids, displays, and so forth?

From an artistic standpoint, you'll want to consider the accuracy of the piano/guitar/vocal copies. Compare them to the record. You'll want to work with a company that is consistently accurate. In negotiating a print deal, try to get a clause that grants you approval of the arrangements, but be reasonable about it. Don't hold up production if you're out of town. Have a friend check the print version out if you can't. Getting it out fast is important, but it's also important that people learn and play your song correctly.

Some writers believe its a disadvantage to have a contract with a print music company affiliated with a regular publishing company. The feeling is that priority will be given to songs signed to the company over those songs licensed from outside. Schiff believes that's a myth and that, in fact, you'll be included in folios of the company's top-selling writers and receive at least equal exposure.

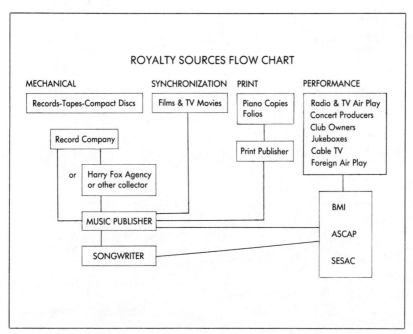

ROYALTY SOURCES FLOW CHART

You can negotiate an educational print deal separately from your pop print contract. To research the effectiveness of those educational market specialists, call on some high school and college band and choral directors and ask them which companies provide the best service and the best arrangements. When you talk to the educational print companies, ask if they do marching band and choral arrangements and ask to see the promotional packages they send to the schools. You'll want to be sure they'll promote your music aggressively.

A maze of deal points can be negotiated in both pop and educational markets, and all print companies have structured a variety of deals for a variety of situations. It's to your advantage to find an attorney or publisher who's knowledgeable and creative in the print area to help you negotiate your deals.

Publishing

The Copyright Law broadly defines "publication," as it refers to songwriting, as the reproduction of a song in the form of any kind of product, printed or recorded, and the offering of those products for sale to the public. The practical concept of music publishing, however, is a lot more complex than any legal definition or theory.

Mention "music publishing" to someone outside the business, and they're likely to associate it with print in the same way they'd think of a book publisher. The business of music publishing in America did, in fact, begin with the manufacture and sale of sheet music copies. But through decades of social, economic, and technological changes, the business evolved with the times. Currently, the sale of sheet music is only a small part of music publishing, and its actual manufacture and sale is carried out by a handful of "print publishers" licensed to do so by music companies whose duties, as we'll see, are now much broader.

Leonard Feist's book, *Popular Music Publishing in America,* traces the fascinating history of the business. Feist chronicles the role of the "songplugger" from the early 1900s in New York's "Tin Pan Alley," where most of the music publishers had their offices. In those days they performed the songs for vaudeville troupes who were putting together shows for their tours; for employees of music stores who, in turn, performed the songs for potential sheet music customers; and for anyone else who might influence sales.

Today, songpluggers are still in the front lines, only now, since the business centers mainly around records and films, they're playing songs (prerecorded on cassettes) for managers, record producers, recording artists, record company A&R personnel, and film music coordinators. Today they're called "professional managers" and songplugging is just one of their duties.

It's important to understand all that publishers do, whether you want them to pitch your songs to their contacts, or if you pitch your own songs but want to avail yourself of the other services publishers provide.

WHAT PUBLISHERS DO

Many different levels and types of activities come under the label of "publishing."

At its best, publishing demands imagination, creativity, intuition, tenacity, and good business sense. A publisher must be willing to make mistakes and face daily rejection of songs he believes in. A knowledge of how the music industry operates, a familiarity with the work of a great variety of recording artists (both established and new), are also required. It's a special combination of ingredients that makes a great publisher, and few have it all. Fortunately, in your own situation, you may not need all of these services or a publisher with all those qualities.

Publishers' activities fall into four categories: creative, promotional, business, and administrative.

Creative endeavors include screening new songs; meeting with new writers; visiting clubs, concerts, and recording studios to hear and make contact with new and established acts; critiquing and otherwise working with staff writers and independent writers who show promise; reviewing songs already in the catalogue; producing demo tapes; initiating or suggesting collaborations between staff writers or lyricists and producer/writers or artists; conceiving new uses for songs.

Promotional duties include calling producers, managers, agents, and A&R reps to learn what songs they need for their artists; reading music, film, and advertising trade magazines, periodicals and tip sheets to discover projects that may need material; making and mailing tape copies; producing lead sheets; conducting casting meetings with professional staffers and writers to determine which songs are appropriate for certain projects; maintaining files on producers, the songs they liked (or didn't), the songs they're holding and for how long; making calls to radio stations, record companies, and managers to work out ideas for promotion.

On the business side, publishers also hire personnel; establish company policies; negotiate contracts with writers, sub-publishers, music print publishers, and producers, artists, managers or film companies; initiate and maintain contacts with foreign sub-publishers; make decisions on "holds," and negotiate and grant licenses to users.

Under administrative duties, they file copyright forms; file notices with BMI, ASCAP, or SESAC for songs released for air play; file notices with agencies that collect mechanical royalties (for record and tape sales) or make collections from record companies themselves; do general accounting, financial planning, and tax accounting; compute and pay writers royalties.

There are other tasks that warrant a little more explanation:

Catalogue evaluation and purchase. This is the level at which the "heavy duty" deal-making machinery gets into gear. Companies merge or one major company buys another. Companies also acquire the catalogues (groups of songs owned by one company) or estates of individual writers. Paul McCartney bought the Buddy Holly catalogue, for instance. Some catalogues contain standards that will probably make money forever. Any time you turn on the radio, you'll hear oldies that are obviously still generating lots of performance royalties. Companies that own those songs are always being assessed by experts to determine their future earning power and looked upon as potential investments not only by other publishing companies but by international financiers.

The people involved in that level of activity aren't generally the ones who are assessing new talent off the street (so you won't have much contact with them), though some "street" experience in evaluating the commercial potential of songs is valuable to those predicting the future value of any catalogue.

Investing in the production of master tapes and the signing of new writer/artist talent is another level of activity that's becoming more and more common for those companies who can afford it. The companies look to sign promising writer/artists and self-contained groups. They'll produce masters and shop the tapes to record companies. Obviously, if they get a record deal, they'll own part to all of the publishing on all the songs their act records, which guarantees them an outlet for the songs and helps them expose the songs to other artists.

In a case like this, a publisher is often acting like a combination manager, producer, and publicist all rolled into one. Trying to find the right producer for an artist involves a knowledge of the work of many producers, playing the writer/artist's preliminary tapes for them, scheduling the project, negotiating the contracts and choosing the songs, studio, and musicians if necessary. After the masters are completed, it involves making appointments to play the tapes for key A&R people, putting together press kits, setting up showcases, and following up. It can also involve finding the act a manager.

These publishing/production deals can be a viable alternative for a writer/artist or group, depending on your situation. (See "Where Do You Start?," page 226.) Publishers are also very interested in signing writer/producers who have the potential to write for or with the artists those producers will be working with.

Writer development is another important aspect of a publishing company's work. The most common way that publishers do this is to sign writers exclusively to their staffs. (For more information, see "Staff Writing Positions," page 177.)

EXPLORING THE POSSIBILITIES

There are major companies who hire people to do individual tasks, and small independents who must, to some degree, do it all. Still others seem to be publishers in name only and, in effect, are "holding companies." This is often the case with managers or producers who use a song once with a particular artist and have no staff or time to exploit the song beyond that first use.

The use of a song is limited only by lack of imagination and perception. The bottom line for any publisher is to make money by finding as many uses as possible for the song. Obviously the big ones are through sales of records, tapes, and CDs, synchronization (the use of songs in films, TV, and video) and air play. If a song is successful in these areas, sheet music can be an additional source of revenue. The song might be suited to a choral or band arrangement for high schools and colleges. It also might have value in advertising, as part of a radio or TV commercial. Manufacturers of autos, audio equipment, and the like compile special tapes and records to demonstrate auto sound and stereo equipment. Public places such as restaurants, hotels, doctors' offices, elevators, and supermarkets use collections of songs for which royalties are paid. Manufacturers of music boxes, musical toys, and video games are also licensed to use appropriate songs. Greeting card manufacturers use song lyrics and electronic melodic devices—and there are more uses on the horizon.

It's not always enough just to be aware of those possibilities. A creative publisher will *initiate* uses for songs already in the company's catalogue and even generate new songs. For instance, the publisher might hear of a new children's book being written, and have his writers or outside writers tailor songs for an album that would be compatible. Instead of griping about how bad business is, publishers could actually be creating new business. Unfortunately there are very few like that around.

It's up to you, with the help of some advice, to assess your needs (they'll differ at different points in your career) and determine which kind of publisher works best for you, or if you should consider an alternative such as self-publishing.

FINDING A PUBLISHER

Though finding a publisher who believes in your material can be difficult, it could be your most important music industry contact.

In the major music centers there are many organizations that can give you information about publishers. The main organizations are listed in the following section, "Checking Out a Publisher." Beyond that, even outside the major music centers, if you hang out at songwriter organizations and events and college music business seminars, you'll get information from instructors and fellow songwriters. Read the trade magazines' *(Billboard* and *Cash Box)* list of publishers of hit songs. *Songwriter's Market* (published by Writer's Digest Books and available through most book stores) will give you profiles of companies open to listening to new songs including contact names, what they're looking for, and how to submit tapes.

MAJOR PUBLISHERS VS. INDEPENDENTS

In looking for a publisher, the most important elements to consider are the individual's credibility, whether he or she is independent or works for a major publishing company, and your own relationship with that person. Has he earned the respect of producers by consistently bringing them high-quality, appropriate songs for their projects? Does she respect you, love your songs, and believe you'll be successful? Those are the key questions.

Sometimes it's easier for a professional manager (with the emphasis, when you say it, on "professional") to open the doors of producers and artists if they have the name of a major company behind them. A major publisher may also have the cash flow to invest in master tapes and record promotion if you're a writer/artist.

The debate over whether to go with a small or large publisher usually gets around to the well-worn axiom that "A small company can give you more individual attention. You'll get lost in a big company." That's not always the case.

Depending on the ratio of professional staff to staff songwriters, you *can* get individual attention at major companies. By the same token, a small company may have so much to do that they don't have much time to spend working with you on a personal basis. It all depends on the company and the individuals there.

There are many small but aggressive independent publishers with great contacts and experience. Many independents formerly worked for major companies but wanted the autonomy of making their own business decisions. They may not have the cash flow to hire staff writers, but can do a great job on a "song by song" basis.

Major publishers are also interested in hearing new songs even though most of their "new" material comes from staff writers or from re-demoing old songs already in their catalogue. They're interested in keeping in touch with the "street" to get a feeling about new trends and to make sure they're not missing out on any hot new writers, writer/artists, or writer/producers. You may, however, find them less accessible than independents.

Many major publishers are affiliated with record companies. Is this a positive or a negative? Do the publishers hold off pitching songs to artists on other labels in favor of those on the affiliated label? No. Each of those companies has its own financial bottom line. Though the publisher will certainly attempt to get songs to artists on the "home" label, it's in his best interest to aggressively pitch them to other artists, as well. (There's also no guarantee that an artist on the affiliated label will record the songs.)

CHECKING OUT THE PUBLISHER

You're offered a contract by a publisher. Maybe you've submitted a song by mail. Questions rush through your mind. What if this publisher is a rip-off? What if he doesn't do anything with my song? How do I find out about him? Relax! If you want to know what the publisher has done in the past, you have every right to ask. He'll be glad to brag about his success. If he wants your song he should be able to sell you on his abilities.

He may tell you who he wants to pitch the song to but sometimes he won't—he's afraid you'll pitch it yourself, or he may not be able to reveal privileged information. Don't necessarily take reluctance as a sign of deviousness. You can negotiate a reversion clause in your contract (see "Negotiable Contract Clauses," page 166) so that if the publisher is unable to get your song recorded, you'll get it back.

If a publisher is just getting started and doesn't have much of a track record, it doesn't mean he can't do the job. Just ask him why he thinks he can do a good job for you, and get a reversion clause of two years or less. If he has few songs to pitch and is serious about the business, he'll be aggressive and, hopefully, will soon be able to give you a list of producers he's pitched your song to.

If you want to check out a specific publisher, you can call one of the national songwriter organizations. Check with the Los Angeles Songwriters Showcase or the National Academy of Songwriters if the publisher is in Los Angeles. Call the Nashville Songwriters Association in that city, and BMI, ASCAP, SESAC, or The Songwriters Guild of America at their respective offices. There may be someone in those organizations who can give you feedback about individual publishers or companies. There is no "Good Housekeeping Seal of Approval" for publishers except that songsharks (those who charge to publish your songs) are not allowed to be affiliated with ASCAP, BMI, or SESAC.

You can talk to other songwriters who have worked with the company. The problem with seeking someone else's approval is that one writer may badmouth a publisher for not getting a song recorded, and the next writer may praise the same publisher because her song *did* get recorded. It's hard to sort out these types of subjective evaluations when you don't know all the details. In the end, you have to do as much research as you can and use your own best judgment and choose a publisher who suits your individual needs.

WRITER/PUBLISHER Q&A

Is it good to send songs to a publisher by certified mail?

No, it scares them to death. They feel they're being set up for a lawsuit and they don't feel it's worth it to take a chance on accepting them. It's also inconvenient for both parties.

May I show my song to several publishers at once?

Yes, and you should. It is an ethical and common practice. You have a song you believe in and want everyone to have an opportunity to hear it. You also want feedback from as wide a range of publishers as possible.

What if more than one publisher says she wants it?

This is a "problem" you'll hope to have. Get more information from each of them. What are their recent successes? Will they give a reversion clause, pay for a demo, give you an advance? Who do they envision recording the song? Can they get to those artists? Let them know who else is interested. (Don't lie. They may know each other.) If you get satisfactory answers to all your questions but want to check them out further, tell them you want to think it over. If they pressure you to sign a contract immediately, walk away. Call other writers they publish and ask about their reputations.

If I have a publisher, is it okay if I also show my songs to producers?

Yes, you should. The publisher will probably appreciate the help. After all, he gets his cut whether he gets the song recorded or you do. Remember to let him know what you're planning, so you don't both promise the same song to different producers. The publisher may also be able to help you get in the door or provide useful info about the producer you want to pitch to.

GETTING FEEDBACK FROM A PUBLISHER

I often ask writers how they've been received by publishers I know. Though I've heard stories about publishers who were long on ego abuse, in all fairness, that's a rarity. It's not as rare, though, for publishers to avoid offering any feedback or constructive criticism. More often they give a stock answer: "That's not the type of song we're looking for," "I wouldn't know who'd record a song like that," "I don't think the song is marketable." All those lines, though probably true, don't help you know how to write better or more marketable songs. I decided to ask some publishers why this is the case and got some fairly typical responses.

One publisher said, "I won't give writers a critique anymore unless they're very close to writing hit songs and I know I want to get involved as their publisher. Otherwise, it's more hassle than it's worth. I used to do it all the time because I wanted to help, but I stepped on too many egos and got into arguments. Songwriters don't really want to be criticized. Even when they ask for it, they just argue with me."

On the other hand, he said, "Bob [a writer we both knew] is the kind of writer I *will* work with. He's come a long way because he listens. The first time I heard his tunes I knew he had a basic grip on how to write a good song. I told him one of the tunes was close but I thought it would be stronger with a bridge. Next day he came back with two different versions of a bridge and we published it and got it recorded. He didn't say, 'What do you mean, it needs a bridge? I wrote it without a bridge and it sounds okay to me!' He just gave it a shot and because he did, we both won."

Another publisher explained, "Hey, if I wanted to spend all my time teaching people how to write songs, I wouldn't have time to deal with the songs I'm already committed to. Besides, most writers don't even want to hear it!"

Len Chandler and I once suggested to a writer a change we felt would clarify a particular lyric. The writer couldn't believe his song was being critiqued and replied incredulously, "But I wrote that song in *Topanga Canyon!*" To that writer, the act of writing the song was akin to receiving a sacred message from the Great Spirit. To suggest any change by himself or someone else was unthinkable.

I'm not going to tell you that it's wrong to feel so personally about your songs, or that you should operate with the attitude that there's something wrong with your songs and all you have to do is find some publisher to tell you what it is. That's destructive to your self-esteem and, in music, you need all the self-esteem you can get. But it's also self-destructive to assume you have nothing to learn from anyone. Nothing will stop your creative and professional growth more surely than that. You need to be able to look at feedback from industry pros as an *opportunity to learn* either or both of two important things. (1) You can learn something valuable about improving that song, about writing in general or writing more commercially in particular. (2) You can learn about the needs and tastes of that particular person, so even if you decide not to act on the criticism, you'll have learned what to bring or what not to bring that publisher or producer next time.

In any case, you need to at least be receptive to criticism and to know that most industry people won't even bother to give it unless they think you have enough talent to begin with. If you're defensive and argumentative, you may have a problem finding a publisher who will want to work with you. There are simply too many other good writers around who *are* open to criticism and willing to rewrite.

There's another angle to this that should also be brought out. Publishers aren't infallible, and you don't need to believe their every opinion as gospel. You'll definitely find, in going from one publisher to another, a great diversity of tastes and opinions. Pay attention to the criticism and don't let their experience and willingness to help go to waste. You may learn more from those you disagree with than you will from those who see things the way you do. You need them both. Those who agree will give you support and confidence. Those who challenge you, especially if they're articulate about it, can give you the opportunity to grow.

UNCONTRACTED SONG PLUGGING

Songplugging without a contract is a practice that writers occasionally ask me about and wonder how to deal with. Most publishers want a contract, at least a letter of intent, before they commit their time and energy to pitching your song. But for those who don't, here's how it works.

A publisher might say, "Just let me run with your song for a month, six months, or whatever you agree to, without a contract, and see what happens. If I can get you a record on it, I get the publishing. If not, you've got the song back." The publisher may suggest this for a variety of reasons:

(1) He doesn't want to sign your song, not be able to do anything with it, and have you hounding him forever.

(2) He's not sure enough about the song to commit his money or his company's money to do demos, copies, and all the attendant things that go with it.

(3) He has a specific artist in mind for the song and if it's rejected he doesn't know anyone else who would cut it.

In any case he's trusting you not to take it to another publisher and allowing you to get the song back if he can't get it recorded. The danger of *not* having the deal on paper is that one of you may forget the terms of the agreement. Make sure you clarify what happens if an artist or producer puts a *hold* on the song (asks that the publisher not show it to anyone else for a period to give him a chance to cut it or decide if he will cut it). The producer may want to hold the song for longer than you had originally agreed with the publisher. Fairness would dictate that you wait, along with the publisher, until the producer makes up his mind. Since the publisher made the initial contact with the producer, it would be unethical of you to take it to other publishers or publish it yourself. Remember that the music business is like a small town, and word gets around if you abuse the trust people place in you.

It often happens that a publisher won't ask you not to show it to other publishers because he assumes you know the ethics involved and doesn't want to insult you by suggesting your ignorance. But writers who know little about the publisher's job, or the industry in general, may not even consider that there's an ethic involved here. They may actually look at the situation as an adversarial relationship rather than a partnership to be built on mutual respect. (See "Ethics in the Biz," page 237.) I've run across several writers in the past couple of years who told me, quite innocently, that they planned to let several publishers try to market the song, or said "I'll let publisher 'A' run with the tune for a couple of weeks and if he doesn't get anything happening I'll take it to publisher 'B,' who's also interested." The problem was that he hadn't told publisher "A" that he intended to do that.

Imagine what would happen if both publishers pitched the song to the same producer. In other words, they'd both be doing their job as publishers on your behalf, using their hard-earned expertise and credibility. Suppose the producer likes the tune for his artist and wants to cut it immediately. If the producer realizes that both publishers pitched him the tune, he'll probably call both publishers and tell them. They aren't going to be happy about your game, but if you don't have contracts with either, they both might want you to sign one immediately. There's also a good chance that the producer will want to sign the song to his own company.

Who will you choose, and what do you tell the other publisher, who may have worked as hard for you? If you had a contract with "A" and none with "B" then "A" is the winner and "B" is mad at you for using him unethically. "B" assumes you knew your contract with "A" gave "A" *exclusive* right to publish your song. (He may also decide that he'll never again pitch a song without a contract.) If you're unfortunate enough to have signed contracts with both "A" and "B" on the same song, you're in serious legal trouble, because you're lying on the contract when you gave exclusivity to two publishers at once. Would you sell your car to two different people? Basically, the rule of thumb is "Be up front." Let everyone know what's going on. If a publisher wants to plug your song without a contract, agree on a specific period in which no one else will plug the song, and stick to it!

SINGLE-SONG CONTRACTS

Songwriter-publisher contracts covering one song are the ones you'll most frequently come in contact with as a songwriter. I use the plural because there are probably hundreds of different single-song contracts that say "standard" at the top of the page. Publishers come up with these contracts in various ways. Some come right "off the rack" from music supply stores. Some publishers will get a contract from their attorney and work out modifications based on that publisher's philosophy of doing business. Well-established companies will have contracts that they've developed over the years. The only things you can count on as "standard" are that, if a publisher hands you a contract, it will be biased to the publisher's advantage, and that it will be negotiable. Don't ever believe that because a contract's typeset and says it's "standard," that it can't be changed.

How contracts are worded and how they can be negotiated are very important areas to explore. Paranoia is common among songwriters due to a lack of understanding about contract clauses and how to negotiate them. Most of that fear persists because the songwriters don't always understand the reasons why some of the clauses exist. Many deals have gone out the window because a writer has been told never to accept this or that deal point.

NEGOTIABLE CONTRACT CLAUSES

The National Academy of Songwriters (NAS) has published a list of song-by-song contract recommendations that I'll use as a basis for discussion. I'll talk about each contract clause in an effort to illuminate some pros and cons.

NAS cautioned that the recommendations are "suggestions to some of the negotiable points in certain songwriter contracts. Ability to obtain these recommendations depends on the bargaining strength of the writer." I'll add that I'm not an attorney and, not knowing your individual situation, I can't advise you about what clauses I think would be more or less important in your specific circumstance. I *can* discuss what I feel are the important issues from both sides so you can look at this agreement with some perspective. The best advice always is to have a music business attorney look over your contract. Also keep in mind that although a single song contract is important, unless you think this is the only publishable song you'll ever write, it's not exactly the end of your creative career if you can't get all the clauses recommended here. You will need to be flexible.

What makes negotiating so crazy is that it's difficult to get any perspective about your bargaining strength. Even if you've been successful in the past, your current material will be judged for its commercial potential in *today's* market. The only thing you can do is try to negotiate these clauses to your own advantage and hope for the best, keeping in mind that the best contract is one in which each party's needs have been addressed and neither party feels he's been "had."

Reversion for non-publication. In the event no commercial recording is released within a year—no more than two years—the copyright ownership should be reassigned to the writer. The reversion clause was introduced on behalf of writers many years ago by the American Guild of Authors and Composers (AGAC), now The Songwriters Guild of America, in their model writer-oriented contract. It's always been a bone of contention with publishers, but the past few years have seen most publishers accepting it in order to be competitive. It also keeps disgruntled writers off their backs if they're not getting their song cut. The length of time granted to the publisher is a major negotiating point in this clause. It can be any length you agree on, but it commonly runs as short as six months or as long, in current practice, as three years. Personally, I agree with NAS that two years should be adequate. Six months or a year is not always enough time for publishers, for several practical reasons. It frequently happens that an act may be interested in a song but won't be recording again for another six months. Touring commitments or other circumstances may delay the recording *or even the release* of the record. If that were to happen, then technically, the writer could get her song back and take the publishing credit herself after the record was later released, leaving the publisher with no reward for the job done. That fact has soured publishers on short reversion periods, unless they know they're hitting the one or two acts most likely to cut the tune at a time when they're in the studio and looking for songs.

A producer may also put an "exclusive hold" on the song, asking the publisher to refrain from pitching it to anyone else until a final decision is made. That "hold" may last weeks or months.

The producer may also have collected fifteen or twenty songs as possibilities for the project, whittled them down to ten, and your song gets whittled out. Or, it might actually get recorded but fail to live up to the expectations of the producer, artist, or label and end up "in the can" (not released) as they say. The record might be released someday, but by that time, the reversion period is up and the publisher has had to return the song to the writer.

So, you see, publishers face problems with short reversion periods. Given that, I feel it would be fair to negotiate a one- or two-year reversion clause with the stipulation that the period be extended for the length of time a producer has the song on "hold." (This, of course, would require an agreement in writing between the publisher and producer as well.)

By the time the reversion period is up, the writer should also have had adequate opportunity to assess the amount of activity the publisher has expended on the song. If the writer sees that the publisher has been taking care of business, she should grant the publisher an additional reversion period.

Early in the history of this clause, some publishers would subvert its intent by pressing up a few copies of the demo, sending them to radio stations, and say, "Okay, I released the song on a record, so that means I can keep the publishing." Currently, the wording goes an extra step by saying the publisher is responsible for the song's "commercial recording and release for distribution and sale to the public."

There are other reasons for a song to revert back to the writer besides the inability of the publisher to get it recorded. The clause can prevent the publisher from reassigning your copyright to another individual or company without your consent. Or you can also have the song revert back to you if the publisher refuses to allow you or your representative to audit his books regarding royalties.

Be sure your contract states that at the end of the reversion period, the song automatically reverts to you without requiring you to send a registered letter by a certain time to demand it.

If royalties are not paid fairly and/or on time, the copyright should revert to the writer. This recommendation can make publishers very nervous since everyone is aware of the possibility, even probability, of mistakes and delays. A change of accounting personnel, computer errors, fire, vandalism—any number of other disasters could blow ownership of copyright. Frankly, your chances of getting this clause are zilch. This recommendation stems from the point of view that a writer should be able to protect herself in the event that a publisher tries to deliberately cheat. It provides an automatic "out" for a writer without the necessity of costly litigation. Proving that royalties are paid "unfairly," however, may involve an audit of the publisher's books, an expense to you. If, by some miracle or the power of your negotiating position, you could obtain this clause, it carries with it the responsibility that you be very discreet and understand its application. New writers, in particular, can sometimes be paranoid, expecting a rip-off at every turn and jumping to conclusions too quickly. The possibility then is that a publisher will ask, "Why should we put any more work into this song when it looks like the writer is eventually going to find some excuse to get the copyright back from us?" So it behooves you to be careful about making threats and accusations. With such a big stick to wield, you can afford to speak softly in reminding them of an overdue payment or apparent discrepancy.

Mechanical Royalty Rates. A publisher may not grant a licensee a rate lower than the current statutory rate without the prior consent of the writer. (See chapter 9, "Where Your Money Comes From.")

It's wise to have such a clause added to the contract. This practice of allowing a company to pay you less than the statutory rate is called "giving a rate." The rate refers to the current mechanical rate effective at the time the license is granted to the record company for use of the song.

Here's the problem that prompted this clause. Let's say, hypothetically, that your publisher has interested an artist in your song and the record company says, "We'd like Sally Superstar to record the song you brought us, but we don't want to pay the current rate. Would you allow us to pay only three quarters of the rate if I give you (a) two songs on her next album (also at three quarters of the rate), (b) the B-side of her next single." Any combination of the above or any other negotiable item they can think of could be offered. Some of these suggestions may be acceptable to the publisher because he represents many other songwriters and is involved in a lot of other projects. But none of those suggestions are in your best interest. If Sally's record, with your song on it, is a hit, the quarter of the rate given up could add up to some very big bucks. On a million-seller, the difference between the mechanical royalties on a full rate cut and a three quarter rate cut is $12,500.

To be fair, giving a record company a break on rates might benefit your publisher's business as a whole, but, generally speaking, you can be sure that publishing companies do not want to negotiate rates. They want the maximum, just like you do, but will occasionally make concessions in order to get the songs cut, which naturally benefits you, too.

The issue here is whether or not you have the right to be a part of the publisher's decision. It probably wouldn't be difficult for the publisher to convince you of the wisdom in his approach if, indeed, it was the best deal he could make on your behalf. This clause may be difficult to get for obvious reasons. Without it, you need to have a lot of faith and trust in your publisher. Record companies will usually try to "get a rate" whenever and however they can, which makes it tough on both publishers *and* writers. (See "Controlled Composition Clauses," page 147.) One of the things publishers object to about this clause is that they may not have a lot of time to make a decision on rates and if you're in an ashram in India, they don't want to have to call in the FBI to find you. Make sure you're always easy for them to locate.

If you can't get the clause, you should at least get one that limits the reduction to a three quarter rate. The clause should also state that no less than the full statutory rate should apply to licenses granted to any "person or business entity owned, controlled or affiliated, in whole or in part, by or with the publisher," because there's the chance that an unscrupulous publisher might give a *very* low rate to an affiliated record label.

Writers royalties should be paid within 30 days—no more than 60 days—after receipt by the publisher. Statements should show computation in reasonable detail and writer should have the right to audit the publisher.

Since a major problem for publishers is timely payment of royalties *to* them *from* record companies, you'd think that publishers might be a little more conscientious when it comes to timely payments to their writers. Though many publishers do pay like clockwork, a lot of others play the same games record companies play, the main one being to hold on to your money to build up interest. One of their most common dodges is, "We don't seem to have a current address on you; you must have moved." All too often, that excuse is really true, pointing out again the importance of making sure that when you move or change phone numbers, you notify your publisher.

Most publishers prefer a quarterly or semiannual pay period and many now insist on paying 90 days after the end of each six-month period, to simplify and organize their accounting routines. Big publishing companies often have such huge volumes of paperwork that it would be hard for them to change their pay schedules to accommodate individual writers. (It's my belief, however, that computerization might make that possibility more feasible.)

Regardless of the publisher's problems, however, it's *your* money he's holding and it could be in *your* bank account earning interest for *you.* One clause you might get if you've got enough clout is an agreement in which the publisher pays you the prevailing interest rate on your money for the length of time he keeps it *beyond* the agreed pay period. This would discourage any interest-earning motivation. On their side, they shouldn't be responsible for paying that interest past the time they actually send that payment to your last known address. If it gets returned to them "address unknown," that's *your* problem.

NAS further suggests that statements should show computation in reasonable detail. But what's "reasonable"? Reasonable and ideal are a long way apart. Ideally, the statement would show:

a) Names of songs for which you're being paid royalties;

b) Names of artists, albums, or singles and record companies on which the songs appear (if there is more than one recording);
c) Number of units sold on which the royalties are based;
d) Date of receipt from the record company;
e) Whether the royalties are from foreign or domestic sources;
f) Itemized deductions, if applied, for demo costs, mailings, advances, and other publishing expenses.

Now, when we return from dreamland, we find that we're lucky if it shows essential items a) and e). Part of the problem is that record companies all seem to have different methods of reporting information to publishers. That lack of standardization makes it difficult for publishers to promise to give *you* that info. It's not in the record companies' best interests to give publishers that much detail because the vaguer they are the harder it is to accurately trace your royalties. Companies also usually lack the manpower needed to give you that detail. All in all, it doesn't seem practical to insist on an elaborate statement.

So, the big question is, "How do you know you're getting paid what you're due?" You make sure that, in your contract, you have a clause that gives you or your accountant the right to audit the publisher's books. It's a standard clause in all contracts, and if it's refused, you can always take your business elsewhere. If you do decide you want an audit, find an accountant who specializes in them. This procedure is expensive, so it's usually only done in situations in which large numbers of record, tape, and CD sales are involved. Unless you've got a hit, the cost of hiring an accountant to do an audit may not be justified by what he'll turn up in extra royalties. So, short of that approach, you should be able to speak to your publisher or your publisher's accounting department for an explanation of your royalty statement.

Unless you have reason to doubt your publisher's competence on the business end, you can be reasonably assured that everything possible is being done by the publisher to collect from the record companies. The publisher should be using a mechanical rights licensing organization (see "Mechanical Royalties," page 145) to collect what's due. Those organizations will audit the record companies on behalf of the publisher.

If you have doubts about the sales figures on which your publisher is basing royalties, here are some ways for you to get an *approximate* indication. If the song has a cowriter who's with another publishing company, you could check to see what that writer received. Others whose sales figures you could check would be the artist who recorded the song, his or her manager, the record company (slim chance to see their figures unless you have a friend in the accounting department) or the writers and/or publishers of other songs on the same album. Other writers may have more or fewer deductions on different percentages of those royalties, so at best, you'll get a rough "guestimate" from this type of search. I should add that there's no reason any of those people should feel obligated to give you that information, so be diplomatic about asking. However, they may also be interested in knowing *your* figures, too.

You could also do a little detective work by trying to find out from the pressing plant how many albums were pressed. (Don't forget to check on foreign pressing plants, too.) To get any close-to-accurate figures on actual sales (on which you're paid), though, you'll have to wait to subtract the "returns," records returned to the company that retailers haven't been able to sell. It usually takes about nine months before those records are returned.

In regard to changes in title, words, or music, NAS recommends, *No changes should be made without the approval of the writer.* Here's a scenario that illustrates the value of this type of clause. You have a contract with a publisher on a song. The publisher pitches the song to an artist. The artist wants a piece of the publishing before he records the song, but the publisher refuses. The artist says, "I basically love the song and I'll record it, but I think the second verse is weak and I'd like to rewrite it. Of course, I'll have to have half of the writer's royalties to do that." The publisher says to himself, "What the heck. I still get all my publishing and the writer should be grateful that he gets co-writing credit with this famous artist. I'll go for it."

Your second verse may not have been bad at all. The artist may write a terrible second verse and destroy the integrity of your song (which *you* have to live with), or make it so personalized that no one else would want to record it. If the publisher had refused and had stuck to his guns, the artist might have recorded it anyway. If the artist genuinely felt the second verse was weak and could explain why, *you* should have been offered the first opportunity to rewrite it. This publisher has just deprived you of half your writer's share of royalties and will come back to you and say, "100% of nothing is nothing. I thought you'd be glad to get half of what could be a big writer's royalty." This may be a compromise you're willing to make, but the fact is that without this clause in your contract he has every right to do just what he did without your permission.

There have also been cases in which a publisher/writer with greed and a big ego wants his name on your song as cowriter and will put it there on the flimsiest of justifications. He may decide to change your title, change a couple of words here and there, change a melody line, and cut himself in as a cowriter without your permission. The publisher may also insist on unnecessary changes in your song if he's getting flak from his staff writer(s) for signing an "outside" song (from a nonstaff writer) and to appease them, he might have one of them "rewrite" the song and take cowriter credit!

Those are some of the situations that happen. When those types of proposals are made *before* the song is signed to a publisher, you have the choice to forget it or to go along for the sake of your career. The reason to include a "no change" clause is to make sure you still have that choice *after* the contract is signed. And if a cowriter is still forced on you under any of the above circumstances, there should at least be a clause that provides that no more than 50 percent of your writer's royalties can be split with anyone else.

Sometimes a publisher will want to take writer credits himself. It's a part of a publisher's job to help inspire, guide, edit, critique, and make suggestions for writers. If *you,* the writer, feel that the creative contributions of the publisher are substantial enough to warrant inclusion as a cowriter, then *you* should offer it. There are times, of course, when the publisher does deserve a writer credit, so if you see a publisher's name on a song, you should reserve your judgment about how it got there until you know the real story.

You might ask why a publisher would not want to give you a "no change" clause if he's such a good guy. Well, here's another scenario. The publisher gets a hot tip that a major artist is finishing up an album and a couple of her songs didn't turn out so well at the session, or the artist decided the songs weren't right after all. The publisher remembers your song and rushes over. The producer loves it and so does the artist *except* that a) she wants the melody to be a little more rangey to show off her voice, b) it was written as a man's song and a couple of lines therefore need to be changed and c) the title has to be changed too, to reflect all the other changes. They want to do it *right now.* The publisher calls the last number he had for you and it's disconnected or you're out of town and can't be reached. The publisher, at that point, has to risk losing the cut and incurring your wrath for it or risk your taking back the copyright because he allowed the change without your permission. Chances are the publisher will risk the latter and pray that you don't turn out to be an ungrateful person.

As an aside here, it should be mentioned that most publishers will insist on excluding foreign translations and new foreign versions from any prohibition on changes or royalty reductions.

Addition of lyrics. On occasion, when a promising instrumental is assigned to a publisher, cowriters have been added, thus reducing the royalties to the composer. Lyrics should not be added to an instrumental without consent of the composer.

This situation is a lot like the one I just described. Very seldom does an instrumental become a hit, unless it's a movie theme. The commercial viability of the piece may be enhanced appreciably with a great lyric. The right lyric is very important though. Some great instrumentals could easily be trivialized and cheapened by any lyric, let alone a bad one. Many dynamic orchestrations can be written for an instrumental without having to be conscious of "leaving space" for the vocals. Also, without language barriers, an instrumental can be internationally successful. So there are a lot of factors to consider. I believe the original writer, with the input of the publisher, should have the last word on which, if any, lyric should be written for his or her melody.

Publisher's collection fees. It is customary for the publisher to deduct a portion of the commission paid to the Harry Fox Agency (or other collection agencies) from writer's royalties. The percentage paid the agency is 4½ percent (in 1987). No more than half that fee should be paid by the writer.

Many publishers feel that it's their responsibility to assume all administration costs such as these agency fees. An exception would be in the case of a copublishing agreement between the publisher and the publishing company owned by the writer, in which case, those fees could be split. The writer should never be asked to assume complete payment of the fees, but it's not unfair to split it between writer and publisher if it's agreeable to the writer.

Demo costs. On occasion, publishers will charge the cost of making demos against writer's royalties. The publisher should absorb the costs, or the amount charged to the writer should not exceed 50 percent. Also, demos may not be used as commercial recordings.

What's happening more and more is that writers are approaching publishers with good, appropriate demos—complete and already paid for. In that situation, I think the publisher should pay you up front for all, or at least half, of the demo costs you incurred. Your negotiating position on this point may be weakened if you're also asking for a reversion clause. Most publishers are reluctant to lay out cash on a song if there's a chance they'll have to give the song back to you. They'll have to spend money anyway on postage, tape copies, phone calls, and all that's necessary to promote the song, and they want to minimize their risk. I believe that a reversion clause is more important than front money in general, but that depends on how badly you need the bucks. If you can't get them to pay you for your demo right away *and* give you a reversion, negotiate to have them reimburse you for your demo when they get the song recorded.

As for demos being used as commercial recordings, today's technology makes it possible to create master-quality demos in a home studio that can and are used as commercial recordings and in films and TV. In fact, it's an advantage for you to have master/demos if you have opportunities to get songs into films and TV movies. Film and TV producers and directors, especially in low-budget productions, like to have something ready-made. They don't have to gamble on how well it'll turn out. They may also pay less to get the synch rights from you or your publisher than they would to produce something from scratch. You don't want the tracks and vocals to be used without your permission. A fee should go to the producer, and if other singers and musicians were used (unless you did it all by yourself) they should also be paid for this additional use. In fact, if the company wanting to use your masters is a union signatory, and if there were union musicians on your original session, those players must be paid union scale for the new use.

Where a contract does not specify the percentage of royalties to be paid the writer for a particular use, the writer should receive 50 percent of the publisher's receipts for that use (i.e., synchronization licenses, foreign licenses). As I write this, somewhere in the Silicon Valley or in some kid's basement, a whole new technology is being developed for delivering music to the public. In fact, many in the industry believe that vinyl records will be obsolete by the mid 1990s. Compact Disc (CD) and Digital Audio Tape (DAT) technology are succeeding them as the primary information and music storage and delivery systems. With every innovation, however, new problems arise in getting writers their share of royalties. Every new system, to be fair, should have a built-in method of monitoring its sale and/or use and a way to compute royalties. We're now wrestling with the problem of assessing and collecting royalties on cable TV music use and home video cassette rentals. You can bet the publishers are doing everything possible to make sure that they're able to collect on these uses and new ones to come. It's in your best interest to make sure your contract covers these uses, too. If it does not include *"any other use now existing or used in the future from which the publisher receives royalties,"* you may be out of luck. If that clause isn't in there, the publisher doesn't have to pay you for a use that's not listed on your contract.

Adding that all-inclusive clause with a specified percentage (it shouldn't be less than 50 percent) will make sure you share in the wealth.

Division of writer royalties. The writers' share of royalties is not necessarily divided equally. Percentages can be predicated on the value of each writer's contribution.

Royalties can be divided between several cowriters of a song any way you choose. It must be specified for the benefit of the publisher and of the performing rights societies (BMI, ASCAP, SESAC) so they'll know how much to pay you and your cowriters (see chapter 7, "Collaboration").

Limitation of assignment by the publisher. The writer must be notified if the publisher assigns any of his or her copyrights to someone else.

Strictly speaking, NAS's explanation only says that the writer must be notified *after* the copyright has been assigned to someone else and does not deal with limitations. Limitation would mean that the original publisher *can't* transfer the copyright (though they own it) to anyone else without your permission. Limitation is a tough clause to get because, if your song is successful, it makes the publisher's catalogue valuable and sought after. It should be much easier, however, to get a clause requesting notification of the transfer after the fact. You have a right to know the whereabouts of your child. If the song was not successful with the first publisher, you may be able to generate the interest of the new owner to actively promote it.

OTHER NEGOTIABLE CONTRACT CLAUSES
There are additional clauses and wordings you should watch for in song-by-song contracts.

1. "No royalties will be paid for ... *copies disposed of as new issues...*" It's common practice in print music to send *new issues* of all new sheet music to dealers to let them check it out. Publishers will get paid for it by the print publishers with whom they sub-contract but, with this clause, you, the writer, won't. This clause is usually connected with a clause that mentions not getting paid for *promotional copies* of records, which your publisher will *not* get paid for, so it's all right to leave it in. But make sure *new issues* gets deleted.
2. Instead of the traditional 5¢-10¢ (you'll be asked to take) for "regular piano copies," or "dance orchestrations," you should get 50 percent of what the publisher receives.
3. "Publisher shall *reasonably* pro rate such royalties ..." Watch out

for vague language. "Reasonable" to the publisher may not be reasonable to you. Pro-ratio formulas should be specifically defined, for example: "In such event, the royalties payable to writer shall be computed by a fraction, the numerator of which shall be one (representing the writer's song) and the denominator of which shall be the total number of copyrighted musical compositions contained in the (folio, book, etc.)."

4. "A royalty of _____ percent of the *net* cash proceeds . . ." Always make sure that you have, spelled out, what *net* means. Does it mean after *administrative* costs? If so, forget it. It's the publisher's *job* to administer and those costs should not be deducted "off the top" (from the gross) before your writer's royalties are paid. If you're co-publishing the song, though, it's certainly fair to split the costs between your company and theirs.

Does net mean after demo costs? That should be something you agree to, through discussion. Do they mean after promotional costs? Again, those costs may include the publisher's flying cross-country to pitch the song, also part of his job. Be sure to get it spelled out.

YOUR CHANCES FOR ADVANCES

An advance is, essentially, money paid to you before it's been earned. One of the big questions when you negotiate any contract (whether a single song, a staff writing contract, or recording contract) is "How much of an advance can I get?" A couple of general philosophies operate regarding advance money. One is that the more money a company puts out in advances, the more committed they are to recouping it, so naturally they'll work harder. But only to a point. And once a company decides that your project is a loser, another philosophy may kick in, called "don't throw good money after bad." They'll just stop trying. An advance may be the only money you'll see on the deal if they drop your project.

A philosophy you'll hear from small independent publishers is "instead of giving you an advance, I spend that money doing great demos and other things that will help us both make more money in the long run." In that situation, you have to rely on a most important consideration, which is whether you feel the publisher can do the job for you. Starving to death is also an important consideration, but I would hope you have enough sense to get a day job rather than relying on single-song advances to keep you alive.

VARIABLES REGARDING ADVANCES

Here are some variables to consider regarding cash advances in a writer/publisher deal.

An advance is money paid ahead of time against future royalties, not a payment for the song. The money they give you now comes off the top of any future royalties due you. Despite this fact, I'm surprised at the writers I talk to who are very upset a couple of years down the road when their statement from the publisher doesn't yield them a check. They've conveniently forgotten that the publisher will pay himself back for the advance. The computer doesn't forget!

Reversion clauses in your publishing contract may be affected by an advance. The most common reversion clauses state that if a publisher does not obtain a nationally released recording of your song within a specified period of time (e.g., two years), the publishing rights revert (return) to you. Such a clause ensures that if the publishers don't do the job for you, you can take your song elsewhere and it won't sit in their files forever with nothing happening.

So how does it relate to advances? Here's the basic principle. The more money a publisher puts out in front, before actually getting a record cut on the song, the more he gambles. So he is not going to want to give you back the song *and* lose the money if the song doesn't get recorded. Oh yes, he can just write it off, but of course, he'd rather not. If the song never earns money, you're not expected to pay back the advance. So he will probably tell you that he can't give you a reversion clause if he gives you an advance. That's just a good business practice. However, you should try to get both.

Remember though, that if someone working for a major publishing company offers you an advance, it's not their own money and there's a company budget for those expenses. A small, independent publisher doesn't get a salary. If he doesn't get songs recorded, he doesn't eat, and that advance would come directly out of his pocket. He's less likely to give you one for that reason. You may be able to get both an advance and a reversion clause if you agree to return the advance if the song reverts. Some publishers will even want you to pay back their demo expenses on reversion.

Going in with a good demo enhances your chances. Based on the same principle as above, if you go to a publisher with a good, usable demo and that saves him the cost of producing it ($100 to over $4000), you're in a much better position to ask for an advance. You're also in a much better position to ask for a reversion clause but you still may have to decide between the clause and an advance. It's a good idea to ask for at least enough of an advance to cover your demo costs.

If you want to keep a part of the publishing, they're unlikely to want to give you an advance. Here again, you're reducing the potential income for them because they'll now only be keeping a portion of the publishing royalties. In fact, they're likely to ask you to split the demo costs if you want to split the income. Not unreasonable at all, because you'll be business partners.

Writers under exclusive contract receive not a weekly *salary* but a weekly *advance* against future writer's royalties, and there's very little chance of their getting a reversion clause. They want every song you write during the term of the contract and previous to it. (A discussion of "Staff Writing Positions" follows.)

How much of an advance can you get? Whatever you can negotiate. Ultimately, everything depends on how badly the publisher wants the song and how much he feels he can afford to give you. The risk is that you'll take it somewhere else if he doesn't give you what you need. If you need an advance, you should ask for it, but the enthusiasm of the publisher and his willingness to give you a reversion clause are ultimately worth more. Publishers' ability to assess the commercial viability of your song is their game, and if you raise the stakes they lose more if they're wrong. Bear it in mind since they're bound to hit a limit at some point. Be prepared to be flexible.

STAFF WRITING POSITIONS

A staff writer may be at one company for several years. During that time, all the songs he or she writes become the property of the publisher, generally with the standard 50/50 writer/publisher royalty split, though copublishing deals are also possible if you have a successful track record. The writer is paid weekly (or monthly, quarterly, or annual) advances against future royalties, rather than a salary. The publisher gambles that he'll be able to recoup that money by getting some of those songs cut. If the songs never recoup the investment, the writer doesn't owe the publisher and the publisher loses his investment.

So, why would a publisher gamble like that rather than sign songs off the street? A writer signed to a staff position is obviously very talented, dedicated, and prolific. Having a writer under contract for several years makes it worthwhile to invest a considerable amount of time and money in developing that writer's reputation. During that time, the publisher hopes that a substantial catalogue of material is developed which will continue to be recorded. That writer's resulting success attracts other good writers as well. And having these writers under contract also prevents their songs from going to another company.

CONTRACT ISSUES

You should *never* sign an exclusive long-term staff-writer contract without the counsel of an experienced music industry attorney. However you can get a general idea beforehand of what the publisher will usually want from you. Here are a few points:

1. The publisher will want to publish all the songs you've already written that aren't already published. They'll want (at least) to have first refusal. You can argue that any advances in the deal are for future writing services only and that a separate payment should be made for back catalogue, especially if the publisher will be using the demos you paid for yourself.

2. Some publishers will expect a certain quota of songs per month or year (twenty per year is common.) Others feel if you deliver a great song every now and then, they won't be pushy. You both need to have an understanding of your creative habits. Some writers need deadlines. Some need to be left alone. Sometimes a publisher will set a quota of "acceptable" songs. This is not a good idea for you, es-

pecially if they can extend your contract indefinitely until the quota of "acceptable" songs is fulfilled.

3. The publisher will want a one-year contract with at least four one-year options. *Their* options. Try to limit it to three. You can build performance clauses into your contract that keep them from picking up the option unless, for instance, they secure a certain amount of recordings during the previous year. You can also negotiate to have your weekly advances increase every time they pick up the option.

4. Advances range from $1,000 to over $4,000 a month, depending on how successful you've been or (they *think*) you will be. These are "advances" against future royalties. There may be someone out there getting a straight salary (on a standard 50/50 writer/publisher deal) that's not recoupable from future royalties. But if there is, it's extremely rare because, by the time you're a valuable enough writer to command that kind of a deal, you either don't need the money or you're better off just getting an administration deal for your own publishing company.

BENEFITS OF BEING A STAFF WRITER
The following are benefits that may or may not all be offered by any particular publisher and are listed as the benefits you'd find in an ideal situation.

1. You're often provided a working environment with instruments and recording equipment. This is great if you don't have a good setup elsewhere.
2. You're given a weekly "draw," an advance against future royalties so you don't have to worry about the rent.
3. The publisher may pay for all your demos.
4. You're in an environment where you're encouraged and expected to be productive. Being around other productive writers can help your motivation.
5. You'll receive critical feedback that will, hopefully, help you grow as a writer.
6. You'll be made aware of upcoming recording projects so that you can tailor songs for those artists.
7. Your publisher will hook you up with film and theater assignments, album projects, and collaborators—often artists or producers with projects of their own.
8. If he feels you have artist potential, he may be motivated to find you a producer, a manager, and a record deal.
9. Because of his belief in you and his financial investment, he'll do all he can to promote your career.

DRAWBACKS OF BEING A STAFF WRITER
Though the staff writer situation can be wonderful and productive (and certainly has been the best way to go for many hit writers) it's a mistake

to assume it's the best situation for everyone. Many staff writers and ex-staffers complain about company policies that they knew about ahead of time but thought that "if the money's good enough, I can deal with it." They later found they couldn't. Some problems could not have been anticipated and were the result of personality conflicts or policy or personnel changes. It's often difficult to fix the blame but here are a few complaints:

"My publisher hasn't placed any of my songs. I got all the cuts myself." Maybe they signed you because they realized you *could* get your own cuts. If so, maybe you should have split the publishing. Hopefully, you signed with the company because they offered other services beyond securing recordings of your songs. It should be noted that publishers can often do their most valuable work *after* the song is recorded by securing *additional* covers and uses of the song and by making sure you get paid for all those uses.

"My publisher demands that the company gets 100 percent of the publishing when I collaborate with another writer, even when that writer has his/her own publishing company." That's one you should know about going in. The bad thing about this policy is that it seriously restricts the number of outstanding writers you can cowrite with since the best so often have their own companies and naturally are reluctant to give up their publishing royalties to your company.

Most major publishers are more liberal, though, and are willing to do a 50/50 split with the other writer's publisher. The belief is that another strong company involved in the song provides more contacts to get it recorded. You run into problems when you collaborate with a great writer who has his own company and your publisher doesn't think it's worth giving up half to someone who may not be actively pitching the song.

"The company seems to have lost interest in my songs but they won't let me out of my contract." Occasionally the person at the company who was responsible for signing you (and was the most enthusiastic about your material and your potential), leaves. Others at the company are pitching *their* favorite writers' songs because they feel more accountable to the writer he or she signed. Since you can't force someone to like either you or your material, it's sometimes a losing battle. It usually happens with writers who aren't getting many cuts yet. (Another good reason for you to be pitching the songs yourself.) It's much more rare for this situation to develop with a writer who's a consistent money-maker for the company.

Sometimes a company won't let you go because they've invested a lot in you and figure you'll hit with something eventually. What they risk is that you'll stop turning in songs to force them not to pick up your option. This tactic has been used before but it's not a great idea. It's self-destructive to deliberately stop creating for that reason, and if you continue to write songs without turning them in to your publisher you may find yourself in serious legal difficulty later since they legally own everything you write during the time you're under contract to them. If you're having problems, it's time for a serious heart-to-heart talk.

"My company is great with my pop and rock songs but doesn't seem to know what to do with my country material" (or vice versa). It's possible that you're not nearly as good at country writing as you think you are and that's the real reason they're not pitching those songs. It's also possible that your publisher doesn't know a good country song when he hears one. Or maybe he does and sends it to the company's Nashville office where *they* may think your publisher doesn't know what he's talking about.

In general, the major publishers have a pretty good ability to deal with a variety of styles though, as always, it depends on the contacts and expertise of the *individuals* at the company.

"My publisher's criticism is destroying my self-confidence and killing my motivation." Positive, constructive criticism, given sensitively and encouragingly by someone whose opinions you respect, can help you develop very quickly. There are publishers who can do that. You need to find them if you feel you need a nourishing situation to help you be a better writer. If you don't need that, it's not important. Among publishers, as among the public at large, there is a wide spectrum in individual talents for giving good criticism. Some publishers, though they're very definite about what they like or don't like, don't seem to have the vocabulary or the frame of reference to be specific about why or what you could do to improve your song. For them to say "It just doesn't get me," won't help you to be a better writer.

Consistently, though certainly not exclusively, the best critiquers are those who've been writers, musicians, or producers, have had good criticism, and have experience in restructuring songs. An inability to critique doesn't make someone a less effective songplugger but it does make him an ineffective developer of writers.

A publisher can also overcriticize. Hit writer Alan O'Day ("Angie Baby," "Undercover Angel") has a great metaphor for this syndrome: "When you're a hammer, everything looks like a nail."

"There are songs I believe in but my publisher doesn't. I can't stand to see them orphaned." One of the problems with the basic staff deal is that there are no reversion clauses that give you the song back if they don't get it recorded. You can negotiate for all the songs that haven't been recorded by a certain number of years after your contract ends to revert back to you. The publisher will attempt to limit this to the catalogue you brought with you when you made the deal, and only ones from that catalogue that haven't been commercially promoted. These deals and contract clauses may be very difficult to negotiate unless you're already a successful writer. Also, if you love the songs, you should always be out there pitching them yourself.

"I wrote fifteen songs last month and they only demoed one. I'm getting

discouraged. Why should I keep writing when they don't even demo what I give them?" It may be hard for you to accept that everything you write may not sound like a hit to them. There also may be budget problems. Someone in the company has to decide which songs are worth spending the money on and there may be several other staffers turning out fifteen songs a month. Figure a bare *minimum* of $200 per song and they're into big bucks. One possible remedy for this problem is that, if a certain number of "acceptable" songs have to be turned in each month, you have a clause in your contract that any songs rejected from that "quota" become your property, free and clear of any interest of the publisher.

ADVANTAGES OF INDEPENDENCE
Along with the relevant advantages and disadvantages of being a staff writer, you should consider the following:

1. As an independent songwriter you're free to offer financial incentives to individuals who can help you place your songs (see "Negotiating," page 189) that, if you were under contract, your publisher may not be likely to offer.
2. If you can publish the song yourself, you're looking at a lot more potential income.
3. You're never in competition with other writers on the publisher's staff (unless, of course, you're pitching songs to that publisher) as to whose songs get pitched to a particular producer.
4. You can pitch an individual song to any publisher you think can do the best job.

(For more information, see chapter eleven, "Self Publishing.")

HOW STAFF DEALS HAPPEN
Dreamy-eyed writers who've written ten songs come to my office and say they're shopping for a staff-writing deal. Far be it from me to discourage them. In fact, if all (or even some) of those songs sound like hits and the writer also has great artist potential, he/she is likely to have offers.

More often, songwriters and publishers build a relationship one song at a time. Don't let your dreams keep you from getting a day (or night) job so you can afford to let that process take place in its own time. It's important for you to work with a variety of publishers on a "song by song" basis to find those individuals whose opinions and business practices you respect and who are aggressive about pitching your songs. It's also important for a publisher to have the opportunity to size up your creative output, your willingness and ability to rewrite, your mutual personal chemistry, and, obviously, the reaction to your songs from producers. It also can't hurt your negotiating position to have more than one company wanting to sign you. This "sizing up" process is very important in any long-range partnership. Very few marriages succeed when you go to the altar after knowing each other a week.

ELEVEN

Self Publishing

WHY PUBLISH YOUR OWN SONGS?

In the last chapter I discussed what a publisher does. Now let's discuss the advantages of having your own publishing company. It's important, because the publisher's share of royalties could represent a lot of money. The information in this chapter is primarily geared to those of you who want to go full out into being your own publisher and actively pitching your own songs and possibly those of other writers. However, there are a lot of situations for which you'd want to self-publish without getting into it that deeply. You may only have occasion to self-publish a few songs. You may, by a stroke of luck, get a song recorded and not be asked for the publishing by the producer or artist, or the recording of the song may only be released in the U.S. or with a minor artist for which the collection could easily be handled by an administrator. (See "Administration Deals," page 195.) In those cases, only a part of this information may apply to you. Here are some other reasons why you might want to publish yourself and some qualities that would help you do a good job for yourself.

- You're a good commercial songwriter whose tunes are very coverable (suitable to be recorded by other artists) and you already have a lot of contacts among producers and artists who're interested in your songs. In other words, you're in a position to fulfill one of a publisher's major functions: getting covers. You should be aware, though, that it takes a lot of time, and follow-up is very important.
- You have the ability to "sell" yourself. Some people represent others better than themselves. You should be an aggressive self-starter. You should have the ability to be both creator and businessperson. (Yes, it can be done, and yes, it's a myth that creative artists always make poor business people.)
- You have a great casting sense that lets you present the right song to the right artist at the right time. Publishers' reputations are built on their credibility.
- You have your own production company or record company and you're releasing your own product.
- You're a recording artist who's recording your own songs and therefore already doing part of a publisher's job.
- You've already written commercially successful songs and it's easy for you to get in those doors.

182

- You're writing with someone who does well as his own publisher and you can negotiate a portion of the rights for your own company. If your cowriter is a staff writer with a major company, you may find this very difficult unless you also have great contacts and are aggressive about pitching your songs.
- You're a writer/artist whose style is so unique that your songs are unlikely to be recorded by other artists. You don't need a publisher to get your songs recorded. Be sure not to sell yourself short on the potential for other artists to record your songs, though.
- You're independently wealthy or have financial backing. You write coverable tunes and you can afford the alternative of *hiring* someone with experience and contacts to promote your songs.

If you're capable of hustling for yourself, you'll have the satisfaction of knowing that someone with your best interest at heart is on the job. You won't be constantly wondering whether the publisher is "sitting on your song," or why he's avoiding your calls. If someone is not on the case, you have only yourself to blame. Can you handle that?

STARTING YOUR OWN PUBLISHING COMPANY

Assuming that, for whatever reason you feel your best plan of action is to start your own company, here's how to proceed:

1. You're eligible to have BMI, ASCAP, or SESAC process your application as a publisher if: (a) a record is being released containing a performance of the song; (b) a motion picture is being released that includes the song; (c) a television program will be or has been broadcast using the song; or (d) a radio program has been broadcast that played the song.
2. You must clear the name you've chosen for your publishing company with BMI, ASCAP, or SESAC. Remember that you can't have a company with the same name as another publishing company. Unless you intend to publish the songs of other writers who may belong to other performing rights organizations, you need only set up a company with the one you're affiliated with as a writer. Give them three alternate company names in your order of preference. If your first choice is already being used by someone else they'll select the next choice that is not already taken, so be creative and pick something unusual.

    There is a $50 annual fee for being a publisher-member of ASCAP. There is a one-time $25 application fee to be a BMI publisher, and no annual fee. There is no fee for SESAC publishers.
3. Once the name(s) have been cleared, go to your local County Clerk's Office and obtain the forms to register a Fictitious Business Name Statement, also known as a d/b/a (Doing Business As _____). Then go to your bank and open an account under your new business name. Your County Clerk will refer you to a local publication who

will publish a "fictitious business name" statement that gives the required notice that you are now officially doing business as "Crass Commercial Music" or whatever you've chosen. The notice must be published once per week for four weeks in a paper of "general circulation" in the county where the business is located. You can use the same d/b/a to list more than one company if you want to add another publishing company, production company, etc. The cost of publication varies from city to city, but is generally under $50.

A name using the legal name of the individual owner, as long as the business name does not imply other owners, does *not* require a d/b/a, regardless of the insistence of some misinformed bank employees. "John Braheny Music" would not require any fictitious name registration. "Braheny & Associates Music" or "Braheny & Company Publishing" probably would.

4. Copyright all the songs you wish to have in your company on a PA form assigned to your company. (See "Copyright Registration," page 133.) If you have already obtained copyright registrations on your unpublished songs, you will now register them again as published works.

5. For songs being released on records, or for songs that will be or have been performed in a motion picture, television program or radio program (regardless of whether the song is included on any record), fill out both the writer's and publisher's clearance forms from the performing rights organization involved (BMI, ASCAP, or SESAC). These forms notify the organization that a specific song is being released on a specific album so that, when it's performed on the radio, TV, or elsewhere, the organization will know who to pay, what percentage to pay the writer and the publisher, and where to send the checks. Directions are included on the forms and in publisher's manuals provided by the organizations. Keep a photocopy of everything you send out for your files.

6. Matters such as the legal form under which you should operate your publishing company (e.g., as a corporation, partnership, or sole proprietorship), whether you need to obtain any kind of business license, and whether you need to obtain a Federal employer identification number and report wages and withhold taxes for employees can be complicated issues and are beyond the scope of this book. You should consult an attorney or accountant for such matters.

7. Organize yourself to be able to keep track of your "song shopping."

BUSINESS EXPENSES

You'll incur many expenses in the process of setting up and maintaining your business, both as a songwriter or publisher. Keep records of all your expenses (receipts with date, vendor's name, amount of purchase, plus sales tax, if applicable), and income records. Use your business checks and arrange for a separate business credit card, if possible, for those expenses. Here are a few:

- Services of a graphic artist and printing for company logo, tape box inserts, tape labels. Costs vary.
- Bank account and check printing—$100+
- Subscriptions to trade magazines—$250 a year
- Music business and songwriter organization dues. (Some people belong to several.) Costs vary.
- Postage for letters and tapes mailed to producers
- Photocopies of lyric sheets, cover letters, lead sheets, forms, business correspondence, and anything else you'll need to keep a copy of
- Stationery—letterhead, envelopes, mailing labels, tape mailing envelopes, card files, business cards
- Lead sheets—about $25 each
- Copyrights—$10 each
- Demo costs—about $200 per song minimum
- Blank tape—Buy these in bulk to save money
- Tape copying—Costs vary. Save money and do it yourself.
- Sound equipment—tape decks, stereo system, car stereo, and maintenance of all of these
- Records and tapes—to research artists you want to pitch your songs to
- Nightclubs—to check out new talent and possible collaborators. You'll need to document this for the IRS.
- Business lunches—also need to document for the IRS
- Computer costs—If you write, keep records, and accounting ledgers, and research with your computer, you can write it off. (Check with your tax preparer.)
- Travel expenses—for that trip to L.A., Nashville, or New York to meet with publishers, producers, or record companies. Keep good records of gas, mileage, food, lodging.
- Telephone—If you're aggressive, these can run $600+ per month. Check out the lower-cost long distance services. Installing a second phone for business helps tremendously to document those expenses for the IRS.
- Answering service—to make sure you don't miss any calls, about $40 per month. Or purchase a phone answering machine and take it as a business deduction.
- Attorney fees—to put together contracts that reflect your business philosophy and protect your interests, you'll need: publisher/writer single-song contracts, split publishing or copublishing contracts, and staff writer contracts (if applicable).
- Accounting fees—Find an accountant experienced in the music business to make sure you get all the deductions you're entitled to.
- Check with your city or county clerk regarding any business filing fees for your company.
- Any seminars, classes, workshops, songwriter-related showcases, and other educational activities (including those on how to run your business better).

CASTING

Casting is the art of knowing the right song to pitch to the right person at the right time. It's a skill essential to a publisher and to you, if you're doing that part of the job yourself. To be able to cast effectively, you'll need to research several things:

Does the artist you want to pitch to ever record "outside" songs (those not written by the artist or producer)? If so, is the artist currently looking for outside songs on this project?

Is the artist's stylistic direction the same as in previous albums, or is it changing? How?

When is production on the album scheduled to begin? Is there a tentative completion date? This is important information, because you want to get to producers when they're seriously dedicating time to finding the right songs before the sessions are scheduled to begin. As mentioned earlier, another good time to pitch is about midway through the project, when they've possibly discovered that the songs they thought would be great aren't working out so well. Other than those critical times, if a producer knows he will be producing an act, he's *always* looking and will store away great songs to be listened to again as a project gets closer.

One of the most common mistakes inexperienced writers make in casting their songs is to say "That artist could really sing this song," or "She'd really sound great singing my song." That artist may actually sound great singing the phone book. What you should be asking is, "Does that artist really *need* my song?"

For the artistic questions relative to casting, see "Writing on Assignment," page 89, and use the guidelines described to do your research on the acts in question.

See "Research: Trade Magazines and Tip Sheets," page 230, for information on researching artists regarding their use of outside songs.

SUCCESSFUL PITCHING STRATEGIES

Be prepared to send out a lot of tapes in your pitching efforts. It's not uncommon for publishers to pitch a particular song over 100 times. Be prepared for 100 rejections.

As your own publisher, your first job is to get your songs to artists. Here's a strategy that works:

1. **Establish priorities.** Research the trade charts and tip sheets and compile a list of currently successful artists who record the style(s) of songs you write, and who record songs by other writers. Choose a particular song and determine which of those artists would be appropriate to send the song to. Make those artists your "A" list. Make other lists of artists in order of priority. These might include: B— new artists with record deals. C—new artists and former hit artists who have production deals with established producers but no record contracts. D—recording artists with past hits but no recent success, no producer nor record deal. E—new artists with new produc-

ers and no record deal. F—new artists with no producer and no record deal.

Even though this is a logical priority list in terms of playing the odds, and spending your time, energy and money accordingly, the music business isn't known for succeeding on logic. In this case, the situation with any artist on any of those lists could totally change on any given day. "A"s become "D"s, "D"s become "A"s, and "F"s become "A"s overnight. Don't underestimate the value of pitching to new artists. We didn't get a great turnout at the Songwriters Showcase when Arista Records' reps were looking for songs for a new, unknown artist named Whitney Houston. "Whitney who? Never heard of her. I'm saving my best stuff for superstars." There's a lot to be said for the personal and political rewards of being there when they need you, when nobody else will take the chance. It's also easier to get to new artists, and you're more likely to be heard when they're desperate for hit songs because the major publishers may not be giving them their best material.

2. **Surround the act with tapes.** By that, I mean get the song to their manager, attorney, producer, recording engineer, A&R person at the record company, musicians, roadies, hairdresser, chauffeur, secretary, gardener, relatives, lovers, anyone who is a potential contact. But don't do this unless you've done your homework very well and feel confident that this is an outstanding and an appropriate song. It will annoy them no end to keep getting the wrong song.

3. **Check the club and concert listings in your local paper and try to find out where the acts are staying.** Go to the club early when the act does a sound check and try to connect with the artist, road manager, or musicians. You should be aware that for their legal protection, many writer/artists are cautioned by their attorneys not to personally accept any unsolicited tapes. With artists who don't write, it's not as much of a problem.

4. **If you're in a recording center, introduce yourself to some recording engineers at the hot studios in town.** Several of the major trade magazines have sections on who's recording, where, and the names of the engineer(s). Let them hear your songs and offer them financial incentives if they can place songs with acts that record there. You may, in fact, make an offer to any of the above mentioned contacts. Ten percent of the mechanical royalties on a recording they secure for you is a good place to start, but higher percentages are not necessarily out of line. Use your best judgment and offer whatever feels right. Read "Negotiating," page 189, for more information on this.

5. **Be aware of the successful bands in your area.** Maybe there's a great Top 40 "cover" band in which none of the members write. They may want a record deal but have no original material. You might be able to cowrite with someone in the band, maybe the lead singer or keyboard player. It's always a good idea to pay attention to acts that

may have a shot at a record deal. If they hit with your songs, it may result in a long and lucrative relationship.

6. **Get involved in every musical project you possibly can,** including student films and video projects, background music for a play, commercial jingles, anything! In every project, you may meet someone who likes your work and likes working with you and who will refer you for another project. It's called "networking," and it's one of the best ways to develop a reputation and contacts. When you find good musicians, singers, or writers, refer them to projects. What you give comes back!

7. **Think of some creative ways to stand out from the crowd.** Legendary stories abound about writers and publishers pulling outrageous stunts like dropping tapes from helicopters or by parachutes or delivering them via strippers or in cakes. A friend of mine sent tapes to A&R departments in sealed soup cans with the songs listed as ingredients. Very clever, but he neglected to send along can openers. Some still sit unopened in A&R offices as a lasting testament to his ingenuity.

   Those are the stories that get passed around in the industry and usually end with, "Yeah, fantastic! If only the song had been good. . . ."

   The point is that if you can think of an imaginative way to present your material, you'll definitely make a lasting impression, but it's useless to you unless the people who receive your package are also excited about the music.

8. **Make your packaging as professional as your song.** Let's assume your music is worth pitching and talk about what you can do to make an eye-catching professional-looking package. Atlanta songwriter Diane Pfeiffer's trademark is hot pink—the color she uses for lyric sheets, cover letter, tape label, and tape box insert. Publishers or producers can pick it out of a stack or basket of tapes immediately. Using good graphics with a logo, professional typesetting, and an artistic layout with possibly a picture on the tape insert (particularly for performers) can strengthen your presentation. With the advent of desktop publishing it's becoming more common to see lyrics that are beautifully typeset. (See "How To Present Your Demo," page 222.)

   Regarding logos, a common question comes up. If I have my own publishing company, should I send materials out under company letterhead? If you're sending songs to publishers, no, unless you're suggesting a copublishing agreement in your letter. If they're going to record companies, yes. In sending songs to producers, you have this to consider. It might help to get your song through the door, or it may make the producer skittish. A producer usually has his own publishing company and will prefer to record a song he at least partially owns. He may opt to pass on your song if he thinks the publishing rights are not available. However, it all depends on how good the songs are. If he wants to record them and also wants a piece of the publishing he'll probably try to negotiate. So, use your company logo and take your chances.

9. **Be prepared.** Never leave the house without tape copies and lyric sheets. If possible, carry a portable cassette player and headset. You never know who you're going to meet.

NEGOTIATING

A writer I know happened to get to the manager of a major R&B/pop crossover group. The manager loved her song and felt it was so good that the group wanted to record it despite the fact that they usually wrote their own songs. He asked her if the group could have the publishing if they recorded it. She said "No." He said, "Goodbye." She told me later she was totally unprepared to deal with the situation and had no idea what to say. She was excited that he liked it but when he wanted the publishing, she thought he was trying to rip her off.

There are three schools of thought on this situation. The first is, "Right on, don't let them have the publishing. You did right! You did the job of a publisher by getting it to the group in the first place. Does anyone seriously believe that the manager is going to do anything with that song beyond this group's recording of it?"

The second is, "My God, do you know that there are writers who'd sell their kids for just an *album cut* on that group? The writer's royalties alone are worth thousands, especially if it's a single. So what if you *do* give them the publishing, if you can get a guaranteed release? If you give it to a 'real' publisher, it might never get cut because they're not going to give up *their* piece of the action to that group. Either way, *you* wouldn't have been able to keep any of the publishing anyway! It's just one song and it'll help build your career."

The third point of view is, "Why didn't you *negotiate?*" She answered, "I don't know. I didn't even think of it. What's to negotiate? Either you give them the publishing or you don't, right?" *Wrong.*

Let's look at each of these attitudes. The first is certainly defensible and, in fact, it *is* important to analyze whether this manager (or producer or artist) has an active publishing company with employees who will spend time trying to get other recordings of your song, even after the group has recorded it. If he does, it might be a good situation. If not, you'll know that any subsequent covers of the song will be entirely up to you and though you'll get your writer's royalty, you won't share any of the publisher's royalties for doing the publisher's work. If they insist on owning the publishing, you could point out that you'll want to be actively pitching this song to other artists after this recording and try to get them to split the publishing with your own company. If that doesn't work, see if they'll give *you* a portion of the mechanical or performance royalties on any new recordings of the song that *you* are responsible for placing.

Even active publishers (as opposed to holding companies) have different philosophies about splitting the publishing with an artist or producer in order to get a recording. They range from "Under no circumstances will

I give up anything. I'm doing the work and I deserve the royalties," to "I'll give up what I have to to get the tune recorded." It depends a lot on the individual circumstances. How important is this recording? Is this the only artist who could cut the tune? Would this cut be very important in the development of the writer's career in generating interest in the rest of his/her catalogue? If I give this producer a piece of the action, am I setting a precedent with him that I'll regret later? And always, how badly do they want this song? If you're going to be your own publisher, those are the questions that *you'll* have to consider.

The second attitude is also defensible. This may be a major act and your first recording. One hundred percent of zero is zero. If the manager or producer is adamant about having the publishing and you know it will make you a lot of money for the writer's share of the royalties, it might be best to let them have it. Is this the last or only good song you'll ever write? If they want it that badly, chances are the song is good enough that you should have more confidence in your own ability. Maybe you won't need to make a deal like that with your next song because you'll be in a better bargaining position if this one turns out to be a winner. There is a danger in being too attached to a song, too protective. It's the classic situation of the bird in hand. If you do decide to give them the publishing, however, and the company is basically a holding company and not an active publisher, *make sure that you have it in writing* that the publishing doesn't get officially assigned to them until the record is actually released. That way, if they decide not to record the song after all, it doesn't end up in limbo because they own it but won't do anything with it.

But don't give it up so fast. There *are* other negotiating positions you can take.

Two major sources of income (mechanical and performance royalties) are negotiable without transferring your ownership of any of the copyright. Generally, when someone says they want "the publishing," they want ownership of the copyright. In the "standard" writer/publisher agreement, you assign the copyright to the publisher in a contract which gives you half the total income as writer, the other half going to the publisher. But the publisher *owns* the song and can sell it to anyone else if he wants to (unless the agreement includes a nonassignment clause). A good businessperson will always want to own the copyright. It's a commodity whose value will increase with the song's degree and length of popularity. So you can't blame them for going for it. They're not trying to rip you off, just looking out for their own interests. You need to do the same.

"Mechanicals" are the income from the sale of records, tapes, and compact discs at the current rate of 5 cents per song per unit sold payable to the copyright owner. (See "Mechanical Royalties," page 145.) For a million-seller, that's $50,000. As the writer, you'll take half off the top right away and from the remainder (referred to as the "publisher's share of mechanicals") you can offer percentages as an incentive for someone to record the song. The advantages of offering, say, 50 percent participation in the "publisher's share of mechanicals" (25 percent of the total) on *that particular record* is that you still own the copyright and you give them incentive only for their limited use of the song. This is referred to as a "cut in" or a "participation agreement." If someone else later records the song, you still own the copyright so you can make a better deal. You can get *all* the publisher's and writer's royalties for future recordings.

Another negotiable item is "performance royalties." That's the term for all the money received through BMI, ASCAP, or SESAC for the performances of your songs on radio, TV, juke boxes, and in clubs. Those organizations, called performing right societies, pay directly to the publisher and to the writer. This is a different situation from "mechanical" royalties which are paid directly to the copyright owner. If you have a hit song, particularly one that gets played on the radio long after it's been a hit, your "performance" royalties can amount to considerably more money than your "mechanicals."

For the purpose of negotiation, another important difference exists between "mechanical" and "performance" income. When you receive your quarterly earnings statement from BMI or ASCAP, they don't note which recording of your song you're receiving royalties from (SESAC does, however). You can't say, "I'll give you X percent of the publisher's share of the performance income on this particular record," since, in some cases, two different versions of the same song (e.g., a country and a pop version) have been on the charts at the same time. You *could* say, "I can give you X percent participation in the publisher's share of performance income:

a. for the first _____ quarters in which royalties are received; or
b. until the quarter before the next recording of this song is released."

Another approach is to negotiate a percentage of the mechanical or performance royalties *until a specified maximum dollar figure is reached.* In other words, "I'll give you X percent of the money up to (until you've received) X dollars."

Here are some other points to keep in mind when negotiating with anyone regarding mechanicals and performance income:

1. The percentage or dollar amount you offer is totally negotiable. There are no set rules. You may offer any percentage of the income from the song that you want to offer and still maintain ownership of the copyright.
2. On an album cut, your performance royalties won't amount to much unless it's a piece that DJs take particular interest in. With the exception of the small percentage of stations that specialize in playing albums, radio will play singles. There are times, though, when an album cut unexpectedly gets enough radio excitement going that it forces the company to release it as a single.
3. On a hot act with good album sales, mechanical royalties on album cuts are worth a great deal. Singles are still worth more because your song will appear on both the single and album and because the single will earn performance royalties if it gets air play. Remember,

too, that the B-side of a hit single makes as much in mechanical royalties as the A-side. If it's an A-side single, your song may also be included on an eventual "Greatest Hits" album.

4. On pop records (including R&B/pop) by established artists, you'll
get the highest mechanical *and* performance royalties.

On country records, mechanicals are low because sales here are
usually low except for country/pop crossovers like Kenny Rogers
and Anne Murray and a few country superstars. But performance
(air play) royalties on a country *single* can be very high because of
the great number of country radio stations. These are generalities to
give you a rough estimate of the relative popularity of styles, but the
bottom line is determined by the popularity of the individual artist.

5. It may be wise to offer one percentage of royalty participation for an
album cut and an additional percentage if it becomes a single (even
a B-side). This approach could work for a situation in which the artist or producer to whom you're offering the incentive can influence
the choice of the record as a single. Their increased financial participation, if your song is chosen as a single, could be a factor in that
decision.

6. Make sure the "cut in" or "participation" goes into effect only upon
release of a specified record by a specified artist on a specified label.

If you choose to deal with producers and artists directly and they
want some financial incentive, just keep in mind that, as they say,
"there's more than one way to skin a cat" or "everything is negotiable."

A word of caution in making these deals: If the person to whom
you're offering this incentive is employed by a record company and
makes this agreement without the permission of the company, your
deal may constitute commercial bribery. Check it out!

"HOLDS"

If a producer feels your song is right for his recording project, he'll ask for
a "hold" on it. It means he'll want to have the first opportunity to record
the song. He doesn't want you to pitch it to anyone else in the meantime
because he doesn't want to spend the money to produce the song, only to
have his release beaten out by another artist. Producers commonly have
exclusive holds on more songs than they need to go on an album because
it frequently happens, as I've mentioned before, that even if they get
around to recording a song, it may turn out to be less exciting than they
thought it would.

Aside from that, there are several other reasons why your song may not
end up on an album. A writer/artist may have written new songs since
yours went on hold and the artist will decide to record those instead of
yours. Maybe it was decided that other writers' songs chosen since yours
were stronger or better suited to the project. It also happens that a musical direction or concept for the project may emerge from the material
that's gathered and it inevitably becomes clear that certain songs just

don't fit with the others, no matter how good they may be. There aren't enough ballads, or there are too many. The artist, producer, or A&R person at the record company may change their minds about the song at the last minute.

Since any of those things can and do happen and because selecting the right songs is crucial to an album's success, you can see why a producer wants to hold on to as many songs as possible until the project is finished.

On the other side we have the writer and publisher who may want very much for the producer and artist to record the song. In granting a hold to the producer there is a risk for them that the producer does not share. It can't hurt the producer if he decides not to record the song but the publisher may be forced to turn down some other equally good, if not better, offers in honoring the hold. In being your own publisher, this is a situation you'll have to deal with, and with great diplomacy. There are several different attitudes among publishers regarding holds:

"If I think the project is worth it, I'll always let them hold it. In the process, I'm building my relationship with the producer."

"I never give holds. They all know that if they want the song they'll have to hurry up and record it. I'll stay in touch with the producer and let him know about any other interest in the song as it comes up, and I'll let him know I want him to record it, but I'll keep pitching it."

"It depends on my relationship with that producer, how long he wants to keep it, and whether I know if he'll be honest with me about the status of the project—not lead me on by telling me it'll be just a little longer when he knows he'll need a lot more time."

"I'll tell them they can have a hold, but if another major project comes along, I'll give it to them too. I know the odds are that when it gets down to it, only one of them will end up wanting to record the song anyway." Be careful with this one. You could burn some bridges if they discover you've given them both holds, particularly if one of them has spent some of his budget to record it.

If more than one producer wants to hold your song, ask yourself some questions: Is one of the acts likely to sell more records and get more air play than the other? Is the song to be released as a single or an album cut? Do the producers plan for a major artist or a newcomer to record your song? Is it being considered for a country artist (good for performance royalties but not so good for mechanical royalties, as country music fans aren't avid record buyers) or for a crossover artist (good for performance *and* mechanical royalties)?

How long do they each need to hold it? If one will be able to tell you in two weeks whether he's cutting it and the other needs six months before his act is ready, off the road, or on the wagon before he can get into the studio, tell him you'll let him know in two weeks! Stall for time.

FOREIGN SUBPUBLISHING

Foreign subpublishing has become an important aspect of the publisher's business. It's estimated that 60 percent of the world music market is outside the United States. The international market for American songs has grown tremendously in the past several years. A publisher with any chart success at all, and a strong catalogue of songs to back it up, won't miss the opportunity to capitalize on it in other countries. Most publishers, including the small independents, have affiliations with foreign publishers in countries where their songs are viable. In the simplest terms, it works like this: American publisher "A" contacts foreign publisher "F." "A" has done research which shows him that "F" has had success with songs similar to those in "A" 's catalogue. He's also learned that "F" is very aggressive about getting cover records, promoting the songs of their U.S. affiliates, and collecting the money.

Publisher "A" contacts "F," often at MIDEM (the international music industry conference held in France each year), and gets together with "F" to play him the catalogue, listen to "F" 's catalogue and get a sense of the activities of "F" 's company, their personalities, and business knowhow. "A" needs to feel that "F" is genuinely excited about the songs, and has good ideas about which artists in his country would be likely to record them. "F" is also interested in having "A" represent his songs in the U.S., so he also has to be satisfied.

Assuming that both publishers are in tune with each other, a contract for a number of years (usually three) is worked out, usually including an advance from "F" to "A." The amount of the advance is based on several factors, including "A" 's track record, current hits, and the strength of the overall catalogue, particularly the number of songs that would be viable in "F" 's territory.

The musical tastes of listeners and record-buyers can be very different from one country to the next. Check out the international charts in *Billboard* and you'll see what I mean. Part of the jobs of both publishers may be to come up with a translation of the song for a new artist or a translated version by the original artist. Barbra Streisand, Kenny Rogers, and Sheena Easton are among the American artists who've done foreign language versions of their hits.

Royalty splits in such cases vary from 90/10 to 75/25 for "A" and "F," respectively, including both performance royalties from that country's version of BMI or ASCAP and mechanical royalties from local record companies. That is the case for songs by the original American artist or cover records obtained by "A." If "F" obtains a new cover of the song by an artist in his territory, "A" and "F" usually divide the royalties received from that recording anywhere from 70/30 to 60/40. The higher "cover splits" are easier to obtain if the overall deal split is in the higher range. That, by the way, is the reason why you receive a lower royalty from foreign recordings on your writer/publisher contract. You're only getting 50 percent of *what the publisher receives in this country.*

It's possible to lose out on an enormous amount of money on an international hit if the foreign subpublishing deals are not in place or are not good ones. Foreign royalties may be generated that you won't even know about. It's one of the areas that get neglected by writers who retain their own publishing rights and have a big hit. It's well worth the trouble for you, your attorney, or other representative, particularly if you have a hot catalogue to go to MIDEM, do your research, and pick publishers from Japan, England, Australia, Italy, Scandinavia, Argentina, and other countries where you think your songs are viable. The advances you could receive from the deals you make, could more than pay for the trip. Next best is to contract with another American publisher, or attorney, who has already set up foreign subpublishing contracts, to make that trip on your behalf and have them deal with all other countries, excluding the U.S. Don't attempt to negotiate foreign subpublishing deals without the assistance of an attorney experienced in that area. There are many potential difficulties caused, for instance, by constantly shifting currency exchanges that need the advice of an expert.

To find foreign publishers on your own, check the international charts in *Billboard* to see which hits are stylistically compatible with yours and in which countries they're popular. You can get lists of publishers in those countries from *Billboard*'s *International Buyers Guide* and the annual *Songwriter's Market.*

A creative foreign publisher can be valuable by helping to set up tours and TV exposure for the U.S. writer/artist or group whose songs he represents. The more popular he makes the act and songs in his territory, the more money he makes. He can also arrange interviews on radio, TV, or in newspapers, provide interpreters if necessary, concoct promotions that would work in his own country, but maybe not the U.S., find the best lyric translators and adapters or maybe even facilitate cowriting situations with his own writers.

Obviously, the agreement works both ways. U.S. publisher "A" will also become familiar with the songs in "F" 's catalogue and advise him as to what type of songs "A" could get recorded over here, maybe assisting "F" in finding an American record deal or producer for one of "F" 's writer/artist acts. The agreement also gives "F" the opportunity to sign songs in his country that may not be viable there but that could get recorded in the U.S. It's always important to remember that the whole world loves a great song.

ADMINISTRATION DEALS

If you want to publish your own songs, don't need advances on royalties or any other benefits of a copublishing contract, but want to find someone else to take care of the business end, your best course of action is an administration deal. An administrator doesn't own the copyright or any percentage of it. He is paid a fee of 15 percent (or less) of the royalties in a contract usually of one to three years. In order to make it worthwhile for an administrator to work with your catalogue, you'll need, of course, to have recordings that are generating income.

Some "full service" publishing companies will administer your catalogue for a fee (instead of copyright ownership) and there are also administrators, usually attorneys or accountants, who will charge you for their services on an hourly basis.

Administrators do the following (to varying degrees, depending on your needs):

1. **The paperwork and negotiations** of granting mechanical (recording) and synchronization (film/TV/commercials) licenses and registering copyrights.
2. **Digging up royalties** that you may never have received from previous recordings of your songs worldwide.
3. **Subpublishing,** setting up publishing or administration or administration affiliates in foreign countries to pitch your songs locally and assist in royalty collections there.
4. **Collecting money from record companies.** Some hire the services of a mechanical licensing organization and some do the collections themselves. (See "Mechanical Royalties," page 145.)
5. **Pitch your songs to producers and artists.** Some administrators won't do this at all and are basically accounting firms. Others consider that the more action they generate on your catalogue, the bigger their 15 percent becomes. Since they don't own any of the publishing rights, they can't look down the road and say, "Someday this tune will get recorded and make me money for a long time." They're working for you on a short-term contract and need to make your songs pay off now. Some administration companies will actively pitch songs for an extra overall percentage of the entire catalog or for a percent of the publishing royalties on any recording they secure.
6. **Follow-up.** If you're acting as your own publisher and making the contacts with producers or artists who you want to keep as friends, the administrator can handle the hassles of follow-up, though he will want a higher fee to do it. If an administrator wants more that 15 percent, you should be assured that you'll receive more benefits, and that they'll be spelled out. It's best to "comparison shop" administrators and talk to others who use their services.

Demos

WHY YOU NEED THEM

Demonstration tapes—"demos"—are used to show your songs to publishers, producers, record companies, and other music industry people who may want to use your songs. Those people will rarely look at a lyric without music, and even the few who can read music won't be able to get the full impact of the song by just looking at a lead sheet (lyrics with musical notation). Since the end product (the record) is to be heard, they need to evaluate your song by hearing it. So you're left with the options of performing the song for them live (a long shot) or giving them a demo tape.

Most publishers feel a live audition of a song is impractical and inefficient. To paraphrase what many publishers have said to me:

"My major responsibility as a publisher is to devote myself to the songs I've already signed and to the writers on our staff. There's not much time for me to schedule appointments in my workday. The few appointments I make are referrals from people whose 'ears' I respect. I know there are some great tunes just walking around out there looking for a publisher and sometimes I'm too busy to see the writer. So in order to be able to listen to new songs, I need to have tapes or records. Then I can listen when my head is into it and I'm not distracted. What I'm actually listening for is a song that will be a hit record, so it's easier for me to hear it on tape since I won't be distracted by watching the performer."

So unless you have good contacts in the music business, you probably won't get an appointment to sing your songs "live" and will need to make a demo. Even if you can get a live audition your contact will want to have a demo to listen to later or play for someone else at the company.

A very practical reason why publishers prefer a demo tape is that it allows them to listen to a lot of songs in a short time. It's hard for any sensitive person to give you the "gong" thirty seconds into your song while you're looking at him. So handing them a demo tape is both a time-saver and a convenience.

A demo can benefit the writer as well. Creating a demo is an education in itself, whether you're actively producing it or observing someone else putting it together. If you're producing your demos at home, you can learn about the recording process at your own pace. You can experiment and work out arrangements without the pressure of paying for studio time.

The more familiar you become with the finished product, the better perspective you have on the writing process. You can more easily imagine a singer performing the song. You learn more about the use of space and density in your lyric writing, and become more conscious of the role that arrangements play in enhancing a song's emotional impact.

One of the great thrills of songwriting is to watch your song bloom into a full-blown musical production, to make it fulfill your vision or surpass it. Your failures as well as your successes become great teachers.

On the business side, demos are efficient. Once you get a good demo of your song, you can make an unlimited number of copies and within a couple of weeks, have them in a hundred different offices, assured that everyone will hear the same top-quality rendition of your song. That's quality control.

TYPES OF DEMOS
Different kinds of demos serve different needs.

Basic song demos. A most basic kind of guitar/vocal or keyboard/vocal with maybe the addition of a bass or drum machine (depending on the equipment you own or have available; or, at its simplest, *a cappella* (unaccompanied) vocal. These can be used as a kind of "pre-demo" to be critiqued before spending money on a more elaborate version; to show the emotional, rhythmic, or energy "feel" of your song as a guideline for musicians or demo production services who may do a more elaborate production; to play for publishers or producers who you already *know* will accept simple demos.

More elaborate song demos. Studio demos or more elaborately produced home demos either a) produced by the writer to play for publishers or to pitch directly to producers and artists or b) produced by the publisher to pitch to producers and artists. These demos usually have a basic rhythm section—drums, bass, guitar or keyboard, lead vocal, and sometimes background vocals. What goes on the demo in addition to that is based totally on the writer's or publisher's perception of the style of the artist(s) and the "ears" and personal tastes of the producers it will go to. Often the demo will be mixed in several different ways, leaving in or dropping out various instruments or parts (string or horn parts, for instance) to accommodate different styles and tastes.

Artist demo. One used by an artist or band to shop for a record deal, manager, or producer. It highlights the strengths of the act, including not only the songs but the arrangements, performances, vocals, instrumental virtuosity of individual members and the overall style and energy of the group. Even in the case of an individual writer/artist, this is almost always a demo using a group in order to show the artist in the musical environment that best suits her style. This is a studio tape but, depending on the style of the group and how well rehearsed they are, it could be done with a minimum of expense.

Master demo. The same function as an artist demo, but with the high quality of studio, engineering, production, and attention to detail that would make it acceptable for release as a record or to be included in a movie soundtrack.

WHO GETS WHAT AND HOW ELABORATE DOES IT NEED TO BE?

In creating your demo, it's important to know what purpose you want it to serve. One way to sort it out is to decide who's going to get it. These are the major groups of people who you'll be sending demos to.

PUBLISHERS

Though it's actually part of a publisher's job to produce appropriate demos to pitch to producers, the truth is that you have a competitive edge if you can produce your own demos well enough for the publishers to use. There are several reasons for this: 1) More writers today, in all styles, are conceiving and writing songs with a vision of how they want them to sound as a finished record. In producing their own demos, they can realize that vision. 2) More of them also have access to state-of-the-art home recording equipment. 3) Songwriters, pitching songs simultaneously to *both* producers and publishers, need good demos to give them a competitive edge.

One of the advantages in presenting well-produced demos to publishers is the increased ability to negotiate reversion clauses (see "Negotiable Contract Clauses," page 166). Publishers are reluctant to return songs they've had to lay out much money for, and demo costs represent a good share of the initial expense. If you give them a high-quality demo, that expense is eliminated (unless, of course, you're asking them to reimburse you up front).

Another advantage is that your chances of interesting a publisher in a song based on a simple guitar/vocal or piano/vocal demo are slim. Though some publishers can "hear through" such a sample, others need more elaborate production to help them imagine how the finished product might sound. In most cases you won't know ahead of time what a particular publisher needs to hear. Your basic demo is likely to be sandwiched between two or more elaborate demos that sound like records and yours will suffer in comparison.

There *are* exceptions. Country music publishers are still accustomed to hearing guitar or piano/vocal demos and since the focus of most successful country songs is the lyric, a simple demo will work with a great lyric. In another arena, keyboard/vocal demos of pop ballads can work *if* you have an excellent lyric, melody, keyboard player, and singer. Those are exceptions, though, and no longer the rule. If you have any kind of rock, R&B or pop rhythm ballad or up-tempo song, you *need* a basic rhythm track—drums (or drum machine), bass and keyboard synthesizer or guitar—because the groove is an essential ingredient in its appeal.

PRODUCERS

Record producers come from a great variety of backgrounds. Some evolve into producers from being recording engineers and their skills may be focused on how records sound. Others are former studio musicians who may focus mainly on getting the right players and putting together great arrangements. Others, closer to the function of film producers, excel in the overview. Their skill is in putting together the magic elements—the artist, the arranger, the musicians, the engineer, the studio, the money, and most importantly, the songs.

No matter what their backgrounds, their success depends on recognizing great and *appropriate* songs for the artists they produce. However, as you might guess, their initial impressions when hearing your tape may vary based on their own particular areas of expertise. An engineer/producer may have a negative reaction to a poorly recorded tape. A studio musician/producer might cringe at an out-of-tune vocal or guitar, though he *may* be more adept at hearing the arrangement possibilities of a rough or simple demo. The "overview" type of producer may not have the musicians' sophisticated ability to visualize a finished production—he may just know what he likes when he hears it. Obviously, these categories are oversimplified for the sake of illustration, and any individual producer will possess his own unique combination of tastes and skills.

The point is that, in order to deal with that diversity, your best approach is to make sure your demo is technically "clean" and well arranged. I've heard a successful musician/producer say, "I can hear it from a piano/vocal," and at another time say, "The demo sounded just like the artist—the right key, the musical hooks, and everything were right there. I hardly had to do anything, so we cut it." One statement doesn't necessarily contradict the other but illustrates the fact that the more you give them, the more *easily* they'll hear it. Of the utmost importance in pitching a song to a producer for a specific act is that the song is *appropriate* for the act. (See "Casting," page 186.) Do your research!

If you're an artist or band looking for someone to produce *you,* it's most important that the producer hears your best *performance* and your best *material.* He should be able to hear all the voices and instrumental parts clearly. A well-recorded live performance will work just fine if the vocals can be recorded cleanly.

RECORD COMPANIES

In most cases, the person at the record company you'll be pitching tapes to is the A&R person. A&R stands for "artist and repertoire," and in times of old when almost nobody wrote his own songs, they were the ones who told the artists what they'd record. Alas, for better or worse, those days are gone. A&R executives have a wide variety of tasks to perform and, like producers, come from diverse backgrounds. Different record companies have different philosophies in hiring them.

Each of these philosophies has potential advantages and disadvantages. Some companies want people who know music intimately, such as musicians, producers (in some companies all the A&R executives *are* producers), music journalists, and critics. Producers may become "studio bound" and lose touch with "the street," though they usually have the respect of the artists, managers, and other professionals they deal with and a decent ear for raw talent.

Others ascribe to the "man on the street" theory and hire an opinionated young rock fan to be their rock A&R representative. That philosophy sees an "A&R person as a general public record buyer." The "man on the street" has been exposed to records and masters all his life, may have trouble "hearing" less than finished product and, because of a lack of music or production experience, may not easily gain the respect of artists.

Other companies tend to hire from within the company. The former secretary of a producer (who screened all his material anyway) or the guy from the mailroom who used to hang out in the A&R department may be next in line for the job. The advantage is that he or she pretty much knows how the company operates and the company knows them. There's no dealing with an outsider who already has his own methods and philosophies, which may clash with the company status quo (unless the company *wants* a change). Each of the above philosophies, by the way, has produced outstanding A&R people.

The basic functions of an A&R department today are to find new talent and sign it, when needed, to find the act a manager, booking agent, or band members, to supervise and oversee production and budgets of recording projects, and to find suitable hit songs for the artists signed to the label. The latter is not as important as it used to be since most new acts come to them as self-contained units who write their own material or have producers who write or find it. Some record labels, like Arista, do have artists like Whitney Houston and Aretha Franklin who don't write and are always on the lookout for songs. And, in fact, A&R people also look for hits for artists on their labels who *do* write, though maybe not enough or not commercially enough. So though record company execs are probably not your first line of attack in pitching your songs (unless you're pitching yourself as an artist), they should not be ignored. Again here, you need well-produced demos and the song must be right for the artist they need songs for.

Never waste good tape by sending a song to an A&R department "just in case they might have an artist who could do this song." Target a particular artist, know the artist's work, have the correct label, and know the song is right or don't bother. If you're pitching the song to a specific artist, write "for Tina Turner" or whoever, on the package *and* in a cover letter *and* on the tape. They'll either turn it over to the artist's producer without opening it, or listen and decide for themselves whether to pass it to the producer, or send it back unopened (more on that later).

If you're pitching yourself or your group to an A&R department as an artist, the best way is to go in with two to four finished masters of the best songs you can write *or find* in your style. Whether they're masters or demos, your performance on these tapes must honestly be the best you're capable of. Excuses like "I know I can do it better but I had a cold that day," or "Our regular bass player went on the road and this new guy only had one rehearsal," just don't make it. This may be your only shot, and it's better to postpone your session till your cold is cured and your bass player is back. You can't expect a record company to sign you if they don't know exactly what they're getting. It's not absolutely necessary, but if possible, include the following with your tape: Your personal bio or bios of group members, pictures, a press kit with reviews, list of clubs played, a graphic design or logo on your press kit cover and tape insert, and a video of you or the group (please don't spend a lot of money on this). All this says, "We're ready and we're serious!"

CLUB OWNERS

If you're looking for a live gig in a club, your demo tape should be live, too. Most club owners won't trust studio demos alone because they've been burned so many times by hearing a great studio tape of an act that sounded very different in person. It doesn't hurt to include studio cuts, but your demo should contain at least part of a live set with your between-song rap, audience interaction, applause, etc., intact. Along with the tape, send them photos and bios with a list of clubs previously played, letters from owners of other clubs where you've worked, and, if it's a Top 40 gig, a list of the songs you're prepared to play. If you have a live video, it's much better than a live audio tape, but it's ideal to have both.

WHAT YOU CAN DO AT HOME

Once you've decided what kind of demo you need and who you're going to submit it to, you have to plan the actual production of the demo itself. It's important to plan ahead because you can waste a lot of time and money going into a recording project cold. One of the ways many songwriters cut the expense of demo production is by doing their own recording at home.

Recording at home has many obvious advantages. Sometimes you don't just get a great idea for a lyric. You also hear that drum groove and a bass line. Sometimes inspiration hits at 2 A.M. when your left brain is winding down and your right brain is starting to talk to you. If you've got your studio in the next room, you can plug in your headset, turn on the drum machine and keyboard, crank it up loud, and catch that idea before it gets away! Within hours you not only have a new song, but you've got the demo done the way you heard it in your head. You didn't have to write out chord charts for other musicians, worry about whether everybody would show up on time for the session, talk the guitar player out of doing a solo, buy lunch for the band at rehearsal, or spend your time in the studio watching the clock ticking away dollar signs. These advantages alone may make it worthwhile for you to invest in your own home studio, particularly if you write a lot of songs. For what it would cost you for a few demo sessions in a pro studio you could buy a good little home studio setup.

You will, of course, be saddled with maintenance of the equipment and the ever-present desire to buy the next piece of state-of-the-art gear to upgrade your setup. No matter how convenient and versatile your equipment, there will always be something you want to be able to do with it that you just can't achieve without one more gadget. Another problem also goes with the territory. Getting hung up in the engineering, forever fiddling with equipment to get the right sound, can actually rob you of spontaneity. There's always a trade-off. Your individual needs will really be the key to your decision to have your own studio. But you have a lot of options to choose from to let you enjoy the best of both worlds.

If you're a musician with even minimal skills, present-day technology (which is increasing at a dizzying rate), can make it possible for you to create master-quality demos at home. Companies like Roland, Oberheim, Yamaha, Korg, Kawai, Casio, Sequential Circuits, Fender, Akai, Ensoniq, and others manufacture synthesizers, sequencers (which record any rhythm, chord, or melodic pattern you create) and drum machines (programmed with changeable digital computer chips which electronically generate actual drum sounds). As the electronic components become easier to mass-produce, their cost comes down and their versatility increases.

Another contribution of the computer age is digital recording, in which you can perform many of the functions of a major recording studio using your personal computer and specially developed software programs. Included in the new instruments is the capability to program/record one note of the melody at a time (called "step time") which can later be electronically played back in its entirety at any speed. This is a great boon to those with limited keyboard skills because it can make you sound like a virtuoso. If you rush or are a little late on a beat, it can also correct your time (called "quantizing"). The drum machines can be inspirational, especially if you're having a hard time getting into writing an up-tempo groove.

Other computer-assisted capabilities include the ability to digitally sample and record any sound, correct single notes, change pitch, or transpose to another key without changing speed and (vice versa) and change the duration of a note after it's recorded. To take advantage of this technology, you need equipment with MIDI (Musical Instrument Digital Interface) capabilities. There are also adapters available that will convert or retrofit any instrument to MIDI.

These miracles of electronics make it possible for you to get your musical and rhythmic concepts down on tape without limiting you to the boundaries of your own adequacies as an instrumentalist. What happens then is that your abilities to *conceptualize* musical ideas are also tremendously expanded, because you know you can record anything you can think of without needing to be able to actually play it all. Learning to manipulate electronic instruments and computers is a valuable skill. Songwriters who have a solid education in music theory will save much trial-and-error time in creating arrangements, but that kind of formal education is not as necessary as it used to be to write and record contemporary songs.

Developments in synth and computer technology occur so fast that I can't be specific about what to buy—the equipment might be obsolete by the time this book hits the stores. It's safe to suggest, though, that any synthesizer you buy should have MIDI (Musical Instrument Digital Interface) capability so it can be connected to other synthesizers and to computers.

The best thing you can do to keep up with latest developments is to subscribe to or periodically pick up a copy of *Keyboard; Guitar, for the Practicing Musician; Guitar Player; Electronic Musician; Musician; KCS, Keyboards, Computers and Software;* or *Music Technology.*

You might think, "That's great if you write synth-styled songs, but what if I want to write acoustic country songs?" Again, technology makes it easy. Fostex, Teac, Yamaha, and others make very portable, easy-to-use, recording equipment with very good specifications in 4-, 8- and 16-track formats. They've also developed educational books to help you get the most out of them. The books deal not only with recording techniques but with shaping the acoustic properties of your home environment.

It's possible to record and make copies of your demo from start to finish in your own home studio. But many writers choose to record at home all those electronic instruments that don't depend on the use of microphones and an acoustic environment. They then take what they have to a professional recording studio, transfer it to the studio tape, and use the studio's selection of microphones and outboard gear (reverb, limiters, compressors, etc.) to record acoustic instruments and vocals and to mix the tracks. This method can save a lot of money and still produce a high-quality demo. It allows you to spend your creative, experimental time at home without the studio pressure, and to plan the best use of your studio time. If you can get the rhythm tracks down at home with drum machines and synths, you can also give your singer a chance to work with the tracks before the studio session.

Electronic instruments and recording gear can be too expensive for many writers to buy on their own. A little cooperation and planning with others, though, can often get you what you want. Some friends of mine bought different components and periodically bring them together for a demo marathon weekend, pooling all their equipment and helping each other to produce their demos. Others I know borrow from and loan each other equipment.

The digital recording you can do at home using MIDI and computer technology is usually so clean it can be used in studio masters. Today it's not unusual to create many components of master tracks outside the studio and then combine them with the advantages of the studio environment and technology. Most studios have the computer electronics to "read" what you bring them. In fact, the old joke about the studio musicians "phoning in" their parts is now a reality.

CHOOSING A STUDIO

Many songwriters use the facilities of a professional recording studio to put the finishing touches on their demos. Other writers like to work in a studio from the start. If you should decide to do all or part of your recording in a studio, there are several factors to consider in choosing one. It's very important to pick a studio where you can get the services and equipment you need to achieve the sound and quality you want.

Your first move should be to decide what kind of demo you want and how much recording you'll do there. Then you want to decide what you need from the studio in order to do it. The amount of money you have to spend is also very important, though we'll discuss other options later. How do you decide what you need? Here are some points to consider:

What style of music do you play? If your music is primarily electronic (electronic drums, keyboards, etc.), some studios have excellent facilities for plugging "direct" into the recording equipment but offer little if you need an acoustic environment for vocals or instruments that you'd record with a microphone. It may be best to go elsewhere to do your acoustic recording.

A small room is adequate if you play quiet, acoustic music. If you play loud rock and roll you need to decide whether you want a big, open concert-style sound for which you'd look for a big, high-ceiling room (also good for live string sections) or the tight, "present" sound you get in a smaller, acoustically "dead" room. Most studios, however, offer some versatility by the use of "baffles" (also called "gobos"), which are movable screens that can be placed between instruments or amps. The baffles often offer a choice of sound-absorbent or reflective surfaces to give you a choice of "live" or "dead" sound. The studio may also give you a choice of curtains or reflective walls or rug-covered or hard floor surfaces to achieve the same effects. The baffles can also isolate the sounds from "bleeding" into the mikes of other instruments.

The way songs are "miked," recorded, and mixed is different in each style of music, so no matter what your style, you'll want to find an engineer who's experienced with that type of music, or make sure that the studio would allow you to bring in your own engineer.

Do you want to record demos or masters? You don't really need masters unless you're shopping your act to record labels and you are (or have) a good producer and a very clear idea of how you want to sound on record. Otherwise, go for more simple demos. If you're producing masters, you're going for a "radio ready," finished product. Consequently, every detail of the recording must be the best—the sounds of all the instruments, the performances, audio quality, everything. Many times during the process of recording a master some little thing goes wrong, and you need to decide whether it's worth the time and money to do another "take" or otherwise fix the problem. With a demo, while it's important that it sounds very good, you'll decide fewer times to spend the money to fix little things or you'll opt for a less than perfect, but more economical solution to the problem. That's because a demo is understood not to be a finished product.

"You get what you pay for" is a good maxim to keep in mind when you shop for studio time. If you find a studio with unusually low prices, don't feel awkward about asking them how they can afford to offer such inexpensive rates. *Ask if they have a maintenance person on duty.* If they say, "No, but we have someone we can call if anything goes wrong," determine how that might affect your session. If it's just you and a couple of buddies who don't have anything else to do but wait to see how fast those repairs can happen, it may not matter to you. If you have fifteen musicians all getting union scale who have another session booked after yours, you're in very big trouble and may end up having to pay them and not get anything on tape.

Don't book too much time in a single block. Sometimes you can get a better deal if you book a large block of studio time, but there's a "burn-out factor" that takes place after long periods of tension and concentrated listening, particularly if you're into a time period that runs counter to your personal "biological clock" (e.g., 4 A.M., if your regular bedtime is 11 P.M.). You may actually waste money by the mistakes you make because your perceptions and high-frequency hearing are not operating efficiently. Avoid the temptation to use drugs to compensate. They only further damage your perceptions and complicate matters by making you less aware that you're not functioning at your peak. Make sure your engineer is also working at his peak.

The number of tracks a studio offers should not be the basis of your choice. More is not necessarily better. Studios can offer anywhere from 2 to 48 tracks to serve many different needs. I've heard "live" 2-track demos of bands that rival the excitement of a 24-track master because they have more "presence." On analog (as opposed to digital) recording, a small amount of tape noise is added with each track recorded and the quality of the recording, regardless of the number of tracks, is dependent on the quality of the equipment used and the ability of the engineer to get the best use from it.

May you bring your own recording tape or are you required to buy tape from the studio? They'll charge you more than you'd have to pay at a tape and recording supply store. You may live in a place where you have no choice, but if you're in a major recording center, buy your tape outside the studio. If you do that, however, be sure to check with the studio first to find out what type of tape their machines are biased for or you may end up losing your tape savings on studio time spent on the engineer realigning his recorder.

The amount of tape you need will depend on the purpose of your session. If you're recording masters, you need the best fidelity possible. Because the faster the speed, the better the fidelity, you'll want to record at 30 i.p.s. (inches per second). Standard tape lengths are 2500 and 3600 feet. At 30 i.p.s., you'll get 15 minutes from the former and 22½ minutes from the latter. If you're doing a demo, you can record at 15 i.p.s. or even 7½ i.p.s., which of course, gives you much more recording room.

If you're recording on a 16- or 24-track recorder, you'll need 2" (wide) tape. With 8-channel 8-track, you'll need 1" or ½" tape (check with the studio). With 4-channel 4-track, you'll need ½" tape and with full track, 2-channel 2-track, or 2-channel 4-track, you can use ½" tape, so bring enough for the possibility of several different "takes" to choose from.

On demos, if you're strapped financially you can also buy used, bulk-erased tape. The quality may be adequate for a demo, though it won't be good enough for masters.

Always count on using more tape than you think you'll need. It's better to be prepared. You can always use the extra tape at another time. Remember that you'll use up a lot of tape doing multiple takes if you're recording live, so you'll need plenty of room for each song.

STUDIO DEALS

If you do decide to work in a studio, you can make special deals to lower your costs, but you'll need to be careful not to let your eagerness get you into trouble.

In your search for your next career break you encounter local studio owner Harry Sessions. He says, "I like your tunes and you're a good performer. I think you've got a shot at getting a record deal. I own a studio and I'd like to take you in and cut some of your tunes just to see what we could come up with."

This is just what you've been waiting to hear. You've been trying to see A&R people at the record companies with your home demos and getting nowhere. Even though they say they can listen to a simple demo, you know they're listening to finished radio-quality masters every day and that those probably have a competitive edge. You've been waiting for a deal like this to come along and say to yourself, "Just do it, don't ask questions."

You finish the four-song project with help from your (or Harry's) musician friends who learned, rehearsed, and recorded the songs with you. You've got no written or verbal contract regarding the ownership of the masters or demos. You figure Harry is a friend helping you out and in some kind of way he'll get paid when you make a deal with the record label. But then he drops the bomb: "Of course, you understand that I get the publishing on all these tunes. I assume you're hip enough to know that's the way these deals are done. I get the production points[1] and the publishing."[2]

You're a little shocked but you don't want to appear unhip, of course, and Harry has been so nice to you that you don't want to seem ungrateful. You're behaving exactly the way he wants you to. Now he wants you to sign the contract.

This is a familiar scenario and periodically someone calls me and asks, "Do I have to give him my publishing? He says he has a right to it because he did the tapes." The answer is NO, assuming that you made no written or verbal agreement ahead of time regarding the publishing or production points.

Another situation you'll run into is when a studio owner offers to produce your demos or masters "on spec." The studio owner "speculates" that the time and sometimes the money that he, as producer, puts in will be recouped when you sell your master to a record label. He hopes he'll end up as a) the producer of the whole album project, b) your producer for the life of your record contract, and/or c) publisher of all the

---

1 A percentage of income earned by the producer paid from your artist royalties. If we assume that your artist royalty is 10 percent of the suggested retail price of the record, 3 to 5 percent is the customary split. The latter are referred to not as percentages, but as "points," to avoid the impression that it's 3 percent of 10 percent.

2 Ownership of the copyrights and 50 percent of the income from the songs.

songs he produces on you. That's his maximum payoff and he'll need a production and publishing contract with you to achieve it. At minimum, without a production contract, the producer/studio owner hopes the record company would like you *and* the production enough that you'll "buy out" the masters (with your record company advance) with enough money for a profit beyond what he put into the tapes. He also hopes he'd get production points and credit on those recordings the label eventually releases.

If the record company likes you as an artist but doesn't like him as a producer, without a production or publishing contract between you and him, you may get a record deal and he won't get anything. In fact, for the very reason that the record company may not like his production and would want you produced by someone they choose, you should *never* guarantee that the "spec" producer will be hired by you or the record company to produce any product released in your future record deal.

If he doesn't present you with a production contract until after the masters are complete and you don't like the deal he presents you with then, you're under no obligation to accept. If the studio owner hasn't gotten together with you ahead of time and laid out the conditions under which he's speculating his time and facilities, then he's gambling that you'll like his work enough to go along with him or that he can intimidate you like Harry Sessions.

The reality is, though, that if you walk away you won't be able to take your tape with you. The producer/studio owner physically owns the tapes. He doesn't have to give you the masters or copies. After all, he figures, why should you be able to use the results of his production expertise and time without his being compensated for it? He can't release the tapes without your permission or sell them to a label without owning the rights to your performances unless you later sign with a label who wishes to buy them from him or unless he has actually paid you to perform on the masters. If you later publish and release those songs, he can't collect any royalties on your publishing without a specific contract to do so. Obviously, without a record out, there aren't any royalties anyway, but writer/artists often worry that some time in the future someone will make a claim based on this studio situation.

In this case both the studio owner/producer and the writer/artist are responsible for the unpleasant situation because they didn't let it be known what they both expected from the deal before the recording took place.

The preceding example is one I come across more than I'd like to, but many other studio deals can be made which are fair to both the studio and the writer/performer. With an agreement up front in writing, this could have been one of them. The fact is that *you're* also speculating that all the hard work and time *you* put into this project will pay off for you, too. If you're happy with what you accomplished in the studio together and enjoyed working with the producer, you don't want those ugly, unexpected, after-the-fact business realities to damage a promising relationship.

MAKING "SOUND" DEALS

Now that we've got an idea of what can go wrong in negotiating a special studio deal, let's talk more constructively about a better way to approach this situation.

As I said earlier, you have to decide whether you need demos or masters, whether you need a "state-of-the-art" studio and engineer, or if you can get by with lower quality and less experience for less money. If you can get by with a less expensive demo, you may not need to worry about making a deal.

If you decide that you need a more elaborate demo than you can afford to pay for outright, the next question to ask yourself is, "What do I have to offer that a studio owner/producer or an engineer/producer might want?" The variables are cash, services, or participation. Musicians sometimes barter services in exchange for studio time. Maybe you're a builder or painter, decorator, graphic artist, electrician, secretary, or have some other skill that would be of use to a studio owner. As a musician, you might play on some of his other in-house productions. You may also own a piece of outboard equipment or a unique instrument you could exchange for studio time.

Participation refers to percentages of production or publishing deals and gets a little more complex. In the case of an artist, by "participation" I'm talking about production points as discussed in the previous section. In the case of a writer or writer/artist I'm talking about ownership of your copyrights or receipt of royalties (without ownership) from your songs. Generally speaking, *if you just need a demo, don't give away percentages of production or publishing.* The only exception I can think of is if you're making a deal with a major producer who has a great track record— someone who can walk into a record company, play them a demo and get a budget on the strength of his reputation.

Writers with limited funds may encounter studio owners or engineer/producers who will ask for your publishing even for producing a simple song demo, but consider that any legitimate publisher who will be actively shopping your tunes will make demos as part of her job.

It's possible too that all you need is a simple, not an elaborate, production. If you sign with a full time, experienced publisher, he'll decide what's an appropriate demo for the producers he'll approach with your song. The problem with engineer/studio owners acting as publishers is that even though they'll sometimes come across opportunities to pitch a tune to a producer in their studio who needs a song, they may not actively be publishers on a daily basis. That's why it would be better to offer them a percent of the mechanical royalties on any record they secure, but only on that record, without giving them ownership of any percentage of your copyright. (See "Negotiating," page 189.)

If you're going for masters as an artist (ready to be pressed and radio quality), and determine that the studio is equipped to give you master quality, *participation in production or publishing is a common deal to make.* You'll need a producer unless you're already a good, experienced producer and have the rare ability to be objective with your own work. It's only fair, in lieu of cash, to offer a producer production points. In fact, he usually gets both but in a "spec" deal, the cash in front is what he's giving up. A percentage of the publishing on *only* the tunes he produces is also a common deal in lieu of cash. With either of those deals, though, make sure there's a time period involved in which you are returned your copyrights and your option to work with another producer if the record deal doesn't happen. It ranges from 6-18 months and is most often a year (but ultimately, whatever you agree on) after the masters are completed. The studio or independent engineer will still own the actual master tapes (unless you paid for them) so that if a record company wants to use something you've already done, they can buy the tapes, giving the studio or engineer the opportunity to get back their investment. They may also want to be compensated if the tapes are used to obtain a record deal, even though the masters are not bought by the record company. Since there are many contingencies to these agreements, you should always have an experienced music industry attorney help you negotiate them.

Studio rates, whether you're paying cash or bartering services, are always flexible. When you call a studio for rates, they'll always give you their "book" rate, so dig a little deeper. Here are some of the factors involved in lowering that rate.

Block booking. The more hours you can guarantee them, the cheaper you usually can get studio time. As I mentioned earlier, though, spending hours in the studio when you're over-tired can be counterproductive.

Late hours and down time. You can make a better deal if you can work at the studio's convenience. If you let the owner know that you'll be able to come in on short notice in their "down time" (when the studio isn't booked) it helps them by keeping money coming in and they're liable to give you a better rate. Tell them to call you if someone cancels and the notice is too short to book another session at their full rate, or if the studio has to cancel a session because a piece of equipment broke (just make sure you don't need to use that particular piece of equipment). In some of these deals, the studio reserves the right to bump you out when they get a "book rate" session in your time slot. Late night or early morning hours can also be cheaper in some studios.

Up front cash will get you better rates. The more you can give the studio in advance of the session, particularly if you've blocked out a large number of guaranteed hours, the better the rates you'll get.

The engineer you choose will have a bearing on your studio costs. Some engineers are still in training and some are well-experienced pros. If you're doing a simple demo, it may be cheaper to hire a beginner (if you can get him to admit it). What you have to weigh is the possibility that a beginner's mistake may cost you time/money.

If you bring along your own favorite independent engineer, it may involve extra time for him to learn the idiosyncrasies of a new studio, though you're saving time by using someone you've established communication with.

Make sure when you use any engineer that he hasn't already been working for twelve hours and is too burnt out to react or hear properly. Engineers work more hours under stress than is healthy for human beings anyway. So always find out how long your engineer has worked before your session. If their own staff engineers are unavailable during the hours you want to work, most studios can recommend independent engineers who have worked in their studio before.

Though most seasoned engineers are fairly versatile, some have experience primarily in country music, R&B, heavy metal, or some other style and who will be more familiar with the way instruments and vocals are recorded and mixed in that style. Find one who will understand what to do with your music.

When you're pricing a studio, you may be quoted the studio time rates *without* the engineer, though most demo studios include it. Fees for engineers run about $10 per hour for demos. Engineers fees for masters can run from $25-150 per hour. Make sure you find out exactly what the fees are and figure them in your budget. Independent engineers are usually paid separately, and staff engineers are paid with the same check you pay the studio. Get it straight ahead of time. In fact, talk to the engineer you'll be working with before the session so you can feel a little more relaxed and confident about what you intend to do.

Many demo studios advertise "production assistance," but people are sometimes disappointed by the minimal assistance actually available. Ask the studio *exactly* what is meant by "production assistance." Is it five minutes with the engineer before the session, or is it playing your songs for someone and discussing a musical direction, musicians, and budget? Regarding the latter, remember that the studio is in business to make money, and therefore may be inclined to make suggestions that will result in your use of more studio time than you need. Try to at least determine whether a simple or a full-blown production is appropriate before talking to the studio. The more "overdubbing" or "tracking" (adding instruments or vocals to the initial recording) that's done, the more studio time you need. Playing the instruments yourself and building the tracks one by one is most time-consuming. When you work out your budget you have to decide whether it's cheaper not to pay other musicians and spend the money on more studio time or use less time and pay more musicians.

Equipment. The cost of the studio time is also determined by the equipment you need. If you're doing a piano/vocal you may only need a two-track studio. Cheap! If you're cutting masters with a big production, you may want 24 or more tracks with automated mixdown capabilities, or maybe you want digital recording. Very expensive! You may need some signal-processing devices that the studio may or may not have available the quoted hourly rate. This is referred to as "outboard" equipment and includes such things as phasers, flangers, limiters, compressors, various types of reverb and delay, harmonizers, DBX or Dolby noise reduction, graphic or parametric equalizers, and many others. Discuss your needs for this equipment *before* the session so you aren't surprised by, "Oh, you want to do *that!* You need a thingamajig and we don't have one, but we can rent one for you for $100 a day!" Don't be fooled by the brand names of outboard equipment that many studios advertise, unless they specify the model number and you're familiar with that model. The brand name alone doesn't tell you if they have the specific piece of equipment you need.

Getting all the info before the session will save you money in the end. In fact, knowing what questions to ask ahead of time and knowing what everyone needs to make them happy on the business end is the key to also saving your peace of mind during and after the session.

THE RECORDING PROCESS
Once you've decided on a studio, engineer, and equipment you'll need, here are a few things to keep in mind about the recording process:

1. Remember to double your estimated recording time (for listening to playbacks).
2. Test your mixes on your car stereo/cassette player. Switch back and forth between your song and the radio or a familiar tape for comparison. Listen for the clarity of instruments and vocals.
3. If you have several days in which to record, in the first session, record your basic drum, guitar, bass, and keyboard tracks first with a temporary "scratch" vocal. That temporary vocal is used so that the musicians can create parts that support but don't get in the way of the vocal. At the end of the first session, "scratch" (eliminate) the vocal and do a rough mix. "Mix" refers to the relative *volumes, placement* (right, left, or center for stereo), and *"EQ"* (equalization), the amount of treble, bass, and mid-range emphasis, on each of the instruments. You'll then take home a tape with which the vocalist can rehearse her performance and with which you can work out and rehearse "overdubs," additional parts such as instrumental solos and harmony parts, background vocals, orchestral parts, etc. During the next session, record the vocals and the overdubs and get a rough mix or two of that session. Take them home and listen to the mixes so you can make decisions about them at your leisure outside the pressure of the studio. It's generally not a good idea to do more than a rough mix at the same session in which you record. It's difficult to have a good perspective on this important process when you and your ears are fatigued.

This is a common, though not necessarily the best, approach to the recording process. If you're a self-contained group, you're well rehearsed, and want to preserve a spontaneous sound, you'd record everything "live" at the same time, though it still may be advisable to have a separate mixing session.

You may not have the luxury of recording over a several-day period. If you must do it all at once, prepare very well, rehearse the musicians and singer(s), and make sure your engineer knows ahead of time what you want to do and how you want to do it.

SAVING MONEY BY BEING PREPARED

The best way to cut down on time, aggravation, and expenses is to have a solid idea of what you want for your demo and a good plan for getting it. In preparing for the session there are some things to consider that will save you a lot of time and worry.

Choose the right musicians and rehearse ahead of time. One of the most difficult aspects of doing demos is choosing the right musicians, because one of the properties of a good demo (directed at publishers and producers) is to be able to suggest possibilities for arrangements without actually doing a full arrangement. Demos require musicians with an ability to exercise restraint, to control their egos, and to control the desire to "show off all their chops." Sad to say, that kind of self-control is a rarity in most young musicians. Many are still too wrapped up in learning their instrument to be able to direct their creativity toward playing something simple that fits and *complements* the whole arrangement or *supports* a vocal. In a rock demo, it's more important to get across an infectious, danceable rhythm *feel* than to feature a great guitar solo. You want the person you're pitching the song to, to be able to say, "Man, I could really do a great solo there!" Always try to suggest just enough for them to think it's *their* idea.

The ideal in choosing musicians is that you've had an opportunity to work with or listen to a lot of them and can afford to pay $10 to $60 per tune (extra to overdub other parts), which is the range of demo rates. You'll then choose them according to the style of songs you're recording and the way you'll predict that they'll interact with other musicians when left to their own creativity. The result is that you'll need to exercise a minimum of direction and get maximum creative contribution from each of the musicians involved. In fact, you'll ideally want to find a number of musicians who play together in the same group, or at least have played together often enough that they have their own intercommunication well tuned.

What usually happens, though, is that you don't have that much money and you can't afford to be choosy. You should know, then, that there are a lot of musicians around looking for something to get involved in and willing to do sessions for the experience or "on spec" (on the speculation that if and when *you* get paid, *they* get paid). Make signs explaining your situation, the type of music you're interested in, and put them in music stores, colleges, music departments, and clubs. Advertise in musicians' magazines. Offer to trade your own services as a musician, singer, or whatever. You're bound to go through some trial and error to find the right people, but that's what you need to do.

When you find the musicians you want, rehearse with them as much as possible before doing the session. It'll save you lots of money in studio time. If you can afford to pay the musicians, agree on the fees before the session and pay them promptly. You'll feel much better about directing them if you've taken care of business and, psychologically, you'll eliminate "bad vibes" and have an eager team working with you.

If you don't feel you have the inclination or experience to find and direct musicians and only have a basic idea of how you want your demo to sound, a great alternative is to hire an arranger. You can find one through your local musicians' union or check out the local Top 40 "cover bands" in your area who are used to playing a broad range of contemporary styles. At least one person in the group usually has a good head for arrangement. Whoever you hire should be able to write out master rhythm charts, select musicians, find the studio, help you prepare a budget, and make sure everyone gets paid.

Prepare master rhythm charts of the songs for each musician before you rehearse or before the session if there's no rehearsal. Master rhythm charts don't necessarily need to have the melody written out, but should contain the chord changes and all the directions *you've* thought of ahead of time, such as when certain instruments enter or exit, a specific bass line you want to hear, etc. Singers should have a "lead sheet" that contains melody line and lyric.

Have your musicians check their instruments and amps before the session to eliminate unwanted hums, buzzes, noisy pedals, or other obnoxious sounds. Listen up close to the amps where the mikes will be placed. This is frequently a problem with musicians who are used to playing live. A slight hum in an amp that might ordinarily go unnoticed in a live situation will make you crazy when it's miked and magnified in the studio. You may end up spending lots of costly time trying to fix a buzzing guitar string or having to call an instrument rental company to send over a new pedal.

Get your "sounds" established on the instruments during rehearsals. Do you want the bass and guitar to be mellow or biting? "Tune" the drums the way you want them for the song or the session. For the studio, producers usually prefer the snare to be deadened somewhat with pads of cloth and masking tape near the edge of the head. They'll also deaden the kick drum as well, by removing the front head and pushing a pillow against the inside head. This is, however, a matter of personal taste. Those creative decisions should be made as much as possible before the session. You may change your mind later when you hear them over the studio monitors, but at least you'll have a concept to start with. If you're using a drum machine, program it for each song before the session.

It's part of the engineer's job to "get a sound" on the instruments before recording, and you should be prepared to explain the concept you're going for. (Try taping examples of the drum, bass, or other instrument sounds from radio or records to show the engineer what you want.) Find out from the engineer whether this procedure is included in "setup time" before the clock starts running on your session. Sometimes it is, but usually it's not. Know in advance how much setup time you're allowed. (It varies from ½-1 hour.) Make sure your musicians understand this and don't waste time setting up.

Everyone should have spare strings, drum heads, etc. I don't know a professional musician who hasn't learned that lesson on his first gig, but I thought I'd bring it up anyway, just in case.

Decide the order in which you want to do the songs. Is one song more difficult and another more fun? Find out how the musicians feel about it, assuming you have time to do them all. Be careful to figure realistically how much you can get done. The engineer can help you decide when you meet with him before the session.

Make sure the musicians all know exactly where and when the session is, how long it'll take them to get there, and that all have transportation.

CHOOSING THE SONGS

Whether you decide to produce your demos at home or in the studio, there are a few decisions that must be made before you begin. The most obvious one is choosing which of your songs to record.

All the songs you write don't have to be commercial, but the ones you present to publishers and producers must be. Many writers have difficulty determining the commerciality of their songs. How do you know? You start by asking your friends, most of whom will be so knocked out that you wrote a song that they'll automatically love it. Tell them to be critical, and don't try to explain the song before playing it. Ask them if they can sing the chorus back to you. Can they tell you what the song is about? Did they understand all the words? Do they remember any lyrics? Which of your songs do they like the best? Which do they remember? Why? Which ones can they sing the melodies to? Those songs are your best shots.

Get as many opinions as possible. If people are critical, thank them and don't get defensive. Keep a cool head and know that they're not attacking you personally. The rewards of letting them help you grow and find success in your craft far outweigh the short-term ego damage.

What if you write a lot of different styles of songs and get good critical response on all of them? Your decision is then based on whether you have the desire or the potential to become a recording artist. You have the best chance at it if you have an easily identifiable voice and style. (See chapter 15, "Getting a Record Deal.") If that's your direction, limit your selections to the style you feel most at home with. If you love to sing rhythm and blues-styled tunes, but also write good country songs, stick with R&B for demos to show record companies. It's confusing to them to hear a lot of different styles from one artist and it presents a marketing problem: "Do we market this artist country or R&B?" It's good, however, to show some variety within the style.

For publishers it's different. Though they're happy if you specialize, it's a plus for you to be able to write well in many different styles. So it's okay to present them with your best songs in several different musical genres.

ARRANGEMENTS

We'd all like to believe that a great melody and lyric are all that's necessary to make people pay attention to a song. In some cases that may be true, but in most cases, the melody becomes more appealing in the context of the harmonies and countermelodies around it, and the meaning of a lyric can be conveyed even more strongly by framing it in the right way.

In recording demos or records, you can do several key things to help make them clean and powerful.

One of the most common problems in demos is the conflict between vocal and instrumental tracks. Demos are uncomfortable to listen to if the vocal is buried under the instrument tracks. It sometimes seems that the writer or artist is so insecure about the lyric or vocal that it's intentionally obscured. Or whoever mixed the demo knew the lyric so well, there was no perspective left about whether anyone else could understand it. One of the functions of a producer is to provide the right perspective to the mix. If you don't have a producer, let the engineer do it or call in someone who doesn't know the song when you're close to the final mix. Ask him if he can understand the words.

Letting the whole band mix the tracks will cost you money in studio time because everyone will want his own instrument to be loudest.

The arrangement is also crucial in achieving clean vocals. Here are some important considerations:

Melodic movement of instrumental parts relative to the vocal melody. One of the things that make demos sound busy or cluttered is the conflict of too many melody lines moving at the same time. Our natural tendency as listeners is to focus on the vocal melody. A harmony on that melody (instrumental or vocal) may enhance it, but a different single line melody on, say, an electric guitar at the same time may be distracting. A slow moving chordal "pad" of strings or synthesizer will work fine because these don't command our attention like a single-line melody. Rhythm instruments and repeated short rhythm parts on the instruments aren't usually a problem because once your brain realizes that they'll keep repeating, you take them for granted. Your body responds automatically, but your mind focuses on the movement of the melody.

Cutting basic tracks or overdubs without being able to hear the vocal phrasing or melody can produce a busy, cluttered sound. That's why it's best to at least use a "scratch" vocal (to be removed later) during a "head" arrangement (not written previously) and during production of both rhythm tracks and overdubs. That way you can tell if your arrangement works and if any of the instrumental parts are competing with the vocal melody. If there are any problems, they can be fixed while the musicians are still there.

Linear placement of instrumental parts relative to the vocals. The idea is to make a "window" for the vocals, to highlight them and to create expectation and tension. Drum "fills" perform this function going into a chorus, for instance. Instrumental "fills" should "bracket" the vocals, ending when the vocal phrase starts and starting when it ends. See the diagram at the top of the next page, where the top line represents the vocal phrase (with accompaniment), the notes represent the ongoing pulse, and the bottom line represents an instrumental "fill" that picks up where the vocal stops and drops out where the vocal begins again. If, for instance, you have a two-bar, eight-beat phrase and the vocal phrase takes the first five beats, the fill might start as early as that fifth beat. Even if a vocal is holding a single note past that point, a fill will work because the melody line isn't moving.

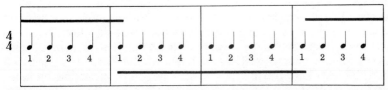

Vertical placement of the instrumental parts in the audio frequency range relative to the range of the vocals. Again, rhythm instruments and parts aren't usually a problem, but with melody instruments, you can make cleaner tracks and highlight the vocals more by separating the ranges in which the instruments are played. Keyboards and guitar commonly get played in the same midrange area as the vocals. Experiment with moving the parts up or down an octave or two to keep that vocal "window" uncluttered. (See the diagram of instrument ranges.) Other ways to enhance that window are to mix the volume of the instruments lower in that range, to deemphasize the EQ (equalization, treble/bass/midrange frequencies) in that range, and to pan the instruments (place them apart from each other in the left/right/center spectrum).

If you have a lot of tracks available, you may try to think of ways to fill them. There are *always* ways to fill empty tracks, but "less is more." Try to have fewer parts and make each one sonically interesting.

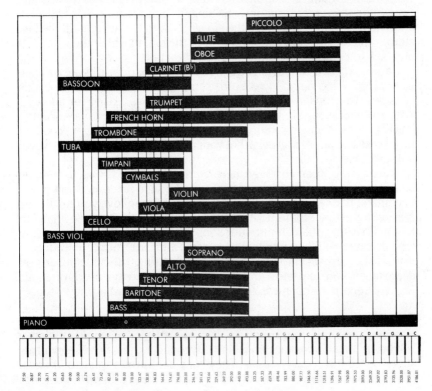

VOCALS

The emotional impact of a vocal may well be *the* most important factor in the effectiveness of a demo. Most writers who can sing automatically assume they should be the one to sing on it. Sometimes it's a simple question of economics. You feel it costs too much to hire another singer. Or it could be simple ego. You figure you *know* the song; you *feel* the emotions that went into it. It's part of you. Who could do it better? Even if you're not a great singer, you feel you can at least do it adequately. You may be right. Then again, you may be wrong. You'll never know if the performance of a great singer could have made the difference between acceptance and rejection. Have faith that if the song has emotional impact, a very good singer (perhaps with your direction) should be able to put it across. So the rule of thumb is: *If you know anyone who can sing the song better than you, he or she should be singing on the demo.*

Make sure that the singer is comfortable with the song's musical style—classical or musical theatre-trained singers may be out of their element doing country or R&B, for instance. Stylistically, it must be believable.

The singer should avoid improvising on the melody too much. Stylistic inflections are okay, but vocal gymnastics that tend to obscure the melody are not. What you get is a showcase for the performance and not for the song, making it difficult for an artist to hear what *they* could do with the song without re-creating your demo singer's performance. What you *can* do to highlight both is to have the singer stick to the melody till the last chorus and maybe do a chorus repeat at the end in which the singer improvises to demonstrate some stylistic direction.

If yours is a song that could be sung by either sex, do you choose a male or female for the demo? I've heard some interesting feedback on this question. The consensus seems to be that it's much easier for a female artist to hear herself singing a male demo'd song than for a male artist to imagine himself singing a song he hears from a female singer. Too bad those sexist attitudes still exist, but your odds are better with a male vocal in these cases.

A demo singer can cost anywhere from $20 to $150 a song, depending on how good and how fast she is, how well she sight reads, and how much in demand her services are. Again, if your funds are low, you might suggest barter. Share studio time and assist her to produce her own demo. Remind her that she can put your song on her own performance demo tape and that you'll be pitching your song, with her vocal, to producers. Many major artists have been discovered through their exposure on demo tapes. You may find a great Top 40 cover group that needs originals to pitch record companies. Your songs may be just what they need.

INTROS

How you introduce your song on a demo depends on who your audience will be. In *song demos* for publishers or producers, you *must* keep intros short. Get to the vocal/lyric fast. They consider intros a waste of their listening time because they're only listening to the *song.* In *artist demos* to producers and record companies that's not the case because you're creating a finished product and the creativity of that intro is part of what you're selling.

The length of an intro will vary from song to song. Generally, though, it should be kept under four bars for a ballad because it's more difficult to sustain interest at a slow tempo. An up-tempo dance song that involves a listener's body will generate more excitement simply by increasing the speed of their heartbeats. Consequently, those intros can be longer.

Short or long, an introduction creates an immediate first impression that sets up the listener's expectation for the whole song. It sets the mood, the emotional tone and ultimately, on a record, becomes the "signature" that sets it apart from all other songs. When you go to a concert or hear a live recording, you'll hear the audience cheer in recognition of their favorite songs after only a few notes.

So, in producing your demo and writing the song, pay special attention to developing a unique intro. Some writers have a tendency to throw away that opportunity by "vamping" (repeating the same thing) for four or eight bars between two chords. To bore your audience before even getting into the song is unwise. I've seen publishers angrily push the "stop" button on their cassette player after eight bars of boredom.

Here are some possibilities to explore:

1. Try using a variation or mutation of either your verse or chorus melodic theme as an intro.
2. Work backwards from the first vocal melody to discover a melody or progression that might heighten the impact of the vocal entrance. A big dynamic buildup to a soft, quiet vocal entrance might work well or maybe a gradual build to a strong vocal entrance.
3. Use an interesting repeating instrumental riff that will be heard later under the verse or chorus.
4. Explore your acoustic or synthesizer instruments for a unique sound or blend of sounds.
5. Introduce a new instrument or part every bar or two to thicken the texture and increase tension. This is fairly common, but if your instrumentation and melody are unique it can be a very effective intro.
6. Develop a groove by starting with the simplest component and adding the other rhythmic parts as you go. Sometimes it's easier to develop the whole groove first with drums, bass, rhythm guitar, and other rhythm parts, then figure out later which of those components to start the intro with. If you've layered them onto separate channels of a tape recorder, experiment by punching various combinations in or out every bar or two. You might start with the bass line, then bring in the drums, then the rhythm guitar or vice versa, whatever works best. Try all the combinations you can think of.
7. Consider the possibility, particularly in a ballad, of having no instrumental intro at all, just starting with the lead vocal or an interesting background vocal part.

The bottom line is that, no matter how long it is or what devices you use to create interest, the intro must sustain a listener's attention. Some long ones do and some short ones don't. When you listen to the radio, check out the intros and whether they kept *you* interested.

SOLOS

Solos, like intros, are generally considered by publishers and producers to be a waste of their listening time in song demos. If they're judging the song, they don't care if Eddie Van Halen is playing on your demo. No solos. Just the song, please. Publishers and producers have shut off hundreds of tapes because of interminably long and self-indulgent intros or because they know they're going to hear a solo. Most people include long solos only because they don't have enough lyric and want to fill the space, or some friends are helping do the demo and get to show off with a solo as a compensation for their time. Don't do it!

That's not to say that a short solo of a couple of bars that serves a *definite function* as a transition or a dramatic tension-builder can't be very effective in a song demo. Just don't use a whole verse or chorus worth.

If you're cutting masters or demos to sell your self-contained act to a producer or record company, the above does *not* apply. They *need* to hear the talents of the group, and that long guitar solo better be a killer!

ENDINGS

With endings your have two choices: work out an ending or fade. The fade is usually done to allow you to keep "cooking" on an exciting riff or repetitive vocal phrase or "the hook," without bringing down the energy level and intensity of the music. On a fade, you only bring down the actual volume. You leave the illusion that the band is just going on down the road and even though, after a while, you can't hear them, you know they're still cookin'. A fade works if you have something great to go out on that feels like it has a natural momentum. Commercially speaking, it's always a good idea for the "hook," or chorus, or whatever you want an audience to remember, to be the last thing they hear. With a fade you also give the disc jockeys a chance to talk over the ending, which excites THEM as much as talking over the intro (even though it doesn't excite US so much). It also lets them do their own fade, which may be considerably shorter than yours. Keep in mind that unless you're playing a dance gig, long, repetitive fades tend to get tedious, so the shorter the better. This is particularly true for demos, presentations to record companies, and showcases.

As for working out endings, it all depends on the song. The only thing I can say is: Please, try to be original. I'll grant you that there are times when the best ending for the song is one that has already been well worn. Just TRY to give it the care you give the rest of your song.

DEMO PRODUCTION SERVICES

If you've decided that all you want to do is write songs, and producing your own demos is way too much of a hassle, never fear! Demo production services have sprung up into a whole industry. These services advertise in music trade magazines including *Music Connection, BAM, Billboard, Cash Box,* etc., the L.A. Songwriters Showcase *Musepaper,* and the newsletters of songwriters organizations all over the country. Here are some guidelines for dealing with them.

Only deal with demo production services if you can check out their product ahead of time. Some will send you a tape sample of their work free; others may charge a nominal fee, but it's worth it to know what you're getting into.

Only deal with those who will tell you exactly what you'll get for your money. They should be able to send you a rate sheet that gives you a choice of options from guitar/vocal to full-scale productions with strings, horn sections, and so forth. Extra rates for lead sheet preparation, tape copies, and other services should be spelled out. In other words, no surprises. Some companies, on their demo reels, will give you a choice of singers. Rates usually range between $15 and $30 per instrument or singer per song, although some singers may charge up to $50 depending on whether they rehearse first, on how many overdubs they do on each song, and so on.

Don't deal with companies who offer to *compose music* to your lyrics for a fee or to *publish your song* for a fee. By the rules of BMI and ASCAP, they are not allowed to be members of those organizations. Therefore, if by some remote chance they actually got air play on your song, you'd never be able to get paid for it. (See "Avoiding the Songsharks," page 138.) You can always call or write your nearest BMI or ASCAP office to check them out.

Occasionally there is some confusion among songwriters who think that if they can't write musical notation, they're not "writing" music. If you "think up," "make up," or "compose" a melody that you can sing into a tape recorder, you have "written" the music. Most demo production houses offer such services as translating your melody into music notation (it's called "takedown") or preparing a *lead sheet* (containing the melody and words together) or arranging (in some cases deciding which chords to use and in some cases, much more), and are entitled to receive a fee for their work. But they are, strictly speaking, not cowriters. Whether you recognize them as cowriters depends on *your* assessment of the value of their contribution to the song.

You usually pay extra for a lead sheet. Takedown is usually included in the demo cost because they may need to do it anyway in order to get a roadmap from which to build the arrangement. Arrangement, too, is usually included in the overall cost of the demo.

Most demo services are mail-order businesses though many will let you be on the premises, and some will even let you do your own vocals. Most services welcome any creative input you have about how you would like your demo to sound. They thrive on repeat business and pride themselves on giving you what you want. If you like some sound you've heard on a record and are looking for something like it, send it with your song and it may help them zero in on your needs.

TAPE COPIES

When you've recorded a demo you're happy with and you're ready to make copies to send out to the pros, be professional yourself. Today's music industry operates on cassettes. Rarely does anyone ask for a reel-to-reel tape. Cassettes are cheaper to mail and easier to handle and most industry people have cassette players in their cars where they can listen without being interrupted by telephones.

Don't buy cheap, low-quality tape. It's a bad way to cut corners because it's noisy, subject to dropouts (places on the tape where you'll lose the sound) and may subliminally turn people off. Save some money instead by teaming up with other writers and buying high quality bulk-loaded cassettes and boxes in volume. Find bulk tape ads in music magazines and trade papers and write and ask them for a catalogue and samples. Most companies who deal in bulk-ordered tape can also custom-wind tapes to any length.

Buy 10-, 20- or 30-minute lengths or some of each depending on the number of songs you'll be putting on each tape. Remember that a 30-minute tape has 15 minutes per side, enough for four songs. *Put all your songs on one side.*

Prepare to send a lot of copies and prepare not to get them back. Consider the cost of tapes an investment you may have to "eat."

Check your local phone book for tape duplicating services if you don't have a high-quality copying setup at home. Using studio time to make copies (except for one master cassette from which you can copy) can be very expensive. Check with the studio to find out if they have a copying service at lower than their regular studio rates.

HOW TO PRESENT YOUR DEMO

I think it's always enlightening to get a scenario of what happens behind the scenes in the office of a person who listens to demos. Here's a sample from my own experience and that of friends who torture their brains and eardrums in the all-too-often futile search for that killer song or sound.

If 5 percent of the songs we hear are in the ballpark of what we need, we're doing very well. We engage in this masochism because we know that when we find that one-in-a-thousand song that brings tears to our eyes and makes the hair stand up on the back of our necks, we'll forget about all the bad ones we've listened to. The rejects aren't even all bad. Some have lots of imagination and no craft and some have lots of craft but little to say. The right combination of ingredients is rare but we know it's there somewhere. We're eager to find it as soon as possible.

Some demo reviewers listen in the order they receive the tapes. Most others don't. They look for the most likely candidates: First, for the names of writers they already know are good. That's where the odds are best. Next, for tapes referred to them by other industry people whose tastes (or power) they respect. Next, when faced with a stack of anonymous tapes, they look for a package that is professional, neat, and imaginative. They hope the songs will show those same qualities. The odds still aren't great but they're several points above the lowest.

The least likely candidates are the ones that look like the sender doesn't care. The lyric sheets, if there are any, are scribbled illegibly on the back of a menu, and the cover letter (with no return address) says something like, "I no thees songs wood bee grate for Little Stevie Wonder. Pleez sen them to him." What do you think the odds are that they'll find a really "grate" lyric here? It's not about bad spelling, but about not caring enough to find someone who can check your spelling and not caring enough to notice that Stevie Wonder cuts someone else's song only about once every 10 years. It's easy to get the impression that this person doesn't care enough to find out how to write a good song.

Here is a checklist that will maximize your chances of getting heard and respect the listener's time.

Never send more than four songs unless specifically requested otherwise. Demo listeners like watching the "in" pile diminish and the "out" pile grow as quickly as possible. If the listener has a limited time to listen, which is usually the case, the tendency is to listen to a tape they know they can complete. If you send a tape with ten songs on it and other tapes have one song, you can bet those one-song tapes will be listened to first. There's also the psychology that implies, "I've sent you *the* song you need!" This is particularly true in pitching songs to producers for a specific artist. Along those same lines, most people resent getting tapes with twenty songs and a letter that says, "I know you'll like at least one of these, so just pick out what you want." They want *you* to do that and send them only songs you totally believe in. The fewer the better. If you're not far enough along to be able to decide, you're not ready to submit songs to music business pros.

Place your best and most commercial song first on the tape. If you have a strong up-tempo song it's a good bet to start with that. If they don't like the first one they may not even listen to the rest. *All songs should be on the same side* so the listener doesn't have to turn the tape over.

Never send your original master tape. You may never see it again and it's not fair to saddle its recipient with the responsibility should it be lost or damaged.

Don't send reel-to-reel tapes unless requested. They're expensive to mail and inconvenient to play. Cassettes are best because the listener will have a cassette deck in the office, in the car (where a lot of listening gets done), and at home in the living room, den, and maybe even the bathroom!

Always cue your tape to the beginning of the first song. You don't want to put your listener in a bad mood because you just wasted his time making him rewind your tape. Also, be sure the beginning of the song wasn't cut off. When you make your copies, leave six seconds between songs. Most new tape machines have an automatic search feature which finds the silence between songs, stops the fast-forward, and automatically starts playing the next song.

Send a lyric sheet, neatly typed or printed. Letterhead is impressive, so use it if you have it. It says "This is my business and I take it seriously." Some people don't like to look at lyrics while they listen, but most do. It's a time-saver to be able to see the whole song at once and to see the structure of the song graphically laid out on the page. When you type out your lyric sheet, separate the sections of the songs with a space, and label each section (verse, chorus, bridge etc.) at the upper left side of the section. Don't type your lyrics in prose form. Lay them out with the rhymes at the ends of the lines. (See examples of lyrics elsewhere in this book.)

Lead sheets are not usually sent out with demo tapes. They're good to have at the point where a producer says he wants to record your song and you want to be sure he has the correct melody. Lead sheets used to be necessary to register a copyright, but since the current copyright law permits tapes to be sent for copyright registration, their importance has diminished. They're bulky to mail because they shouldn't be folded, it's difficult to follow the lyric and visualize the song's form, and many industry pros don't read music anyway.

Make sure there's a copyright notice (© 1988 I.B. Cool, All Rights Reserved) on the first page of the lyric or lead sheet and on the tape label. **Make your cover letter short and to the point.** Avoid hype. Let the music speak for itself. A professional presentation will do more to impress someone than "I know these are hit songs because they're better than anything I've ever heard on the radio," or "I just know that we can both make a lot of money if you'll publish these songs." Avoid the temptation to tell your life story, or explain how you have a terminal disease and are the sole support of your ten children. In fact, don't plead, apologize, or show any hint of desperation. It only gives the message that you have no confidence in the ability of the songs to stand on their own.

Here's what should be in your cover letter:

a. Ideally, an address directing it to a specific person in the company.
b. A clear statement of why you're sending the tape. Are you looking for a publisher, a producer, a record deal for you as an artist? Do you want the listener to pay special attention to your production, your singing, your band, or just the song?
c. Any significant professional credits that apply to the purpose of your submission. If you want your song published, list other published or recorded songs, contests won, etc.
d. Any casting ideas you might have. For which artists would the songs be appropriate? (See "Casting," page 186.)
e. A request for feedback, if you want it.
f. A list of the songs enclosed and writers' names in the order they appear on the tape. (Lyric sheets should also be enclosed in the same order the songs appear on the tape.)
g. Thanks for their time and attention.
h. Your address and phone number.

Send a self-addressed stamped envelope (SASE) if you want your tape back. There are two schools of thought about this. If you don't want to lose all those tapes, you can't expect to get them back without an SASE. On the other hand, if you say you want your tape back, will they think you're assuming they won't like it? There's no guarantee that you'll get your tape back even if you do send an SASE, in which case you're gambling even more money (the cost of the tape *and* the return postage). And, so what if they don't return it? Worse could happen than having your tape sitting around a producer's office. Your decision may depend on how many tapes you can afford to lose. If you do send an SASE make sure it's big enough and has sufficient postage for the materials you want returned. **Your name, address, and phone number should be on the tape, box, and on every lyric sheet.** Between listening sessions at the office, the car, and home, it's easy for the tape to be separated from the box or lyric sheet. Once the music professional has gone to the trouble to find your hit song, not finding you is a fate he doesn't deserve. On the tape label should appear your name and phone, titles of the songs, publisher (if there is one), copyright information, bias (normal or CrO^2). Don't send tapes with noise reduction. People seldom check, so they're not likely to adjust for it. **Be sure you have adequate postage.** And, don't send your tape in an ordinary business envelope. It's risky because rough postal handling could force the edge of the tape box through the envelope or crush the tape box. Use a special envelope with an insulated lining. Some people also prefer the soft "bubble" tape box because it isn't easily crushed, doesn't have sharp edges, and it's lighter to mail.

In short, make your tape as easy as possible for the listener to deal with.

Your demo will introduce you to the eyes and ears of many music industry professionals. Take this introduction very seriously. It's your job interview. It should look good, have something important to say, and say it well. There are a lot of other applicants for the job. The pros are looking for the best. Be it!

Marketing Yourself and Your Songs

WHERE DO YOU START?

Whether your sole goal is to be a songwriter or whether you also have aspirations to be a performer, one of the most common and frustrating problems for a novice is not knowing where to start. Do you approach publishers first, or go right to the record companies? Should you find an independent producer or look for a manager?

The first answer you'll get from anyone is "it all depends." No single approach works the same for everyone and that one step-by-step formula you want so badly just doesn't exist. In this section I'll cover some of the assessments you'll need to make of your own personal situation to help you sort out a direction. The best way to find your path is to get a realistic evaluation of your chances through some professional feedback.

Do you want your songs to be, and are they suitable to be, performed by other artists? You may have developed a songwriting style that's too lyrically personal or musically unique to interest artists in recording your songs. However, that uniqueness can be a valuable thing if you also perform your own songs. Some of the most exciting artists write so uniquely that it's difficult for another artist to record their songs without sounding like imitators. It's tough to record a Joni Mitchell or a Laurie Anderson song without sounding like them.

The next consideration is to assess your potential as an artist. Do you want to perform your own songs? Do you have the talent record companies require? Do you have a unique vocal identity? Bob Dylan isn't a great singer, but you always know who he is when you hear him. Gladys Knight, Rod Stewart, Michael McDonald, and Cyndi Lauper all have strong vocal identities and very distinctive styles. For a demonstration of this, listen to the recording of "We Are The World" and see how many of the voices you can identify.

Don't kid yourself about whether you have those qualities. Get specific feedback about it. If you don't your odds for becoming a performer are poor, unless you can create a unique group sound or concept, or have fantastic commercial songs. In other words, to be a successful artist, you need to provide as many ways as possible for the audience to identify and remember you.

Some people may tell you that you don't have artist potential and others may tell you that your songs aren't "coverable." They may be right, but don't let one or two different people make that assessment for you.

There are many different publishers with a variety of tastes. Publishers generally want songs that offer a variety of possibilities for recording. If there's only one artist your song appears appropriate for and they fail to get the artist to cut it, they have a dead song on their hands. Try your songs out on several publishers and others who will give you honest, critical feedback about your songs' overall potential.

If you're an intelligent, perceptive writer who's willing to spend some time on your craft, you can learn to write more coverable songs without sacrificing the factors that make you unique.

The following are some of the potential routes you can take, depending on your own special combination of talents and aspirations. They are, of course, generalizations. Your situation may fall in the cracks somewhere but it should give you a rough idea.

PUBLISHER
If you have coverable songs but don't quite fill the bill as an artist, finding a good publisher who will shop your songs to artists may be the best approach. If you want to be your own publisher and contact producers and artists yourself, that's another option.

If the feedback you get is that you're both a topnotch singer and writer, find a publisher who is also willing to put up money to record and shop masters of you as an artist. Many publishers have production companies through which they'll finance masters and shop them to record labels. If they get you a deal and they own the publishing rights to your songs in the bargain, it's gravy for them. In other words, they don't need to go out and try to get other artists to record the songs (though they often do after you record them).

If you approach publishers first, you will certainly bargain away a part, if not all of your publishing rights. But in exchange you'll get: (1) someone working very hard on your career (since they have a vested interest), (2) a company who can possibly get you a record deal, and (3) someone who can pitch songs that you write. (See Chapter 10, "Publishing.")

RECORD COMPANY
If publishers aren't exactly shoving contracts in your face when they hear your songs but most people feel you've got what it takes to be an artist, or if your songs work well for your unique style, but aren't the kinds of songs publishers think they can place, go for the record companies first.

If your own songs aren't strong enough or you don't have enough potential hit singles to approach a record company, look for great songs from other writers. Though record companies would prefer to sign a totally self-contained artist, the next best thing is that you or your producer know how to pick the right songs. The bottom line is that, one way or another, you have to have material that's considered hit potential by the company. They want to at least feel confident that there's a radio format receptive to the artist's material. (See Chapter 15, "Getting a Record Deal.")

One of the advantages of being signed directly to a major record label is that you stand a better chance of keeping your own publishing rights which, if you become successful, could amount to a considerable income. If you want to make a publishing deal later, you're in a great negotiating position if you already have a record deal, particularly if you've had hits as an artist.   Some labels, however, will want to acquire all or part of the publishing rights for their affiliated publishing companies. Small, independent labels will be especially interested in your publishing. If the company operates on a narrow profit margin, the publishing royalties from the songs could make it a better gamble for them. But don't give anything up unless you're satisfied with what you're getting for it.

PRODUCER

For a writer/artist, finding an independent producer is another option. (There's no point in doing this if you're solely a writer, unless you're pitching a song specifically for one of his artists.) If the producer is putting up the financial backing for demo/masters or an album, he may want half the publishing. It's not uncommon, but restrict it to the songs he records within a time period (six to eighteen months after completion of the masters). If he fails to secure an acceptable record deal, all rights should revert back to you. The producer will still own the masters (if he paid for them) and will recoup his money if you get a deal later, and if the record company wants to use those masters. If he does get you a deal, you're signed to his production company with that producer. If the producer is respected by the record company and dedicated to your career, he can work to your advantage. If not, it can hurt your career because, if you're signed to the production company rather than directly to the label, the label does not have an option to get you another producer without buying out your contract.

Be careful about signing with a producer who has a contract to deliver a certain amount of product annually to a particular label. It's not necessarily a bad deal, but if that producer is guaranteed a certain amount of money per album, his temptation is to record the album as cheaply as possible, put the "override" in his pocket, go on to the next act, and neglect to follow up on your project at the label. If you don't have strong management and enthusiasm for your product at the label to act as a check and balance in that situation, you're at a severe disadvantage. At a major label you may be competing with more than 100 other acts for optimum release dates when the company isn't focusing all its publicity and promotion attention on its superstar acts. If that producer/label team doesn't seem to be looking after your best interests, you may be better off trying to get out of your deal so you can pursue another one. Your attorney will include "performance" clauses that nullify your contract if certain sales figures or other terms aren't met and can protect you from some of these problems.

MANAGER

If you don't have very good artist potential, and aren't already a very successful writer or writer/producer, it doesn't make much sense to look for management. You can pay an attorney a fee to negotiate your deals rather than pay a manager 10 to 25 percent of your income. As in the case of producers, if you're solely a writer you should approach a manager only if you wish to pitch songs to his artists.

At what point a manager should become involved in an artist's or writer/artist's career is subject to debate. A manager might tell you it's very important that your career be guided correctly from the start. They're right: it's important for an artist to have someone to help make career decisions and to coordinate publicity campaigns and club bookings, but does it take a manager to do that? A lot of it you can do yourself. Also, some very good industry attorneys will perform the management functions of shopping your tapes to labels, negotiating deals, and offering career advice. They may not always be right, but no one else is either.

If you don't already have a manager, many record company A&R and artist development departments, after you're signed, perform some management functions for you such as securing booking agencies and coordinating promotional appearances and will also help you find a manager.

It's usually difficult to get a good manager when you're starting, since most of them only want to get involved with artists who already have record deals. If you can find one who's knowledgeable, resourceful, aggressive, honest, and is willing to gamble with you, grab him now, because he won't be available for long.

It frequently happens that a friend of the artist with a minimum of music business experience and an abundance of faith takes on management duties. I've seen some of these situations work out very well, particularly if the manager is aggressive about learning the business. However it does happen that the artist or manager realizes that the latter's lack of expertise and industry clout is holding back the artist's career. A viable option at that point is to look for a comanagement deal with a major management firm. The novice manager obtains the power of the established firm and a great opportunity to learn and establish contacts. The major company benefits by having someone who can deal with details and the artist's needs on a daily basis.

"Where to start," as you can see, involves a lot of variables, and it's important to know what they are before getting started. Still, it's a good idea to test the water in all directions before committing to a course of action. Professional feedback is what you'll need to make a good decision.

WRITERS, WRITER/ARTISTS, AND WRITER/PRODUCERS IN THE MARKETPLACE

You'll often hear songs on the radio that you feel are below your standards and wonder how they got there. You feel your own songs should surely have a chance. You're right, but you may be misunderstanding a basic fact of life. You're judging your standards as a writer against industry standards of making a record (see "A Song Is Not a Record," page 32).

Some writer/artists have high standards; some don't. But they all have access to "the record-making machinery" that allows them to put their visions on vinyl and use production and arrangement to compensate for the dynamic factors that writers who aren't artists need to build into their songs. Usually, it's not a question of songwriting standards of excellence, but about the greater degree of creative latitude available to writer/artists and writer/producers who have a much larger canvas, and more colors and brushes with which they can paint that final picture. In other words, they have arrangement, sound, and production techniques as further ingredients to help them make an appealing product.

An example that comes to mind is writer/producer Jim Steinman's "Total Eclipse of the Heart," a hit by Bonnie Tyler. The song took an uncommon amount of time to get to the chorus, yet Steinman heightened tension with that long verse while providing the necessary repetition of "Turn around bright eyes" by the background vocals.

This is a prime example of a song that publishers would have had a hard time accepting because of its unorthodox form. They'd sign Steinman in a minute as a writer/producer because of his versatile talent, but if a songwriter who was not an artist or producer brought in the song in a bare form, they'd be hard-pressed to think of an artist who'd record it, despite the wonderfully original title/concept. They'd undoubtedly ask for a rewrite to "get to the hook faster" (which may also have worked fine). As a producer, Steinman didn't have to change it, giving himself an opportunity to be innovative.

More and more writers are opening up new creative fields by learning to produce and arrange, finding a singer (if not themselves) as a vehicle, and producing masters or demos that indicate the production possibilities strongly enough to stretch the forms and show them to be "workable." If you're a writer who doesn't have production and arrangement skills, you face the challenge of finding creative ways to express your ideas on a more limited canvas. You need, to a greater extent, to work within established song forms (and variations), and to use your creativity to develop well-crafted lyric concepts and exciting, memorable melodies. Whether or not you ever develop arranging or production skills, you'll have the confidence that you can write a great song.

RESEARCH: TRADE MAGAZINES AND TIP SHEETS

If you were making a cross-country drive on a tight timetable and weren't sure about how to get to your destination, would you just start driving in the general direction and hope everything would work out somehow? No way! You'd be studying maps trying to find the best roads, figuring out when and where you'd be sleeping, and researching any other information that would make your trip as fast, pleasant, and efficient as possible. But it's surprising how many songwriters will make a blind trip into the music industry and spend years just wandering around and going nowhere. They seem to feel that crafting and marketing their songs is one of the few professions in the world that they don't have to know anything about to do successfully. Since you're reading this book, I know you understand the need to learn a lot more about this fascinating and ever-changing business and learn how to improve your odds of success.

It's quite common to hear industry pros say that when they've had an "open door" policy regarding unsolicited material, over 95 percent of the songs they received were not even "in the ballpark" for the artist. It was clear that those writers didn't even bother to listen to the artist or find out the special needs or strengths of the company soliciting the songs. The fact is that there are many ways to research the information and learn about the industry that will put you in that remaining 5 percent.

One of the things a serious songwriter should do is read the music trade magazines. They are a music industry education. If you can't afford to subscribe, you can go to the public library every week and read them. The main branch of most city libraries should carry at least some of these: *Billboard, Cash Box, Radio and Records, Black Radio Exclusive, Country Chart Analyst,* and *Indie Bullet.* (See Bibliography.)

One of the most valuable features of the "trades" is the charts. *Billboard* and *Cash Box* are among the most valuable to writers because their pop, country (*Cash Box* doesn't list country writers), and black music singles' charts list the producer, writer, label and release number, distributing label, publisher, licensee (BMI or ASCAP) and, in *Billboard,* the sheet music supplier. Though the other singles, album, air play and sales charts don't list writers and producers, they are still a valuable barometer of the popularity of artists, records, and record companies.

Album charts feature black, country, inspirational (including all styles of Christian music), Latin, compact discs, Hits of the World, and Album Rock Tracks (i.e., which cuts from rock albums are getting the most air play).

So, what can you learn from all that? First of all, you can get an idea about trends, providing that you're also listening to a lot of radio and are familiar with the songs on the charts. You'll see what artists and songs are most popular in their respective styles and which artists and songs "cross over" between two or more charts. There are also editorial sections relating to those styles, providing analysis and news about artists, labels, and trends. Some columns trace the activities of small independent labels.

Veteran record company executive Russ Regan says he studies the charts for the "gaps." If he sees there are a lot of up-tempo dance tunes crowding the charts, he knows it's time for a great ballad, or vice versa. Also, once the public has bought and feels at home with a "sound," when the group who created it drops out for a while, it may be a good time to release a similar sound. In the '70s, for instance, Barry White filled a gap left by Isaac Hayes and the group America arrived on the scene when we weren't hearing much of those Crosby, Stills, Nash & Young vocal harmonies. Though the time lapse between your writing a song and its being recorded and released probably wouldn't allow you to take advantage of the chart information the way Russ Regan could, it gives you some idea of the way it's used in the business.

There are some other practical applications of that information. The listing of the writers' names can tell you if the writer is also the producer or artist. If that's the case, the percentages are against your being able to place a song with him. (That, of course, isn't cut and dried. Many writer/artists are open to outside tunes, but your songs would have to be better than those written by the artist or artist/producer.) The best bets for song placement are, obviously, with artists who consistently show up on the charts with "outside" material. You can locate the numbers and addresses of the artist's producers or managers by calling the A&R or artist relations department of the listed record company. Then you can pitch your songs to the artist's producers and managers. Though those people may not be open to unsolicited material, your knowledge of their work and ability to discuss it intelligently may get you through otherwise closed doors. It shows them that you're paying attention and you're serious enough to do the research. Consequently, they may guess that you're in that 5 percent that's worth listening to.

The international music market is so important now that it's always enlightening to check out the international charts for the types of English-language songs that are popular in other countries. If you're publishing your own songs and write in a style that is popular in certain countries, you'll know to concentrate on those countries when you look for a foreign subpublisher. (See "Foreign Subpublishing," page 193.)

If you are an artist or group looking for a producer, you can look at the charts for a group that is produced the way you would like to hear yourself and find the listed producer. Since he/she has an artist on the charts, it is reasonable to assume that they have pretty good leverage with a label or labels. It's good to hit these producers when they're hot, though you have to realize the record companies are also trying to get them to produce *their* acts and producing an unknown act (like yours) won't be a priority.

If you're actively trying to get something going, either as a writer or a recording artist, it's important to know the names and meet the people in the business. If you're on the outside looking in and you're not hanging out at any of the industry watering holes, it gets very difficult to keep track of who's who, who's what, and where these people are. It's complicated by a musical chairs game unequaled in any other business, except maybe advertising. In some cases, people didn't know they'd been fired until they read it in the trades. So, *Billboard* calls its column, "Executive Turntable," where you can see where your favorite A&R person, publisher, etc., is working this month. *Cash Box*'s column is called "Executives on the Move."

You may have run into an A&R person who liked your act or your songs but couldn't get anything going for you at his previous label. You see in the "Executive Turntable" that he's at a new company now, so it's worth another shot. In a new company he may have more respect, more power, and a renewed motivation to prove himself. Yours might be the act he'll sign or your songs might be better suited to the acts on his new label. It may also be worthwhile to contact the executive who took his place at the old company. Most of the same considerations also apply to executives and professional managers at publishing companies.

In the case of publishers, keep in mind that if you've already signed a publishing contract on a song and you see that the person responsible for signing your song to that company has made an exit, you should call the company and make an appointment with his replacement. If you don't bring your song to his attention, it may get lost in the shuffle of thousands of others the new person has to represent. It also gives you a chance to make a new contact and expose some of your newer songs. Also call your old contact at his new job, congratulate him, and go to see him at the new company.

Occasionally, a whole company will be restructured by a new president who wants to put together his or her own "team." This is also valuable info for anyone looking for a job in the business. That kind of news will be carried in the trades' news columns and is also likely to be found in a more detailed feature article. You'll learn about new companies forming or branch offices being set up locally, and you'll have a situation where people are eager to prove themselves by finding some great new local artists or songs. Call right away to make an appointment.

Billboard's "Audio Track" is another valuable column for writers. If you're the aggressive, creative type, you can find out, as publishers do, who's recording, at what studio, and who are the producer and engineer. If you're very sure that your songs are appropriate for the artist, you'll know how to get to them.

Here's a good game to play with the trades: Listen to a station that's not afraid to take a chance to add a new song by a new artist now and then. When you hear one you think is a hit, look at the *Billboard* Hot 100 chart or other trade charts to see if it's there. Analyze the song stylistically and predict what charts it'll show up on. Is it a "crossover" that will show up on both pop and R&B or country charts? Pretend it's your song and follow it up (or down) the charts over a few weeks. Check out the Single and Album Radio action charts and see who's adding it to their play lists. What kind of stations are playing it? What other songs are those stations playing? This is a useful exercise for you because it's a game that record companies and publishers play for real and it gets you into the excitement of second-guessing. By comparing these songs to your own, you can second-guess your songs before even taking them to a publisher. It gives you the opportunity to critique your own song in the context of the real music world. Too many songwriters are totally out of touch with what is going on. To be ignorant of contemporary artists and styles is inexcusable when you claim to be trying to write commercial songs.

It's important to develop your critical abilities and you have an opportunity to do that by reading record and live performance reviews, not only in the standard trades but in *Stereo Review, High Fidelity, BAM, Record, Spin,* and other consumer music periodicals. Listen to the same records they do, go to the same concerts, and do your own reviews. Obviously, opinions differ among reviewers depending on their own personal taste and critical abilities. For your own learning process, though, it's as helpful to disagree as to agree, as long as you've paid careful attention to their critique and given some thought to your own.

The trades and consumer magazines contain interviews with music industry people that can be helpful on several levels. First of all, if you see an interview with, say, Tina Turner, and want to write a song for her, you may gain some insight into her likes, dislikes, experiences, and fears that will help you write a song she'll identify with, a song that will "speak" for her.

If you're a performer or group looking for a manager, you can get an idea, through an interview, what a particular manager is like personally and professionally. What does he or she think is important? What kind of acts does he like? Why? What's the nature of his relationship with record companies? Cooperative or adversarial? Is he feared, respected, loved, or all of the above? Through interviews with A&R execs, you can find out what they look for, their company policies, their personal experiences, philosophies, and goals. All managers, A&R people, and others share basic knowledge in their particular field of expertise, but everyone has a little different approach or a few "tricks of the trade" learned from their own experience and from their personal creativity and imagination. There are several "right" ways to do almost anything in this business and it helps to know a number of them. Never be afraid to ask questions of industry people when you have the opportunity. In our Showcase interviews, with few exceptions, music industry people have spoken freely about how they do things and how they feel about what they do. Even as a struggling writer/artist, whenever I expressed a desire to learn about something, there was *always* someone who would take the time to explain.

TIP SHEETS
Tip sheets are periodicals listing producers (primarily), publishers, or record companies who are in need of material for artists. Some are monthly, some biweekly, some weekly. Some are directed to all songwriters in general and some are restricted to publishers or pro writers with proven track records. The reason for the restriction is this. For its credibility, a tip sheet relies on listings by producers of major acts and other established producers with new acts. If the producers don't want to list themselves, publishers and others don't want to buy the tip sheet. If a tip sheet is sold indiscriminately to amateur songwriters who have no casting sense, don't know how to do their research on the act, or don't know what the radio format terminology means, they may end up sending totally inappropriate songs. The producer then calls the tip sheet and says, "Who are you selling this to? I've been getting hundreds of terrible songs and if this keeps up, I'm never listing with you again."

Are tip sheets good sources of information for you? Some tip sheets list producers willing to wade through amateur submissions and if you've got the right song, they'll hear it. Most of the heavy hitters, though, are going for the restricted lists or the lists that are so expensive that only the very serious can afford them, which is how some of them deal with the problem I just described. Others deal with it by cancelling your subscription and refunding your money if they get complaints that your submissions are inappropriate or of poor quality.

With tip sheets, remember that you're rarely going to be among the first to know that someone is looking for songs. Any worthwhile publisher will know it before—or at least at the same time as—the tips, because they or their staffs are calling producers daily. The tip sheet takes some time to collect listings, print, and mail them. By the time you get it, the hot publishers will have their songs on the way to the listed producers. Publishers subscribe to them anyway because they can't afford to miss anything and a new producer may come out of left field that they haven't yet made contact with.

The fact that you're not among the first, however, doesn't necessarily mean you don't have a chance. It's quite possible the producers won't find what they want in the first go-round and will keep looking. It's still important for you to be aggressive about responding to listings.

Every tip sheet will contain its own guidelines for the way you should submit songs. Additional information will also appear on the individual listings like "no ballads," "one song only," "SASE (Self-Addressed Stamped Envelope) required for tape return," etc. Following their instructions will help insure that your tape gets listened to. For further information, reread the sections on assignment writing (see page 89) and presenting your demo tape (see page 222).

Here are a few of the most popular tip sheets (subject to change):

New on the Charts (212)921-0165
1501 Broadway
New York, NY 10036
Monthly; subscription for $165 year
For professional use only.
Special features: Video Spotlight, New Signings; Sub-publishing and master lease deals available; Label Profile (personal bios of record company staff, etc.); Producer Profile; Songtitle index of current hits from *Billboard* and *Cash Box* charts and cross-referenced names, addresses, and phone numbers of producers, managers, agents, publishers, and labels for charted songs and artists.

Parade of Stars (615)320-7270
Chuck Chellman
The Chellman Bldg.
1201 16th Ave. South
Nashville, TN 37212
Weekly; $120 year, $75 half year.
For publishers and pro writers only.
The oldest tip sheet. Lots of country listings, but also lists white and black gospel artists as well as R&B and rock artists.

Song Connection (818)763-1039
Joe Reed
12390 Chandler Blvd. #C
N. Hollywood, CA 91607

Every two weeks; $125 year (26 issues), $225 two years, $70 half year (13 issues).
For publishers and pro writers only.
All styles in addition to international listings.

Song Placement Guide (213)850-3606
Marcia Singer
P.O. Box 189
Pacific Palisades, CA 90272
Monthly; $5 trial issue, $55 year. Three- and six-month subscriptions. All styles. Includes informative interviews with industry pros. Advertising is available.

Songplugger (818)761-5859
Len Latimer
P.O. Box 3839
Hollywood, CA 90078
Every two weeks; $148 year, $79 half year.
For professional songwriters and publishers only. Founded in 1975. All styles.

Tunesmith
Len Latimer
(same address and phone as *Songplugger*)
Monthly; $39 year, $25 half year.
Newsletter for songwriters listing information about publishers and producers looking for unpublished songwriters. Contains descriptions of wanted material as well as occasional trend analyses of charts, how-to tips.

Music City Trax Fax (615)244-7524
Quinton Q. Qualls
1609 Roy Acuff Place
Nashville, TN 37203
Monthly; $75 year.
Features one major interview with a hit songwriter or producer. Also includes 1½-2 pages listing top artists and the type of material they're seeking.

OTHER SOURCES
Besides the trade magazines and tip sheets, other sources of information are:

Songwriter's Market, an annual that gives you an excellent list of publishers, producers, record companies, advertising agencies, and others who *are* open to receiving unsolicited material, how they want the material submitted, and what types of music the company specializes in.

The Los Angeles Songwriters Showcase "Musepaper" contains a schedule of their weekly showcases featuring Pitch-A-Thon sessions in which producers screen songs on cassette for specific recording projects. Members may submit songs from anywhere in the country.

The newsletters of the *National Academy of Songwriters, Nashville Songwriters Association International,* and your local organizations.

Records and tapes. There isn't a better way to familiarize yourself with the style of an artist. Record album jackets usually contain more information than tape inserts. To find out who's managing a particular act, look at the jacket of their most recent album. Often the management company is listed with an address. On the album cover or insert you'll also find the name(s) of the producer(s) of that album or of individual songs on it. Of course, the next album may be produced by someone else. But at least you've done some homework and can call the record company, get the A&R or artist relations department, and ask if so-and-so will be working on the next album (if not, who is?) and how to get in touch. They'll also be able to give you the manager's office address and phone number.

Billboard's Talent and Touring Directory annually lists hundreds of artists, their personal managers, booking agents, and other contacts.

GETTING READY TO FACE THE INDUSTRY

Now that you've got some idea about how the business operates, you're ready to venture out into the real world and start making some contacts. Even when you feel physically prepared, like a soldier going into battle, you need to prepare yourself mentally. No matter which approach you take to get your songs heard and no matter who you decide to contact, knowing what to expect will give you a lot more confidence. There is a professional way to approach the industry and the more professionally you present yourself, the more professionally you're treated.

ETHICS IN THE BIZ

Discussions about ethics in the music business frequently expose a great variety of feelings about it. A business like this that seems so blatant about its powers and pleasures and extravagance draws many people to it who are greedy for those most visible things. It also draws very creative businesspeople. Most songwriters and musicians, though they're certainly enticed by the high stakes involved, are much more wrapped up in the music itself and seem to want to keep "The Biz" at a distance. Managers, attorneys, and others on the business end will say, "You shouldn't worry about anything but the music. Leave all the business stuff to us." It's exactly what a lot of musicians want to hear. They'll say, "I don't want to even know about that! Just go ahead and do it!" Both lines are candidates for "Famous Last Words."

I can't count the number of times I've heard musicians and writers say, after a sour business deal, "I should have checked him out before I signed" . . . "I should have seen an attorney" . . ."But the vibes really felt right!" . . . "He *told* me we'd split the publishing; he'd record masters; he'd get me a record deal; we'd get paid right after the gig; we'd split the advance 50/50, etc., etc." But it wasn't *written* in the contracts.

In many of those cases, I'm sure the businesspeople were quite well in-tentioned and, at the time, really wanted to do what they promised. Oth-ers chronically take advantage of people and have bad reputations for it. Save yourself a lot of grief by doing some research and talking to others who have dealt with them. Don't feel obligated to work with the first peo-ple who show interest in you. Even when the voice of that poor, trampled, part of you says "Oh, thank you, thank you! I'm so glad you like me—show me where to sign," get a grip on yourself. This may indeed be someone you'll want to work with, but if you go into a deal with that frame of mind, you're begging to be victimized. Calm down and check him out and don't sign anything without legal advice.

Also make sure that there is a "performance clause" in the contract, which states that if the terms of the contract are not fulfilled within X amount of time or in X manner, the contract becomes void. This can, quite literally, save you years of creative productivity. Without a performance clause, it's possible for someone to pick up one-year options for five or more years (whatever's in the contract) without doing anything he's sup-posed to do. Meanwhile, someone else may want to sign you but can't without paying some exorbitant amount of money to buy you out of the deal. According to you, you were ripped off. According to him, he made a good business deal. He recognized good talent, got you to sign, and made some bucks. That's *his* gig. You may not consider him to be ethical, but you *did* sign the contract.

Not everyone, of course, does business this way. There are lots of straightforward, honest, up-front people in the business who believe that, in the long run, a good reputation will make them more successful than a bad one. No rigid set of ethics govern practices in the music business short of what's actually illegal. Some industry people follow "situational ethics" or "It seemed like the right thing to do at the time." Some sub-scribe to the basic greed philosophy that says "Anything goes if it gets me what I want." Others hold the "Everybody else is doing it" and "Do it unto others before they do it unto you" philosophies. You're likely to run into any of these anywhere, and the best protection you can have is to get to know enough about the business that you have some idea about whether you're hearing straight talk or jive. If you do turn your business over to someone, you should know enough about what they *ought* to be doing to know whether or not they *are* getting it done. Remember that *they* work for or with you. You don't work for them.

The type of people you associate with in the industry can have a great effect on your reputation, peace of mind, and your creative future. Take it very seriously and find good people to work with. Journalist Paul Law-rence once asked Ken Kravitz of Hit City West Recording Studio if he felt that "Nice guys finish last." "Maybe nice guys sometimes finish last in the rat race," Ken answered, "but that's not the only race there is."

EGO

Also keep in mind, as you approach industry pros, that though your songs may be very personal and expose delicate parts of your being, people in the business must look at them as a *product.* They, in turn, must try to sell your product to someone else on the merits of its commercial potential alone. It's understandably difficult for a writer to keep from feeling that it's him or her who's being rejected, rather than the song. Some of the most powerful songs written are very personal statements and confessional revelations that make the writer's ego quite vulnerable to destruction when rejected. So, don't stop writing those kinds of songs. Just get a grip on your ego and leave it at the door when you go in to show your wares.

Before you can successfully pitch your songs to the industry, you must become a good self-critic. There's a point during or after the writing of a song where you must step away from it and try to look at it as though you were another person—a publisher, a recording artist, a radio program director, a J.Q. Public. Sometimes, in order to get that perspective, writers put a song away for a few days or even a few weeks, so they can get a fresh look at it.

Ask yourself the same questions that, consciously or unconsciously, others will ask: Is this a song about an event or feeling that many people can relate to? Will the people most likely to relate to the lyric be in a certain age group? Will the music appeal to the same age group? Can the lyrics be understood by everyone? Is there a better, more powerful, more graphic way to say what I've said? Is every line of the song important? Is this a song that can compete with the best songs that I hear on the radio?

Doing this kind of self-critique will help you in important ways. It will help you write better songs. It will help you choose, from among your songs, those which are the most commercially viable and consequently, the least subject to rejection. It will help you develop that professional detachment that will make it easier to look at your own work as a product, like someone who makes omelettes or clothes or anything else. In accomplishing that, you'll find it much easier to approach buyers and to welcome their positive and negative comments. They, in turn, will find it easier to work with you.

Play your songs for friends before approaching the buyers. Even if they can't or won't give you honest criticism, it gives you some instant perspective. I've written songs I was perfectly happy with until I read the lyric or sang the song to someone else and it suddenly sounded trite or unclear. Back to the drawing board!

It helps in dealing with rejection if you can sympathize with what happens on the other side of the publisher's or producer's door. It does neither you nor them any good if they publish a song they're not genuinely enthusiastic about and in which they see little commercial potential. They'll have to spend money to demo it and they'll have to put up with your continued questions about what they've done with your song. They'll have to keep telling you nothing's happened or avoid taking your calls altogether. So if they can't really get excited about your song as a product, they *have* to reject it.

You shouldn't want someone to publish your song unless they're *very* enthusiastic about it. When *they* get rejections on your song, you want them to retain enough enthusiasm for the song to continue to pitch it. Several publishers have told me that they had songs in their catalogue that had been rejected over 100 times! In spite of that, they continued pitching them because they totally believed in those songs.

Sometimes songs or styles are simply ahead of their times. In the late '70s, for instance, it was common for L.A. writers to get rejections because their "country" songs were "too country" for L.A. and "too pop" for Nashville. Now many country artists are looking for country crossover (country/pop) material.

There are more reasons why you're more likely to be in the wrong place at the wrong time with the wrong song than vice versa. Probably 99 percent of those reasons have nothing to do with you personally, but with the marketplace, your product, and the buyer's ability and inclination to deal with it.

It's a certainty that, no matter how good your songs are, they *will* be rejected. If you don't adopt some attitudes that help you to deal with that rejection, you can get too discouraged to persevere. And if you quit, there will always be more writers out there to take your place. You're the one who loses, along with all those music lovers out there who will never get to hear your songs.

DEALING WITH REJECTION

It might comfort you to know that, at all levels, a substantial part of what happens in the music industry involves rejection. Rejection of songs, rejection of finished master recordings that people have sunk thousands of dollars into, rejections of record company product by radio stations, and, ultimately, rejection of individual records or styles by consumers.

Every day, for hundreds of different reasons, people in every different facet of the industry are facing rejections. They may accept it as an inevitability, an everyday occurrence, but it is never really easy for anyone to deal with. Egos are bent, reputations questioned, jobs are lost, and friendships are damaged or ended. There are hundreds of rejection stories of major songs. Joe Brooks's "You Light Up My Life" was rejected countless times by both publishers and producers before Mike Curb saw it as a vehicle to launch Debby Boone's solo career. It stayed at #1 for ten weeks and became one of the most played songs ever. Elton John was turned down by twenty-two record companies; the Beatles and Billy Joel were turned down by every major record company. The list goes on and on. I would venture to say that every major artist has been rejected numerous times before attaining any success. In fact, even after an artist is successful and subsequently goes through an unproductive period, he may again face those rejections. There's even an industry joke about being fortunate to be turned down by certain record execs, because they've rejected so many successful artists that you should worry if they *like* you.

For songwriters it's particularly difficult, though, because you're usually creating in isolation, and it's difficult to find good critical feedback. Often your only artistic validation comes from friends and family who are so knocked out that you're doing something *they* don't have the talent for, that the last thing they'd do would be to criticize your efforts. They'll be supportive and keep you in that vacuum until you smash up against the "real world" of the music *business.* Songs that your friends liked because they saw you reflected in them (and they like *you*), songs that audiences seemed to like ("They clapped, didn't they?") are meeting with "Sorry, not strong enough," "not appropriate," "no hook," and other standard lines.

When I ask a writer if he or she has been making the rounds of publishers, I often get the reply, "Yeah, but they passed on all my songs. I didn't have anything they wanted, so they told me to come back when I had some more stuff to show. I know they were just trying to be nice." Wrong!! Publishers don't say stuff like that "just to be nice." They don't have time to keep making appointments with writers they feel have no talent. Believe that if they keep the door open to you after hearing your songs, it's because they think there's a good chance you'll have something later that they'll be interested in publishing. Don't let what *you think* is a rejection keep you from going back. Take them at their word. If you call back to make another appointment and it seems like they're putting you off, don't let yourself believe it. Keep trying! That's the place where it really gets tough psychologically. You're sticking your neck out again and your self-confidence is in danger. With every rejection it gets tougher to put yourself back on the line. But when publishers tell you that the door is open, believe them! It's hard enough anyway without *imagining* that you're being rejected.

There are some ways that you can deal with rejection that will keep you from totally losing your self-esteem.

Cultivate a support group. Yes, there is life outside the music business. Sometimes you can get in a rut, take the whole thing far too seriously, and fail to take comfort in your families and friends who love you whether you write a hit or not. Cultivate friends outside the music business so you can tap into some other worlds and keep yourself from getting too isolated and tunnel-visioned. That cross-fertilization of experiences and ideas is also creatively stimulating. It also helps to hang out with other songwriters who understand what you're going through and can help you get back up when you're down. Stay away from those who will trivialize even your smallest successes. You don't need negativity.

Develop short-term payoffs. It usually takes a very long time for anything to happen in the music business. So that big reward—the recording, the record deal, the hit, the royalty check, the film score, whatever, that's somewhere in the unseen future, isn't always enough to make you feel like a valuable human being today. Yes, you should be able to get that by just writing a good song and feeling good about it. But after you've done it you're likely to set another goal for it that requires the validation of others and a dependence on a timetable and circumstances over which you don't have much control. So it helps to be actively involved in hobbies, sports, another job, volunteer involvement in a cause or even something as mundane as cleaning the garage or organizing your albums that gives you a sense of accomplishment and immediate positive payoff.

Don't let rejection stop you from writing. There's a particular song you keep pitching and it keeps getting turned down. You've already rewritten it twice. You're now so totally obsessed with getting it published or produced that you stop writing altogether. A little, self-destructive voice inside you says, "This is the best thing I've ever done. If I can't get anything happening with this one, I might as well hang it up because, if they don't like this, they won't like anything." So you stop writing "just 'til I get this one cut." Meanwhile, you're forgetting several important things. The next song you write may be much better than this one or, at least, more interesting to publishers. You won't become a better writer, or a more successful writer, unless you continue writing. A song you haven't written yet may be just the song that gets everybody interested in everything else you've done. Just the process of writing can make you feel good about yourself.

In her tape, "Rejecting Rejection," songwriting consultant Molly-Ann Leikin offers the following advice:

Learn self-affirmation. Since you can't always rely on someone else telling you how great you are, you have to take care of it yourself. Make a list of all the good things about yourself. Read the list every day.

Remind yourself that every "no" is a "no" you won't hear again from that person about that song.

Have a long-range plan so that one "no" is no big deal.

Have additional plans of attack so if you strike out on one, you're ready to try something else right away so you don't have time to feel sorry for yourself.

Keep your body in shape. When you're healthy and feel good physically, it's much easier to maintain a positive attitude.

QUERY LETTERS

Now that you know what you're up against, you're ready to contact people and show them your stuff. The easiest way to submit your material, especially if you live outside the major recording centers, is to send your demos through the mail. The problem is that, even though it's the easiest way, it's not as easy as it used to be.

Publishers, producers, and record companies have, in general, tightened up on their acceptance of unsolicited material. If you don't *know* whether or not they'll accept your submission, it makes sense to inquire ahead of time with a postcard before going to the expense of sending a tape. Otherwise, they may send your tape back unopened. This practice also serves to show them that you're methodical and serious. Send a letter with a self-addressed return postcard enclosed.

In the letter, list any credits you might have or anything else that might interest them in your act or your material. That information would include recordings of your songs, reviews of your act, contest prizes or other awards you've won, music education and professional experience. Make sure your letter looks neat and professional. Your self-addressed, stamped postcard can have a choice of replies as shown on the following sample.

_____ Yes, we'd like to hear your tape.
We're looking for _____R&B, _____Pop, _____Rock, _____Dance,
_____Country, (or your description) _____

Address it to the attention of: _____

We're <u>not</u> listening to tapes <u>now</u>. Try us: _____next month,
_____next year, or when? _____

We <u>never</u> listen to unsolicited tapes unless your:
_____attorney, _____manager, _____producer, _____ Uncle Herman
sends them to us.

OTHER COMMENTS: _____

Signed _____ Date _____

Company _____

For your own records, keep a notice like: *Card sent to Megahits Music 11/1/87.*

IN-PERSON INTERVIEWS

We get our strongest impressions of people in person. It's helpful for you to be able to size up the people you do business with, and for them to be able to put a face with a song. That's assuming it's a good song and that you usually make a good impression when you meet people.

Appointments for an in-person audition are usually rare without a referral by someone whose taste (or at least, power) a publisher respects. But there still seem to be unknown writers who just come into town and are able to meet with several publishers in a day. Their success has a lot to do with self-confidence, personality, and timing. Obviously, your best shot is to be able to call ahead of time and say that you're in town for a short while and give them the name of someone who recommended that you see them. But you should call and try to set up an appointment even without a referral, especially if you have any notable credits. Let them know about your success on the initial call. Be nice to the receptionist, secretary, and/or assistant. If you don't get an appointment, ask if you can drop off a tape and don't be discouraged. It's a long shot anyway. If you do get an appointment, find out approximately how much time the person can give you so you can prepare accordingly, and remember the following:

Be there on time, or ahead of time! If *they're* late, they'll likely be more accommodating out of guilt. If you're late, it puts a heavy psychological burden on you. If you're in a strange town, make sure you get good directions from someone and an idea about how long it'll take to get to your appointment. Allow extra time for emergencies.

If something unexpected comes up and you can't be there on time, *call ahead to let them know.* They may have to cancel and reschedule. Personally, I'm extremely reluctant to reschedule if you've set up a meeting with me and didn't call or show up. It shows me that you don't respect my time.

If possible, *bring each song on a separate cassette tape.* This will save time, because it allows you to change the order of your presentation on the spot. If the person says "Play me a ballad," and your ballad is at the end of your tape, you'll have to do a stop-and-start search for that song while you're saying "No, that's not it. I think it's just a little further on," and on and on. When you have a limited amount of time available, you want him to spend his time listening to your songs, not waiting while you look for them.

Before beginning to play your songs, *tell the person conducting the appointment that he's free to turn off your tape* (or your live performance) *and go to the next song whenever he likes.* Be prepared to *give him lyric sheets* with the songs so he can scan your lyric as he listens. This maximizes the value of his time with you.

Take extra copies of everything so if he wants to keep something, you can leave it. Be sure that your *name, phone number,* and *address* are on each *cassette, cassette box, and lyric sheet.* Don't ever leave your master tape.

If you want criticism, ask for it. If not, don't. If they give it to you, thank them for it whether you agree or not. Don't argue! If they like something enough to ask for a rewrite and you like the person and are interested in forming a working relationship, tell them you'll try it. Do it and get back to them—the sooner the better. If you think there's a chance you won't or can't do it, don't make any rash promises. It's better to pleasantly surprise them than to let them remember you as a broken promise.

When you leave, thank them and their secretary. Send a "thank you" card or letter that same week.

GETTING IN THE DOOR

In a business where people's time is at a premium and there are thousands of songwriters out there looking for a share of it, it becomes very important for A&R people and publishers to develop a way to screen which will allow maximum results for a minimum of time spent. It's sometimes difficult for new writers to understand that listening to new songs is not a publisher's main job. His most important job is to make money by exploiting the songs he has already published, especially the songs that are written by staff writers paid by advances. All publishers would agree that building their catalogues by signing new songs and writers is very important, but the priority given to that function differs from company to company and from week to week. A publishing executive may simply make the decision that "We won't accept any unsolicited tapes" or "We're not looking for any new songs at this time."

There are many reasons for those decisions. As an example, one major company recently went through a change in management and personnel. The new president brought in a team of people he'd worked with in the past and fired all but two songpluggers. That meant the new staff, with the help of the remaining original staff, was faced with the monumental task of familiarizing themselves with thousands of songs in the current catalogue. Until they assessed that catalogue there was really no point in spending valuable time looking for new songs.

A company also faces legal jeopardy when opening and listening to unsolicited tapes. The attorneys at many publishing and record companies advise representatives not to open them. Lawsuits frequently occur when a song is a hit and someone says, "I sent you a tape two years ago that had the same line, title, idea. I think you stole it from me." Since one of the major proofs needed for plagiarism is access to the song in question, if the plaintiff can prove it was in the publisher's possession at the right time, it can give a company attorney nightmares. Some publishers aren't too frightened by that prospect, but it remains a common excuse for not accepting unsolicited tapes.

Publishers, producers, and A&R departments with continuous "open door" policies are few and far between. They usually hire people specifically to screen material and if the screener feels it's good, it's passed on to other ears. Other companies are small operations in which there are a limited number of person-hours available and most must be spent seeing producers, going to recording sessions, and performing other publishing duties, leaving little time for screening. Other publishing companies may be merely "holding companies" for a writer/artist's own catalogue and don't accept demo submissions because they're genuinely not interested in shopping other writers' songs.

Regardless of the "we're not listening" policies and the reasons behind them, most publishers and A&R people still do listen to new songs, but very selectively. They want to weed out the writers who haven't learned anything about how the business works, or the hobbyists with two or three songs taking a quick shot at it, and then retreating. The pros size up a writer, his or her attitude and presentation, from the first contact and then decide whether to spend time listening or not. They know that even given all a writer's positive attributes, the odds are still minimal that they'll find something they can publish or a writer with genius-level raw talent they'd like to develop. That's why it's important to them to set up a tough screening process.

On the front lines of that process are receptionists, secretaries and assistants. Unless you have the name of a specific person at the company, your phone call won't get past that point. Even if you do have a name, you'll be referred to that person's secretary. She will say something like, "May I tell her what this is about?" or "He's not in right now. May I help you?" The worst thing you can say is, "Sorry, you can't help. I need to talk to the main man." That person's job is to save the main man's (or woman's) time. How you present yourself to a secretary or receptionist may determine whether or not your tape gets heard.

Here's a typical scenario:

Writer: Hi, I'm a songwriter and I've got a hit for Stevie Wonder and another one that would be great for Billy Joel. Actually, I've written over twenty songs. Could somebody there listen to them?

Receptionist: Could you please drop off a tape? (You'd be very lucky to get this request.)

Writer: No, I won't leave a tape—how do I know you won't steal my songs?

Receptionist: Who referred you to us?

Writer: I got your name out of the phone book. Could you connect me to the man in charge?

What do you think are the odds that the caller will get through? I'd say slim. An important part of a secretary's (and often a receptionist's) job is to screen out this type of call from songwriters. If they recognize your name or you've been referred by someone whose name they know and whose reputation they respect, your chances of getting through the door are much better. In other cases, it's pretty much up to their discretion who to accept tapes from or whose call to put through to their bosses. Consequently, the first encounter you have with the front desk is vital. If you present yourself as a rank amateur, they'll assume your writing is just as amateur and that their chances of finding a great song from you are zilch.

Every secretary or receptionist has his own criteria for figuring the odds in favor of the boss. Let's look at the call again. Only an amateur who has done no research doesn't know that Stevie Wonder and Billy Joel don't do outside songs. If you've written only twenty songs, you're obviously a beginner. You can't be on the scene long and not know you're going to have to leave tapes. Get them protected first so you won't have to worry about songs being stolen. You also haven't done your research if you don't have the name of a person at the company and have to resort to the phone book for the company name. If you don't know the name of "the man in charge" you just might be insulting the woman in charge. Do your homework. (See "Research," page 230.)

I asked the receptionist at a major publishing company how she screens unsolicited calls. She said she tells writers that the company is not listening to tapes now. If they ask when the company *will* be listening (and they seldom ask), she tells them to call back in a month. If she does get a call back from that writer, she accepts his or her tape. It shows her that writer is persistent, professional, and organized enough to follow up the call.

I've gained a lot of insight into this process by going from being a struggling songwriter to the other side of the desk as a screener. It's taught me some important lessons that have been pretty much corroborated by my "other side of the desk" peers.

We always respect persistence, even though we may at times find it annoying and guilt-provoking. We know that no matter how talented you are, you need persistence to succeed. The hardest part of being persistent is continuing to be pleasant about it and not allowing yourself to become bitter or desperate from the rejection you'll experience. It turns people off when they sense that desperation in you.

A secretary I talked with said, "It's a real turn-off to have someone spill their guts out to me that this is their last chance or they need to pay their doctor bills or whatever. I don't want to subject my boss to that either. It's very unprofessional."

There's also a thin line between confidence and arrogance. We like to feel that you believe in yourself and are confident about your talent and abilities even though you're open to criticism and direction. If you come off arrogantly with the attitude, "I'm God's gift to the music world and if you can't recognize it, you're a Neanderthal," it will be difficult for you to find people to work with you.

"The squeaky wheel gets the grease," is a cliché that remains true. If someone calls me looking for a singer for a project "right now," I have no time to research and get to my lists, and you're a good singer I know who I just talked to a couple days ago, your name will jump out of my mouth. If I haven't heard from you in a year, it won't. The lesson here is never to assume that people will remember you and what you're doing if you don't periodically remind them.

Always be pleasant to the "gatekeepers." No matter how many times you call to talk to the boss and she won't return your call (she may have fifty calls to return that day and forty-nine of them are priorities) be polite, never abusive nor arrogant unless you want to be introduced to the boss as "that abusive, arrogant @#*!" Next year the person you abused may *be* the boss! Enlist his aid. Tell him your situation. Ask if *he* can help. Ask *him* to listen to your tape. He'll know what his boss likes or doesn't like. Empower assistants, secretaries, and receptionists to help you by assuming they can.

Always follow up. Two weeks is an adequate amount of time to follow up once you know someone has your tape. That doesn't necessarily mean he should have listened to it in that time. He may have hundreds of tapes to hear, and listening to them is not a major part of his job in most cases. When you call, ask how soon you should call back. Don't get upset and demand your tape back. He'll be only too glad to get rid of it. Leaving a tape somewhere indefinitely means, at worst, you lose the cost of the tape. At best, a producer or publisher goes through a box of tapes in a couple of years, finds your tape, and calls you. Don't think it hasn't happened.

Say "thank you." If someone (a boss *or* gatekeeper) has given you his time, advice, or help in any way, take the time to drop him a "thank you" card. It's another positive way to make contact, to acknowledge the value of his contribution, and to let him know that you're sensitive, caring, organized, and taking care of business. If you knew how seldom it's done, you'd realize what an impact it has.

SURVIVAL

Getting through the door involves continuously and consistently making contacts and being able to support yourself while you're doing it. If you're a writer who isn't working as a performer, don't assume you'll be making it "any day now" and borrow from friends and family to survive till your big break comes. Get a day job so you can spend your evenings writing with others who have day jobs, attending industry events, workshops, and clubs, and be able to afford it. You'll also need money for demos, postage, and other songwriting expenses.

Try to get a job in some aspect of the industry. It's tough because everyone else wants those jobs, too. Don't be afraid or too proud to start on the bottom rung. Kris Kristofferson swept floors in a Nashville recording studio and met lots of important people in the process. If you have good typing or other office skills, get work with temporary employment agencies that specialize in the entertainment industry.

Volunteer! Do volunteer work for songwriter or other industry organizations that put you in action centers where you can keep in touch with what's going on. Volunteer to work in recording studios in exchange for studio time. If you're a dedicated, hard-working volunteer for a music company or songwriter organization, when a paid position comes up, you just might be considered first because the boss already knows you and likes your work. Whether you get a job in the industry or not, the security of a regular paycheck will preserve you from desperation and taking the first deal that comes along. There's definitely an advantage to negotiating a deal knowing that you don't *have* to have the money.

THE OPTIONS OF AN OUT-OF-TOWNER

The best advice if you're serious about a career as a songwriter is to move to a major music center: New York, Nashville, or Los Angeles. The next best advice is to move to a not-so-major but active music center. In the '70s, Philadelphia was hot and may be again. Other cities like Atlanta, Memphis, Detroit, Minneapolis, Chicago, Toronto, Boston, Austin (Texas), San Francisco, and others seem to simmer, then periodically get very hot when a local act or two break nationally. Even when they're not hot, these cities seem to support a thriving live music community. The recording scenes there tend to evolve around local producers and studios that have spawned successful acts. The area also tends to have a characteristic music style based on what those particular producers have had success with. Obviously, you need to find out who those producers are and get their attention if you migrate to one of those areas.

If you stay in your own town, find out if there are any local recording studios, producers, publishers, booking agents, musicians unions, or radio programmers and DJs. Make it a point to meet them and let them know what you're doing. Outside of a specific program that features local talent, the radio people won't give you air play unless you have a record deal. But they may refer you to local record promoters who will refer you to the record companies they represent. This is a good way to "network" from your local scene to industry people in the major recording centers. If you're not a performer, have a hot local act record your demos and pitch *them* to the above. If your musical style is at odds with the local focus, give it a shot anyway. You may be the breath of fresh air they've been looking for. If not, start packing your bags for a reconnaissance trip to greener pastures.

"But," you say, "I have a good day job, a wife (or husband) and five kids, so relocating is not exactly a practical solution. What's the next best thing?"

Try a vacation trip first. Pick up a *Songwriter's Market* (see "Research," page 230) or get some info from your local songwriters association if you have one. Write to some publishers at your destination. Try to get an appointment set up for when you'll be in town. (See "In-person interviews," page 243.) If you can't accomplish that, at least get their permission to send them some songs. Maybe they don't want to meet you till they know they like your material. The point in trying to meet with them is that they'll remember you better when you contact them from home later. Those solid, in-person contacts will make it much easier to continue your long-distance relationship.

When you're far away from recording centers, it becomes more important that you establish an identity by way of your correspondence, packaging, and graphics. Then, when they get your package, they know (from across the room) whose it is. (See "Successful Pitching Strategies," page 186.)

If you're sending in tapes it's better to send one or two songs at a time but send them more frequently so people don't have time to forget you. Better to send a couple songs a month than to send several every six months.

Over the years, I've seen many writers set up long-term business relationships with industry people in this way. On the other hand, I've also seen in-towners get complacent and not form those relationships because they feel as though they can do it any time. Let's face it—no matter where you are, it all gets down to how much you want success and how persistent you are about working for it.

MARKETING YOUR LYRICS

The situation for lyricists in the marketplace has its positives and negatives. On the plus side, it's necessary for you to collaborate to have a suitable melody for your words. I know that doesn't really sound like a plus, but if you're a prolific lyricist, finding several collaborators represents an opportunity to produce a great number of finished songs. Those who insist on writing both lyrics and music, in my experience, are rarely so prolific. As a lyricist, you can develop your lyric skills in a variety of styles without needing to restrict yourself for marketing purposes as do many writer/performers.

On the minus side, it's very difficult for you to get a staff-writing deal. You really have to be an extraordinary lyricist with some commercial success under your belt to get an exclusive staff-writing situation. And it's next to impossible to make a single-song deal on a lyric with no melody. There are audiovisual firms that commission lyricists to write material for them. Check with local firms to see what their needs are, and find additional contacts listed in *Songwriter's Market.*

So, outside of that, what can a lyricist do? Find collaborators. Along with the methods listed in "Collaboration," (see Chapter 7), pay particular attention to political strategy. Find cowriters who are further ahead in their careers than you and still moving forward. Among collaborators to consider are new bands who are getting some industry attention or at least drawing great audiences locally. Good lead singers are usually worth considering because they'll likely write exciting melodies that may need equally exciting lyrics. Find other writers who are starting to get their songs recorded or those who are already on staff at a publishing company. Find writers in strong positions to make contacts with artists, such as studio musicians and recording engineers. With all the above you have the advantage of writing with people who could get good demos made at a reasonable cost, a big plus for you.

If those situations are just not available to you, look for skilled musicians in bands, college music departments, churches, theaters, and so on.

If you speak another language fluently, gather samples of your song translations from, and into, the language. Contact publishers both here and in the countries where the language is spoken. They can be found in directories like *Songwriter's Market* and *Billboard's International Buyers Guide.* The Spanish-speaking market, for example, is enormous.

Make contact with as many potential cowriters as possible, enter lyric writing contests, put notices in music stores, schools, and magazines. Let everyone know what you're looking for and you'll find that your opportunities will grow quickly.

Caution: Do not send your lyrics to companies who advertise in magazines for "song poems" and ask you to pay a fee to have them write melodies to your lyrics. (See "Avoiding the Songsharks," page 138.)

ORGANIZE YOUR SONG SHOPPING

If you plan to actively "plug" your own songs, it's important to keep track of what's going on. You'll want to act as professionally as the successful music publishers who are out there pitching their writers' songs to some of your same contacts. (See "Successful Pitching Strategies" and "Casting.") You'll need to develop a list of producers and recording artists for whom your songs may be appropriate. Keep a card file (5x7 or larger index cards) or a computer file on each of them so that every time you make contact you can note who they're producing, what type of material they need for the upcoming LP, where they're recording, what kind of demos they prefer, whether they usually ask for a percentage of publishing and so on. If you're also shopping for publishers, keep a similar card file for them.

Name of Producer: Lucy Producer
Address:
Phone:

Background: Likes up-tempo country, love songs, happy
              endings. Produced 6 Grammy-winning LPs.

Artists being produced: Proposed studio dates:

Harry Hitsinger   *August*
Art C. Singer   *October - November*

Sent these songs to her: Date: Reaction:

1. *"You are my best"*   *3/87*   *60-day hold*
2.
3.
4.

(Producer card)

Name of Artist: ART E. SINGER   Style: Country

Record Co.: (name, address, phone)
Manager: (name, address, phone)
Agent: (name, address, phone)
Other contacts: (names, addresses, phone numbers)

NOTES:

(Artist card)

TITLE: YOU ARE MY BEST LOVE SONG

WORDS: Suzy Songwriter   MUSIC: Sam Songwriter

Contract: (Name of publisher, address, phone, date)

Copyright: (Date)   Copyright registration #:

Song submitted to: Date: Reaction:

1. *Lucy Producer*   Jan 1987

2. *Harry Hitsinger*

(Song title card)

Information on the artist should include vocal range, what style he or she prefers, and information about personal idiosyncrasies like "hates sexist songs" or "positive lyrics only." This information can be obtained from the producer, consumer and trade magazines, tip sheets, radio and TV interviews, or, if you're one of the more fortunate ones, from the artist personally.

It's also smart to keep a record of personal items about the producer such as "plays golf," "anti-nuke activist," "just had a baby," "going to England in August," and so forth. This type of information is useful in all businesses where personal contact is important. It allows you an instant recap and reminder when you call someone or set up a meeting, gives you an idea for opening a conversation to break the ice, and lets them know that you're concerned about them as people. It doesn't take the place of having good songs, though, since many producers have little time for "small talk" and are best served by a brief presentation of your material. It can, however, create a better climate for you to get feedback on your songs and help you develop as both writer and publisher.

After every meeting or phone call, make notes regarding the outcome, such as "loved 'Don't Take That Away,' doesn't feel it's right for (artist's name) but wants to keep tape for future reference—remind him,"— "didn't like 'Do It Again' but maybe if the hook was stronger, rewrite,"— "will be producing (artist's name) in September—start writing."

Set up file folders with the name of each song you're working on, one song per folder (alphabetical by title, if you have several songs). Each folder will contain:

- Lyric sheets and/or lead sheets for that song. (If you keep your rough drafts and rewrites, mark them accordingly, so you don't send out the unfinished versions by mistake!)
- The names, phone numbers, and addresses of each cowriter on that song AND their performing rights affiliation (BMI, ASCAP, or SESAC).
- If there are any copublishers on that song, include their names, addresses, and phone numbers on a page for reference.
- Photocopies of any correspondence pertaining to that song. (If a letter you receive mentions more than one of your songs, make a photocopy for each respective file.)
- Photocopies of any contracts that pertain to that song (for example, a cowriter's agreement, a copublisher's agreement, an assignment of copyright agreement) or any legal documents that pertain to that song, so you don't have any unpleasant surprises looming over your future about anyone who has ties to your song without your knowledge.
- The copyright registration certificate (or the letter saying you've sent for it) or any forms from other song protection services.
- The performing rights clearance forms (BMI, ASCAP, or SESAC) and any correspondence to or from them.
- Any correspondence or forms from the Harry Fox Agency or other agency collecting your mechanical royalties (or reports from the record company about these).

The value of these files and cards will become apparent after you've called about thirty producers and are preparing for another call or visit when you discover you can't remember whether it was producer X or Y who already "passed" on the song you want to present.

If you have a personal computer, use it to keep these records instead of, or in addition to, your file card system.

Aside from the obvious value in being able to keep track of what you have or haven't done with a song, this organizational process is psychologically valuable in helping you view your songs as product in the marketplace. It takes a little of the edge off rejection by keeping you constantly involved in pitching your songs on an ongoing basis to many industry people.

Keep your tape copies well labeled with the song titles that are on each tape—and once more, don't forget to put your name, address, and phone number on the tape, the insert, the tape box, and your lyric sheets. Have everything ready so you don't need to delay if someone asks you for a copy.

It's also a good idea to keep some 3×5 cards or a small notebook with you at all times so you can write down any info you pick up "on the street." The cards are better than little scraps of paper or matchbook covers because they don't get lost and are easier to file. The street information you pick up is usually about who's recording now or a new producer with an unknown act who might give you the opportunity to get in on the ground floor.

SHOWCASING

Performing your own songs on live showcases, either alone or in the context of a group, is yet another way to expose them for various purposes:

1. For feedback from an audience.
2. For other songwriters as a way to network and find collaborators.
3. To audition for record companies or other industry people (producers, managers, publishers).
4. To audition for booking agents and club owners to get live performing gigs.

Most cities, regardless of how small, have a club where you can play a few original songs. Though most professional club gigs require that you play predominantly contemporary hits or standards, depending on the audience, you can usually get by with throwing in a few of your own over the course of an evening. This is a good way to gauge audience reaction to your songs. You don't always get it right away, but after they hear them a few times, you'll see which ones start to get requests.

In the major music centers there are always "writers' nights" somewhere that are either fairly loose, informal gatherings where you just show up and play, or prescheduled, organized events that you may have to audition for in advance. Talk to whoever's in charge of organizing the talent and get the real story so you don't sign up late and end up showcasing for two drunks and a bartender at 3 A.M.

If money is tight for you, you may have to weigh the value of taking part in these showcases. You will rarely, if ever, be paid for writers' nights types of showcases. Occasionally a club owner might split part of the admissions collected at the door with the performers, but don't count on it. If you're a working band and you have to give up a paying gig somewhere to showcase without pay, you're going to want some assurance that someone will be listening who will be worth showcasing for. If you do it just for fun and performing experience, that may be enough. The deciding factor is the degree of benefit you get out of it.

Established, well-publicized showcases in major music centers that regularly draw industry people are always worth playing at (and attending regularly, even if you don't play). Networking is the most important benefit of these showcases. You not only have a chance to meet and be heard by industry pros, but meeting, hearing, and being heard by other writers and artists can lead to an amazing number of career opportunities. For example:

- Someone likes the way you sing and wants you to play on a demo or master session—or vice versa.
- Someone likes your songs, lyrics, or music and wants you to collaborate with them—or vice versa.
- You make new friends and become part of a mutual support group.
- You find out about resources, organizations, and services that can further your career.

- You get the gossip about local "movers and shakers," recording sessions and other projects needing material.
- You are inspired and motivated by being around other creative people who are being inspired and motivated.

The more people you meet, the more possibilities can open up for you. One person introduces you to a few more who, in turn, introduce you to others. All these contacts increase your odds of finding whatever you're looking for.

If you're auditioning for record companies, it's imperative that you perform primarily original material. A&R people are not interested in the way you play the hits. If you're working a Top 40 gig, make sure to check with the owner to see if you can throw in a set of predominantly originals to play when you know the company reps will be there. Make sure the companies know what time you'll be doing your original set. Hopefully by now, you've developed a mailing list of appropriate music industry people who should be invited.

Get handbills printed. If you're working a regular gig at the club, try to get the owner to help pay for them. Tell him you'll distribute them. Hopefully, you're working at a club that has a mailing list of its own. If not, try to get the club owner to put one together by having his patrons sign a list. If they like you, they'll receive a notice when you're playing there again.

If you're doing a one-shot, one-night showcase at a club you haven't played before:

1. Make sure your appearance is listed on their mailer if the club has one. If it's a regularly scheduled "showcase night" that promotes itself generically it may not mention specific acts.
2. Check with the people who run the showcase for any tips that will help you come off well in their club. Remember, they've seen lots of acts win or lose in their place, and that perspective can be very valuable to you.
3. If you have a band, make sure the stage is big enough to accommodate your instruments, amps, etc., with enough room for whatever stage movement you need to show yourself to best advantage. If there isn't enough room, look for another club.
4. If there is a house P.A. system, talk to whoever runs it. Generally, if you have a sound person you work with regularly and the house system is adequate, it's better for him or her to work with the club's sound person to get the best sound out of the room. If the club's sound system isn't adequate, and you bring in your own, the procedure is riskier. Your sound person should be someone who can tailor the sound output to the acoustic properties of the room with the right E.Q. (treble/bass adjustments) and speaker placement, and who is willing to accept advice from the club's sound person. I've seen some good groups empty the house because they wouldn't listen to advice and played too loudly for the room. *Vol-*

ume must be tailored according to the size and shape of the room and whether the walls are reflective or absorbent. If you're doing a record company showcase, being able to hear clean vocals is important, so start there and mix around it.

5. Make sure you have a sound check to work out all the problems and to set your instrument levels.
6. Show up on time for sound checks and performances.
7. Make sure the lighting is adequate. Will someone be running the lights? Make sure they're aware of any lighting cues you might need. Write them down.
8. See if they have a place to display your photos.
9. Know ahead of time exactly how much time you can have for your set and stick to it.
10. If you need a piano, make sure it's in tune.
11. Be cooperative with everyone at the club, including the waitresses. It's the difference between your coming back to the club or not, between having the employees tell everyone to come and see you or telling everyone you're losers.
12. Talk with the owner about guest lists and guest policies beforehand so you'll know what arrangements to make for them. This will avoid a bad scene at the door involving guests whom you want to be in a receptive state of mind toward your group.
13. Dress with some conscious thought about how you look individually or as a group on stage. No matter what you decide to wear, make it a calculated choice rather than looking like you just got off work as a mechanic and didn't have time to change.
14. Plan your sets carefully, considering the length of the set, pacing, and where you should place your strongest material. Generally, if you have a potential hit single, or other very commercial material, begin and end with it. If you're going to be the last set, put strong material at the beginning of your performance. Record people frequently have other places to go and are in a hurry to leave. If you play a couple of less commercial tunes to open with and think you'll "finish strong," you'll find when you hit the heavy ones that your guests have already gone.
15. Make sure *all* information concerning the showcase is conveyed to the *whole* group.

If you're auditioning for a club gig, most of the above list will also apply, but here are some additional questions to ask that will help you tailor your performance to the needs of the club. What does the club owner want? All Top 40 stuff? Top 40 standards? Top 40 with some originals? Who will be in the club's audience? Under 18? A singles' bar drinking crowd?

Pick a club that wants the kind of music you enjoy playing or you're wasting your time. The audience won't like you and the gig will get old very fast. The attitude "we'll make them dig what we do" is admirably ambitious but chances are the owner knows the audience better than you do.

CONTESTS

Since contests represent an important avenue for exposure, it's important for you to get some information about how to sort out the ones you might want to enter.

There are many different types of songwriting, composing, and lyric competitions—major international competitions, national and local contests, and specialty contests for city, event, campaign, or product themes. Entry fees vary, though the so-called specialty contests are usually free. Contests that offer cash prizes generally require a fee, and some contests require an additional fee for a song to be submitted in more than one judging category.

Though some contests advertise in national magazines, others can be found through songwriter organizations, some of which produce their own contests as well as announcing others for the benefit of their members.

Are contests worthwhile? That's a good question. You'll need to balance the time and money you put into them against what you stand to gain from the effort in each individual case. Your choice will depend on knowing what the contest offers. Media exposure, industry exposure, cash, a publishing deal, a record deal, certificates of merit, scholarships, critiques, studio time, demo production, and musical instruments are all common benefits. In addition, being able to say you won, placed, or received honorable mention in a competition is a good credit to have on your resume because it says, in effect, that someone has already screened your songs and felt they were worth listening to.

An important factor in any contest is the ability to assess your odds. In the case of a songwriter it amounts to being able to be a good critic of your own songs.

This is quite obviously a difficult thing for most writers to do. They get emotionally involved in songs that, to other, more objective observers, may sound simplistic and trite. Other writers think they're creating great works of art, but their efforts may be so self-consciously poetic, abstract, and unfocused that nobody else can figure out what they're about. Still others have sunk a lot of bucks into a demo that sounds great, and because of that commitment, lose all objectivity about the fact that, in a contest, if you don't have a good lyric and melody, the production won't help.

For many writers, the incentive that a contest offers to get organized and quit procrastinating is worthwhile in itself.

Contests can lead to contacts you couldn't have made otherwise. In some contests, the judges can get the names of other writers they liked but who didn't win. Some contests give judges "address request" forms on which they write the entry number and song title (there are no names or addresses on the tapes). These are turned in and, after the contest, judges can get the names and addresses of the writers and request more material. I've seen it happen often. This is a recognition of the fact that a lot of good songs don't win. It also means that there is a broad range of tastes in the industry and an individual publisher or producer may like something that other judges don't like or don't feel is worth pursuing. Judges' reactions in some of these contests can be very telling:

- "This is a great idea and a good hook, but he lost it in the last verse. I can't move it up (to the next judging level), but I want to see if he'll rewrite that verse."
- "This doesn't work as a song, but it's a great *record.*" One of the semifinalists lost this judge's vote because the *song* didn't stack up to the others, but I'm sure he got recording offers.
- "I love this lady's voice! The song doesn't make it, but if I can get her some material, she'd be a killer!" Publishers with good contemporary catalogues often look for a great new artist who can record songs they publish. They then try to secure a record deal for the artist.
- "I know an artist who's looking for just this kind of song." It may be an unusual kind of song that most judges may not "hear" as commercial, but that one publisher or producer with a special project may find is exactly appropriate.

So there are more ways you can "win" than the obvious ones. By all means, though, take advantage of every opportunity promptly. A publisher and fellow judge told me he was very disappointed that after sending out about fifty letters to writers whose songs he liked, only about fifteen bothered to respond.

Be wary of a contest in which a publishing contract is the main prize (or any prize) or a contest in which the contest owns the publishing automatically if you win (or enter) and you have no option to turn it down. What it means is that a publisher just figured out a way to get you to pay him for screening songs for his publishing company, which a publisher should do for free. On the face of it, a publishing contract may seem like a good prize, but if the publisher doesn't have some success already (or great contacts) your best song may be orphaned. Check out *anyone* who wants to publish your song, and never allow yourself to be bound to a contract you can't read first.

Who judges and what do they look for? The preferences of all judges are influenced not only by personal likes and dislikes but by their jobs. For instance, it's often more difficult for publishers to look at a song's intrinsic merit as a work of art when, in their daily business, they must place great value on current commercial potential. It's difficult for a producer not to be excited by great production in a demo or turned off by an unpleasant-sounding tape though good producers reject great demos of mediocre songs as a daily part of their jobs. In the contests I've judged, the criteria for evaluation were clearly spelled out to the judges and we were frequently reminded not to let production (or lack of it) influence our decisions. We even advanced songs that were presented *a cappella* if they had a good melody and lyrics. Blatant clichés and unmemorable melodies weren't going to win, nor were lyrics with bad meter, sloppy or no rhyme, no focus, or no choruses (except for AABA forms). We all had a standard of how good a song had to be to win, so at the first sign of a flaw, the tape usually got turned off.

Current commercial potential is always a factor regardless of what anyone says to the contrary, though it's more important in some contests than in others—usually when industry judges are involved. Also, major contests want to be able to play a part in getting those songs recorded so they lean toward songs that would stand a good chance in the marketplace.

In practical terms, what that means to you is that if the lyric or song doesn't have a commercial structure, it's generally eliminated automatically. We were all aware, for instance, that if there were no chorus, or at least a refrain at the end of every verse, it just wouldn't work commercially, or at least it was not the kind of song the contest wanted as a winner because its chances of being commercially successful were slim.

Some excellent writers, by the way, have hurt their chances in lyric competitions by not labeling their verses, chorus, and bridges. A writer I know who's a first-class lyricist was depressed that she had submitted her best lyrics to a contest and didn't even get an honorable mention. I asked her to send them to me. When I received them, I noted immediately that songs I knew to be ABABCB structures appeared on the page to be AAAAA (a series of verses). She never retyped the chorus or labeled the original chorus and typed "repeat chorus." Consequently the songs were immediately eliminated for lack of commercial structure. Similarly, other lyrics have been eliminated because the writer continued each line on the page, prose style, not making separation between segments. Judges assume the writer is ignorant of form and the chances of the lyric or song being a contender are very poor.

Are the contests fair? Although it's relative, and open to argument, I think every contest tries to do the best it can with what it has to work with. Some of those that charge a fee can afford to hire the best ears in the business to listen, and, in fact, they owe it to you. Even when the most experienced professionals are judging material, you're dealing with a wide variety of tastes.

Since different people prefer different styles of music, some contests ask the screeners to choose only those categories they feel competent to judge. This eliminates those who don't understand, for instance, what makes gospel or country music "work" because of limited experience with it. This categorization is something a writer should consider when entering. A writer with a Southern accent and a guitar/vocal demo may feel that he's written a song that could be Top 40. But there's a risk that the judge in that category may "hear" it as a country song and not have the imagination to visualize it as a Top 40 song. I've seen good songs eliminated because the screener thought the songs didn't belong in the category he was judging. So you need to consider both the sound of your demo and the category you choose most carefully.

Most major contests deal with the problem of divergent tastes by having several judges listen to the same songs. I believe this is the fairest way. When I judged the American Song Festival (no longer in existence), we were given a batch of 100 songs and asked to move up to the second level anything we felt was even remotely worth another listen. That same box of 100 then went to two other screeners. Even at that, we ended up eliminating most of what we heard. For the second level, three of us sat on each panel and two out of three had to agree on one to three songs from a batch of about fifty to raise to the top level. If there were more than three in our batch that we felt were exceptional, we were told we could advance them, too. There ended up being ten to fifteen songs per category in the third level. Thirty judges listened to them over a speaker system and rated them in order of preference.

Other factors that affect a contest's fairness:

Are the judges familiar with the writers? The procedure should eliminate any bias by removing names and numbering tapes before judging or using outside judges, at least on the final round.

How are judges paid? If judges are paid based on how many tapes they listen to, there's a danger that your tape might get all of two seconds so they can quickly move on to the next one. A setup that pays judges by the hour is preferable.

Writer/producer Doug Thiele came up with a valuable set of guidelines, both for those who produce contests, and for those who enter. Use this checklist in investigating any contest you're considering entering or producing.

SONG CONTEST GUIDELINES

1. The contest organizers and/or those responsible for the contest's finances should be listed on the advertising.
2. All contests should have an address other than a post office box (i.e., a street address) and a public phone number available through easily accessible channels.
3. Contest organizers should file with the Better Business Bureau before doing any advertising.
4. The contest officers, owners, representatives, judges, and their families should be ineligible to enter the contest.
5. Prize schedules and amounts should be clearly listed and, where necessary, explained.
6. Deadlines for entries, notification of finalists, notification of winners, and awarding of prizes should be stated and must be adhered to. If a deadline becomes impossible to meet, those in charge must implement a predetermined procedure of notifying all contestants involved. New deadlines must clearly be stated.
7. Those in charge of the contest must place no automatic claim on rights of the song or subsequent royalties therefrom. This does not include the contest organizers' right to have the winning entry performed for promotional purposes.
8. Judges for the contest must be music business people with proven experience in judging or critiquing songs.

9. After the first year, contest literature should list the names and accomplishments of past winners.
10. It is recommended that there be a statement on all advertisements that prize money is either guaranteed personally by those responsible for the contest, or that the prize fund is in an escrow account deliverable to the contest winners only.

For current information on contests contact the Los Angeles Songwriters Showcase office. Investigate thoroughly any contest you enter. Read all the literature carefully. Call the organizers if you have questions about anything. Try your songs out on other people first, and pick your very best shot.

Marketing yourself and your songs can, of course, be a full-time occupation if you're willing to put in the time and energy and to deal with the rejection. But if you believe in yourself and feel your songs deserve to be heard beyond your friends and family, you owe it to yourself to try to make it happen. Pursuing songwriting as a way to make a living can be a rocky road. Hopefully, the information in this chapter will make it a little smoother for you. If you're successful, great rewards are in store. If you're not, you'll have the satisfaction of knowing you gave it your best shot and you'll always have a wonderful way to express yourself, a gift that's its own reward. You also won't grow old saying, "If only I would have tried. . . ."

Additional Markets

Good songs have many different markets. Though most writers seem to think in terms of commercial radio, your skills can be used in a variety of ways.

With a little imagination, you can market even your most "off-the-wall" efforts. A friend of mine once wrote a song about his dog that expressed the sentiments of a lot of dog lovers. He sent the lyric to a magazine devoted to dogs, they printed it and paid him. He also sells a version suitable for framing via an ad in the magazine. He *still* makes money from it. It was a song a publisher would never have been interested in and he knew it, so he took that extra step and asked himself "Who would be?"

The following are some additional markets to be aware of. For more of an in-depth look at each, check the Bibliography.

FILM AND TELEVISION

Film and television, though always important users of music, have become even more important in recent years. The success of MTV and other programs featuring popular contemporary music, and youth market films that spawn million seller-soundtrack albums have combined to create an awareness among film and television producers of the commercial power of contemporary music. That awareness has prompted them to hire, or contract on a project basis, music coordinators and music supervisors with record company and music publishing experience to make sure they get the best contemporary composers and songwriters for their projects.

The two major areas of music usage in film and TV are: 1) instrumental underscoring and theme composition, and 2) songs. Songs are either "featured" (used prominently in strategic places) or used as "source music"—music you hear coming from a radio, stereo, jukebox, or other source on the screen.

SKILLS

If your goal is to do instrumental scoring and themes, you're ahead of the game if you know how to arrange and orchestrate. It also pays to have a good working knowledge of current synthesizer, computer music software, and recording technology. Keyboard players have an advantage in this area because most of the "synth technology" that allows a composer to create and record a substantial amount of the music simultaneously is keyboard-oriented, although MIDI/computer music technology, as I mentioned earlier, diminishes your need to be a virtuoso. The best opportunities are available to those who have the greatest variety of skills, because film and TV producers want a finished product (composed, performed, produced) for as little money as possible. Those who can do it with the least manpower in the fastest time can quote them the best prices. The best-paying, but most demanding of all the jobs in this area are the weekly TV series, which require technical skill, discipline, and speed.

Richard "Koz" Kosinski is a successful scorer and songwriter for both film and TV. He worked on the film *Teen Wolf* and later scored the TV series *Spiral Zone* and HBO's *First and Ten* sports series. He describes the pressure of film scoring.

Typically, a film starts out allowing about six weeks to do the music for, say, an hour-long film. Then it takes a week to choose a composer from maybe six who are up for the job, then another week to work on the contracts. So you might have three to four weeks at the most to write, arrange, produce, record, mix, and transfer (to the magnetic stripe on the film). Then the music, dialogue and sound effects are mixed to the film at a sound stage studio that has been booked six months ahead of time. There are a lot of projects booked in there afterwards, so if you don't make it, you're in deep trouble.

With TV, especially cartoons where it's almost all music, it's a rough situation, too. Sometimes I'll work 36 hours at a stretch. This is a crazy job.

Koz and a partner usually do the complete score electronically. The other method of scoring is for a composer, arranger, and copyist to write out the complete score and record it "live" in the studio. This is sometimes a faster method, but the pressure is still great.

LEARNING

Colleges and universities with film and TV departments offer the best opportunities to learn the craft of scoring. In the major film and TV centers (Los Angeles in particular), there are excellent classes taught by professional film and TV composers. To gain experience with a minimum of pressure there are also opportunities to score industrial and educational films (see "Audiovisuals," page 277), student films and cable shows if you're competent and aggressive. Find out about *student films* by finding your closest college or university film department and posting your credits, skills, and availability on the department bulletin board. For *cable shows,* make a visit to your local cable TV station and find out if there are any local programs that use different music on each show, or new shows being produced that may need theme music. You won't make much money on these projects, but by the time you've done a few of these you should have an impressive demo reel or reels. Whenever you finish a job, transfer the highlights to a reel that you can use as an audition for your next project. Since, in scoring, it's as important to know where *not* to have music, you'll best demonstrate your taste by presenting a video demo that can demonstrate your ability to "spot" (determine the appropriate music for the appropriate spots in the film).

FINDING WORK

You may also win friends and admirers along the way who will turn you on to yet more lucrative jobs. Those who become successful enough to score several series often hire assistants who are orchestrators, arrangers, copyists, and engineers so, if you have those skills, working for a pro is a great way to get "hands-on" experience. Most professionals work in their own studios and can be found through the TV network on which the show is broadcast. Each show has its own office, so always ask for that specific show.

As soon as you've acquired enough credits to interest a film and TV music agent, you move into another stratus where it gets easier to gain access to the big opportunities.

Songwriters have several ways to make contact. Each of the major film and TV studios has a music director or music supervisor who is the liaison with songwriters and film composers. Most prefer to deal with established writers, agents, music publishers, or record companies but "open door" policies exist at some companies. Independent music coordinators and supervisors who deal with film projects are generally more accessible but you can't afford not to try them all.

Reading *Variety,* the *Hollywood Reporter,* and *Drama-Logue* (see Bibliography) will give you leads on what films are casting, in preproduction, and currently shooting.

A back-door approach is to present your songs to the music editors, producers, and directors of specific films so they can use them as "temp tracks" (i.e., songs used in scenes temporarily to establish a mood or set a dance tempo before making a final decision on songs). If they use one of your songs that has the right tempo and groove, they may ultimately want to replace it with a current hit but, in the end, may not be able to negotiate the rights to use the hit in the film and end up using yours.

One of the most common strategies of film producers in obtaining soundtrack songs is to find a major recording artist to sing at least the title song. A hit song in a film can be a major marketing tool for both the song and the film, so they'll look first for hit artists and hit songwriters. But several things can go wrong. The artist or record company may reject the offer because they may not feel that the film will help the artist's career, the release schedule of the film may conflict with the release of other product from the artist, or, in the end, the film company can't afford the artist. The film company can be running out of time—and money—without finding that major song and major artist to sing it. With your "temp track" approach, after hearing your song used repeatedly (even if "temporarily"), the editor and director may begin to feel as though it belongs there and, if other strategies fall through, you're already in position.

It's important to be aware that the decision-making politics in filmmaking is, in most cases, extremely erratic. Financial backers, producers, directors, stars, agents, and others vie for decision power. These are most often people with no musical background who "know what they like" or "have a nephew who's a songwriter," a situation that can be both a blessing and a curse. One day you've got a song in a film, the next day it's out.

Or vice versa. If your song is good and is perceived that day to be appropriate (or perhaps if you're the "nephew") you've got a shot.

On the subject of appropriateness, writers often feel that it's desirable for their song to tell the story of the film. Wrong. It's much better to express the emotion of the scene. The music shouldn't compete with the visuals, but complement and support them.

If you want to write for TV, look for TV series that use lots of new, unknown songs. You have the luxury of "researching" while you watch TV since the credits list the production company and music supervisor.

There are people and organizations who can help you make contacts. The Los Angeles Songwriters Showcase has a Professional Membership category for exceptional writers and arranges special in-house "pitching sessions" with music supervisors looking for songs for film and TV. Film and TV reps at BMI and ASCAP can also help. More and more films are being created with soundtrack record potential in mind, so they're using more contemporary radio-style songs.

HOW YOU GET PAID AND WHAT YOU CAN EARN

The pay in film and TV ranges from ridiculously bad to incredibly good, based, as usual, on your bargaining power and the budgets of the projects. Your bargaining power comes from your talent, skill, speed and your past credits. For already existing songs, synchronization licenses are granted to the film or TV production company by the copyright owner and are totally negotiable, but usually film and TV producers want to own the publishing rights to your song. In cases where they pay you to write a song or score specifically for the project, they want it to be a "work for hire" so they'll own it outright. Either way, you'll probably get an advance, retain 50 percent of the performance royalties from air play, 50 percent of the mechanicals if it gets into a soundtrack album, writer credit, and screen credit. For TV, you want to write themes and score series so that you'll receive performance royalties from BMI or ASCAP every time they're shown. You'll hope the shows go into reruns so you'll continue to get paid. Be sure to check with your performing rights organization regarding proper reporting procedures. The performing rights societies do not pay royalties on American theatrical performances for films, but will collect from their foreign counterparts for theatrical performances in those countries. In the U.S., performance royalties *are* paid if the film is shown on television.

If you're offered a contract to have a song in a film or to score a film, get the advice of an entertainment attorney who specializes in film and TV as this is a complex area.

In "Motion Picture Soundtrack Songwriting and Performing" from *The Musician's Manual: A Practical Guide* (see Bibliography), Mark Halloran (Vice President of Business Affairs at MCA Motion Picture Group) and Thomas A. White (a business affairs advisor in the record and music publishing industries) give a good picture of writer royalties for a chart-oriented single from a film by a writer/artist/producer. The information was gathered in 1986.

Let's assume you make a deal with Paramount, as a writer/performer/producer, for a title song and master. You are paid $25,000 for the song and $25,000 to record. You retain the "writer's share" but Paramount retains the publisher's share. You receive a 12 percent retail U.S. record royalty, pro-rated, on LPs, and 9 percent on singles. Your master is three minutes long. The picture is a blockbuster, your single sells one million copies in the U.S., 750,000 foreign, and hits number one on Billboard's Hot 100 chart. The soundtrack LP (on which you have one of the ten cuts) sells 500,000 copies in the U.S. and 375,000 copies overseas.

We have prepared the following summary which is designed more to alert you to sources of income than to provide exact figures (although we have done our best to be reasonably accurate).

FILM INCOME CHART

A. Writer's Share

1. Writing Fee (non-recoupable)	$ 25,000
2. Song Synch License For Film	-0-
3. Performance Income (Worldwide)	
(a) From Film In Theaters	
(i) U.S.	-0-
(ii) Foreign	$ 20,000
(b) Radio Performances	$100,000
(c) Home Video	-0-
(d) Pay TV	*
(e) Free TV	
(i) U.S. Network TV (two runs)	$ 3,000
(ii) U.S. Syndicated TV (two runs, 150 stations)	$ 600
(iii) Foreign	$ 5,000
4. Sheet Music (140,000 copies @ $.10/copy)	$ 14,000
5. Mechanicals	
(a) U.S. (¾ statutory)	
(i) Single (A side only) (1,000,000 × 1.875 cents)	$ 18,750
(ii) LP (500,000 × 1.875 cents)	$ 9,375
(b) Foreign	
(i) Single (750,000 × 2.25 cents)	$ 16,875
(ii) LP (375,000 × 2.25 cents)	$ 8,438
Total	$221,038

COMMERCIAL JINGLES

Here's some background on the making of commercial jingles and the qualities, beyond creativity and composing and production skills, needed by a jingle music producer to be successful.

To air a single 30-second commercial on prime time network TV may cost a client (sponsor) over $300,000. That's just to pay for the air time alloted to it, not for the time and effort to create it. That's a lot of money, especially when you multiply it by the number of times these spots run. This explains the tremendous responsibility ad agencies have to deliver commercials that bring results to the clients who make that kind of investment. There are advertising agencies with multimillion-dollar-a-year clients without whom those agencies would not exist. This explains the legendary paranoia of ulcer-ridden advertising executives. It also explains why it's so difficult for beginners to get into the business of making music for commercials. Like the old Catch-22, "If you're not already successful, how do we know you can do the job?"

With the stakes so high, ad agencies can't afford to gamble. If they choose music that sounds less than professional and appropriate, they risk losing an account and their jobs. So a composer must not only understand the advertising medium and be thoroughly professional, but must be a kind of psychologist, instilling confidence in his abilities and making agency personnel feel secure in their musical choices.

As a composer, your problems may be compounded by the fact that few ad agency people really understand music and may not have the language to convey their needs to you.

So you need to become adept at translating lines like, "I want something like Van Halen, only softer." (Translation: he wants high energy but low volume.) He may request a musical style in terms of a particular artist or song ("I want something that sounds sort of like Madonna's last single"). It's important that you keep current. Avoid using technical or musical terminology. You don't have to impress them—they already accept that you know your business. You must also learn to mix demographics into your music. In other words, you must target the audience. How old are they? What do they like? What do they already buy? Where do they live? How much disposable income do they have? In general, what are their needs as a group? What style of music appeals to them? Those are some of the questions agency personnel will be able to answer. They'll usually have a "storyboard" already worked out—a series of drawings, like a comic strip, depicting the way they see the commercial from beginning to end. Each section is timed.

They may also be able to give you a script so you can get a feel for the emotional content of the scene, and perhaps a lyric or slogan to work from. (If you're lucky, the lyric is actually singable.) You'll seldom have the opportunity to create the lyric yourself, but will be creating an "underscore" (instrumental background), music for the lyric, or some of each.

You and several other producers will usually be asked to come up with demos to play for the client. Usually you'll be given a minimal budget to cover demo costs, but occasionally you'll be asked to do the demos on spec (your money). On "spec" deals, you gamble that if you skimp on the costs and give them a demo that doesn't sound enough like a finished product to inspire their confidence, you lose the job to someone who puts more money into his demo or actually comes up with a master. That can happen even with ad agencies who know your work and know you can come up with a great finished product. Keep in mind that the client usual-

267

ly also has to be convinced by the demo. It's a good idea, if possible, to come up with two or three variations of instrumentation and sounds so you can let the agency feel they have a part in making the final decision. Always have your own favorite, though, so if they ask, "What do *you* think?" you'll come across as decisive and won't make them nervous. (There's that psychology again.)

Ad agencies prefer to do business with music people with whom they have good rapport, who are professional, who understand their needs and who deliver the goods at an equal or better price than anyone else. They also like to deal with people who are personable and even charismatic, because they can depend on them to impress the multimillion-dollar clients. It won't do to have the client come to your session and have the ad executive who hired you have to apologize for your bad attitude. That's not the way business is done at that level. He wants the client to love you and compliment him on his good taste. A great personality will never substitute for competence in this business, but in this case, at least, it can provide a competitive edge.

THE AUDITION DEMO

Because the competition in commercials is heavy, having a first-rate demo that shows your skill and versatility is essential. Collect not more than ten pieces of music on not more than five minutes of tape. If you've already got legitimate credits, include them. If not, don't be intimidated. The agencies are always looking for new talent because some composers, after a few years, get too expensive and their style gets old. Agencies look for fresh ideas and very contemporary styles, particularly for youth market products. Put a sample of whatever you do best first on the tape. Do a piece of atmospheric background on it, create some jingles for imaginary products, show them some different moods in both vocal jingles and instrumentals, and some different styles. Today many commercials only identify the product on screen and not in the jingle. Create a couple of evocative jingles with lyrics that express some emotional comment on life in general. Typeset a slick label and tape insert so you'll look like a pro. Print some credits or other self-promotion on the insert and don't forget your address and phone number. You want them to keep that tape on file, along with your résumé.

MAKING CONTACT

Everyone I talk to in the jingle business seems to have entered it in a different way. Some started out as singers on jingle sessions, some were musicians and arrangers. I got started when an advertising executive in Montreal heard an electronic music cut on my album and called me in L.A. to see if I'd do something like it for a Toyota commercial. After doing that and a couple more for that agency, I started systematically pursuing jingle jobs. I secured a copy of *The Standard Directory of Advertising Agencies* (available at most libraries) which lists all the ad agencies, their clients, and who to contact at the local offices.

Those people, called "creative directors," are the ones who screen and choose the creative talent for the "spots," including actors and actresses, locations, film production companies, and jingle music composers and producers. I called every agency in Los Angeles that produced commercials for radio and TV (some were print only). The first question I asked was whether they ever used, or were open to using, original music in their spots. Some replied that they only used "library" music (see "Audiovisuals," page 277) that they bought inexpensively by the minute.

After locating the ones who at least occasionally used original music, I made appointments to meet the creative directors or their assistants, who were in most cases quite open and eager to hear something new. My "rap" included the info that I was a recording artist, coproduced my album, and had already composed and produced music for national network spots (which I brought along on a reel to play for them). I'd never been good at promoting myself, but in advertising it is absolutely necessary to go in with all your credits blazing. The competition is fierce! I don't know how eager they would have been if I hadn't had any credits.

If they wished, I also showed the directors film copies I'd gotten of my previous spots so they could see how the music and visuals worked together. I'd leave them a tape for their files, and after the meeting I'd send them a card to thank them for their time. I also made a file card on each company, who their clients were, who I spoke to there and their comments on my music, and the names of their secretaries and assistants. I always asked when I should call back and noted the date on my card. Later, I transferred the information to a calendar and followed up when the date came around. Typically, I'd call back two to five times before I'd get to talk to them but I got to be friends with the secretaries, who often gave me valuable information on upcoming projects.

Even though it's been a while since my "jingle hustle," the process is still basically the same, at least from the standpoint of an independent composer/producer with your own business. You're known to the agencies as a "music producer," and they count on you to deliver them a finished product. If you can do all or most of it yourself, fine. It's important not to kid yourself about your own abilities, though. This is serious business. Hire pros to to whatever you can't do *extremely well.* You may be hiring an arranger, singers and musicians (including filling out union contracts), and booking and paying the studio.

Most major jingle activity is in New York, Chicago, and Los Angeles, so if you don't live near those cities you need to pursue some other options.

Here are some other suggestions for finding work as an independent jingle music producer:

- Place ads in advertising and production trade magazines such as *Adweek, Advertising Age, Advertising World,* and *Millimeter.* (See Bibliography.)
- Contact your state film commission and try to get listed as a music resource in the catalogue they send to companies to solicit film projects in your state. These catalogues are also sent to companies within the state.

- Most major cities have an ad club whose members include ad agencies, media professionals, clients, and music producers in that region. They also have newsletters in which you can advertise.
- The American Advertising Federation is a national organization for advertising professionals. It has periodic conventions in various cities that provide valuable opportunities to show your wares and make contacts. Get information on membership and schedules from: American Advertising Federation, 251 Post St., Suite #302, San Francisco, CA 94108. Or phone (415)421-6867.

START A LOCAL AGENCY

Yet another possibility is to form your own small-scale ad agency and music producer combination dealing with small local accounts. It requires some research, but check out local restaurants, clubs, hotels, tourist attractions, and similar businesses to see if they do or will do radio ads. If you have access to recording equipment and a few musician friends, put together a catchy jingle for some of them. Write a sample script, get a voiceover actor to read it, and present your potential "clients" with a 30-second version of the whole thing. If it sounds professional you'll be surprised at how positively people react to hearing their very own commercial jingle. If you lay down several different kinds of tracks you can just put new vocals and lyrics on them for each different prospect you approach.

Your competition for local radio ads are the radio stations themselves, whose salesmen sell the businesses package deals which include their staff announcer's reading and writing the ad copy. A good plan is to form alliances with the ad sales people at the stations and help them put together those packages. Your advantage is that you can provide the client with an original jingle and can likely do it cheaper than a jingle house, which has more overhead. You would sell the jingle to the client and have the station's announcer write and read additional copy.

A drawback to this approach is that, in order to give the client an inexpensive deal, you'd pretty much have to do it without union help. When you do non-union spots and play on them yourself, you do not receive residuals. You'll charge a one-time fee that includes your creative fee and covers your production cost. You'll hope to create a lasting relationship with the client and periodically create new jingles for him.

"JINGLE HOUSES"

If you're not interested in being in business for yourself, another alternative is to hook up with a jingle music production company or "jingle house." These are established businesses that usually represent several composers. You may not have the potential to make as much money if you choose this route, but you wouldn't have as many expenses and headaches, either. If you're in a major jingle production city, you can find them in the Yellow Pages usually under "music arrangers and composers" or "music producers." If you're not, check out the local recording studios and find out if any jingle production is done there and who is doing it. Compile a demo of your best work and play it for them.

WHAT IF YOU HAVE AN IDEA FOR A MAJOR PRODUCT?

If you think up an outstanding jingle or concept for a particular product, can you sell it to an agency? Your odds are not good. Remember, ad agencies who represent those products pay a lot of money to copywriters and other people in their company to come up with those ideas. There's a good chance they don't want to hear yours. If they do, you risk that they'll borrow your idea or some important aspects of it without paying you. Ideas are not copyrightable. What you can copyright is an actual slogan or jingle (song), but unless it's compatible with the product image already planned by the agency, the odds are against the company using it no matter how clever the idea.

As an example, let's take the telephone company's "Reach Out and Touch Someone" concept that gave us humorous or dramatic human interest vignettes. It was such an effective campaign that it lasted for a long time and is still going as of this writing. It was also one in which the general concept (uncopyrightable) was more important than the actual slogan (copyrightable). So, what if you came up with one of the vignettes? Why should the ad execs buy yours when they can probably get hundreds of ideas from their own staff? It's like, to use an old phrase, taking coals to Newcastle, or to coin a new one, taking songs to Bruce Springsteen.

If you hear a campaign that uses different jingles within the same concept, chances are that there is a company already contracted to create those jingles.

THE MONEY

Today's commercials use a lot of recent or oldie hits (depending on the age of the target consumer), either in their original versions or rewritten for a specific product. In those cases, the ad agencies will negotiate a "synch fee" with the song's publisher, assuming that the writer doesn't have a clause in the writer/publisher contract preventing the song from being used that way. The writer and publisher split the synch fees which, for use of a hit, have been known to exceed $200,000. In addition, if the agency wants to use the original recording instead of a new version, an additional "master use" fee must be negotiated with the record company, which can, in some cases, exceed the cost of the synch license. In either case, the writer and publisher may also receive performance royalties for air play of the song, depending on the provisions of the contract. Check with your performing rights society to make sure you'll be able to receive performance royalties.

Let's assume now that we're not dealing with a previous hit but with the writer of a commercial jingle with lyrics or just instrumental tracks (underscores). These have three sources of income, depending on how you work it: creative fees, union session payments and residuals, and performing rights royalties.

You can negotiate a "creative fee" over and above the cost of production because you're creating the music. Just as it is in any other business, the amount of that fee depends on "clout" and chutzpah (nerve). It takes a lot of chutzpah to ask for twice what you think you can get and negotiate from there. At any rate, figuring out what to ask for is one of the most difficult parts of the business. You don't want to downgrade yourself by asking too little or price yourself out of business by asking too much.

I once bid against two competitors on a job that was to be a series of 30-second spots, variations on a basic theme. My bid was based on my figuring out a low-cost way to do the variations. I lost the bid, and it wasn't till two years later that the agency representative would tell me why. The spots had gone for nearly twice my figure, because the other two bids were in the same neighborhood and the client decided that if my competitors, both well-known pros, were charging that much, he didn't see how I could possibly deliver for half that amount. The ad man tried to convince the client, but the psychology of "If it costs more, it must be better" worked against me and it has since changed my negotiating tactics.

Bid high, and let them tell you it's too steep. You can then say, "Well, let me see if I can figure out some shortcuts without compromising the quality." You get back to them with something like, "I made a good time deal with a new studio so I can knock off a couple hundred," or "I can use three singers instead of six," etc. If you have a solid relationship with the ad agency, they may hint at what sort of ballpark figure they're thinking about, but they'd rather not. Obviously, if you're talking about Coca-Cola, you're dealing with a company that annually spends millions on advertising, as opposed to a local jewelry store which spends thousands. Creative fees, those over and above production costs for a national commercial jingle, can range from $1,500 to $15,000 per spot, depending on your clout, the budget, and how big and time-consuming the job is. It's all negotiable.

If you play on commercials, other money is available to you from union scale payments, from the American Federation of Musicians (AF of M) or, if you sing, even higher payments from the American Federation of Television and Radio Artists (AFTRA) or the Screen Actors Guild (SAG). At the end of every 13-week period in which a spot is run, you'll receive a residual check for the same union scale you made on the original session.

The checks can add up. I used to play three different instruments on some of the spots I did. One of them was designated "leader," which is double scale, so I'd make the equivalent of what four musicians would make! I also did a Borax spot that ran two-and-a-half years and gave me a nice "surprise" residual check every 13 weeks.

The rate schedules are available from your local AF of M and AFTRA offices. They're comprehensive and complex, but anyone involved in producing or playing on commercials should be familiar with them, for their own protection.

The performing rights societies (ASCAP and BMI), have instituted performance royalties for music used in commercials. Since those organizations are continually updating their rates and conditions of payment, you should check with them for current payment schedules.

Except for pre-existing music licensed by the copyright owner to be used in a commercial, nearly all music written for commercials is considered "work-for-hire," in which the client (sponsor) retains all rights to the composition. In that case, performance rights may only be paid if the writer obtains a contract provision from the agency/client that *excludes* the performance rights from the rights granted the client.

In the above-mentioned income sources for jingles, the amounts paid are based on the ways the music is used in the jingle, whether it's broadcast locally or on network, whether it's used regionally or nationally, whether it's played on radio or television, and how often and in what time period it is played.

CHILDREN'S MUSIC

One of the many good things about writing and recording music for children is that it's a stable market. Unlike the pop record business where, if the planets or cards (or whatever you believe in) are aligned right, you can make a lot of money in a relatively short time, the children's market is slow but sure, and doesn't burn out overnight. Walt Disney Productions, for instance, will consistently sell well (many times over a million copies) on just about every record it releases because everyone trusts Disney to have consistently good products. In some cases, they're buying the same records for their kids that they themselves grew up with.

If you establish yourself with a body of work in this market, you can sell a million records over several years. You'll never make the *Billboard* charts, but chances are that if you're genuinely interested in this market, it won't matter to you.

Styles of children's music range from the same contemporary rock, R&B and country that kids hear on the radio, to more traditional folk music styles. Lyrics, however, are directed to kids. There is a strong push for nonsexist, nonviolent (except for some toy manufacturers who create TV programs that sell ray guns), non-racially stereotyped messages that promote positive self-images. There's also the feeling that children should not be "talked down to" but should be treated as intelligent individuals.

Children's music is roughly divided into three main categories: the home entertainment market, educational record companies, and the educational music market.

The *home entertainment* market is made up of the major companies involved in children's music for entertainment purposes though some (such as Sesame Street) cross over into the educational market to some degree. These include Disney; Henson Associates (the Muppets); Children's Educational (Sesame Street); Hanna-Barbera (Flintstones, Yogi Bear, Jetsons, Scooby Doo); Warner Bros. (Bugs Bunny, Road Runner, Porky Pig, Daffy Duck); and Parker Bros. (who also manufacture many children's games).

These companies frequently produce albums based on their characters, so if you're very familiar with them, it may be worthwhile to come up with a story/concept with music and submit it. Individual songs submitted for these characters have little chance of being used, since the companies usually have writing staffs who supply the songs for specific stories. It's best to make your presentation through an agent or attorney.

Do research by going to a local record store featuring children's records and tapes (some large toy stores will have a good selection), copy the addresses from the record sleeves, and send for information about submitting material. Your local library may also have a children's record department.

Educational record companies specialize in records that have a direct educational value for developing children's language, motor and social skills even though they're likely to have entertainment value as well. The greatest share of business in this category is done by mail order. The records are sold through ads in parent's and teacher's magazines and education conventions and are used in workshops, day care centers, parks and recreation departments, public and private schools, and preschools.

Writers such as Hap Palmer, Ella Jenkins, Pete Seeger, Tom Glazer, Shel Silverstein, Raffi, Jim Henson, and Peter Alsop have contributed much to this field, but there are many others breaking in. Children's music, though it may sound deceptively simple, is *not* easier to write than other kinds of music. It helps to have some experience and understanding of current teaching trends, child psychology, and learning processes to be an effective writer in this genre. A good sense of humor is also valuable, since, after all, nothing communicates quite as powerfully to a child (or anybody) as a good laugh.

You can research here by going to the periodicals section of the library and seeking out magazines such as *Early Years* and *Instructor* for ads of companies that supply these records. Buy a few and study them.

The *educational music market* deals primarily with printed music and includes easy choral pieces (two- or three-part) for grade school and junior high and children's musicals or vaudeville/variety shows. Packages for the latter usually come with suggestions for costumes, props, staging, and the like.

Experience in teaching music to children is very important in this category so that you understand their capabilities at various ages.

Canada has a very active and organized children's music market. Contact: The Canadian Society of Children's Authors, Illustrators and Performers, P.O. Box 280, Station L, Toronto, Ontario, Canada, M6E 422.

MUSICAL THEATER

Musical theater is a wonderful art form combining music, drama, dance, design, and who knows what else in the future?

For writers it demands great discipline, craftsmanship, and patience, since it may require constant rewrites to accommodate time, pacing, choreography, and the personalities of the characters and the actors who portray them. Even the best writers discover that scenes they'd visualized won't work quite the way they were supposed to on stage and require quick rewrites.

Though some of the most memorable recorded hits to come from musicals have been ballads, stage musicals depend much more heavily on fast pacing and choreographed up-tempo numbers to generate the visual and auditory excitement that reaches the last rows of the theater.

Launching a major musical theater production is a tremendous undertaking. You must find financial backers willing to gamble large sums of money to bankroll the production, wait endlessly for stars to be cast so the backers will feel more confident about the show's success, negotiate with a choreographer, stage and costume designers, and pray that the critics love it. Despite how intimidating that all sounds, every musical follows this scenario, though sometimes on a much more modest scale.

I've attended many "backer's auditions," presentations of a shortened version of the show for potential producers, directors, and financial backers. Here's how they work. A narrator tells the story and describes the action, while actor/singers do essential dialogue leading into the major musical numbers. Sometimes the music for those numbers is pretaped and the vocals are done live, and sometimes musicians are hired, depending on the budget. The auditions are almost always videotaped so the presentation can be shown again to anyone who couldn't attend. Audio presentations can also be made with a script, lyrics, and a tape of the songs.

TRAINING
Most writers I know who write for musical theater are those who have always loved it, and know all the musical scores. They've been "going to school" in musical theater for a long time, though they may have no formal training. It's definitely an asset to be a fan. The public library, as always, is a great place to do research. Read every libretto you can find and see every musical you can, whether it's a high school production or a major touring company.

New York is the home of musical theater, though an increasing amount of development is happening in Los Angeles as well. The late Lehman Engel founded workshops, sponsored by BMI, in both cities. ASCAP also sponsors a musical theater workshop in New York. For more information on the workshops, contact BMI and ASCAP in New York, and the Los Angeles Songwriters Showcase in Los Angeles. These workshops are good places to find out how to go about writing and marketing your ideas for stage musicals. The annual *Songwriter's Market* also publishes a list of play producers and publishers looking for original musicals.

Take part in any aspect of university, dinner theater, community theater, and summer stock musical theater productions and write for as many original projects as possible. These are great places to try out your ideas. There's no better way to learn.

THE MONEY
Those interested in writing for musical theater will be pleased to know there's a potential to make very big money. The Dramatists Guild has provided a new contract giving composers, lyricists, and librettists (who write story, book, and dialogue) a total of 6 percent split three ways. It may not sound like much, but when you consider the ticket prices charged for stage musicals and the fact that a successful show may have several road companies performing in several cities simultaneously, versions performed in countless high schools and colleges, and albums on

top of that, you're looking at something formidable. Rodgers and Hammerstein's "Oklahoma," after forty-five years, still makes several million dollars a year on college productions alone! For local, regional, and college productions, the pay is on a less grandiose scale and is usually a negotiated percentage (usually 5 to 7 percent) of box office receipts or a per-performance fee.

For up-to-date contract information, contact the Dramatists Guild, 234 W. 44 Street, New York, NY 10036, phone (212)391-3966.

Consult the Bibliography for several excellent books on the subject.

CORPORATE EVENTS

An area that gets little attention but is nonetheless an ongoing opportunity is writing theme songs and other special material for corporate events. They include: in-house corporate events, e.g., regional, national, or international meetings of, say, Toyota dealers, IBM salespeople, etc. There are also trade shows in which various manufacturers display their products for retailers. These involve every conceivable product area, including musical instruments, health food products, automobiles, baby products, hospital and health care products, furniture and appliances, building materials, electronics for entertainment and industry. The list is endless.

MAKING THE CONTACTS

These events usually take place in major hotels with convention facilities or independent convention centers. They'll either have in-house coordinators or a list of outside independent contractors who supply or arrange a variety of services including catering, comedians, dancers, singers, sound, music, staging, and decorating for these events. Call the facilities, find out who the coordinators and contracters are, and contact them. Tell them what your special skills are and, if they're receptive, send them a tape and résumé.

If they need original material, it will usually be for a company that wants a theme written around a slogan for a new product, not unlike a commercial jingle. In fact, I know writers who have done that so successfully that the corporation actually asked them to create the jingle for broadcast. You'll be required to write, arrange, produce, and record the piece, or to write, arrange, and deliver sheet music for a band or small orchestra to play. These are first-class productions and require a high degree of professionalism.

Coordinating these events is a major international business with its own trade organizations and magazines. If you want to pursue this area further, you should subscribe to one of these to get a better picture of the opportunities:

Meeting Manager
c/o Meeting Planners International
1950 Stemmons Freeway
Dallas, TX 75207-3109

Special Events Magazine
2048 Cotner Ave.
Los Angeles, CA 90025
(213) 477-1033

COMPENSATION

You can't really look at this as a big money-maker unless you're in a major convention city, have good writing and arranging skills, feel comfortable dealing with corporate types, and plan to pursue it nearly full-time. Otherwise, it's two or three hundred dollars here and there, or more if you're playing in the band or singing too. The more skills you have, the more valuable you become, since the planners usually would rather only have to hire one person, not several, to get the job done. So, though you won't get rich on it, it's one of those areas in which it can't hurt to make the contacts. Get your résumé and tape out to those services and give them a follow-up call every couple of months so they remember you. It's one of those "You never know where it'll come from" situations where networking can pay off when you least expect it.

AUDIOVISUALS

The area of audiovisuals is very broad. It involves writing songs and composing themes and scores for film and video productions and slide presentations. It represents a valuable "almost entry level" way to get experience in the film scoring field. I say "almost" because you do have to have some basic arranging skills and an understanding of the technical aspects of film scoring, which isn't that hard to get.

In my case, I met Bernard Selling, who wrote and produced educational films as *his* entry level preparation to get into feature films. Selling heard my songs and asked if I could score a short film for the tourism department of the state of Maine. I said I could, then started reading everything I could find about the subject and picked the brains of every friend I knew who had ever had anything to do with film scoring. Fear is a great motivator! Luckily, I had the luxury of time and knew if I got stuck or had a question I could get help. I went on to score two other films with Selling, both film adaptations of short stories for the educational market—Stephen Crane's "Three Miraculous Soldiers" and Ray Bradbury's "The Flying Machine." These films were used as teaching aids in English classes but were also suitable for cable or PBS (public broadcasting).

Video is very strong in this area though most are shot on film and transferred to videocassettes. The enormous increase in sales of videocassette recorders and the ability of videocassettes to be shown in slow motion and freeze-frame has been a boon to "how-to" films. Music, as always, is used in these films.

The audiovisual field covers several categories:

Industrial. Instructions for salespeople; management techniques; "informercials" (extended commercials showing you how to use a product);

state and city government films that "sell" the state or city to tourists or to attract industry; films that introduce a company's new product line at conventions; company propaganda including profiles of executives, company history, and community service; travelogue for the tourist industry, airlines, railroads, passenger ships.

Educational. This crosses over into the industrial category but also includes: "how-to" films for mechanics; new medical techniques; teaching methods; government and military training films; educational aids in all elementary school, high school, and college subjects. In addition, video producers are turning out special programs for home videocassette sales on everything from "How to Make Great Omelets" to "Fix Your Car," "Learn to Play Guitar," and "Defend Yourself." Magazines and catalogues for the home video market list hundreds, and soon thousands, of these special tapes.

Entertainment. One of the heaviest expenses of major theater films is promoting them to the general public. The radio, TV, and print ads represent a high percentage of the overall cost. When a film is made specifically for cable and only needs to be advertised in the cable magazines that go directly to their potential market, much of that cost is eliminated. In addition, many films made for TV and cable enjoy an additional life in home video sales and rentals. This all adds up to increasing production of shows made for cable.

With the increased growth of cable programming and the erratic cable schedules (they run lots of films that don't end exactly on the hour or half hour) there are usually odd bits of time to fill. They'll need a one-, five- or ten-minute film here and there to keep people's attention until the next feature comes on.

I've seen several interesting shorts put together behind story songs. The visuals may portray the story with live action footage, animation, or "dynamic stills" (still photos and slides faded in and out, superimposed, or rapidly flashed). Since these shorts don't involve anywhere near the cost of the feature films to produce, more small production companies can afford to create them. During the World Series I saw/heard a song portraying a short history of baseball. The song was naming the great games and heroes as the visuals ran the original films—a nifty little piece of filler. If you have a knack for writing good story songs, it's something to look into.

Collaboration with video artists. In the future, many of the short-form video productions mentioned above will be equal collaborations between songwriters and composers and video artists. Audio technology has spawned a whole new genre of musical instruments, the synthesizers, capable of creating new sounds that, in many areas, surpass the limitations of conventional instruments. Much the same kind of phenomenon is happening with video technology. The creation of computer graphics programs and innovative real-time manual video controls for manipulating images have turned the TV screen into an amazingly versatile palette for a new breed of artists. Computer technology has made it possible for video artists to control color, texture, movement, form, and spatial perception in a seemingly endless variety of ways. It's allowed them to create an exciting new moving art form that is enhanced greatly by music. Computer graphics are becoming very common in commercials and in science fiction film sequences. Its potential is limited only by the imagination and the tremendous cost of production.

And the two new art forms have been very compatible together. Electronic music in particular doesn't usually fare well in live performance. It's not very exciting to watch someone turning dials. On the other hand, though video art is visually exciting, music always gives it a satisfying sense of form, direction, and predictability. In most video/music collaborations, music is used by the video artist as a starting point and is chosen for its mood, rhythm, and other properties.

An organization in Los Angeles, the Visual Music Alliance, was formed to facilitate the kind of interaction and innovation necessary to expand this new art form. It's for professionals working in music, film, video, photography, and analog and computer graphics. It's a great place for writers to hook up with people initiating video projects. Their address is VMA, 8435 Geyser Ave., Northridge, CA 91324. Phone (818)885-7316.

MAKING CONTACT
The key to connecting with this market is the audiovisual production companies. These are the people who companies pay to deliver a finished product. At times they also originate productions on their own. Start in your own backyard by looking through the Yellow Pages for "Audiovisual Production Services," "Television Program Producers," "Motion Picture Producers," and "Video Production Services." If the types of projects they produce are not made obvious in their listing, call and ask if they use original music in their productions. If they do, ask when you can get an appointment to meet them and play them a tape of your music. They're looking for pros, so the more professionally you present yourself and your material, the better chance you have, even if you don't have a knockout résumé.

Elsewhere, you can find an international list of audiovisual producers in the annual *Songwriter's Market* or in *Audiovisual Marketplace*.

Be prepared to give or send these people a résumé of past writing credits and a cassette, 7½ or 15 i.p.s. reel-to-reel, or a videotape of your best work in a variety of styles if possible. Most will want to keep your tape on file so they can review it when a project comes up. It's to your benefit if you let them do it.

Many productions (commercial jingles, too) make use of "production music" libraries who will license the producer to use a piece of music the producer chooses. The libraries usually have a broad range of music from which to choose, from classical, public domain pieces to contemporary styles. It's also worthwhile to contact these libraries about their using your music. They're also listed in the Yellow Pages. You'll most likely be paid on a one-time buyout basis, but it's also possible to receive royalties for each use, credit for the use, and if the user files a cue sheet with your performing rights organization, performance royalties if it's broadcast. If your music is produced non-union (and most of it is) the library won't be able to license it to companies that are union signatories who are not allowed to use non-union music.

COMPENSATION

For home video you can receive a flat fee per unit sold, a percentage of the wholesale or retail selling price, or a combination of both. In addition, you can also charge an up-front, one-time, unrecoupable flat fee or an advance that's recoupable from future royalties. There is currently no royalty provision for home video rental.

For feature films, industrial and educational films the producer will most likely want a "buyout," a one-time payment that will save them the time and paperwork of accounting to you, and allow them to use it forever in any way they wish. For most audiovisual projects the producer will want to buy all rights or rights for a one-time use. Some will pay royalties.

SPECIAL MATERIAL

When you see the stars of TV specials performing songs that are clearly built around skits, unknown songs designed to open or close the shows, or songs used as transitions between segments of the show, those pieces are called "special material." In their live appearances, major artists frequently use material that hasn't appeared on any of their records. Often it's comedy material that wouldn't necessarily fit their recording concepts but is necessary to spice up their stage act and save them from the potential stagnation of being a "jukebox," playing their hits one after another. The special material helps to establish them as well-rounded personalities and aids the pacing of their shows.

To write this material you need to be good at assignment writing. You need to be able to have someone give you a subject or a personality sketch and craft a song for the situation. You need to be flexible, rewrite quickly, be familiar with many musical styles (as a composer), and be a good collaborator. The situation may call for you to write a lyric to an existing melody or work with a rehearsal pianist or a composer already connected with the show. In many ways, it's a lot like musical theater writing, because you're often tailoring the song for a specific character or dramatic situation.

Given that you have the talents described, the contacts to make are with the music coordinators or supervisors at the TV networks, the major booking agencies that represent the stars you want to write for, or the managers of those stars.

On a local level you can get started by contacting your local television station about writing songs relating to current news stories. There's often a spot for music behind the "crawl" credits at the end of both network and local live news and special event shows. It's also a good idea to develop your talent (and material for a demo tape of your work) by writing special material for local singers, high school and college talent reviews, and community theater productions.

Getting a Record Deal

For the performer or songwriter/performer, obtaining a recording contract is a major step toward mass public exposure. Remember, however, that the real goal is not the record deal. It's only the *means* of manufacturing and marketing your artistry. The recording contract is, at the least, just a piece of paper. It is far from a guarantee of fame and fortune. At its best, it represents the legal basis for a cooperative marketing effort in which a team of experts exposes a product (you) to an audience who will translate their appreciation of your music into purchase of your records and tapes. The record deal is only part of a larger effort by your own personal team to promote your career in as many ways as they can and to earn you (and them) as much income as possible.

When approaching this or any other career decision, it's important to get as much information as possible about the circumstances, needs, and responsibilities of the other parties involved. In this chapter I'll explore the information you need from the point of view of the record company. You'll learn how a record company looks at you as an artist, at your songs, and at your professional team. And since a deal with an established record company is not something every artist can count on (there was a time when even the Beatles couldn't get a deal), we'll look at the very viable, and sometimes preferable "do it yourself" option.

THE ARTIST VS. THE WRITER/ARTIST

Exceptional writer/artists have always been around. Until the '50s and '60s, however, with the increasing exposure of country music, black music, and the birth of rock and roll, most popular songs on the radio were not performed by their writers. With the phenomenal success of the Beatles, record companies began to discover that they could get publishing rights to the songs the artists were writing and thus be able to keep the potentially enormous publishing income along with the recording profits. The self-contained act was an attractive package, because though they would (in most cases) pay writers one of the two cents (the old rate) per side per unit sold, by also owning the publishing rights, they could keep that other penny "in house." They could also participate in the performance royalties collected from BMI and ASCAP.

Today, virtually every record company has a publishing affiliate. But though the business affairs departments of the major record companies and their publishing companies are interested in acquiring the publishing rights of new artists signed by the company, refusal is rarely a deal-breaker. It's so hard to find a great act that has all the qualities a record company looks for, that the publishing rights are less important by comparison. Also, the publishing affiliates operate on their own and have lots of income from other projects, so they don't depend on deals their affiliated labels give them.

Small, independent record companies, however, don't sell as many records. The royalties they receive from the ownership of the publishing rights, along with record sales, can help to offset their overhead, making the publishing a very important consideration in the deal. In that situation, being a self-contained act with publishing rights to offer is an asset.

For both the major labels and independents, an even bigger advantage of the self-contained artist or group is that it eliminates the need to come up with outside material. That's because, even though the record company A&R staff is constantly on the lookout for songs for their artists who are not self-contained, they don't always have enough time to screen songs as well as to deal with the responsibilities to the many other acts on their rosters. So the trend has been to give that responsibility to the producers or writer/producers (sometimes several for the same album) to write (or find) and produce songs for the project. Though that's generally a better gamble, I know of projects that have been doomed by writer/producers who have insisted on writing all the material themselves and ended up with no hits.

As you see, it's a bonus if the artists can also produce themselves, eliminating the need for the record company to look for a producer. Among those who do it successfully are Prince, Kool & the Gang, Huey Lewis & the News, Journey, Talking Heads, Toto, John Parr, Boston, Paul Simon, and Stevie Wonder.

One of the most exciting attributes of the self-contained artist is the potential to create a consistent fusion of style and material that is quite unique and that offers fans the opportunity to get to know the writer/artist in a personal way. With a nonwriting artist, though he or she may have a consistent vocal identity and style, it's much more difficult to achieve a consistency with the material. The most common way has been in the long-term relationships between writer/producers and artists. The collaborations of Burt Bacharach/Hal David with Dionne Warwick, John Farrar with Olivia Newton-John, Jimmy Jam/Terry Lewis with Janet Jackson, and David Foster with Chicago are good examples.

One drawback nonwriting artists face is the never-ending search for hit material that they and their record companies can agree on. The flip side of that problem is that those artists have access to the best writers in the world. Certain companies such as Clive Davis's Arista Records have made a specialty of signing nonwriting artists. His roster includes Whitney Houston, Aretha Franklin, and Dionne Warwick. Davis has always subscribed to "the song comes first" philosophy and has delayed many recording projects until he had what he felt were the right songs for the artist.

So though the self-contained artist will most likely be the first choice of a record company, each situation is unique, and many different factors will be weighed in the decision to sign an act. The following sections will delineate those factors. Remember, while you read them, that these are all presented as ideal situations and the likelihood of a record company finding an act that "has it all" is almost nonexistent. The reality is that they take the best combination of ingredients they can find, try to compensate somehow for what's missing, and roll the dice.

THE PERFORMANCE DEMO

One of the most important elements in a successful campaign for a recording contract is your demo tape. By way of explaining how the demo tape and the act are judged, I'm going to play the part of a record company, with a few asides thrown in to explain what's happening or why.

I'm assuming that you're looking for your first record deal, so I'll ask about things I need to know to make a decision about signing you to my label. I know I'll need to spend anywhere from $100,000 to over $200,000 on the recording alone. Then, maybe another $50,000+ on a video to make enough people aware of you and buy your record. If they don't, I'll have to eat that expense. It might take that much on a follow-up album again next year, but I'll spend it if I'm still as excited about the music as I was when I signed you.

Also, I want to see that you're not sitting around waiting for me to make you a star. I want to know that you're writing and I want to hear new songs on a regular basis.

Are you working on your act? The visuals? Arrangements? Concepts? I want to know that you're working to improve your vocal and instrumental chops. I want to know that if I do invest in you, both you and your manager know what to do to make the most of my investment and that you'll be ready to get out on the road and get those people excited enough to buy that record. We'll get reviewers out to see you and my ulcer dictates that I be confident that you have your trip together.

Let's say, typically, that I received your tape through your attorney, manager, someone in my company, your producer, your publisher, or someone else whose taste I respect. Before I listen to that tape I know what I want to hear:

Songs that I think are hits or that will appeal to a large number of people because of your point-of-view, style, etc. (Randy Newman, Tom Waits, and Joni Mitchell, along with most major heavy metal artists, are good examples of writer/artists who seldom write hit singles but have large followings. They're known as album artists, and it takes more time and money to market them successfully because hit singles and videos are proven to be the fastest and most cost-effective way to promote an artist.)

I'm looking for craftsmanship that tells me that those songs I liked were not just an accident, and that you know exactly what you're doing and can do it again. Otherwise, I risk spending my money on a "one-hit wonder" with little chance of recouping my investment.

I'm looking for identity. I want that audience to be able to recognize you after hearing your record once or twice. As I suggested earlier, listen to "We are the World" for a great example of vocal identity. No one on that record sounds like anyone else. If your voice doesn't have a distinctive character, what you do with it stylistically should be unique. If that isn't happening, I should be hearing an instrumental sound and production concept that are unique. I should know that you and/or your producer can continue to re-create that sound once the public has grown to love it.

I want to hear something that has an emotional impact. I want to be moved by the way you sing your song. I want to know that you are totally involved with what you're saying in your song. If *you* don't believe it, why should I? If it's not the kind of music that's lyrically oriented, I want it to move my body. If you've been playing your songs at your lounge gig every night for the last three years, there's a danger that they'll sound tired and unenthusiastic. I want to know that you can get into those songs every time you perform them.

I will assume that what I'm about to hear on this tape is the very best that you can do. I have no evidence to believe you'll ever perform it any better than on the tape, so don't tell me "That was a bad day for me" or "It's just a demo. I'll do it better on the master."

When I'm spending this company's money, I'm not taking your word for it; I need to know. I'll have control over the technical quality of the final record, so if it's a convincing *performance,* it won't bother me that the technical quality of your demo isn't up to par unless you're also trying to convince me that you're a producer. (See "Who Gets What and How Elaborate Does It Need to Be?," page 199.)

If you show me a record you produced and distributed yourself and can show you've developed a marketing strategy for it as well, it tells me you're very serious about your career, you have a realistic view of the process, and you're proceeding with your career whether I sign you or not, so I'd better pay attention. Obviously I'll be more impressed if you've sold a few thousand records.

THE LIVE PERFORMANCE

As a record company executive, my bottom-line question has to be, "Can my company make money on this act?" Other related questions are, "Will this act enhance the prestige and contribute to the image of the company?" and "Will I be a hero or lose my gig on the success or failure of this act?" For those reasons, I need to hear the right sounds, ask the right questions, and get the right answers. Let's assume that I liked what I heard on the tape. I thought the songs had commercial potential and the performance was excellent. Those are really the basics. Now I also have to ask another series of questions, not necessarily in order of importance, but all, nonetheless, very significant:

How is your live performance? It would impress me to know that you had spent a few years as a live performer. I'd like to see some great reviews of your performances, preferably by recognized critics (your high school or college newspaper won't quite do). But most of all, I want you to excite a tough audience—not one where all your friends are stacking the house. So I'd prefer to see you perform in a club or in concert rather than in a special showcase just for me.

Are you visually interesting? If you're good looking, it helps, but it isn't necessary. There have been many artists whose talent transcended their looks.

Do you move and speak confidently? Remember that we retain more information with our eyes than our ears, which is one reason we can sell a lot of records to people who attend your concerts and see your videos. Do you have a good sense of your personal identity? I want the audience to go away from your performance with a feeling that they know who you are and like you, or that you've given them enough pieces of yourself in your musical visual presentation to create an intriguing mystery that makes them *want* to know who you are.

If you're a group act, I want to see you all involved and interacting with each other, not standing there like robots, each in your own little world. That doesn't mean you have to do the splits, moonwalk, and choreograph dance steps if that's not your style. But I do want to sense that there's a real, honest chemistry between the group members that inspires your music. I want to know you're giving me something and enjoying it. I'll also be looking at your stage movement, your choice of songs and their placement in the set, your arrangements, and the way you dress.

Can you reproduce your tape sound in person? I'll want to know that the things I liked on tape can be reproduced live. I don't expect to see an orchestra, but the basics have to be there. For example, if a significant degree of your appeal to me is based on your group vocal sound, I'd better hear it in your live performance.

Do you love to perform? I want to know that, ideally, I'll be working with an experienced professional who knows and understands (and accepts) the hardships of the road and loves to perform. I know that in spite of TV exposure and hit records, there's no substitute, in the eyes of fans (and potential fans), for the magic of a great live performance.

Live performance sells a lot of records and is a great marketing tool for us. It gives us reviews in the press, it helps us to keep your name in front of the public, and gives local DJs and fans something to talk about. It gives you contact with your audience so you'll know what they like about you. It gives you a kind of high that can't be duplicated.

Are you willing to sacrifice? Though it may take a couple of years of money-losing opening-act status, touring can eventually provide a major source of income (as can concert merchandising of T-shirts and other items), particularly for group members who don't receive songwriter's royalties.

THE ACT'S MARKETABILITY

Now I have to assess how, if I sign you, I'm going to make people aware of you. It's easier for me if you're the brother or sister, son or daughter of somebody famous, though after the curiosity of the first album wears off, you'd better be able to deliver something substantial and very much your own. It also helps if you have famous friends who would like to sing or play on your record. That in itself doesn't get you signed, but it does give me something of an incentive.

That's what I need: PR (public relations/publicity) potential! "He/she has been in the background as a musician, a backup singer, or a writer and is now coming up front to make his/her own music." That's a good hook for us because there may be quite a few people out there who remember you when you were doing whatever you were doing in the background. If not, then maybe we can arouse their curiosity by association. "Oh, yeah, if he played with that artist, who I really like, he must be something like him. I'd probably love his stuff."

Beyond all those old familiar PR approaches, I want to look for things about you personally that enhance the mystique; that reveal you as a human being of substance, strangeness, virtue, or character, or ideally, all of the above. Eddie Money was a policeman. You have to say, "Hey what kind of great rock and roll singer was a cop?" or vice versa. It's a great interview opener. A "one hook" publicity campaign can wear thin fast, but it's a good start.

Can you speak well and confidently and do you have something interesting or funny to say? If not, I'll make sure David Letterman doesn't invite you to talk to him after you sing and that you don't do interviews. If you have strong and well-articulated opinions, on the other hand, I might want you to be. Are you willing to do radio and TV interviews and in-store appearances?

Do you have an unusual or interesting background that will intrigue people? Some artists like to tell stories about growing up in poverty. Did you get your start driving a cab/collecting trash/waiting tables/writing songs in jail?

Have you had some kind of previous success that we could use for PR? Were you part of a successful group? The writer of a well-known hit? Do you now or have you ever had a successful TV show? Do you have an interesting and flamboyant personality or hang out in social circles that automatically attract attention from the press?

Those things are important in that they give us "hooks" that we can use to let people know about you, and the press needs that kind of stuff to work with. More important, though, is the marketability of your music itself. It's important that the music has a unity of style so that, when we do find the audience, you're the same artist from album to album, and still show artistic growth and change within your general style.

Writer/artists frequently ask if record companies like to hear stylistic variety. "I can write country, R&B, pop, anything! Why don't I give them a little of each and see what they pick up on?" That's commendable if you want to be a staff songwriter, but a record company will no doubt say, "But really now, who are you?" If country music is what you write and perform best and enjoy most, what's the point in their trying to market you as an R&B artist and release an R&B single on you? If it takes off, are we going to be trying to sell half an album of country tunes to a rock or R&B audience, or vice versa? So it's a marketing problem. Of course, we don't want all your music to sound the same and we do want you to grow, we just need for you to have developed your style to the point where you're the same, identifiable artist from one album to the next. Ideally, you know who you are and how you want to be presented to the public.

PERSONAL FACTORS
Considering the tremendous investment the company will make in your career, it's important for us to know that we're not going to be flushing it down the drain due to your lack of commitment or other personal factors beyond our control. These are important questions that I have to weigh.

I don't want to worry that you're a heavy drug user and that you'll die of an overdose or you'll spend all your advance on drugs or that the drugs will ruin your health or your relationships with your group. I'd like to know you're responsible enough to show up for gigs and interviews.

I'd be glad to know that you have a reasonably stable domestic situation, that your wife/husband/live-in can deal with your being on the road or that family problems won't interfere in any other way with your career.

Ideally, I want to like you since we'll probably be spending a lot of time together. I like to enjoy my work and don't look forward to putting my neck on the line for someone I don't like and respect.

If you're a group, I want to see that you've established a strong bond between band members and that each knows and accepts his function within the group. I expect that there may be strong egos involved but I also know that if they're out of hand, they can ruin the band. Money changes everything and if you're successful and doing heavy touring, the pressures of both can do more to break up the group (and lose our investment) than anything else. So, I need to get a sense of who you are as individuals and how you interact with each other.

THE PROFESSIONAL TEAM
Now we get to a subject which, in my assumed role as a record company executive, is very important for me to consider, the people on *your team.*

I'm likely to be impressed if you have a team of professional people who believe in you, particularly if they are people whose work I respect. If you come to my attention through the efforts of your manager, producer, and attorney, who have been generating energy and momentum on your behalf, it will tell me important things: 1) that if I sign you, my company will have lots of competent aid from your team, to insure your success and 2) that if I don't sign you, someone else probably will. First of all, let's assume that all my questions until now have been answered to my satisfaction and I'm very excited about you as a writer and an artist. Another thing that will impress me and tip the scales in your favor is knowing that you have a competent manager and producer. Let's talk about the best situation for me as the record company and, consequently, what's best for you.

YOUR MANAGER

A manager, among other things, should be able to initiate publishing, record company, and production deals, know what clubs or concerts you should play and what radio and TV shows you should do and when. She should oversee or coordinate the activities of your booking agent, road manager, publicist, accountant, attorney, business manager, publisher, and producer and be your official contact with the record company. She is the buffer between you and the business, your advisor and alter ego and the captain of your team. Ideally, your manager is also excited about you and your talent and is dedicated to helping you become a successful artist. I'd be more impressed if she is a manager with a record of successes, one who has managed other successful acts, one who knows the record business and understands the functions of all the component parts of the talent machine and the need for coordination and teamwork. I'll want to know that your manager knows you, your strengths and limitations, and has a plan for the development of your career.

What if your manager does not have a heavy track record and is not knowledgeable about the record business? Unless she is willing to learn and take direction, I know I'm going to have lots of problems. Enough arguments erupt between record companies and managers who *do* know the business. It's particularly crazy to try to deal with someone who has no way of knowing when I'm making important concessions to her or suggesting a course of action that from our experience is advisable, but one that the manager does not understand.

Inexperienced managers may also assume adversary roles to cover their ignorance, rather than finding ways to work with the company. I would rather you had a manager with whom I already have a good working relationship because our problems may have already been worked out, or at least we've learned how to argue with each other. I might even sign an act that I'm not *totally* sold on if I believe in the abilities of the manager.

So, if you have an inexperienced manager, I'd try to hook her up in a comanagement situation with a successful manager so that she could learn and you wouldn't have to suffer from her inexperience. Otherwise, I'd rather you didn't have one, so I could help you find a good one.

General information. Managers get paid between 10 and 25 percent of your gross income, though some are paid on the net. It's difficult, but not impossible, to get a good, experienced manager unless you already have a record deal. The best managers don't have to take on the burden of building a career totally from scratch, since they can afford to be choosy. But it's not an impossible situation. There's no accounting for human chemistry and a manager's basic gambler's instinct. If she thinks you've got star quality, she just knows she can get you a deal!

Some artists need a manager they can relate to on a very personal basis. Others just need a manager to take care of their business and stay out of their personal life. You should know which one you need before you start looking and let him or her know what you're looking for right away.

You find an established manager by looking at the credits on records and tapes of artists who do, very generally, your style of music (though some managers like to diversify). You ask other artists. *Billboard* annually publishes a list of artists, their managers, and booking agents. Your local songwriters organization or music association may also have a list.

YOUR PRODUCER

If the tape I first listened to was a finished master recording, ready for the radio, and produced by someone with a successful track record, it gives me another way to hype you to radio and the press, as well as ensures that the rest of the product will be competently produced. With a successful producer as part of the package, it isn't even necessary to bring me finished masters, just demos of exceptional songs and performances.

If you bring demos produced by yourself or an unproven producer, even if like them I have no way of knowing that I'll get a well-produced finished product. It's a judgment call that depends on the strength of the various ingredients in that particular situation. It's possible that I'll want to hear a finished master before I decide or I'll want us both to find you a producer who I *know* can deliver a great record.

If you've produced masters I love, I'm happy because I truly have a self-contained package and don't have to worry about your having problems with your producer (though the potential for you to be less objective in your choice of material will make me keep a close eye on it).

If you're already signed to producer "A," who I believe to be incompetent or inappropriate, then I know I'll either have to buy out your contract with that producer, convince him to allow another producer ("B") to work on the project through "A" 's company, or not sign you at all.

Your producer should know your strengths and weaknesses and have a plan for how he will produce you to make you as commercially viable as possible.

General information. Producers have a dual responsibility, to deliver the record company a record it can sell and get the best performance from the artist or group. Part of this includes choosing the best components needed for that particular project which may mean: songs, studio(s), musicians, arranger, engineers and recording equipment. The producer bears the responsibility for both the technical and artistic quality of the record.

The worst way to find a producer is to send your tapes randomly to producers whose work you don't know. The best way is to buy records of artists in your general style of music and listen to the sound of the record. If you like it, try to find out what other records that producer has worked on and listen to them. Often the production company's address is listed on the record. If not, call the record company A&R or artist relations department and ask for it. Also, *Billboard* lists the producers of hit records on its charts in all styles of music. If you read it on a regular basis you'll get to know who's producing your favorite records. Some producers have their own characteristic style no matter who they produce and if you need a stylistic direction look for one whose style feels right for you. Others work to enhance the unique qualities of the artist or group, and a producer with that philosophy may suit you better. So beyond the question of liking their work is the question of compatibility.

Producers come from a variety of backgrounds. Some are recording engineers who went to "producer school" by engineering hundreds or thousands of sessions in which they've observed and participated in the workstyles of many different producers. If you're a writer/artist/arranger with a unique sound based on your arrangement ideas, your vision may be enhanced more by an engineer/producer than by an arranger/producer.

Studio musicians and arrangers go to that same producer school and benefit from the same exposure but from the other side of the glass. They'll excel in creating the musical dynamics and hooks that may have already helped launch some hits. If you're a singer or singer/songwriter who needs the most assistance in creating an instrumental sound, check out the musician/arranger/producer. Many of them are also writers who like to cowrite with the artist. This could also be advantageous if you need material and like to collaborate. That producer may also be attracted by the additional royalties he'd receive for his writing contributions.

Regardless of his background, a producer needs to be able to choose the best songs for a project whether choosing from among your own or finding appropriate songs from other writers. Some are better than others at this, and if finding or writing strong commercial songs is a problem area for you, it'll be necessary to have an expert working with you. As you can see, an assessment of your own strengths and weaknesses is essential to be able to find a producer who can make up for your weaknesses and enhance your strengths.

As an artist without a record deal, your chances of getting a major, established producer to work with you are slim. They usually have projects booked far into the future. Though you shouldn't abandon that approach, you should also check the charts for new producers who have recently had their first hit(s). It's more likely that they're not booked so far ahead and may be looking for their next project.

Producers get paid a royalty as percentage "points" based on record sales, a flat fee per song or, most commonly, a combination of the two.

ATTORNEYS

As a record company executive, I will frequently be approached by attorneys with product. This is happening more and more frequently. Since attorneys are negotiating many contracts with record companies, they have made good contacts at the labels and find themselves in a position to know if and when a company is looking for a certain type of act. Since they have an inside track, it's easier for them to "shop the product" than, for instance, an out-of-town manager or a new one who doesn't know his way around yet. From the record company point-of-view I want to deal with an entertainment attorney and, in particular, a record business attorney. When he comes to me or my company attorney to negotiate a deal, he must speak the language and have up-to-date knowledge of current record industry practices. If not, we will end up engaged in needless hours of fruitless negotiations and we'll end up having to educate your attorney (at your expense).

For instance, you're presented with a production or record contract and you call your uncle, whose specialty is suing auto manufacturers. He *should* refer you to an entertainment specialist, but suppose business is slow this month, he knows there are lots of bucks in the music business, he has visions of his nephew being a big rock star, he thinks it would be great to get involved in a more glamorous business, and figures, "What the hell, how hard could it be to negotiate a record contract?" He gets the contract and the first thing he objects to is the fact that this big record company wants all recording costs recouped off the top from your royalties. He thinks it's terrible (not knowing that it's a firmly established practice in the industry) and decides he should try to negotiate that point, thereby exposing his ignorance. The record company attorneys will either not want to negotiate with him at all or eat him alive for breakfast.

Needless to say, none of this helps you at all. Entertainment law is very complex, and just knowing law academically is not enough to make one a good attorney in that field. Personal experience, good contacts (politics), and a knowledge of current industry practices as well as a knowledge of the policies and contracts of specific record companies are equally important. As a record company, I want to deal with an attorney whose philosophy is that the best deal is one that comes closest to being fair for both parties. Obviously, I'll negotiate for my own advantage but if that means it's unfair to you, I know I'm going to have problems with you later and you won't be happy with the deal. So, as you can see, it's very important to choose this team member well.

General information. In relationships with attorneys, fees are always a major concern. Attorneys in this field are expensive, and fees range from $50 (not many) to $250.00+ per hour. They'll log all the time spent on your behalf on the telephone, in meetings with you, with the record company or whatever, and bill you for that time. Some attorneys, in lieu of an hourly rate, will offer to shop your tapes and negotiate your deal for 5-10 percent of your income from that contract for the life of the deal. Some may also want to include other types of income in the deal including touring and merchandising and, in a sense, operate as if it were a management commission. On the surface, this may seem like a good deal, particularly if you're broke, but you should consider that maybe in a couple of months you'll become disenchanted with your relationship and want to get another attorney. You'll then be paying two attorneys, and that original 10 percent is part of your income that you might find a better use for.

An attorney working on a percentage may also be tempted to "front load" a deal. Here's a simplified scenario for the sake of illustration: In negotiations, the attorney has an opportunity to obtain maybe a $200,000 advance from the record company for you, the artist, by trading it off for a 10 percent artist royalty instead of 12 percent. Let's say that for 12 percent there would only have been a $150,000 advance. If the attorney is getting 10 percent of that advance (because he gets 10 percent of all your income from the deal he negotiated for you), he may have a quick fantasy about $5,000 with wings on it, flying out of his pocket if he gets you the higher royalty and lower advance. If he decides to act on that fantasy, he can go back to you and say "Great news! I got you a $200,000 advance" and never tell you about the extra 2 percent artist royalty he gave up for it, which down the road could mean a·substantial amount of money. If he were ethical, he'd give you the pros and cons and let you make that decision. The bottom line is that if he helps you earn more money, he'll earn more money, too.

Attorneys will sometimes work on "spec" or "deferment," which means that they'll keep track of their time spent on your project but defer payment until they've made a deal for you and then collect their accumulated fees from the front money. They're most likely to do this if a producer or record company has shown enough interest in you to present you with a contract, or if they have good ears and feel you've got a favorable shot at a deal. It is a risk for them though, because they could conceivably spend a lot of time, the deal wouldn't happen, and they'd risk not getting paid.

Here are some additional tips on dealing with attorneys:

1. Never sign a contract without some legal advice. I'm sure you've heard this before, but I'm still appalled by the number of unfortunate situations I come across in which people who knew better ignored the advice. They say something like, "The people were so nice ... ," "They said they would ..." but, unfortunately, what they said they would do wasn't written into their contract and consequently, they don't have to do what they merely said.

2. If you or your manager are discussing your deal with a company, take notes on the verbal points they're offering you. Relay this information to your attorney so he can incorporate it into the contract in case the company selectively forgets. Most companies already have their own contracts that they've worked out over the years from their own legal battles, and those of associates, reflecting industry practices as well as innovating their own terms. A good reason for hiring an experienced music industry attorney is that he's had to negotiate with a great variety of companies and is familiar with the negotiating practices and contract terms of most of them. If your attorney has already negotiated deals with a particular company, that experience could save a lot of the attorney's time and your money.

3. Don't ask the company with whom you're negotiating to recommend an attorney. Never go to an attorney for advice who also represents those who are offering you a contract. To avoid conflict of interest, your attorney should have no connection with your manager, producer, record company or anyone else with whom you are doing business. An ethical attorney will always let you know that, but ask anyway.

4. Always ask an attorney what his/her fees are and try to get some

sort of estimate of how much the service you need could cost. It will sometimes be hard to tell you exactly, but you should at least have a ballpark figure. That way you can determine whether it's out of your league. It could cost $2,000 to $10,000 to negotiate a recording contract.

5. Your conversation and business with your attorney is confidential unless you consent to "leak" information as a business tactic (such as the amount of money another company is offering you).

6. If you "discharge" your attorney and decide to get a new one, the new attorney has the right, with your authorization, to copy your files from the previous attorney. They're your files.

7. Communicate in writing whenever you can. It documents and dates your requests and comments and avoids communication breakdown due to self-serving lapses of memory and human error.

8. Keep a photocopy of all correspondence with anyone you do business with, including a copy of every contract presented to and signed by you *before* you return it. You do this because it is possible to add a clause to a contract *after* you sign it and you'd otherwise not be able to prove that you didn't consent to the added clause.

9. Ask an attorney what he's done lately. If you're looking for an attorney to represent you in negotiating a record deal, you'll want to find one who has had *recent* experience in negotiating that kind of contract and uses up-to-date contracts.

10. Shop for an attorney with expertise in the area in which you need help. There are many specialists among entertainment attorneys. You may want different attorneys to negotiate management, publishing, production, film music, or recording contracts. Ask them what they specialize in.

BOOKING AGENTS

Back to my role as a record company exec. Even though it's essentially your manager's job to find the right booking agency for you, I may be able to help, since here at the record company we have ongoing relationships with many of them. Sometimes they help me "discover" new acts. I'll get tapes of hot new acts from them because they're constantly being approached by artists and bands looking for work. They may also be booking acts in parts of the country that I don't have much regular access to for scouting talent. If you already have a good agency and you're working regularly, it's a plus for me because you may already have a strong following of potential record buyers.

If you're an artist who loves to perform, the booking agent is an important part of the team. The decisions you make with her about where and when you play could be very important to the success of an album. In the coordination of album releases and touring schedules, timing is critical. **General information.** Booking agents (also referred to as talent managers, as opposed to personal managers) are those who secure work, negotiate contracts, and collect your money for live performance gigs, film work, and so on. Though major agencies like William Morris, ICM (International Creative Management), ABC (Associated Booking Corp.), CAA (Creative Artists Agency), and APA (Artists Performing Agency) occasionally work with unknown artists without record deals, it's rare. If you're a new act, you're better off finding a small or medium-sized agency that deals with unsigned or newly signed acts because they regularly deal with clubs and concert venues (clubs, concert halls) that feature talent at your level of development. Those agencies may be difficult to find unless you're primarily a cover band who can earn some money. "Showcase" clubs for acts with original material seldom produce profits for the act.

Booking agents, with a career development plan in mind, can do a lot to advance your career. Major agents can assist by bringing you to the attention of record companies who they deal with on behalf of other major clients. Their approach is to tell the label that if the group gets a record deal, their company is committed to represent the act.

It's also to the advantage of smaller agencies that you get a record deal even with a small independent label, because they can then charge more for your appearances. However, acts who are on the road constantly and making $5,000 or $6,000 or more a week may find that their agents balk at the time off the act may need to produce an album. For every week you don't work, your agent doesn't make (at 10 percent) $500 or $600 or more. Those agents truly concerned with your growth will not obstruct your career. In the long run, the additional fees the agent will be able to charge once you have a record out will more than make up the temporary loss.

One of the best ways to locate a reputable agent is through your local AF of M (American Federation of Musicians), AFTRA (American Federation of Television and Radio Artists) or AGVA (American Guild of Variety Artists), who keep an up-to-date list of those agents who they've licensed and who comply with their regulations. Another way to find them is through other musicians who seem to work regularly. Finding an agent who deals with college concerts is a good way to go if you just want to play primarily original material. (Club gigs, in general, discourage a predominance of originals in favor of a "Top 40" or "standards" repertoire.) You can find such agents by calling some college student activities directors and asking which agents they like to deal with.

Agents customarily charge from 10 to 20 percent (depending on the union involved, length of contract, and other factors) of the gross receipts from the jobs they secure for you. If you sign exclusively with an agent, they'll want that percentage on all the gigs you get, regardless of whether you or they secure the job. If you already have formed your own relationships with clubs or colleges where you've performed in the past, you may want to exclude them from the clubs where the agent can collect a percentage. If you can get them to agree to this you'll need to put it in your contract with a specific list of excluded clubs. All contracts sanctioned by the unions have clauses that get you out of the contract if the agent doesn't get you work within specified time periods.

Booking agents obviously look for a combination of musical talent and the desire and ability to entertain in the acts they consider representing.

Some agents specialize in specific musical styles. Some are "full service" agencies for those who also have the talent to expand their careers into acting, modeling, writing, and other directions. Some also represent composers for film and TV music. There is only beginning to develop a type of agent who represents songwriters who are not necessarily performers. These usually ask for either a small percentage of your writer's royalties, a percentage of royalties until a certain fee is reached, a flat "finder's fee" for placing the song with a publisher or artist, or a weekly retainer. Those who get songs recorded are, in fact, performing a major publisher function and usually want a publishing contract.

THE CAMPAIGN

If you want a record deal, you can't afford to wait for it to find you. You and/or your representatives need to plan an effective campaign to make sure you get heard by those companies in which you're interested.

A&R people at record companies seldom go to clubs at random to see acts they've never heard before. They'll respond to a "buzz" (talk on the street or in the industry about a hot, new act). They'll also go to see an act whose songs and sound they liked on a demo tape they've heard. They have little time to see an act otherwise. They'll always try to improve their odds of finding a great act and waste as little time as possible in the process. So, if there's such a thing as a standard campaign that makes the most efficient use of your time and theirs, it's close to this:

1. Put together your package with masters or high-quality demos, press kit, photos, reviews, and bios.
2. Send or deliver your tapes, preferably via an attorney, manager, or agent, to whomever that person knows in the record company A&R department. It's not necessary to see the vice president of A&R unless you know him. Staff A&R representatives may be much more accessible.
3. Schedule a showcase for the act about three or four weeks after delivery of the tapes. Announce the showcase, if possible, in the package you present.
4. About two weeks before your showcase, send out a special invitation to the people who have your package, the press, booking agents, producers, or anyone else you'd like to be there.
5. Follow up a few days later with phone calls to find out: a) if they have heard the tape, b) if they like it, c) if they got the invitation, d) if they're coming to the showcase. If so, tell them you will put their name(s) on the guest list. If not, ask if they'd like to be notified of future appearances. (Keep your mailing list current with their present job addresses and phone numbers.)
6. If they attend the showcase, follow up immediately with a "thank you" card and a phone call to find out what they thought.
7. If all that fails, cut some new demos and try it all again. Persist!

THE ALTERNATIVE: PRODUCING YOUR OWN RECORD

For the past several years, as it's been increasingly difficult for acts to get signed to major record labels, a grassroots movement has emerged toward independent record labels. You're a good candidate for this approach if you fall into these categories:

- In your process of pitching yourself to major labels you constantly hear, "I really like it personally, but the company doesn't see it as something they can sell," or, "This is really good, but I don't know what radio stations would play it."
- You find yourself difficult to categorize stylistically and so do others. You sort of "fall into the cracks" now, though what you do might be very hip in two or three years. Innovative artists are usually ahead of the marketplace. At one time, this was true of the Eagles (too country for pop radio, too pop for country radio) and Prince (too black for rock radio and too rock for black radio). "New Age" artists (a very broad category) are consistently in this category, but Windham Hill Records, which started as a two-person operation and is now distributed by A&M Records, has shown the way to opening up that market.
- You're an excellent live performer with a strong, enthusiastic following. This is very important if you're going to make your own record because, if you don't get radio or video play or create a style of music with an established marketing network, you must rely on live performances for people to sample your wares. People don't just walk into a record store and buy an album by someone they've never heard. The press is very important but if you're not playing somewhere, they can't review you.

It's my firm belief that there is an audience out there for anything that's done well, from hard-core punk to ethnic music, to the most esoteric jazz and arythmic "space music." The problem of the major labels is that the cost of their star-making machinery, including their offices, personnel, and studios, dictate that it takes a quarter- to a half-million dollars to record and market a new artist's album to the public. They have to sell a lot of records to recoup that investment and according to the latest statistics I've heard, only 17 percent of the albums released ever do recoup. That fact makes major labels very cautious that they sign only acts that appear to have a clearly defined market and fit an existing radio format.

However, a sort of "farm team" approach has developed within the record industry and many small independent labels that have managed to find their own markets successfully have been picked up for distribution by major labels. Artists developed from those labels include The Police, Elvis Costello, George Winston, George Thorogood, Laurie Anderson, and many more. Many dance music and rap artists have been launched nationally through the dance club market.

Apart from that development, new networks and avenues of exposure and distribution have developed, particularly for focused genres such as women's music, children's music, new age music, blues, reggae, and other non-mainstream genres that are already served by a network of fans, clubs, magazines, and underground and college radio stations and shows. Through these networks, independent labels have become increasingly sophisticated in finding their audiences.

Mail-order forms, astute ad placement, exposure at conventions and music festivals, all contribute to marketing plans for independent labels. When you consider that, unlike the major labels, you may be able to recoup your investment after sales of as few as one thousand records (depending on how low you keep your recording costs), the prospects look very good. In fact, it's quite likely that your odds are better to make money doing your own record than making money with a major label contract.

For more information on the subject, see the Bibliography.

Bibliography

ON CREATIVITY

Amabile, Teresa. *Growing Up Creative.* New York: Crown Publishing, 1988.

Amabile, Teresa. *Social Psychology of Creativity.* New York: Springer-Verlag Publishing, 1983.

Glover, John A. *Becoming a More Creative Person.* Englewood Cliffs, N.J.: Prentice-Hall, Inc., 1980.

Pao, Karin Mac, and Eric Skjei. *Overcoming Writer's Blocks.* Los Angeles: J.P. Tarcher, Inc., 1979.

Rico, Gabriele Lusser. *Writing the Natural Way.* Los Angeles: J.P. Tarcher, Inc., 1983.

Zdenek, Marilee. *The Right-Brain Experience.* New York: McGraw-Hill, 1983.

THE IMAGINATION

Block, Ned. *Imagery.* Cambridge, MA.: MIT Press, 1981.

Gombrich, E.H. *The Image and The Eye.* Ithaca, N.Y.: Cornell University Press, 1982.

Griffitts, C.H. *Individual Differences in Imagery.* Princeton, N.J. and Albany, N.Y.: The Psychological Review Company, 1927.

Konner, Melvin. *Emotions—Physiological Aspects.* New York: Holt, Rinehart, and Winston, 1982.

Kosslyn, Stephen Michael. *Image and The Mind.* Cambridge, MA.: Harvard University Press, 1980.

Lyons, William E. *Emotion.* Cambridge, England, and New York: Cambridge University Press, 1980.

Moore, T.V. *Image and Meaning in Memory and Perception.* Princeton, N.J. and Lancaster, PA.: Psychological Review Co., 1919.

Paivio, Allan. *Imagery and Verbal Processes.* New York: Holt, Rinehart and Winston, 1971.

Richardson, John T.E. *Mental Imagery and Human Memory.* New York: St. Martin's Press, 1980.

Shepard, Roger N. *Mental Images and Their Transformations.* Cambridge, MA.: MIT Press, 1982.

Shorr, J. *American Association For The Study of Mental Imagery, Imagery, Its Many Dimensions and Applications.* New York: Plenum Press, 1980.

Sommer, Robert. *The Mind's Eye.* New York: Delacorte Press, 1978.

Strongman, K.T. *The Psychology of Emotion.* New York: Wiley, 1978.

SONGWRITING

Citron, Stephen. *Songwriting.* New York: William Morrow & Co., Inc., 1985.

Davis, Sheila. *The Craft of Lyric Writing.* Cincinnati: Writer's Digest Books, 1985.

Flanagan, Bill. *Written in My Soul.* Chicago: Contemporary Books, 1986.

Kasha, Al and Joel Hirschhorn. *If They Ask You, You Can Write a Song.* New York: Simon and Schuster, 1979.

Lees, Gene. *The Modern Rhyming Dictionary.* Port Chester, NY: Cherry Lane, 1981.

Leikin, Molly-Ann. *How to Write a Hit Song.* New York: Perigree Books, 1987.

Martin, George, ed. *Making Music—The Guide to Writing, Recording and Performing.* New York: Morrow Books, 1983.

Roget's International Thesaurus, Fourth Edition. New York: Harper & Row, 1977.

Smalley, Jack. *Lyrics, Lyrics, Lyrics (And How to Write Them).* New York: Simon and Schuster, 1987.

Wentworth, Harold and Stuart Berg Flexner, eds. *Dictionary of American Slang.* New York: Thomas Y. Crowell Co., Inc.: 1975.

Wood, Clement. *The Complete Rhyming Dictionary.* Garden City, N.Y.: Doubleday & Co., Inc., 1943.

THE MUSIC BUSINESS
Baskerville, David, Ph.D. *The Music Business Handbook and Career Guide.* The Sherwood Co. (Box 21645, Denver, CO 80221), 1985.

Csida, Joseph. *The Music/Record Career Handbook* (Revised Edition).

Feist, Leonard. *Popular Music Publishing in America.* New York: National Music Publishers' Association, Inc., 1980.

Erickson, J. Gunnar, Edward R. Hearn and Mark E. Halloran. *Musician's Guide to Copyright.* Bay Area Lawyers for the Arts (Fort Mason, Building 310, San Francisco, CA 94123), 1979.

Halloran, Mark, ed. *The Musician's Manual (A Practical Career Guide),* Revised Edition. Beverly Hills Bar Association Committee for the Arts (300 S. Beverly Dr., Ste. 201, Beverly Hills, CA 90212), 1987.

Krepack, Benjamin and Rod Firestone. *Start Me Up: The Music Biz Meets the Personal Computer.* Mediac Plus (Box 3315, Van Nuys, CA 91407), 1986.

Monaco, Bob and James Riordan. *The Platinum Rainbow.* Sherman Oaks, CA.: Swordsman Press, 1985.

Pomerantz, Susan and Teri Muench. *Attn. A&R: A Step By Step Guide into the Music Business.* Alfred Publishing, 1987.

Shemel, Sidney and M. William Krasilovsky. *This Business of Music,* Fifth Edition. New York: Billboard Publications, 1985.

Siegel, Alan H. *Breakin' in (to the Music Business).* Port Chester, N.Y.: Cherry Lane Books, 1983.

Songwriter's Market, Annual. Cincinnati: Writer's Digest Books.

Wacholtz, Larry. *Inside Country Music.* New York: Billboard Publications, 1986.

Weissman, Dick. *Survival: Making a Living in Your Local Music Market.* New York: Hal Leonard, 1988.

RECORDING
Anderton, Craig. *Home Recording for Musicians.* Music Sales Corp., 1977.

Everard, Chris. *The Home Recording Handbook.* Music Sales Corp., 1985.

Huber, David. *Audio Production Techniques for Video.* Howard Sams & Co., Inc., 1987.

Lubin, Tom. *How to do a Demo Quality Recording in Your Bedroom.* Alexander Publishing, 1987.

Rapaport, Diane Sward. *How to Make and Sell Your Own Record,* Third Edition. Jerome Headlands Press, 1988.

Tobler, John and Stuart Grundy. *The Record Producers.* New York: St. Martin's Press, 1982.

Williams, George. *The Songwriter's Demo Manual and Success Guide.* Music Business Books (Box 413, Riverside CA 92502), 1984.

FILM AND TV SCORING
Hagen, Earle. *Scoring for Films.* Criterion Music, 1971.

Mancini, Henry. *Sounds & Scores.* Los Angeles: Columbia Pictures Publications, 1974.

MUSICAL THEATER
Engel, Lehman. *Their Words Are Music: The Great Theatre Lyricists and Their Lyrics.* New York: Crown Publishing, 1975.

Guernsey, Otis L. Jr., ed. *Playwrights, Lyricists, Composers on Theatre.* New York: Dodd, Mead & Co., 1974.

Hart, Dorothy and Robert Kimball, eds. *The Complete Lyrics of Lorenz Hart.* New York: Alfred A. Knopf, 1986.

Kasha, Al and Joel Hirschhorn. *Notes on Broadway, Conversations with the Great Composers on Theatre.* Chicago: Contemporary Books, 1985.

Lyrics by Oscar Hammerstein. New York: Hal Leonard Books, 1985.

MUSIC/SOCIOLOGY
Bowling Green University. *Popular Music and Society.* Popular Press (Bowling Green, OH 43403, tel. 419-372-7866).

Psychomusicology Society, Inc. *Psychomusic—A Journal of Research and Cognition.* Stephen F. Austin State University (Box 13022 SFA Station, Nacogdoches, TX 75962, tel. 409-569-2801).

JINGLES
Standard Directory of Advertising Agencies, Annual. National Register Publishing Co. (Available in the reference section of most public libraries.)

Woodward, Walt. *An Insider's Guide to Advertising Music.* Art Direction Book Co., 1986.

ON MIDI
Anderton, Craig. *MIDI for Musicians.* Music Sales Corp., 1986.

DeFuria, Steve. *The MIDI Book.* Ferro Technologies, 1986.

OTHER RESOURCES
The Mix Bookshelf, 2608 Ninth St., Berkeley, CA 94710 (800)641-3349; (800)233-9604 (outside California)

One of the most comprehensive mail-order collections of music craft and business books and tapes. Many of the above-mentioned books are available here in addition to audio- and videotape courses, music software programs, sound sampling and sound effects libraries.

Billboard International Talent Directory, 1 Astor Plaza, 1515 Broadway, New York, NY 10036

Billboard International Buyers Guide (same address as above)

Bronson, Fred. *The Billboard Book of Number One Hits.* New York: Billboard Publications, 1985.

Brosta, Joseph IV. *BPM, a Beats Per Minute Guide to Dance Music, 1980-85.* Time Warp Publishing (7956 White Oak Ave., Northridge, CA 91325), 1986.

Whitburn, Joel. *The Billboard Book of Top 40 Hits.* New York: Billboard Publications, Inc., 1985.

THE TRADES
Billboard, 9107 Wilshire Blvd., Ste. 700, Beverly Hills, CA 90210 (213)273-7040

Black Radio Exclusive, 6353 Hollywood Blvd., Los Angeles, CA 90028 (213)469-7262

Cash Box, 330 W. 58th St., New York, NY 10019 (212)586-2640

Country Chart Analyst, Johnny Bond Publications, 7 Music Circle North, Nashville, TN 37203 (615)242-6875

Dance Music Report, 33-39 22nd St., Long Island City, NY 11106

Indie Bullet, 3318-E SSW Loop 323, Tyler, TX 75701

Radio and Records, 1930 Century Park West, Los Angeles, CA 90067

MUSICIANS AND MUSIC TECHNOLOGY
Music Connection Magazine, 6640 Sunset Boulevard, Ste. 201, Hollywood, CA 90028 (213)462-5772

Music & Sound Output, 220 Westbury Ave., Carle Place, NY 11514 (516)334-7880

BAM Publications, 5952 Canning St., Oakland, CA 94609 (415)652-3810

Discotech Magazine, 333 S. La Cienega Blvd., Los Angeles, CA 90048

Electronic Musician, P.O. Box 3747, Escondido, CA 92025 (415)843-7901

KCS (Keyboards, Computers & Software), 299 Main St., Northport, NY 11768 (516)754-9311

Musician, P.O. Box 701, 31 Commercial St., Gloucester, MA 01930 (617)281-3110

Keyboard, 20085 Stevens Creek, Cupertino, CA 95014

Guitar Player (same as above)

Frets (same as above)

Guitar for the Practicing Musician, 110 Midland Ave., Port Chester, NY 10573

Overture, The American Federation of Musicians, 1777 Vine St., Hollywood, CA 90028 (213)461-8111

Music Technology, Music Maker Publications, Inc., 7361 Topanga Canyon Boulevard, Canoga Park, CA 91303 (818)704-8777

RECORDING
Home & Studio Recording, 7361 Topanga Canyon Blvd., Canoga Park, CA 91303 (818)704-8777

Modern Recording, 15 Columbus Circle, New York, NY 10023

Recording Engineer/Producer, P.O. Box 2449, Hollywood, CA 90078 (213)467-1111

FOR SONGWRITERS

Words & Music, U.S. Publishing, Inc., 17 Sylvan St., Rutherford, N.J. 07070 (201)460-8666

American Songwriter, 27 Music Square East, Nashville, TN 37203 (615)244-6065

The Musepaper, c/o The Los Angeles Songwriters Showcase, P.O. Box 93759, Los Angeles, CA 90093 (213)654-1665

Songtalk, National Academy of Songwriters, 6381 Hollywood Blvd., Ste. 780, Hollywood, CA 90028 (213)463-7178

Song Hits, Charleton Publications, Inc., Division St., Derby, CT 06418

Country Hits (same as above)

ADVERTISING TRADES (for jingle research)

Millimeter—The Magazine of the Motion Picture and Television Industries, 826 Broadway, New York, NY 10003 (212)477-4700

Advertising Age, 740 N. Rush St., Chicago, IL 60611 (312)649-5200

Advertising World, Directories International Inc., 150 Fifth Avenue, Ste. 610, New York, NY 10011 (212)807-1660

AdWeek/West, 514 Shatto Pl., Los Angeles, CA 90020

Media Profiles: Audio Visual Marketing Newsletter, 70 Hudson St., Hoboken, NJ 07030 (201)963-1600

FILM/TV TRADES (for scoring research)

Hollywood Reporter, 6715 Sunset Blvd., Hollywood, CA 90028 (213)464-7411

Daily Variety, 1400 Cahuenga Blvd., Los Angeles, CA 90028 (213)469-1141

Weekly Variety (same as above) (213)467-8164

Drama-Logue, P.O. Box 38771, Los Angeles, CA 90038

SONGWRITER ASSOCIATIONS

Akron Composers and Musicians' Exchange, 625 Hillsdale Ave., Akron, OH 44303

Arizona Songwriters Association, P.O. Box 678, Phoenix, AZ 85001 (602)841-6397

Arkansas Songwriters Association, P.O. Box 55128, Hilcrest Station, Little Rock, AR 72225 (501)835-8707

Arkansas Songwriters Association, Route 1, Box 693, Pine Bluff, AR 71603

Atlanta Songwriters Association, 2091 Faulkner Rd., Atlanta, GA 30324 (404)634-2610

Austin Songwriters Group, Texas Music Association, 2306 Lake Austin Blvd., Austin, TX 78703 (512)478-2209

Bloomington Indiana Songwriters Workshop, 5095 N. Old Street Rd., #37, Bloomington, IN 47401

Central Valley Songwriters Association, 1042 Pierce Dr., Clovis, CA 93612 (209)299-6309

Chicago Songwriters Association, 5141 S. Archer, Chicago, IL 60632, (312)981-0198

Composers, Arrangers & Songwriters of Kansas, 117 West Eighth, Hays, KS 67601 (913)625-9634

Composer's Guild, 2333 Olympus Dr., Salt Lake City, UT 84124

Composers Workshop Hawaii, P.O. Box 22368, Honolulu, Hawaii 96822

Connecticut Songwriters Association, P.O. Box 2995, New Haven, CT 06515 (203)387-8081

Florida Songwriters Forum, 1501 Seventh Ave., Ybor City, FL 33605 (813)247-1300

Hudson Valley Songwriters Association, P.O. Box 176, 159 W. Mair, Goshen, NY 10924

Indianapolis Songwriters Association, P.O. Box 176, McCordsville, IN 46055

Las Vegas Songwriters Association, 1650 Cookson Ct., Las Vegas, NV 89115 (702)452-0954

Los Angeles Songwriters Showcase (LASS), P.O. Box 93759, Hollywood, CA 90093 (213)654-1665

Louisiana Songwriters Association, 4775 Arrowhead, Baton Rouge, LA 70808 (504)924-0804

Middle Atlantic Songwriters Association, 444 Rocky Run Rd., Midway Park, NC 28544

NAS Midwest Chapter, 20 N. 4th St., Minneapolis, MN 55401 (612)371-9401

Missouri Songwriters Association, 693 Green Forest Dr., Fenton, MO 63026

Muscle Shoals Music Association, P.O. Box 551, Sheffield, AL 35660

Nashville Songwriters Association, Intl. (NSAI), 803 Eighteenth Ave. S., Nashville, TN 37203 (615)321-5004 (call for chapter locations)

National Academy of Songwriters (NAS), 6381 Hollywood Blvd., #780, Hollywood, CA 90028 (213)462-7178 (call for chapter locations)

New Orleans Songwriters Association, 2643 DeSoto St., New Orleans, LA 70119

Northern California Songwriters Association, 855 Oak Grove Ave., Ste. 211, Menlo Park, CA 94025 (415)327-8296

Ohio Songwriters Association, 27801 Euclid Ave., Euclid, OH 44132 (216)731-7664

Ohio Songwriters Association, 3312 Petzinger Rd., Columbus, OH 43232

Pacific Songwriters Association, 944 Howe St., Vancouver, B.C., Canada V6Z 1N9

Pacific Northwest Songwriters Association, P.O. Box 98324, Seattle, WA 98188

Pacific Rim Songwriters Association, P.O. Box 02520, Portland, OR 97202 (503)775-8845

Rocky Mountain Music Association, 231 Harrison St., Denver, CO 80206 (303)355-7426

San Diego Songwriters Guild, 13828 Tobiasson Rd., Poway, CA 92064 (619)748-5138

Santa Barbara Songwriters Guild, P.O. Box 2238, Santa Barbara, CA 93120

Songwriters Association of Jacksonville, P.O. Box 10394, Jacksonville, FL 32247

Songwriters Association of Washington, D.C., 1377 K St., N.W. #632, Washington, D.C. 20005 (703)660-9254

The Songwriters Guild of America (West Coast), 6430 Sunset Blvd., Ste. 317, Hollywood, CA 90028 (213)462-1108

The Songwriters Guild of America, 50 Music Square West, Ste. 702, Nashville, TN 37203 (615)329-1782

The Songwriters Guild of America (East Coast), 276 Fifth Ave., Ste. 306, New York, NY 10001 (212)686-6820

South Colorado Songwriters Workshop, 2023 Vinewood, Pueblo, CO 81005

Southwest Virginia Songwriters Association, P.O. Box 698, Salem, VA 24153 (703)389-1525

Spokane Songwriters Association, S. 623 Denver, Spokane, WA 99202

Tulsa Songwriters Association, P.O. Box 571004, Tulsa, OK 74107

Whitewater Valley Songwriters Association, R.R. 4, P.O. Box 112, Liberty, IN 47353 (317)458-6152

CANADIAN PERFORMING RIGHTS ORGANIZATIONS
Composers, Authors and Publishers Association of Canada, Limited (CAPAC), 1240 Bay St., Toronto, Ontario M5R 2C2 (416)924-4427

Performing Rights Organization of Canada Ltd. (PRO Canada), 41 Valleybrook Dr., Don Mills, Ontario M3B 2S6 (416)445-8700

Permissions

AUTOMATIC
Words and music by Brock Walsh and Mark Goldenberg
Copyright © 1983, 1984 by MCA Music, A Division of MCA Inc.,
Music Corporation of America, Inc. and Fleedleedle Music, New York,
N.Y. 10019.
Used by permission. All rights reserved.

TOTAL ECLIPSE OF THE HEART
Words and music by Jim Steinman
Copyright © 1982 by Lost Boys Music
Administered by Edward B. Marks Music Co. for the U.S. & Canada.
All rights reserved. Used by permission.

BILLIE JEAN
Words and music by Michael Jackson
Copyright © 1982 Mijac Music. All rights reserved. Used by permission.

(JUST LIKE) STARTING OVER
Words and music by John Lennon
Copyright © 1980 Lenono Music. All rights controlled and administered by Blackwood Music, Inc.
All rights reserved. Used by permission.

WITH A LITTLE HELP FROM MY FRIENDS
Words and music by John Lennon and Paul McCartney
Copyright © 1967 Northern Songs Ltd.
All rights controlled and administered by Blackwood Music, Inc. under license from ATV Music (Maclen).
All rights reserved. Used by permission.

HEARTBREAKER
Words and music by Barry, Robin, and Maurice Gibb
Copyright © 1982 by Barry Gibb, Robin Gibb, and Maurice Gibb.
Gibb Brothers Music, Owner of publication and allied rights throughout the world.
Administered in the USA and Canada by Unichappell Music, Inc.
All rights reserved. Used by permission.

WE ARE FAMILY
Words and music by Nile Rodgers and Bernard Edwards

REAL LOVE
Words and music by Patrick Henderson and Michael MacDonald

SAME OLD LANG SYNE
Words and music by Dan Fogelberg

SOMETIMES WHEN WE TOUCH
Words and music by Barry Mann and Dan Hill

ELEANOR RIGBY
Words and music by John Lennon and Paul McCartney

WHAT'S LOVE GOT TO DO WITH IT?
Words and music by Graham Lyle and Terry Britten

YOU'VE LOST THAT LOVIN' FEELIN'
Words and music by Barry Mann, Cynthia Weil, and Phil Spector

WORKING GIRL
Words and music by Dolly Parton

Appendix

GUIDELINES FOR THE EDUCATIONAL USE OF COPYRIGHTED MUSIC MATERIAL

In a joint letter dated April 30, 1976, representatives of the Music Publishers' Association of the United States, Inc., the National Music Publishers' Association, Inc., the Music Teachers National Association, the Music Educators National Conference, the National Association of Schools of Music, and the Ad Hoc Committee on Copyright Law Revision, wrote to Chairman Kastenmeier as follows:

During the hearings on H.R. 2223 in June 1975, you and several of your subcommittee members suggested that concerned groups should work together in developing guidelines which would be helpful to clarify Section 107 of the bill.

Representatives of music educators and music publishers delayed their meetings until guidelines had been developed relative to books and periodicals. Shortly after that work was completed and those guidelines were forwarded to your subcommittee, representatives of the undersigned music organizations met together with representatives of the Ad Hoc Committee on Copyright Law Revision to draft guidelines relative to music.

We are very pleased to inform you that the discussions thus have been fruitful on the guidelines which have been developed. Since private music teachers are an important factor in music education, due consideration has been given to the concerns of that group.

We trust that this will be helpful in the report on the bill to clarify Fair Use as it applies to music.

The text of the guidelines accompanying this letter is as follows:

GUIDELINES FOR EDUCATIONAL USES OF MUSIC

The purpose of the following guidelines is to state the minimum and not the maximum standards of educational fair use under Section 107 of HR 2223. The parties agree that the conditions determining the extent of permissible copying for educational purposes may change in the future; that certain types of copying permitted under these guidelines may not be permissible in the future, and conversely that in the future other types of copying not permitted under these guidelines may be permissible under revised guidelines.

Moreover, the following statement of guidelines is not intended to limit the types of copying permitted under the standards of fair use under judicial decision and which are stated in Section 107 of the Copyright Revision Bill. There may be instances in which copying which does not fall within the guidelines stated below may nonetheless be permitted under the criteria of fair use.

A. PERMISSIBLE USES

1. Emergency copying to replace purchased copies which for any reason are not available for an imminent performance provided purchased replacement copies shall be substituted in due course.
2. For academic purposes other than performance, single or multiple copies of excerpts of works may be made, provided that the excerpts do not comprise a part of the whole which would constitute a performable unit such as a section, movement or aria, but in no case more than 10 percent of the whole work. The number of copies shall not exceed one copy per pupil.
3. Printed copies which have been purchased may be edited or simplified provided that the fundamental character of the work is not distorted or the lyrics, if any, altered or lyrics added if none exist.
4. A single copy of recordings of performances by students may be made for evaluation or rehearsal purposes and may be retained by the educational institution or individual teacher.
5. A single copy of a sound recording (such as a tape, disc or cassette) of copyrighted music may be made from sound recordings owned by an educational institution or an individual teacher for the purpose of constructing aural exercises or examinations and may be retained by the educational institution or individual teacher. (This pertains only to the copyright of the music itself and not to any copyright which may exist in the sound recording.)

B. PROHIBITIONS

1. Copying to create or replace or substitute for anthologies, compilations or collective works.
2. Copying of or from works intended to be "consumable" in the course of study or of teaching such as workbooks, exercises, standardized tests and answer sheets and like material.
3. Copying for the purpose of performance, except as in A (1) above.
4. Copying for the purpose of substituting for the purchase of music, except as in A(1) and A(2) above.
5. Copying without inclusion of the copyright notice which appears on the printed copy.

Filling Out Application Form PA

Detach and read these instructions before completing this form. Make sure all applicable spaces have been filled in before you return this form.

BASIC INFORMATION

When to Use This Form: Use Form PA for registration of published or unpublished works of the performing arts. This class includes works prepared for the purpose of being "performed" directly before an audience or indirectly "by means of any device or process." Works of the performing arts include: (1) musical works, including any accompanying words; (2) dramatic works, including any accompanying music; (3) pantomimes and choreographic works; and (4) motion pictures and other audiovisual works.

Deposit to Accompany Application: An application for copyright registration must be accompanied by a deposit consisting of copies or phonorecords representing the entire work for which registration is to be made. The following are the general deposit requirements as set forth in the statute:

Unpublished Work: Deposit one complete copy (or phonorecord).

Published Work: Deposit two complete copies (or phonorecords) of the best edition.

Work First Published Outside the United States: Deposit one complete copy (or phonorecord) of the first foreign edition.

Contribution to a Collective Work: Deposit one complete copy (or phonorecord) of the best edition of the collective work.

Motion Pictures: Deposit *both* of the following: (1) a separate written description of the contents of the motion picture; and (2) for a published work, one complete copy of the best edition of the motion picture; or, for an unpublished work, one complete copy of the motion picture or identifying material. Identifying material may be either an audiorecording of the entire soundtrack or one frame enlargement or similar visual print from each 10-minute segment.

The Copyright Notice: For published works, the law provides that a copyright notice in a specified form "shall be placed on all publicly distributed copies from which the work can be visually perceived." Use of the copyright notice is the responsibility of the copyright owner and does not require advance permission from the Copyright Office. The required form of the notice for copies generally consists of three elements: (1) the symbol "©", or the word "Copyright," or the abbreviation "Copr."; (2) the year of first publication; and (3) the name of the owner of copyright. For example: "© 1981 Constance Porter." The notice is to be affixed to the copies "in such manner and location as to give reasonable notice of the claim of copyright."

For further information about copyright registration, notice, or special questions relating to copyright problems, write:

Information and Publications Section, LM-455
Copyright Office
Library of Congress
Washington, D.C. 20559

PRIVACY ACT ADVISORY STATEMENT Required by the Privacy Act of 1974 (P.L. 93-579)
The authority for requesting this information is title 17, U.S.C. secs. 409 and 410. Furnishing the requested information is voluntary. But if the information is not furnished, it may be necessary to delay or refuse registration and you may not be entitled to certain relief, remedies, and benefits provided in chapters 4 and 5 of title 17, U.S.C.
The principal uses of the requested information are the establishment and maintenance of a public record and the examination of the application for compliance with legal requirements.
Other routine uses include public inspection and copying, preparation of public indexes, preparation of public catalogs of copyright registrations, and preparation of search reports upon request.
NOTE: No other advisory statement will be given in connection with this application. Please keep this statement and refer to it if we communicate with you regarding this application.

LINE-BY-LINE INSTRUCTIONS

1 SPACE 1: Title

Title of This Work: Every work submitted for copyright registration must be given a title to identify that particular work. If the copies or phonorecords of the work bear a title (or an identifying phrase that could serve as a title), transcribe that wording *completely* and *exactly* on the application. Indexing of the registration and future identification of the work will depend on the information you give here. If the work you are registering is an entire "collective work" (such as a collection of plays or songs), give the overall title of the collection. If you are registering one or more individual contributions to a collective work, give the title of each contribution, followed by the title of the collection. Example: "'A Song for Elinda' in *Old and New Ballads for Old and New People.*"

Previous or Alternative Titles: Complete this space if there are any additional titles for the work under which someone searching for the registration might be likely to look, or under which a document pertaining to the work might be recorded.

Nature of This Work: Briefly describe the general nature or character of the work being registered for copyright. Examples: "Music"; "Song Lyrics"; "Words and Music"; "Drama"; "Musical Play"; "Choreography"; "Pantomime"; "Motion Picture"; "Audiovisual Work."

2 SPACE 2: Author(s)

General Instructions: After reading these instructions, decide who are the "authors" of this work for copyright purposes. Then, unless the work is a "collective work," give the requested information about every "author" who contributed any appreciable amount of copyrightable matter to this version of the work. If you need further space, request additional Continuation Sheets. In the case of a collective work, such as a songbook or a collection of plays, give information about the author of the collective work as a whole.

Name of Author: The fullest form of the author's name should be given. Unless the work was "made for hire," the individual who actually created the work is its "author." In the case of a work made for hire, the statute provides

that "the employer or other person for whom the work was prepared is considered the author."

What is a "Work Made for Hire"? A "work made for hire" is defined as: (1) "a work prepared by an employee within the scope of his or her employment"; or (2) "a work specially ordered or commissioned for use as a contribution to a collective work, as a part of a motion picture or other audiovisual work, as a translation, as a supplementary work, as a compilation, as an instructional text, as a test, as answer material for a test, or as an atlas, if the parties expressly agree in a written instrument signed by them that the work shall be considered a work made for hire." If you have checked "Yes" to indicate that the work was "made for hire," you must give the full legal name of the employer (or other person for whom the work was prepared). You may also include the name of the employee along with the name of the employer (for example: "Elster Music Co., employer for hire of John Ferguson").

"Anonymous" or "Pseudonymous" Work: An author's contribution to a work is "anonymous" if that author is not identified on the copies or phonorecords of the work. An author's contribution to a work is "pseudonymous" if that author is identified on the copies or phonorecords under a fictitious name. If the work is "anonymous" you may: (1) leave the line blank; or (2) state "anonymous" on the line; or (3) reveal the author's identity. If the work is "pseudonymous" you may: (1) leave the line blank; or (2) give the pseudonym and identify it as such (for example: "Huntley Haverstock, pseudonym"); or (3) reveal the author's name, making clear which is the real name and which is the pseudonym (for example: "Judith Barton, whose pseudonym is Madeline Elster"). However, the citizenship or domicile of the author **must** be given in all cases.

Dates of Birth and Death: If the author is dead, the statute requires that the year of death be included in the application unless the work is anonymous or pseudonymous. The author's birth date is optional, but is useful as a form of identification. Leave this space blank if the author's contribution was a "work made for hire."

Author's Nationality or Domicile: Give the country of which the author is a citizen, or the country in which the author is domiciled. Nationality or domicile **must** be given in all cases.

Nature of Authorship: Give a brief general statement of the nature of this particular author's contribution to the work. Examples: "Words"; "Co-Author of Music"; "Words and Music"; "Arrangement"; "Co-Author of Book and Lyrics"; "Dramatization"; "Screen Play"; "Compilation and English Translation"; "Editorial Revisions."

3 SPACE 3: Creation and Publication

General Instructions: Do not confuse "creation" with "publication." Every application for copyright registration must state "the year in which creation of the work was completed." Give the date and nation of first publication only if the work has been published.

Creation: Under the statute, a work is "created" when it is fixed in a copy or phonorecord for the first time. Where a work has been prepared over a period of time, the part of the work existing in fixed form on a particular date constitutes the created work on that date. The date you give here should be the year in which the author completed the particular version for which registration is now being sought, even if other versions exist or if further changes or additions are planned.

Publication: The statute defines "publication" as "the distribution of copies or phonorecords of a work to the public by sale or other transfer of ownership, or by rental, lease, or lending"; a work is also "published" if there has been an "offering to distribute copies or phonorecords to a group of persons for purposes of further distribution, public performance, or public display." Give the full date (month, day, year) when, and the country where, publication first occurred. If first publication took place simultaneously in the United States and other countries, it is sufficient to state "U.S.A."

4 SPACE 4: Claimant(s)

Name(s) and Address(es) of Copyright Claimant(s): Give the name(s) and address(es) of the copyright claimant(s) in this work even if the claimant is the same as the author. Copyright in a work belongs initially to the author of the work (including, in the case of a work made for hire, the employer or other person for whom the work was prepared). The copyright claimant is either the author of the work or a person or organization to whom the copyright initially belonging to the author has been transferred.

Transfer: The statute provides that, if the copyright claimant is not the author, the application for registration must contain "a brief statement of how the claimant obtained ownership of the copyright." If any copyright claimant named in space 4 is not an author named in space 2, give a brief, general statement summarizing the means by which that claimant obtained ownership of the copyright. Examples: "By written contract"; "Transfer of all rights by author"; "Assignment"; "By will." Do not attach transfer documents or other attachments or riders.

5 SPACE 5: Previous Registration

General Instructions: The questions in space 5 are intended to find out whether an earlier registration has been made for this work and, if so, whether there is any basis for a new registration. As a general rule, only one basic copyright registration can be made for the same version of a particular work.

Same Version: If this version is substantially the same as the work covered by a previous registration, a second registration is not generally possible unless: (1) the work has been registered in unpublished form and a second registration is now being sought to cover this first published edition; or (2) someone other than the author is identified as copyright claimant in the earlier registration, and the author is now seeking registration in his or her own name. If either of these two exceptions apply, check the appropriate box and give the

earlier registration number and date. Otherwise, do not submit Form PA; instead, write the Copyright Office for information about supplementary registration or recordation of transfers of copyright ownership.

Changed Version: If the work has been changed, and you are now seeking registration to cover the additions or revisions, check the last box in space 5, give the earlier registration number and date, and complete both parts of space 6 in accordance with the instructions below.

Previous Registration Number and Date: If more than one previous registration has been made for the work, give the number and date of the latest registration.

6 SPACE 6: Derivative Work or Compilation

General Instructions: Complete space 6 if this work is a "changed version," "compilation," or "derivative work," and if it incorporates one or more earlier works that have already been published or registered for copyright, or that have fallen into the public domain. A "compilation" is defined as "a work formed by the collection and assembling of preexisting materials or of data that are selected, coordinated, or arranged in such a way that the resulting work as a whole constitutes an original work of authorship." A "derivative work" is "a work based on one or more preexisting works." Examples of derivative works include musical arrangements, dramatizations, translations, abridgments, condensations, motion picture versions,or "any other form in which a work may be recast, transformed, or adapted." Derivative works also include works "consisting of editorial revisions, annotations, or other modifications" if these changes, as a whole, represent an original work of authorship.

Preexisting Material (space 6a): Complete this space and space 6b for derivative works. In this space identify the preexisting work that has been recast, transformed, or adapted. For example, the preexisting material might be: "French version of Hugo's 'Le Roi s'amuse'." Do not complete this space for compilations.

Material Added to This Work (space 6b): Give a brief, general statement of the additional new material covered by the copyright claim for which registration is sought. In the case of a derivative work, identify this new material. Examples: "Arrangement for piano and orchestra"; "Dramatization for television"; "New film version"; "Revisions throughout; Act III completely new." If the work is a compilation, give a brief, general statement describing both the material that has been compiled and the compilation itself. Example: "Compilation of 19th Century Military Songs."

7,8,9 SPACE 7, 8, 9: Fee, Correspondence, Certification, Return Address

Deposit Account: If you maintain a Deposit Account in the Copyright Office, identify it in space 7. Otherwise leave the space blank and send the fee of $10 with your application and deposit.

Correspondence (space 7): This space should contain the name, address, area code, and telephone number of the person to be consulted if correspondence about this application becomes necessary.

Certification (space 8): The application cannot be accepted unless it bears the date and the handwritten signature of the author or other copyright claimant, or of the owner of exclusive right(s), or of the duly authorized agent of the author, claimant, or owner of exclusive right(s).

Address for Return of Certificate (space 9): The address box must be completed legibly since the certificate will be returned in a window envelope.

MORE INFORMATION

How To Register a Recorded Work: If the musical or dramatic work that you are registering has been recorded (as a tape, disk, or cassette), you must choose either copyright application Form PA or Form SR, Performing Arts or Sound Recordings, depending on the purpose of the registration.

Form PA should be used to register the underlying musical composition or dramatic work. Form SR has been developed specifically to register a "sound recording" as defined by the Copyright Act—a work resulting from the "fixation of a series of sounds," separate and distinct from the underlying musical or dramatic work. Form SR should be used when the copyright claim is limited to the sound recording itself. (In one instance, Form SR may also be used to file for a copyright registration for both kinds of works—see (4) below.) Therefore:

(1) File Form PA if you are seeking to register the musical or dramatic work, not the "sound recording," even though what you deposit for copyright purposes may be in the form of a phonorecord.

(2) File Form PA if you are seeking to register the audio portion of an audiovisual work, such as a motion picture soundtrack; these are considered integral parts of the audiovisual work.

(3) File Form SR if you are seeking to register the "sound recording" itself, that is, the work that results from the fixation of a series of musical, spoken, or other sounds, but not the underlying musical or dramatic work.

(4) File Form SR if you are the copyright claimant for both the underlying musical or dramatic work and the sound recording, and you prefer to register both on the same form.

(5) File both forms PA and SR if the copyright claimant for the underlying work and sound recording differ, or you prefer to have separate registration for them.

"Copies" and "Phonorecords": To register for copyright, you are required to deposit "copies" or "phonorecords." These are defined as follows:

Musical compositions may be embodied (fixed) in "copies," objects from which a work can be read or visually perceived, directly or with the aid of a machine or device, such as manuscripts, books, sheet music, film, and videotape. They may also be fixed in "phonorecords," objects embodying fixations of sounds, such as tapes and phonograph disks, commonly known as phonograph records. For example, a song (the work to be registered) can be reproduced in sheet music ("copies") or phonograph records ("phonorecords"), or both.

315

FORM PA
UNITED STATES COPYRIGHT OFFICE

REGISTRATION NUMBER

PA   PAU

EFFECTIVE DATE OF REGISTRATION

Month   Day   Year

DO NOT WRITE ABOVE THIS LINE. IF YOU NEED MORE SPACE, USE A SEPARATE CONTINUATION SHEET.

1 TITLE OF THIS WORK ▼

PREVIOUS OR ALTERNATIVE TITLES ▼

NATURE OF THIS WORK ▼ See instructions

2 **a**

NAME OF AUTHOR ▼

DATES OF BIRTH AND DEATH
Year Born ▼   Year Died ▼

Was this contribution to the work a "work made for hire"?
☐ Yes
☐ No

AUTHOR'S NATIONALITY OR DOMICILE
Name of Country
OR { Citizen of ▶ —————————
{ Domiciled in ▶ —————————

WAS THIS AUTHOR'S CONTRIBUTION TO THE WORK
Anonymous? ☐ Yes ☐ No
Pseudonymous? ☐ Yes ☐ No
If the answer to either of these questions is "Yes," see detailed instructions.

NOTE

Under the law, the "author" of a "work made for hire" is generally the employer, not the employee (see instructions). For any part of this work that was "made for hire" check "Yes" in the space provided, give the employer (or other person for whom the work was prepared) as "Author" of that part, and leave the space for dates of birth and death blank.

NATURE OF AUTHORSHIP Briefly describe nature of the material created by this author in which copyright is claimed. ▼

b

NAME OF AUTHOR ▼

DATES OF BIRTH AND DEATH
Year Born ▼   Year Died ▼

Was this contribution to the work a "work made for hire"?
☐ Yes
☐ No

AUTHOR'S NATIONALITY OR DOMICILE
Name of country
OR { Citizen of ▶ —————————
{ Domiciled in ▶ —————————

WAS THIS AUTHOR'S CONTRIBUTION TO THE WORK
Anonymous? ☐ Yes ☐ No
Pseudonymous? ☐ Yes ☐ No
If the answer to either of these questions is "Yes," see detailed instructions.

NATURE OF AUTHORSHIP Briefly describe nature of the material created by this author in which copyright is claimed. ▼

c

NAME OF AUTHOR ▼

DATES OF BIRTH AND DEATH
Year Born ▼   Year Died ▼

Was this contribution to the work a "work made for hire"?
☐ Yes
☐ No

AUTHOR'S NATIONALITY OR DOMICILE
Name of Country
OR { Citizen of ▶ —————————
{ Domiciled in ▶ —————————

WAS THIS AUTHOR'S CONTRIBUTION TO THE WORK
Anonymous? ☐ Yes ☐ No
Pseudonymous? ☐ Yes ☐ No
If the answer to either of these questions is "Yes," see detailed instructions.

NATURE OF AUTHORSHIP Briefly describe nature of the material created by this author in which copyright is claimed. ▼

3 YEAR IN WHICH CREATION OF THIS WORK WAS COMPLETED This information must be given in all cases.
◀ Year

DATE AND NATION OF FIRST PUBLICATION OF THIS PARTICULAR WORK
Complete this information Month ▶ _____ Day ▶ _____ Year ▶ _____
ONLY if this work has been published.
◀ Nation

4 COPYRIGHT CLAIMANT(S) Name and address must be given even if the claimant is the same as the author given in space 2.▼

See instructions before completing this space.

TRANSFER If the claimant(s) named here in space 4 are different from the author(s) named in space 2, give a brief statement of how the claimant(s) obtained ownership of the copyright.▼

APPLICATION RECEIVED

ONE DEPOSIT RECEIVED

TWO DEPOSITS RECEIVED

REMITTANCE NUMBER AND DATE

DO NOT WRITE HERE
OFFICE USE ONLY

MORE ON BACK ▶ • Complete all applicable spaces (numbers 5-9) on the reverse side of this page
• See detailed instructions • Sign the form at line 8

DO NOT WRITE HERE

Page 1 of _____ pages

EXAMINED BY _____

CHECKED BY _____

☐ CORRESPONDENCE
   Yes

☐ DEPOSIT ACCOUNT
   FUNDS USED

FORM PA

FOR
COPYRIGHT
OFFICE
USE
ONLY

DO NOT WRITE ABOVE THIS LINE. IF YOU NEED MORE SPACE, USE A SEPARATE CONTINUATION SHEET.

PREVIOUS REGISTRATION Has registration for this work, or for an earlier version of this work, already been made in the Copyright Office?
☐ Yes ☐ No If your answer is "Yes," why is another registration being sought? (Check appropriate box) ▼
☐ This is the first published edition of a work previously registered in unpublished form.
☐ This is the first application submitted by this author as copyright claimant.
☐ This is a changed version of the work, as shown by space 6 on this application.
If your answer is "Yes," give: **Previous Registration Number** ▼   **Year of Registration** ▼

5

DERIVATIVE WORK OR COMPILATION Complete both space 6a & 6b for a derivative work; complete only 6b for a compilation.
a. Preexisting Material Identify any preexisting work or works that this work is based on or incorporates. ▼

b. Material Added to This Work Give a brief, general statement of the material that has been added to this work and in which copyright is claimed. ▼

6

See instructions
before completing
this space.

DEPOSIT ACCOUNT If the registration fee is to be charged to a Deposit Account established in the Copyright Office, give name and number of Account.
Name ▼   **Account Number** ▼

CORRESPONDENCE Give name and address to which correspondence about this application should be sent. Name/Address/Apt/City/State/Zip ▼

Area Code & Telephone Number ▶

7

Be sure to
give your
daytime phone
◀ number.

CERTIFICATION* I, the undersigned, hereby certify that I am the
Check only one ▼
☐ author
☐ other copyright claimant
☐ owner of exclusive right(s)
☐ authorized agent of _____
    Name of author or other copyright claimant, or owner of exclusive right(s) ▲

of the work identified in this application and that the statements made
by me in this application are correct to the best of my knowledge.

Typed or printed name and date ▼ If this is a published work, this date must be the same as or later than the date of publication given in space 3.

_____ date ▶ _____

☞ Handwritten signature (X) ▼

8

**MAIL
CERTIFI-
CATE TO**

**Certificate
will be
mailed in
window
envelope**

Name ▼

Number/Street/Apartment Number ▼

City/State/ZIP ▼

Have you:
• Completed all necessary
  spaces?
• Signed your application in space
  8?
• Enclosed check or money order
  for $10 payable to Register of
  Copyrights?
• Enclosed your deposit material
  with the application and fee?
MAIL TO: Register of Copyrights,
Library of Congress, Washington,
D.C. 20559

9

* 17 U.S.C. § 506(e): Any person who knowingly makes a false representation of a material fact in the application for copyright registration provided for by section 409, or in any written statement filed in connection with the application, shall be fined not more than $2,500.

☆ U.S. GOVERNMENT PRINTING OFFICE: 1986—491-560/20,014

February 1986—200,000

Index

AAA form, 71, 76; variations, 72. *See also* Form

AABA form, 67; example of, 70; variations, 72. *See also* Form

A&R (Artists & Repertoire) personnel, 30, 232; and demos, 200-2; getting a response, 295; interviews, 244-47; and management functions, 229; and publishers, 158-59; and showcases, 254-56; and song shopping, 187-88

a cappella, 32, 84, 198, 258

administration deals, 182, 195-96

advances, cash, 175-78

alliteration, 51, 58, 80-81

antithesis, 59

AOR (Album Oriented Rock), 20. *See also* Radio station format

arrangements, necessity of, 215-17

arranger, 77, 290

artist, identity, 226, 287; point of view, 89-90

ASCAP (American Society of Composers, Authors and Publishers), 34, 110, 121, 142, 148-51, 158, 162, 174, 183-84, 191, 194, 221, 231, 253, 265, 272, 281

assignment, writing on, 89-90, and deadlines, 10

assonance, 51, 58, 80-81

attitude, 36, 52; and point of view, 50

audience, writing for, 36-37

audio-visual market, 277-80; earnings, 280; educational films and videos, 274, 278; home entertainment, 273, 278; industrial films, 277-78; instrumental underscoring, 262; making contacts, 279-80; special material, 280; theme composition, 262; video, 277-79

Automatic (Brock Walsh, Mark Goldenberg), 80

"B" section. *See* Pre-hook

Billboard, 75, 111, 160, 194-95, 221, 231-33, 289

Billie Jean (Michael Jackson), 98

blues, 99, 108

BMI (Broadcast Music Inc.), 34, 121, 142, 148-51, 158, 162, 174, 183-84, 191, 194, 221, 231, 253, 265, 272, 281

booking agents, 293-95; responsibilities of, 295; showcases for, 254-56

bridge, 67-69, 71; examples of, 69-70, 74; and rhyme scheme, 85

Careless Whispers (George Michael), 59

casting, 158, 186, 200

"catchy," 51, 81, 91

Cat's In The Cradle (Harry and Sandy Chapin), 25

censorship, 23

charts, the, 231-34. *See also* Trade magazines

children's music, 273-74

chords, 100-106; progressions of, 84, 103, 105; intervals, 99-103. *See also* Harmony; Song dynamics; Triads

chorus, 66, 77, 220; and the hook, 67, 91; construction of, 67, 69, 78-80; examples of, 69-70; forms of, 73-75; hook chorus, 77-83; melodic changes, 84; refrain, 67-68; repetition, 81-82; rewriting, 86-87; rhyme scheme, 85. *See also* Hook; Pre-hook; Song dynamics

Christmas songs, 28-29

classical music. *See* Radio station formats

"climb." *See* Pre-hook

club owners, 30, 254-56

collaboration services, 113-14

comanagement, 229, 288

commercial jingles, 266-73; demos of, 268; earnings from, 271-73; jingle houses, 270; skills needed for writing, 267

contemporary Christian music, 29. *See also* Radio station formats

contests, 257-61; guidelines for entering, 260-61; publishing contract from, 258

contracts, collaboration, 123-25

contracts (publishing) and advances, 175; staff writing, 177-81; exclusive contracts, 176; foreign subpublishing, 193-95; limitation of assignment by

318